Product Analytics

Product Analytics

Applied Data Science Techniques for Actionable Consumer Insights

Joanne Rodrigues

✦✦ Addison-Wesley

Boston • Columbus • New York • San Francisco • Amsterdam • Cape Town
Dubai • London • Madrid • Milan • Munich • Paris • Montreal • Toronto • Delhi • Mexico City
São Paulo • Sydney • Hong Kong • Seoul • Singapore • Taipei • Tokyo

For information about buying this title in bulk quantities, or for special sales opportunities (which may include electronic versions; custom cover designs; and content particular to your business, training goals, marketing focus, or branding interests), please contact our corporate sales department at corpsales@pearsoned.com or (800) 382-3419.

For government sales inquiries, please contact governmentsales@pearsoned.com.

For questions about sales outside the U.S., please contact intlcs@pearson.com.

Visit us on the Web: informit.com/aw

Library of Congress Control Number: 2020940464

Cover image: Mad Dog/Shutterstock

Page 6: "By 2018, the U.S. . . . deep analytic talent." McKinsey & Company.

Page 21: Introduction to Bayes' Rule, Thomas Bayes.

Page 51: "if people are . . . adversely and resist." Thaler, R. H., & Sunstein, C. R. (2008). Nudge: Improving decisions about health, wealth, and happiness. New Haven, Conn.: Yale University Press.

Pages 256-257: "1. Strength of the . . . you could easily test?" Hill, Austin Bradford (1965). "The Environment and Disease: Association or Causation?". Proceedings of the Royal Society of Medicine. 58 (5): 295–300.

Page 271: "Fewer variables are better: There is . . . number of chimneys swept in a day to determine dosage effects." Radcliffe, Nicholas, and Surry, Patrick. "Real-world uplift modelling with significance based uplift trees." White Paper TR-2011-1, Stochastic Solutions, 2011.

Page 281, Figure 14.1: Screenshot of R Studio window with four panels © 2020 Apple Inc.

ISBN-13: 978-0-13-525852-1
ISBN-10: 0-13-525852-9

1 2020

❖

*To my children Sahana and Ronak, whose infectious laughter
kept me focused.*

❖

Contents

Preface

A point of view can be a dangerous luxury when substituted for insight and understanding.

—Marshall McLuhan

This book is a practitioner's guide to generating *actionable* insights from consumer data. *Actionable* in this context refers to *extracted* insights used to drive change in a web or mobile product or within a broader organization. Many organizations have terabytes of user-generated data from their web products or internal organizations. However, much of the data goes unused. How should they use this data to make changes that will foster user growth, increase revenue, improve engagement, and engender efficiency in an organization?

Product Analytics will take you step-by-step on the journey to extract insight from user data. The reader will traverse the peaks and valleys of theory building, navigate the waters of designing experiments, drive the meandering roads of developing models, and finally embark on translating these results into actionable insights. This book is a primer on the product data science toolkit. Data science is a multidisciplinary field whose goal is to extract insights from data. Product data science is focused on harnessing user data to drive product and organizational changes to meet core business goals. It emphasizes the use of advanced analytics to understand and change user behavior to help start-ups and large companies alike to build engaging products and exceed revenue targets. As a side note, this book does not address other data science workflows, such as building scalable recommendation systems, computer vision, and image recognition, or other types of applications.

The analyzed data can come from a variety of sources. While it's often user data from web products, it could also be data from emails or mailing campaigns, survey data, internal company data, or integrated data from marketing channels, demographic, or census data, and a variety of other types of data.

The Audience

The core audience for this book consists of entrepreneurs, data scientists, analysts, or any other practitioners who are using user data to drive growth, revenue, efficiency, or engagement in their web or mobile products. This book is useful if you are or want to become a product data scientist, an analyst, or an entrepreneur building a website or web product, or if you just have an interest in working with the terabytes of behavioral data available on the web.

The book is not written for an academic audience, but rather with the practitioner in mind. If you're looking to understand real-world product data, look no further than this book.

Product data science relies on multiple disciplines to extract insight from human behavior. While the analytical toolkit is somewhat more modern, it relies on computing and statistical methods, based on some of the latest machine learning and causal inference techniques. Social scientists have been studying human behavior for the last 400 years. Social science methods and analytical tools need to be adequately integrated to drive "actionable insights."

Often, practitioners work with one toolkit, but not others. Many data scientists are well versed in the latest machine learning techniques, but lack the user expertise and qualitative skills to apply those techniques to extracting insights from human data. They often get stuck while developing sufficient theories of social processes and operationalizing conceptual ideas into measurable quantities.

In contrast, many user experts with a sufficient understanding of human behavior lack the statistical and machine learning rigor to adequately test their ideas and model data. The goal of this book is to bridge the gap between the subject-matter expert and the machine-learning guru. Merging the contextual insights of the subject-matter expert and the sophisticated methods of the machine-learning guru can generate useful insights in the web or mobile analytics space.

The Content

Using practical examples from the world of web analytics, readers will discover how to

- Think like a social scientist to contextualize individual behavior in social environments, explore how human behavior develops, and establish the conditions for change

- Develop core metrics and effective key performance indicators for user analytics in any web product

- Understand statistical inference, the differences between correlation and causation, and when to apply each technique

- Conduct more effective A/B tests

- Build intuitive predictive models to capture user behavior in product

- Tease out causal effects from observational data, using the latest quasi-experimental design techniques and statistical matching

- Implement sophisticated targeting methods such as uplift modeling for marketing campaigns

- Project business costs/subgroup population changes by using advanced demographic projection methods

Themes of the Book

This book has three subthemes that permeate the text: (1) qualitative tools from sociology, psychology, and demography integrated with quantitative tools from statistics, machine learning, and computer science applied to the domain of web analytics; (2) methods for causal inference (rather than prediction) since causal inference is integral to altering human behavior; and (3) nonmathematical explanations and demonstrated application in the R language for machine learning and causal inference topics, since most texts in these spaces are not written for practitioners.

Theme 1: Qualitative versus Quantitative Techniques

The first subtheme goes to the heart of this text. The goal is not just to provide analytical tools, but also to provide the resources needed to apply these analytical tools and examples where they are best applied for web applications. Many books within the data science or machine learning realm simply cover the underlying algorithms. While algorithms do play an important role, the cliché "Garbage in, garbage out" comes to mind. Without appropriate data, the algorithms themselves are useless. Applying the wrong algorithm to the wrong problem can lead to a whole host of problems.

To properly apply an algorithm or design an experiment, we must go over the full process of theory building, conceptualization, operationalization, metric building, hypothesis testing, falsification, and more. A large number of qualitative tools are available that we can use to model human behavior and social processes accurately. If we fail to use these tools, we lose out on a great deal of information, nuance, and insight. We also might completely misunderstand "why," "how," or "what" users are doing in our web products. Chapters 1–3 examine the qualitative tools needed to understand and model behavior in web products.

Obtaining actionable insights requires understanding the context and the information stored in each variable. If one cannot connect broader conceptual ideas to analytical results, we're not left with much of anything. A good friend who had a PhD in physics and who worked as a data scientist at a women's clothing company illustrates this disconnect best. He loved physics and loved applying physics algorithms to any data set, but struggled to connect their results to the business context of interest. I would often ask him what insights he had derived about the women's apparel business. He always answered that he had applied the latest "X" model with "some extremely complex tuning." While applying complex, well-tuned algorithms to the right context is awesome, those algorithms can also be applied to the wrong set of data or used to hide the lack of true insight into a topic.

In practice, "actionable insights" do not rely on using the latest algorithm. Better algorithms generally will only slightly improve your results, but bad data will destroy any hope of gaining valuable insights. What is even more common than bad data is misinterpretation of accurate data—a surprisingly frequent occurrence in industry.

For this reason, it's essential to have good qualitative methodologies in place before any data analysis begins, so we don't end up with "garbage out." Since raw data is often not well documented, it's easy to misunderstand what a variable is measuring or counting. It's imperative to understand exactly which steps users must take to get to a particular variable and what they have done to get a particular variable outcome. If you're using a variable as a proxy for a conceptually complex idea, what pieces of that idea is this variable actually measuring? Having theories and good qualitative frameworks in place will allow for the most robust interpretation and actionable use of your data.

Theme 2: Causal Inference

The second theme is this book is the preference for causal inference over prediction. Many data science books are focused on predictive algorithms. This book provides a basic predictive toolkit consisting of the following algorithms: k-means, principal components analysis (PCA), linear regression, logistic regression, decision trees, support vector machines, and some time-series modeling techniques. The more advanced topics, such as difference-in-difference modeling, statistical matching, and uplift modeling, are related to causal inference.

The only exception is found in Chapter 9, which covers advanced predictive techniques from demography on population forecasting. In Chapter 9, we use predictive modeling techniques in a somewhat novel way to create better core user metrics (e.g., retention), understand subgroup population changes in our web product, and forecast future population. Generally, for the analysis of user behavior, causal inference is preferred to prediction.

Theme 3: Layman's Explanations

This book was written because most books about data science, statistical causal inference, or demography are extremely academic and proof-laden. While that is necessary in some contexts, mathematically heavy texts are inaccessible to the common person. Most of these tools don't need mathematically heavy explanations and can be extremely easy to apply with a minimal understanding of R. Statistical data science and causal inference tools are useful in many business contexts, but are rarely applied in those settings due to their inaccessibility.

The goal of this book is to make all of this information accessible to anyone who has completed high school–level mathematics and statistics. This is a little bit optimistic, since some of the topics—such as statistical matching, uplift modeling, and population forecasting—are extremely mathematically complex. The goal is to make them conceptually understandable first. Those readers with a minimal math background should get a general idea of how the algorithm works and when to apply it. After reading the book, readers should be able to find the right design and/or model to apply to their own specific use-cases. After determining the right setup and algorithm, they should be able to run their analysis in R. The core goal of the book is to teach readers how those algorithms generally work, in which situations they should apply particular algorithms in the user or web analytics context, and which tools in R they can apply to get the answers that they're looking for.

In this book, we'll sparsely use mathematical notation as it turn's away non-mathematically inclined readers. Chapter's from 1-6 will use as little mathematical notation as possible and we'll verbally describe equations. After Chapter 6, the material becomes too mathematically intensive to not rely on not using mathematical notation and later chapters will occassionally use mathematical notation in the text.

Organization of the Book

The goal of this book is to better model, understand, and change user behavior in web and mobile products. The book is organized in the following way:

- Chapters 1–3 explain qualitative tools and theories to model user behavior.
- Chapters 4–6 cover introductory statistical methods in product analytics.
- Chapters 7–9 explore predictive modeling and forecasting methods.
- Chapters 10–13 cover causal inference methods for real-world data.
- Chapters 14–16 implement the methods explained in the quantitative chapters in R.

Chapter 1, "Data in Action: A Model of a Dinner Party," is an introductory chapter, which uses the metaphor of a dinner party to showcase common pitfalls that hinder understanding of user behavior. These pitfalls include that social data is often viewed as a "process," rather than a problem. Social data often has no clear outcomes, has rampant problems of incomplete information, has large numbers of variables that are strongly interconnected, is a system that can be easily perturbed, and prevents us from easily inferring causality.

Chapter 2, "Building a Theory of the Social Universe," reviews the scientific method and walks you through sociological tools of quantifying human behavior. Exploring ideas of conceptualization forces us to spend time thinking about "quantifying"—both what that means and what is lost in the process. Today, everything is moving toward metrics. The difficulty with replacing complex qualitative metrics with a few quantitative measures is that these measures can rarely capture the level of sophistication of the original human heuristics or the sophistication that a human expert would expect. Practitioners rarely delve deeply into the shortcomings of their metrics, which leads to even more misguided strategies.

Chapter 3, "The Coveted Goalpost: How to Change Human Behavior," is about human behavior change. User analytics has shifted from demographic profiling to sophisticated methods of targeting and altering user behavior in your web product. What features are most likely to change user behavior? This chapter explores current theories of behavior change, the factors that are most likely to cause change, and the magnitude of a given change.

Chapter 4, "Distributions in User Analytics," takes you through basic statistical tools to start working with user data. In Chapter 5, "Retained? Metric Creation and Interpretation," we explore the nitty-gritty of developing quantitative measures of key ideas. This chapter uses demographic ideas of period, age, and cohort to inform our metric development and expands our toolkit for measuring populations. In addition, Chapter 5 explores the benefits and shortfalls of working with commonly used metrics by working through examples from the four key areas in user analytics: acquisition, retention, engagement, and revenue.

Chapter 6, "Why Are My Users Leaving? The Ins and Outs of A/B Testing," is a practical how-to guide to A/B testing. What is an A/B test? How do you set one up? How do you analyze the results? This chapter also goes through statistical testing and simple power analysis. Finally, it explores the complexities of A/B testing, such as best courses of action for conflicting results between short- and long-run indicators.

Chapter 7, "Modeling the User Space: k-Means and PCA," and Chapter 8, "Predicting User Behavior: Regression, Decision Trees, and Support Vector Machines," explore the basics of supervised and unsupervised learning. This introduction to pattern recognition focuses on graphical descriptions and examples to drive understanding. It's a basic toolkit to help you with everyday explanatory or predictive analysis. It also underlies the more sophisticated statistical techniques in Chapters 10–13. Topics covered include k-means, PCA, linear regression, logistic regression, decision trees, and support vector machines.

Chapter 9, "Forecasting Population Changes in Product: Demographic Projections," covers ways to forecast general and subgroup population changes in your web product. It relies on tools of demographic population prediction to model user behavior in a multidimensional and unique way.

Most data produced is observational, meaning that we must tease out causal relationships. Chapter 10, "In Pursuit of the Experiment: Natural Experiments and the Difference-in-Difference Modeling," and Chapter 11, "In Pursuit of the Experiment, Continued," go through some elementary techniques for deriving causal insights from observational data. These techniques include natural experiments, the difference-in-difference design, and regression discontinuity— all of which can help us derive actionable insights from real-world data. Chapter 12, "Developing Heuristics in Practice," explores statistical matching and situations where causal inference is not possible or is not easy.

Predictive modeling with A/B testing can be a powerful combination. Chapter 13, "Uplift Modeling," explores uplift modeling, a technique that combines the two and leads to improved user targeting.

The final section of the book implements all these techniques in R. Chapter 14, "Metrics in R," runs through statistical distributions and metric calculation in R. Chapter 15, "A/B Testing, Predictive Modeling, and Population Projection in R," discusses A/B testing, predictive modeling techniques, and population projection techniques in R. Chapter 16, "Regression Discontinuity, Matching, and Uplift in R," introduces difference-in-difference modeling, statistical matching, and uplift modeling in R.

Final Thoughts

This book provides an intermediate guide to user analytics and relies on both causal and predictive inference. After reading this book, you should be able to build theories about user behavior, test those theories, and generate actionable insights to improve your product. The tools and practical advice from this book can be used in almost any role—from marketing and project management to business analytics and entrepreneur.

Register your copy of *Product Analytics* on the InformIT site for convenient access to updates and/or corrections as they become available. To start the registration process, go to informit. com/register and log in or create an account. Enter the product ISBN (9780135258521) and click Submit. Look on the Registered Products tab for an Access Bonus Content link next to this product, and follow that link to access any available bonus materials. If you would like to be notified of exclusive offers on new editions and updates, please check the box to receive email from us.

Acknowledgments

I'd like to acknowledge the following people. Debra Williams Cauley, the book's acquisitions editor, guided the book's development and greatly improved its content. I'd also like to acknowledge the help and excellent feedback of the reviewers, particularly Lawrence Rodrigues, Jared Lander, Luda Janda and Nick Cohron, who read entire sections of the book word-for-word. All of these reviewers provided rich feedback that greatly improved or transformed the book in their own way. Finally, I'd like to acknowledge the general feedback of Sohini Sircar, Cloy Rodrigues, Hubert Lee, Rajesh Mascarenhas, and Paul Chung.

About the Author

Joanne Rodrigues is an experienced data scientist and enterprise manager with master's degrees in mathematics (London School of Economics), political science (University of California, Berkeley), and demography (University of California, Berkeley), and a bachelor's degree in international economics (Georgetown University). Her passion is to analyze large sets of structured, semi-structured, and unstructured data to solve real-world problems. She has six years of experience applying machine learning/statistical algorithms to derive business insights (in health care and gaming). She pioneered new analytics techniques at Sony PlayStation, and led all of MeYou Health's data science efforts. She is also the founder of ClinicPriceCheck.com, a health technology company.

Qualitative Methodology

Data in Action: A Model of a Dinner Party

Never in human history have we had access to terabytes of social data in a variety of settings. Such data can lead to amazing, *revolutionary* insights into human behavior. The goal of this book is to take you on a *journey* to gain the skills needed to generate those insights to grow your business and improve your products.

Let's start with the basics. This book is about analyzing customer behavior in a web or mobile product. In the context of this book, a web or mobile product is defined as any product or service available online or through your phone. It includes real products sold online, like a website selling snowmobiles, as well as web and mobile products like social networks. The Internet has changed the game: It allows us to collect lots of data on customer behavior—more than was ever possible before—based on everything from what they clicked on to what they told their friends.

We can use this data to improve our product. Social data is powerful because it allows us to analyze thousands, often millions, of simple behaviors that were unknowable even ten years ago and to then work to change and alter that behavior.

Why is user analytics important? User analytics is the lifeblood of the modern economy. Understanding user interactions with web products often determines whether a company will succeed or fail, even when that firm sells real products. As everything moves online, from retail transactions to doctor's visits, one must understand why users do what they do and rapidly work to improve user experience.

In the last ten years, the data explosion has allowed us to rapidly iterate and improve social and traditional product marketing, sales, and delivery.

This chapter explores the user analytics space, identifying six core ways in which applications in user analytics differ from traditional data science and statistical applications. Using the example of a dinner party, this chapter will illustrate some of the unique aspects of working with user data. Few technical skills will be learned in this chapter; instead, it primarily lays the framework for how to approach theory building and experimental and/or model design for testing hypotheses in web and mobile products.

The following sections delve into this divide between intuitive insight and advanced analytics, which currently exists in many industries. The rest of the book takes you on a journey to bridge that expansive divide.

1.1 The User Data Disruption

Understanding user behavior in a variety of contexts can lead to better-targeted campaigns, increased revenue, and greater user satisfaction and engagement for any product. A myriad of professionals, from data scientists to product managers, are tasked with understanding, altering, and predicting user behavior. However, even with generous investment, most organizations have difficulty effectively utilizing their data. Leveraging data is difficult, and many analysts do not ask the right questions, utilize the appropriate context, or employ the best tools to make inferences about human behavior. This book will show you the most effective tools in the social sciences and statistics to derive *useful insights* from your users.

In this chapter, we'll go over common problems with analyzing user data, an example of a social process (in this case, a dinner party), and common pitfalls when drawing conclusions from complex social processes. At the end of this chapter, you will have a better sense of some of the difficulties of user analytics. Later chapters will help you solve or work through some of these problems.

1.1.1 Don't Leave the Users out of the Model

Most modern web products have embedded social components that make them microcosms of society. Social hierarchy, friendship, culture, and a litany of interesting interactions and behaviors drive the lives of these products. The complexity of the human behavior involved makes social products incredibly difficult to analyze without the correct toolkit. Even simple purchasing websites can have gigantic stores of behavioral data and complex behavioral processes that can be analyzed, such as user clicks, sessions, purchasing behavior, and churn.

Clickstream data is the path of clicks through a website or model product ordered by time. User sessions comprise a pattern of consistent use from the first to last interaction on a site. Churn is the number of users or rate of leaving the site over a particular period. All of this data is present in almost all web products, and it can be extremely useful, when combined with the right context, for understanding what your users are doing in your product.

To add context, all this clickstream and web data is behavioral data. Sometimes this reality is lost because it's present in a web context, where you cannot view your users engaging with your product.

Why is understanding the behavioral aspect of this data useful? Having a model of human behavior will help us to organize, derive insights, and change user behavior. From a business perspective, when you understand who your users are, what they are doing with your product, and what drives them to purchase and engage with your product, then you can try to modify their engagement and revenue behavior.

For instance, as an analyst, you might ask the following questions: How can I make this web product *sticky*—that is, increase user retention? What causes my users to buy? If we make changes to the product, will users adapt?

First, let's understand how many people initially work with data. A very easy way to look at your data is to focus on *description*. Most analysts stop at this level. Description simply means that you collect data about what people are doing with your product. For instance, suppose the average person visits your site three times in the first month. Users spend 30 seconds looking at listings during the average session. Only 10% of users progress past the homepage. There are a large number of potential descriptive tidbits that you can collect from a web product. Most people's first inclination is to weave a story together from disparate descriptive facts or to create a story and then search for descriptive facts that support it.

Spoiler Alert

Weaving a story together from disparate facts is not a good way to understand your product. Why? We don't have a holistic picture of what's happening with our product and our inferences are probably not correct. This book will walk you through the process of moving from description to real statistical inferences that will improve your web product. Before, we start this process, let's explore some common problems with analyzing user data.

1.1.2 The Junior Analyst

When starting out, many analysts try to answer questions about user behavior without exploring the larger context. They silo a certain behavior and then try to explain why that behavior is occurring. However, siloing a certain set of behaviors often does not work, because human behavior and web processes are often complex and deeply interconnected. We also have no "causal linkages," making any connections proposed very dubious in nature.

For instance, let's say you have a website that sells snowmobiles. You have great products on your site for snowmobile lovers, but most users never seem to progress past the homepage. Your bounce rate is very high. The bounce rate is the proportion of users who leave the site after viewing only one page. An analyst might spend weeks trying to answer why there is so little progression deeper into the site.

To address this question, the analyst might pull a variety of descriptive statistics. Let's call her Ana. Ana latches onto one descriptive statistic: 40% of users coming from the search engine Google progress past the homepage compared to only 30% of users coming from the search engine Yahoo. She might then start crafting a story to fit this descriptive data. Google users are richer and worldlier than Yahoo users, and richer, worldlier users are more interested in our snowmobiles, so they progress past the homepage at higher rates. Ana, proud of her work, then shares this nicely crafted story with you.

Okay, you think, this story makes sense. So, to sell more snowmobiles, we simply need to figure out how to better target rich users. But before you invest in better targeting, you ask your analyst what evidence she has that supports this story. She mumbles an answer, "Err ... well, we know Google users are richer on average." Okay, you say, but we do not know what subset of Google users make it to our website. Are they richer than the average Google user? Google users are also more likely to be international, male, and millennials, so how did Ana deal with these potentially conflicting attributes? Any of these attributes might explain some of the difference in rates.

So you ask Ana how she settled on wealth as the driving factor. Ana looks worried, and you realize that she has not thought about this issue. This scenario is not atypical in many industry settings. Without a sound background in statistical inference, it's often difficult to make sense of conflicting descriptive information.

Cherry-picking descriptive statistics also often leads to frustration. Exploring a single behavior can feel like a game of whack-a-mole, where you try to explain away one fact, only to have another conflicting fact pop up in its place. When we focus on only a couple of descriptive facts, we do not get a holistic picture of what is happening in the product—and eventually we just get lost in the details.

Even worse, we may find that our conclusions are incorrect. Since we do not know why more users are coming to our product from Google than Yahoo, we make up a story: *Here they are progressing because they are supposedly richer.* This reasoning makes it seem like these users would be more likely to purchase our snowmobiles.

However, we never even looked at whether they are *actually* purchasing at a higher rate. This comes to the second problem. As we figure out the reasoning for one behavior, another measure of user behavior emerges that fails to make sense in this context.

Let's say that Google users are less likely to purchase snowmobiles than Yahoo users. This information seems to contradict our analyst's story. This often happens in industry when descriptive tidbits are cherry-picked to explain a phenomenon. We do not know why this descriptive feature exists, so we need to do more analysis to figure that out. As you can tell, this is not a good way of exploring user behavior in products. However, coming up with crafted stories around descriptive information is a common practice in many companies and industries.

Executives often want stories that clearly elucidate and explain phenomena. While storytelling is useful when we know what is happening with our products and we can justify those conclusions, faux storytelling can be destructive, leading to the misallocation of resources and failure to effect real change within a web product.

This book explains how to build a model of user behavior, test out that model, and make accurate inferences about what causes that behavior—to help you tell accurate stories about your users. What is *actually leading* to higher purchasing of snowmobiles?

Going back to our example, another question that you may want to ask your analyst is about the size of the effect. Often, this question gets asked in industry, but without understanding the broader relationships between variables, the answer is often wrong.

Let's keep the numbers simple. You have 1,000 organic (or without ads) users daily who come to the site, 50% from Google and 50% from Yahoo. You note that 30% of Yahoo users make a purchase, while 40% of Google users make a purchase. Your analyst theorizes that if all users came from Google and none from Yahoo, it would increase the number of new purchases. On an annual basis, she suggests, you'd see 36,500 more purchases. You tell her great work—let's invest in buying Google ads!

Let's say your ads are so effective that now 1,000 people come directly from Google daily (you meet the criteria for your theory). However, you see only 150 more new purchases total yearly. What happened? Your ads are targeting a different group of users from Google than a simple Google search was driving, and those ad-driven users from Google may not be buying at the same rate. This happens a lot. Measuring the size of the effect is often useless when the relationships between variables are not clearly understood.

As we can see from this example, determining what's happening in a product and making inferences that improve the profitability of the business often require both determining what causes behavior and understanding the size of its effect. We'll come back to these core ideas throughout the book.

1.1.3 The Opposite of the Misguided Analyst: The Data Guru

In 2011, McKinsey Global Institute published a report stating that there would be a massive shortage in analytics professionals in almost every organization because of the sheer amount of data being collected. In this report, titled *Big Data,* the authors wrote: "By 2018, the U.S. alone may face a 50% to 60% gap between supply and requisite demand of deep analytic talent." McKinsey theorized that the data scientist would fill this gap. A data scientist, who is supposed to be a hybrid of a statistician, a computer scientist, and a business guru, was the answer to dealing with the massive growth of behavioral data.

The analytical portion of the data scientist toolkit is primarily composed of Machine Learning/Artificial Intelligence (ML/AI). Why is ML/AI not always that useful? Although other methodologies are also part of the toolkit, ML/AI is generally focused on the problem of prediction. Prediction can be very helpful in forecasting population growth, offering product recommendations, and finding your population at risk for churn. However, prediction is not as useful as causal inference in *deriving insights* or *changing user behavior* because it does not help us find variables that *cause* a user to behave in a certain way, such as deciding to purchase.

As was discussed in the preface, causal inference does not necessarily improve with more data. Causal inference relies on having a valid counterfactual or "placebo" test. Conversely, massive amounts of data do improve predictive models. For this reason, justifiably prediction is in the midst of a renaissance of sorts.

Causal inference is much harder than predictive inference to conduct, and is more appropriate for one-off cases than for overarching models. Although causal inference is the backbone of scientific inquiry, because it does not improve with more data, it's been left at the wayside in this Big Data movement.

Prediction also allows for generalization and validation based on external or new data. Causal inference is difficult to generalize and validate outside of an experiment. We'll discuss which types of questions are best answered by which method, and the differences between the two, in more detail throughout the book.

The very first step in understanding your users is building a conceptual model and collecting the right metrics or descriptive statistics to verify or falsify that model. Next, we use metrics, experimentation, and statistical inference to derive insights about users. Finally, we focus on user behavioral change in a web product based on understanding what causes behavior, or answering the *why* question. Understanding causation is often not a large part of the traditional data science toolkit because many of the original applications of ML are focused on very different problems. We'll discuss this issue more later in the chapter.

The statistics of causal inference has rapidly developed in recent years and can provide us with a whole host of new tools to deal with these seemingly intractable problems in understanding user behavior. Further, by couching this book in social science methods, we can rely on this field's best practices and qualitative tools to build quality descriptive metrics and better theoretical models. Overall, by integrating social science methods with statistics and machine learning models, we will enhance our understanding of customers.

1.2 A Model of a Dinner Party

Let's change the focus for a moment and explore a simple thought experiment. Imagine that you want to host a dinner party to celebrate a recent promotion at work. You want to host a great party, but this is your first-ever dinner party and you are not sure what *great* means. As you prepare for the party, you spend a few moments pondering that question: What makes a *great* party? You think there are some important elements to a *great* party—the food, people, and location.

First, you think about the food. Do you want to have comfort food or fancy food choices? A little or a lot of variety? Lots of alcohol or none? You're not sure. It really depends. Second, you consider the people. Will the people whom you have invited get along? Should you invite all your friends or just the ones within a given social circle? Again, you are not sure what the best course of action is. Finally, where should this party be held: in your house or at a restaurant? Hmm, not to sound trite, but you're not sure.

You make some decisions and decide to evaluate the party after it occurs. In the end, you decide to have lots of comfort food and alcohol. You invite friends, family, and coworkers from a variety of social circles, and decide to have the event at home to keep costs low.

The party begins at 5:00 on Saturday afternoon. Sadly, it's a little bit of a rainy day, so your guests are forced to stay inside. The guests start arriving around 5:30. Your brother, a few of his friends, and two of your coworkers stop by first. They bring some appetizers with them and start talking about the latest college basketball game.

As more people start arriving, your guests filter into different rooms, sticking with their respective social circles. There's a little bit of interaction between circles, as when your brother meanders through your coworker and friend circles. But, most of your friends, family, and coworkers stay relatively separated. People also slowly filter into the kitchen, generously filling up their plates. You get a few compliments on your home-made food and delicious appetizers.

As the party progresses, you can tell that your guests have had more to drink and start to interact with people they do not necessarily know. A variety of conversations are occurring, and you wonder what each group is talking about. You walk around and try to overhear some of the conversations. A few people in the living room are talking about schools in the area, another group is discussing the latest hockey game, and two friends are exchanging numbers.

At 11:00 or so, the party dies down as people filter out. By midnight, you're left with just the remnants of a party: cups full of soda, plates with dessert, paper on the floor, and chairs strewn about. You and your partner slowly clean up while ruminating on your original question: Was this a *great* dinner party?

First, let's start with the outcome. How do you define *great*? Let's say you're a very analytical person and want to quantify this notion of *greatness*. You think of a few different ways. The most obvious approach is to apply some version of the majority rule: Did the majority of your guests have fun? But, to use this metric, you realize that you need an outcome: *fun* or not *fun*. What is the cutoff for *fun*? Would different people define f*un* differently? If so, could you aggregate individual people's different definitions of *fun* into one result indicating whether the party was *great* or not *great*? You think it could get even more complex. Could you have changed the composition of guests or steered certain guests to certain rooms to maximize their level of fun? That's kind of a weird, very utilitarian thought to have.

Could people have fun on a spectrum that can be maximized? Hmm … well, you'll never know your guests' fun spectrum. Some guests could have extreme preferences that overwhelm the quality for the other guests. For example, perhaps one guest derives extreme fun from watching movies, but all the other guests have slightly less fun watching movies.

Let's explore another direction. You could assess the *greatness* of your dinner party in terms of whether your guests talk about it tomorrow. Or you could just ask them all if it was *great* or not. But what if your friends do not feel comfortable sharing their true feelings with you?

Maybe fun is defined by achieving a goal. Some of your guests might have come to meet new people, trade recipes, or find a new romantic partner. Achieving their goals could contribute to their definition of *great*. You could survey your guests on their goals.

Utilitarianism

Utilitarianism is a philosophical theory that explores the maximization of utility. The founder of utilitarianism, Jeremy Bentham, described utility as the sum of all pleasure that results from an action, minus the suffering of anyone involved in the action. Utility theory is the basis of the field of economics. There are some problems with utilitarianism, however, in that some people's utility could be infinite and overwhelm the preferences of the majority.

You have a better idea. What if you had another party—then you could define whether guests had fun at the last one by whether they choose to come again. But what if the next party is held on a weekend when most people are out of town or the COVID-19 is going around and no one shows up?

Okay, this seems like a fruitless endeavor, but we've established that assessing the greatness or outcome of a dinner party is hard and we haven't even discussed all the events and interactions that occurred at the party.

Outcomes

When building simple models, there are generally two types of results: (1) binary and (2) regression. A binary outcome is a class decision. For instance, we have two classes, tall or short. We classify all individuals into either of those classes. We could base their class specification on a simple decision rule: If people are taller than 5 feet 9 inches they are **tall**; otherwise, they are **short**. Then, Michael Jordan, at 6 feet 6 inches, would be classified as tall and comedian Kevin Hart, at 5 feet 4 inches, would be classified as short.

The other type of outcome is regression, which is a real-valued outcome. For instance, let's say we take the exact height of each person. This would be a real-valued outcome. There would then be a spectrum of people with no cutoff between what is considered short or tall.

There are other types of outcomes such as multiclasses, a more complex version of the binary outcome, and count variables, which must be an integer or a whole number.

1.2.1 Why Are Social Processes Difficult to Analyze?

Social events, like a dinner party, are very difficult to reclassify as problems with a clear outcome. What are the vital features of these complex events and what are we trying to derive? Understanding human behavior, in any context, even within a web product, has unique complexities:

- Social behavior is a process, not a problem to be solved.
- Social systems are open systems, meaning there are omitted or unmeasurable variables that can affect outcomes.
- When exploring social behavior, there are often no clear and defined outcomes.
- Social systems have rampant problems of incomplete or one-sided information.
- Social systems consist of millions of potential behaviors.
- Inferring causation or why something happens is *almost* impossible.

1.2.2 A Party Is a Process

Let's explore what each of these complexities means within the context of a dinner party. First, as we discussed earlier, a dinner party is *not* a simple classification problem. For instance, suppose we want to classify whether a picture is of a human or a dog. In this simple classification problem, we could look for descriptive features to determine if the image is human. For instance, does the object have a skin or fur, and is the object walking upright or on four legs? Let's say we have some images of humans and dogs. We could then classify these pictures into the best category by just asking those two questions.

There is one clear outcome in this example—the underlying classification. But what about a dinner party? It was an event with lots of different interactions and behaviors. Individuals at the party went through a variety of stages—entering, interacting with a whole host of people, eating and drinking, interacting more, and then leaving. Those events and their interpretation differed by person.

Is there a problem here? A problem is "an inquiry started from stated assumptions to a result or outcome." There is no one clear problem in this case because the party is a process characterized by a series of events. There could be thousands of defined problems. Some might make more sense given context than others, but all will be insufficient for describing the full event—the dinner party.

Similarly, human behavior within a web product is a series of social processes, rather than a problem with a clearly defined methodology. Your users are coming to your product repeatedly and interacting with people and content. They are also creating content, building communities, reinforcing norms, and building culture, which in turn affects the environment that other users interact with. **Norms** are social patterns of behavior that are accepted within the community. What problems you may choose to look at within this broader context are often narrowly defined and not easily extractable from the background environment.

1.2.3 A Party Is an Open System

In a social event like a dinner party, an outside variable could affect the whole system. What do we mean by "outside variable"? Suppose three variables in our mental model define a party—food, people, and location. As an analyst, you must simplify the context or you cannot build a model of a dinner party. Remember, even for our simple dinner party, if we could collect data on every interaction, individual, and event, we'd have millions of variables.

However, the human brain cannot deal with this level of complexity. The problem with simplification, however, is that any variables omitted could greatly affect the model in certain circumstances. For instance, weather and sickness are potential outside variables that could greatly affect the quality of the social event. Variables reflecting events that happen rarely can greatly affect social processes, are very difficult to predict, and are often left out of models. Because many variables are present in social systems, and we have little understanding of their complete effect, some will always be left out. For instance, bad publicity under some circumstances for Facebook or some other social community could greatly affect the growth of its user base. The quality of that publicity, either good or bad, is probably not accounted for in most companies' growth forecasting models because of the rarity of extreme negative exposure.

1.2.4 A "Great" Party Is Hard to Define

There are often no clear and defined outcomes for social processes. This all harkens back to our original question: Was our party *great*? We can't answer that question if we have not defined *great*. Once we have defined *great*, the question becomes: Is that the right outcome? Maybe we care more about how long people stayed at the party or whether they drank at least one glass of wine.

Most social behavior is a process, not a problem. Is it singular outcomes that we should focus on, or underlying incentives and causal relationships that better define what occurred during the dinner party? In a web product, you're left with similar problems. In a social process, behavior is easier to understand if you can understand your users' incentives and the causal impact of different actions on user behavior. Causal effects and user incentives are key to understanding what is happening with your product, but are left out of predictive frameworks. We'll talk a great deal in later chapters about causal inference and determining outcomes.

Which social processes define your product, and how do you find the right outcomes or structure to examine? Often in industry the outcome variables are relatively random, defined by historically chosen variables, outcomes that are easily collected, or variables that are easy to explain. This does not mean that these variables are the "right" ones to look at or test.

1.2.5 Party Guests' Motives and Opinions Are Often Unknown

Even at your dinner party, you face the often intractable problem of incomplete information. Incomplete information is truly a nasty problem because it often flies under the radar. Many analysts, data scientists, and other practitioners assume that the variables that they collected clearly define the system they are interested in modeling.

Let's say you have captured thousands of variables about user behavior. It's easy to mistake quantity for quality. However, often data on the most important variables in describing user behavior is not easily collected. The primary variable that is left out of analyses but is vital to determining behavior is motivation or user goals.

Going back to the dinner party, it's essential to know how your guests define fun, what goals or expectations they had prior to attending, and how the party measured up to those expectations. All three pieces of data are vital information for accessing dinner party *greatness* or underlying incentive structures, but not something that you'll likely ever be privy to, except maybe for your closest friends or family members (see Figure 1.1).

Figure 1.1 A hypothetical dinner party.

Consider the dinner party depicted in Figure 1.1; let's assume for the moment we're omniscient and can see the goals of each of the patrons. In a web product or in life, you will never have this information—but that does not make it any less vital. The more you can infer about the motivations of others, the more successful you will be at understanding your web product.

Users of our web product probably have a variety of motivations, and these motivations impact how they access and view the web product. Having an understanding of the individual goals and motivations can help us improve our product. When the host of the dinner party knows the motivations of each of his guests, he can optimize their experience. He can share recipes with Lisa and help Paul make some new friends. Understanding motivations is important to improving experiences, but is almost always left out of models.

1.2.6   A Party Presents a Variable Search Problem

Another key feature of a social process is the large number of potential variables that could define the process. What aspects of the party are important to determining quality? Is it the alliteration of guests' first conversation? Is it how many people they interacted with? How much food they ate? The order in which they did various things? Some variables might make more sense than others, but there are many potential variables and it's not clear which ones are the most important.

You might be able to keep track of who talked to whom at your dinner party. But you might struggle to remember the actual conversation topics, and the length and quality of their discussion. Similarly, in web products, some features are much easier to capture, but it doesn't necessarily make them the best features. As we have seen, omitted information like goals and expectations is very important, yet information we may never obtain. Instead, we could have thousands of much less useful variables that we need to sift through to find the right ones to describe the process. As we will discuss later, having a theory or mental model of the process can help us to potentially narrow down the pool, organize variables, and identify missing variables.

1.2.7   The Real Secret to a Great Party Is Elusive

Let's think about a very hard-to-answer question: What could you have done to make the party better? Should you have spent time getting better food, inviting different people, or choosing a different weekend? If we knew what *caused* a *great* party, as crazy as that sounds, then we could maximize the quality of our party. For instance, suppose we knew that having copious amounts of alcohol *caused* people to stay longer at the party and have more fun. No other factor affected the quality of the party. In that case, we could optimize our party simply by having lots of alcohol available.

While we may have some thoughts as to what may *cause* a better party, we cannot test our assertions, because we have no counterfactual. A **counterfactual** is an alternative situation where everything is the same except the variable that influences our outcome; it allows us to determine how this one difference would change the result. For instance, if we could hold two parties that were exactly the same, but one had copious amounts of alcohol on hand and one did not, the party where we did not have lots of alcohol available would be a counterfactual. We could then assess the effect of copious amounts of alcohol on our dinner party. For most social events, many other factors would almost certainly come into play, making it impossible to have a counterfactual. With web products, the prognosis for causation is a little better, especially to determine simple factors, but for larger factors creating a valid counterfactual is very difficult. We will discuss this issue in detail in subsequent chapters in the book.

We'll spend a great amount of time dealing with situations where experimentation is possible and those where it is not. One very traditional experimental set-up is a split-test, where people are randomly assigned to groups, with one group getting a given treatment and another group acting as the control. The control group is analogous to a counterfactual. Many medical studies are conducted this way, with half the group getting a new drug or treatment and the other half getting a placebo pill or control (a fake pill that doesn't contain any drug). A split-test in a web product is called an A/B test.

For instance, suppose you wanted to test green versus red for your website's background. You can test the background color by using a counterfactual, a red background, because your site is normally red. Half of the users who visit your site would be randomly assigned to the new green background and the other half to the old red background. You could then determine whether there was an increase in user retention with your new green background.

Conducting an experiment or an A/B test is often not feasible, because of various constraints such as an inability to randomize or the fact that the event already occurred. Thus, we often need to use other methods for causal inference. Tools used to deal with situations when an A/B test is not feasible include natural experiments, regression discontinuity, and statistical matching; they are discussed in the causal inference section of the book. This book will provide you with tools on how to infer causation in situations where you are unable to conduct an A/B test.

Exploring human behavior in a web product is like analyzing a real-life social process, albeit with one major difference. During social events such as a party, these social processes and interactions are taking place in a real physical location. Being able to see and experience those social interactions even as an observer makes it easier to see and identify the underlying process. It also makes it easier to identify them as social events.

In the past, there has been little focus on the social dimension of web products because many analysts and data scientists do not view web products as analogous to other social events. Part of the reason is that we're dealing with data: We're not able to watch the user experience the product and the subsequent interactions that take place within our web product. *But human behavior in web products is human behavior*. After reading this book, you should be able to work with large data sets, identify the core underlying social processes at play, and test your inferences.

1.3   What's Unique about User Data?

In this section, we walk through each of the six essential aspects of social data discussed in the prior section in greater detail and in relation to web products. We also provide some practical examples of each of these potential obstacles. Throughout the book, we'll come back to these core concepts as we delve into more sophisticated tools to deal with each of the six problems.

1.3.1   Human Behavior Is a Process, Not a Problem

A **social process** is defined as a "mutual interaction experienced by an individual or group in their attempt to achieve desired goals or further norms of interaction." Let's unpack this definition. First, an interaction is driven by either *goals* or *norms*. As we discussed in the last section, human beings are motivated to carry out certain behaviors during an interaction. Understanding what motivates them is crucial to explaining behavior. The second driver is norms or cultural mores.

Here is an example of a norm. In a social product, let's say you have two ways that you can "friend" other users. You can send a friend request and the users must accept it, or you can just click the "follow" button and the users do not need to accept your follow request. A user can initiate either social interaction with just one click. Let's say both are equally easy to do on your social platform.

Assessing descriptive data for this product, you find two times more follow actions than friend requests. Why the difference? Well, there are social norms around "friendship." Friendship might denote interaction in real life or some level of commonality, which may be a higher threshold than a follow action.

Some of your users may fear rejection or nonresponse. Both of these factors could be socially meaningful, leading to lower levels of friending behavior or replacing friending actions with follow actions.

Those norms are present in your social community, and they *absolutely* affect behavior. As you control the functionality of the product, you can encourage users to break social norms (at least to some extent) or create new norms.

A social process encompasses multiple—sometimes thousands or more—ordered events over time, rather than a single event or occurrence. By contrast, problems are often focused on a single outcome or occurrence. For instance, classifying whether a picture is a dog or a human has one clear outcome. A singular process results in that outcome—that is, finding features that differentiate humans and dogs. By comparison, the underlying complexity makes modeling social behavior much harder.

In addition, in a social process, individuals and groups can learn and adjust to future events by changing their behavior. When you build a model, you often assume that behavior remains the same over time. However, starting from the assumption that most of human behavior in a web product is *learned* and adjusted will lead you to completely different results, methodologies. and best practices. Learned behavior is often *changed* behavior. In Chapter 3, we'll explore behavior change in more detail.

Overall, a process is different from a problem. A problem is defined as "an inquiry from certain conditions to demonstrate or investigate a fact, condition or law." A problem is often focused on deriving a solution. With human behavior, there is no clear solution. Instead, the underlying process is often just as important as any potential chosen outcome. This is what makes the problem framework less useful in this context—although in some cases we can divide processes into smaller pieces that might fit better into a problem framework.

How do we go about exploring a social process? The first step is usually qualitative: understanding what is happening in your application. Do you have descriptive information that completely describes what is happening in your web application? Start collecting as much information as possible about what users are doing in your product and how they are doing it.

Social behavior is also multidimensional, so the second step is setting up a testable mental model. We'll discuss this in much greater detail in Chapter 2 on theory building. Basically, your mental model should have a few characteristics: It should be broad, lead to useful conclusions, and be falsifiable. Once you have a testable theory, you can develop core metrics that you can track over time and across different cross-sections of your user population.

Practical Examples

Here are a couple of practical examples:

- **The Enigma of the Profile Picture.** When a company developing a web product hires its first data scientist or analyst, the first area of focus is often product retention or how long a user remains in a product. Product retention is a complex process. However, there are two common ways of looking at it in industry: (1) through descriptive metrics and (2) by the factors that predict retention.

  Perhaps users with a profile picture remain in the product much longer than those that don't. A product manager seeing these results might say, "Let's force all our users to upload a picture or make the profile picture upload the first step of onboarding. It'll increase our product retention."

  When the team makes this change to the product, it only slightly increases retention. What does this mean? The profile picture likely did not *cause* retention, but was only correlated with retention. Maybe some other variable is driving both retention in the product and the desire to upload a profile picture. Retention is a much more complex process than we originally anticipated, and the tools that we are currently using are not sufficient to understand what actually *causes* an increase in retention.

- **A Middle School Dance?** In many social web products, particularly social networks, the vast majority of users create very little content. Instead, they mostly consume content. A small number of users dominate the platform, having many connections, creating most of the content, and using the full functionality of the product. They might even know the product better than its designers do! It's like a middle school dance where most attendees are wallflowers standing against the gym wall and a few gregarious, adventurous sixth-graders are dancing in the center. The others watch cautiously, not daring to make their way to the center of the dance floor.

  The question then becomes: Can you get these wallflowers off the wall and into the center of the dance floor? Most likely you can't drag most of them onto the dance floor. Then should you make a product that caters to the silent majority or one that serves the most vocal, most active users? Every product must deal with this inherent tension between the majority of passive, low-key users and the vocal minority. It's a problem that highlights the reality that a web product is a social system. Creating, maintaining, and trying to optimize that social ecosystem are key to having a healthy product. Some products like Instagram and Snapchat have solved this problem by using filters instead of creating unique content. Although, there are many ways to deal with this inherent tension.

1.3.2   No Clear and Defined Outcomes

As we touched on in the last section, there are no clear and defined outcomes for social processes. Many techniques in machine learning and artifical intelligence were built for problems with clear and defined outcomes. Let's talk about some famous problems in ML/AI and how the outcomes for those problems are vastly different than those for understanding human behavior.

First, one of the defining problems in computer vision is digit classification. Digit classification is the problem of having a computer place any one of the ten handwritten digits {0, 1, 2, 3,4, 5, 6, 7, 8, 9} into the correct class—that is, correctly identify handwritten numbers. It's a difficult problem because people may write their 4s, 9s, or other digits in different ways. Historically, a postal carrier would read the address on a letter and classify it. However, that's not true today because of the power of machine learning.

Certain machine learning algorithms are extraordinarily good at solving this problem. A human classifier gets substantially less than 1 wrong out of 100—and that's comparable to the best machine learning algorithms. These algorithms are so good that the U.S. Postal Service uses them to classify the millions of letters that pass through its mailrooms daily. Imagine the cost if a postal worker had to classify all these letters.

Digit classification has a clear and defined outcome. When creating a practice data set, human digit creators were asked to write and then type the digit. There is a correct outcome for every single element in the practice data set. For human data, this is not necessarily the case. We may never know if your guests enjoyed the dinner party. *They* may not even know if they truly enjoyed the dinner party. *There is not always a correct answer.*

There are also various definitions, levels, and aspects of *fun*. Each person may mean something very different by *fun*, but all of their interpretations would be classified into the "had *fun*" category. It's a very "fuzzy" outcome that contains error. The degree of error cannot necessarily even be assessed. Imagine trying to apply the same type of algorithm used to solve the digit classification problem when classifying dinner party fun. It's a much less powerful algorithm in the latter case because of the lack of clarity and error in our outcome variable.

Why do we assume that algorithms created to solve problems with clear and concrete outcomes would be great at dealing with fuzzy outcomes and human heuristics or simple approximate solutions? They aren't.

Another famous problem is the traveling salesman problem, a very simple challenge. A salesman wants to travel to a few cities like Boston, San Francisco, and New York. He wants to find the shortest path by which to visit these cities. Should he head to New York, Boston, and then San Francisco, or should he head to New York, San Francisco, and then Boston? Obviously, the first ordering is shorter than the latter. However, this problem can get tricky with lots of cities. Note that this problem has an optimal solution, which can be found by calculating all the paths through different orderings of cities. Again—surprise!—it's a clear and well-defined solution.

We can find fuzzy solutions that are pretty good, too. It's easy to eliminate the worst path of NY, SF, Boston. The other two choices are similar: NY, Boston, SF and Boston, NY, SF. Okay, so we have two potentially acceptable results. With either option, this problem has a clear and defined outcome: We can assess whether the option is an acceptable result by comparing it against the optimal result. However, we cannot do the same for social data. Even if we have a "fuzzy" acceptable result in our head, we can't measure it against some correct result. Suppose we've decided to assess our dinner party by counting the guests who come to our second dinner party. Seventy-five percent of the original guests show up at the second party. But we don't really know what the cutoff is for a successful dinner party: Is a 90% rate of attendance good? And we don't know how much that second-attendance number varies for different successful dinner parties. There are a lot of potential problems with using algorithms that assume singular, optimal outcomes for social processes.

The most "fuzzy" conceptual question in modern computing is the Turing test. Alan Turing, the father of modern-day computer science, was interested in the question of whether machines can think. To answer this question, which is rather fuzzy, he suggested a well-structured experiment. The experiment was supposed to resolve this question. It sets up a narrow, clear, and defined outcome to a fuzzy, broad question. The idea behind the Turing test is to create a computer that is so "human-like" that it gets mistaken for human. In the modern conception of the experiment, a computer program must convince more than 30% of judges in five-minute keyboard conversations that it is a human.

Does this experiment fundamentally answer the question "Do machines think?" Not necessarily, but it allows us a framework in which to make advancements toward answering this question. When the Turing test is passed, it means we have a machine that can convince 30% of judges that it can think. In many ways, social behavior is the same way: We must define a theory, create metrics, and develop narrow experiments to get at aspects of a process. This will move forward our development or understanding in a significant way and help us reframe and better formulation theories, metrics, and experiments.

Practical Examples

Here are a couple of practical examples:

- **The Trap of Unclear Goals.** Often, it's not clear what is the goal(s) of a given analysis. It's useful to determine the possible product changes or business goals that could be assessed with this analysis and find outcomes that are useful to reaching these goals. While this might seem obvious, it is difficult to do in practice.

  Why? First, the organization may have competing goals. For example, suppose you have a product whose goal is to enhance healthy behaviors among its users. The business does not necessarily make money directly from healthy behaviors, but rather from engagement and size of the user base (how many times a user may visit the site each month). In this scenario, the goals may be contradictory in that some product changes that you make may increase engagement, but decrease healthy behaviors. You need to be able to quantify the relationship between the two goals to find the optimal outcome for the company, which is often difficult in practice.

  Second, the stakeholders themselves may not understand what is possible with a given analysis. You need to be able to communicate what is and is not possible. For instance, with A/B testing and experimentation, we can test only small changes. A/B testing will not search the millions of potential features for the best to test, but it will test the few features we chose as candidates. The potential changes to a web product could be infinite, so how do we decide what to test? Well, A/B testing will not help us there. Stakeholders may not understand this fact and have different expectations.

- **Limited Documentation.** Often, the analysts and the developers who write the production code to collect data are not the same people. When we see variables in Google analytics or in internal databases, we often do not know exactly what they are capturing. To make matters worse, often companies have limited documentation. Commonly in industry, analysis is done before there is full understanding of what a given variable is capturing. This painful problem can be found in both the largest and the smallest companies. It's often understated and might be embedded in work that's already been done.

1.3.3 Social Systems Have Rampant Problems of Incomplete Information

Incomplete information is present in situations in which there is asymmetric information, where one side has more information than another, or where both sides lack complete understanding of the motivations, payoffs, and behavior of the other side. Incomplete information is a problem in many web products, because users might have different amounts of information about a product and it may define their behavior. The analyst may also lack complete information about the underlying social behaviors of the participants.

From the definition of a social process ("any mutual interaction experienced by an individual or a group with others in their attempt to achieve desired goals ..."), it's clear that understanding participants' goals is highly important when explaining social processes. Impetus drives action. But motivation, like other important social variables, is based on information and not always easy to obtain from both the user's and the analyst's perspectives.

User research is one way the analyst can get at what motivates users and other important social dimensions. But user research (including surveys, focus groups, and other ways to speak to gain feedback) is often plagued with biases or misconceptions. You may never truly know what motivates your user base—they may never tell you, and it may never truly be observable. In later chapters, we'll discuss techniques to deal with problems of incomplete information.

Practical Example

Pedometer Data

For most products, it's very clear that you'll never have full data. For instance, suppose you have pedometer data available. An individual user's number of steps can greatly vary by day, and you may never know why.

You may suspect that users are not wearing the pedometer every day. Conducting surveys, focus groups, and other methods to solicit user feedback is an important part of the process of solving the problem. Qualitative data can be very useful in potentially answering this type of question. Quantitative survey data can be integrated with product data, but it still may not answer all our questions and it may contradict our product data.

There may be another reason for the variation in daily steps. Perhaps it reflects changes in the user's schedule—a user taking a day off work, running a marathon, or traveling.

You may make assumptions about when your users are wearing their pedometers or that each day's schedule is similar. Is there any way to evaluate these assumptions?

We cannot ask every user about their individual patterns, so we must make some assumptions. The quality of those assumptions can greatly affect our ability to understand and change behavior related to our product.

1.3.4 Social Systems Consist of Millions of Potential Behaviors

Working with a social process inevitably means working with lots of variables. Think of any social product. There are potentially hundreds of actions that you can take in any order. You can interact with other users and their content, and they can interact with you and your content, which can lead to thousands, if not millions, of variables. Some variables are useless, like the degree of alliteration in the first conversation with another user in a web product. Other variables are very useful. For instance, maybe the timing—that is, when a piece of content is posted—is relevant. The relationship between social feedback and time posted could be very important to understanding whether that post triggers feedback. We know that finding the right metrics and features to track is often more important to building quality products than using sophisticated modeling methods.

Having millions of potential features leads to a large search problem. We're left trying to find a needle in a haystack. How do we solve the search problem and find the right variables?

A user expert may be able to find core variables in a space that you were not aware of. Human beings tend to create great heuristics like the one that solves the traveling salesman problem. We may not be right, but we might come very close. Sometimes the proverbial "smell test" may not be a bad first pass at accessing variables that should be included. Of course, these variables should be tested (we don't want to fall into problems of confirmation bias), as we'll discuss more in later sections.

Confirmation bias is a skewing of data that occurs when we explicitly search for results or build patterns based on what we already believe. The key is to let user experts alert you to variables not on your radar and help you navigate the search problem. Even so, you must always test the proposed variables or inferences.

Try to contextualize how large the number of potential variables is and organize the variables by type. In a product, you may have solo behavioral variables, game variables, social network variables, social interaction variables, and more. Organizing them into conceptual hierarchies helps you to organize the search space and potentially identify areas that you are missing. There are numerous ways to then explore the space—relying on a user expert, using randomness, engaging in trial and error, and consulting the academic literature may all be useful for identifying the quality variables.

Practical Example

Motivation in Smoking Cessation

We'll see an example later in this text about the use of digital coaching to help people quit smoking. In that example, hundreds of variables were collected and used to build a matching model. But something was always missing; the variables just weren't that predictive. While reading some academic literature on smoking cessation, we realized the most important variable related to smoking cessation was actually *motivation to quit smoking*. Intrinsic motivation is vital to understanding social processes and is often left out of data science models.

1.3.5 Social Systems Are Often Open Systems

A **closed system** is a system that doesn't exchange any matter with its surroundings, and isn't subject to any force whose source is external to the system. Social systems are not closed, however, so an outside variable can affect the underlying system. Many physical processes and algorithmic processes are closed systems, and we assume in most models that the underlying system is closed.

For instance, the traveling salesman problem is a closed system. We assume that no other outside variables can affect the length of the paths to the different cities. However, road closures, weather, and other factors could all potentially affect the distance from city A to city B. When creating a model of a process, we must assume we are working with a closed system. The trick is to assess the quality of that assumption. How large would an external shock have to be to change this underlying system? Also, we need to think about which variables that we are not including, yet might affect this system.

When dealing with a closed system, we must look for variables that are potential disrupters to a social process. In the dinner party example, illness, weather, and uninvited individuals might all affect the quality of the party. Variables that do the most damage to our models are rare event variables that have a large effect when they occur.

Also, we need to focus on what assumptions we are making to create a closed system. Can you assess how large the effect would need to be to disrupt your system? What is the mechanism by which it could affect your system? It's important to explore these questions, even if you cannot answer them perfectly.

Practical Example

Can We "Game" the Game?

In many mobile games (and really any game), "cheats" exist to help the gamers get into a more advantageous position than they would otherwise deserve. Often, awareness of a "cheat" among game participants starts as a drip, and quickly burgeons into a flood. If a cheat is large enough, like immediate leveling or amassing infinite resources, it quickly changes your entire game ecosystem.

In multiplayer games, if the game becomes too unequal or skewed toward certain players due to this sort of cheating, it turns off new users. Cheating can turn a great multiplayer game into a bad multiplayer game and needs to be addressed immediately. Outside variables or phenomena not accounted for, like bugs that cause cheats or unexpected patterns of play, can drastically change the social dynamics and difficulty of a multiplayer game. It's important to address major variables that can cause an exogenous or outside shock to your product or change the way the community functions immediately.

There will always be users who try to "game" the system. The question is how important these "cheats" are and how widespread knowledge of them has become. The gaming community can be close-knit, allowing knowledge of "cheats" to spread quickly.

1.3.6 Inferring Causation Is *Almost* Impossible

Causal relationships between variables lead to actionable insights and changing user behavior. For instance, how do we get users to purchase more? If we can understand what makes them purchase more, then we can build a very profitable business.

1.3.6.1 Types of Inference

There are a few ways to validate our inferences, causal or otherwise. As discussed earlier, one way to validate a causal inference is to compare it against a counterfactual. Most of scientific experimentation is validated this way.

Think of running an experiment in a Petri dish. Let's say we want to test the effect of penicillin on the growth of bacteria in two Petri dishes. We apply penicillin to one Petri dish and not the other, keeping both dishes in analogous environments and observing the effect. This is one way to validate an inference—in this case, the inference that penicillin limits the growth of bacteria. After running our experiment, we can determine penicillin's effect. Sadly, not all situations are conducive to this form of inference. When that's the case, we can use other types of inference.

Statisticians often rely on inference based on randomness. Inference from randomness can be set-up to test causal linkages, but more must be done with the design to ensure causal inference. How does it work? Suppose an event is very unlikely to occur randomly; if it then happens, it likely occurred because of some reason (that is, not randomly).

Think of it this way. An earthquake hits a remote island every two years. The island is uninhabited, so no one was around to observe if an earthquake occurred in the last month, but we can observe and measure the current algae growth. The month after an earthquake, we tend to see a high growth rate in algae. It's very rare to achieve this high level of algae growth naturally without an earthquake—let's say that random algae growth to this level happens one month in every hundred years naturally. Back on our island, we observe a very high level of algae growth, so can we infer that an earthquake took place in the last month?

Okay, this sounds like a brainteaser question—but it's not. It's so rare that this algae growth rate would occur randomly that we can infer that it likely occurred due to an earthquake in the last month. We could also calculate the probability that we are incorrect via Bayes' rule (see the sidebar "Introduction to Bayes' Rule"). With inference based on randomness, we will never know for sure that there was an earthquake. It's just very, very likely, so much so that we assume that it's true, and in most cases it is.

Introduction to Bayes' Rule

Bayes' rule describes the probability of an event, based on prior knowledge of conditions that might be related to the event:

$$P(A \mid B) = \frac{P(B \mid A) \cdot P(A)}{P(B)}$$

Going back to the earthquake example, let's infer the probability that there is an earthquake using Bayes' rule. The probability that there will be an earthquake given algae bloom can be rewritten in a way to take advantage of the probabilities that we know. We know the probability of an algae bloom given that there was an earthquake and given that there was no earthquake. These probabilities are 1 and 1/1,200, respectively. We also know that if an earthquake occurs, it is always followed by an algae bloom, so the probability of an algae bloom given an earthquake is 1. We know that an algae bloom occurs naturally 1 out of every 12 months every 100 years, so 1/1,200 is the probability of a natural algae bloom. The probability of an earthquake is 1/24 since it happens every two years (24 months).

Now that we know those probabilities, we can use Bayes' rule to find the conditional probability that given an algae bloom, an earthquake has occurred recently. The denominator of the Bayes' rule equation is the probability of an algae bloom, which is the probability of an algae bloom given an earthquake and the probability of an algae bloom occurring naturally. The chance of this event occurring due to an earthquake is 1/24. We also have to account for the probability of an algae bloom occurring due to natural causes, which is 1/200 * (23/24). The numerator of the Bayes' rule equation is simply the probability of the reverse conditional—that is, the probability of algae given an earthquake, which as we said earlier is 1. This quantity is multiplied by the probability of an earthquake. This is simply 1/24 since the earthquake occurs every 24 months. If we multiply this out, we get about 98% chance that we had an earthquake given the algae bloom.

$$P(earthquake \mid algae) = \frac{P(algae \mid earthquake) * P(earthquake)}{P(algae)}$$

$$P(algae) = P(algae \mid earthquake) * P(earthquake) + P(algae \mid no\,earthquake) * P(no\,earthquake)$$

$$P(earthquake \mid algae) = \frac{(1)*(1/24)}{(1)*(1/24)+(1/1200)*(23/24)}$$

$$P(earthquake \mid algae) = \sim 98\%$$

With inference based on a counterfactual, as we used with the bacteria in Petri dishes, we are explicitly testing for causation. When we rely on randomness, cause and effect are an element of the design. We can design the parameters to determine whether the difference from randomness suggests a causal link. However, using inference from randomness does not have to be causal. In the earthquake/algae case, we are assessing whether an event occurred, not a causal link.

Another way to validate an inference is through prediction. If we can predict an outcome, it can validate our predictive model. Predictive inference is useful when predicting an outcome has some importance. For instance, demographers have focused on predicting total population. Being able to predict total population five or ten years in the future is useful because we need population estimates to assess societal needs. For instance, a school district may need an estimate of children who will enter kindergarten through 12th grade in the next five years so it can build the right number of schools, hire adequate numbers of teachers, and purchase enough books.

Similarly, the government may need to estimate the retiree population so that it can build nursing home facilities and train medical staff to provide care. Predicting population by age is useful in itself. With the example of population, we do not necessarily need to understand what factors cause population to grow; rather, the accuracy of the estimate of the future value is most important.

Sometimes analysts think the best way to validate that you understand user behavior is to predict it. In industry, many companies use predictive models to find good predictive variables and assume that they cause outcomes or are important to a system because of their predictive power.

Predictive inference is not the same as causal inference because variables can be correlated, or quantitatively related, without having one variable cause another. We'll discuss why this is bad practice in later chapters. Predictive inference validates our estimates of the future value of a quantity or the underlying quality of the model that we are using compared to other models, but not the causal links between variables.

In this section, we have introduced three separate types of inference: inference from experimentation, inference from randomness, and inference from prediction. We go into much greater detail on these approaches in later sections of this book.

1.4 Why Does Causation Matter?

Do job programs help workers get jobs? Does a high-quality education cause a higher income in the long run? Does drinking red wine lead to a longer life? Answering causal questions such as these is vital. It helps us make decisions about our health, helps the government build effective programs, and can help us build effective web products.

As discussed earlier, to assess causation, we rely on experimentation, having a convincing counterfactual or statistical design. Causal inference is incredibly powerful, because it can change behavior and outcomes. If we know that red wine leads to a longer life, we can start drinking more red wine and as a population we will live longer. Or if we know job programs work, the government can fund more of them. Understanding causation leads to *actions* that can be taken to *enhance* outcomes.

The magnitude of the effect—that is, how large it is—while not always considered or accurately estimated, is also important. If drinking red wine three days a week on average lengthens life by one year, then on average the people in our red wine drinking group will live a year longer. Hurray! That's a great effect. We'd want everyone to start drinking red wine three days a week!

If you can find factors that cause an outcome and on average have a large effect, then you can start pulling those levers. Think of causation as a cartoon machine with levers popping out of all angles and an output. Let's say we know the effect of each lever on the output. We can start pulling the levers that we need to create the perfect output. With social processes, as we discussed in the prior section, millions of variables or levers could potentially cause an outcome. We need to find (deal with the large search space) and isolate the levers we suspect are most powerful and test them.

This is clearly easier said than done—but if we can find those levers, we can change behavior and outcomes in our product. In a social product, suppose you want your users to purchase snowmobiles. If we can find the potential levers that lead to greater purchasing, then we can start pulling those levers.

Now consider an individual's purchasing behavior of snowmobiles. There could be a variety of nature and nurture variables—your genetic predisposition to love cold weather, whether your parents took you snowmobiling, your location, education, age, income, friends' interests, free time, quality of the website, models of snowmobiles available, and more. There are so many factors that it's hard to choose which ones to even look at.

Let's say we find that taking a ride on a snowmobile, walking into a snowmobile showroom, and whether your friends have a snowmobile are *causally* related to purchasing a snowmobile on average. If the magnitude of each of these factors is large, then we can try to pull these levers. We can offer this advice to the business owner, and he can better entice customers and target snowmobiles to the right customers to increase revenue.

Experience with social products shows that most variables tend to have a small causal effect. Finding those variables with a large causal effect is quite hard and takes either great insight into user behavior or running a lot of tests. We'll come back to this problem of changing user behavior in later chapters when discussing A/B testing, statistical matching, natural experiments, and other ways to access causal variables.

Practical Example

Last Call: Any Valid Counterfactual

There are lots of times when we will not be able to run an A/B test, but still desire to know the causal effect. It could be that a campaign has already run or the costs to A/B test a large marketing campaign are too high. Whatever the reason, we may be able to still infer causal relationships by finding a valid counterfactual. For instance, we can exploit geographic variations. Often, media campaigns (for instance, TV campaigns) are run only in certain designated market areas (DMAs). If you can find two DMAs that are very similar based on the qualities that could affect the efficacy of a media campaign, except one had a media campaign and the other did not, you might be able to use the DMA without the campaign as a valid counterfactual. It's possible to use geography (here in terms of DMA, but also by county, state, or country) or other dimensions of an analysis (i.e., time or random cut points) to create valid counterfactuals to assess the causal effect. While these estimates of the causal effect might not be perfect, they can provide substantial evidence to support a future campaign that is A/B tested. These post hoc efforts to test causal effects can be particularly useful in industry.

This chapter has introduced some of the unique problems associated with analyzing user behavior in a web product context. Social processes are processes, not problems. They are open systems with large numbers of potential variables and outcomes, rampant problems of incomplete information, and no well-defined outcomes. Of course, these issues make inferring causation exceedingly difficult—but causation is core to behavior change and understanding your social system. This book will provide you with a comprehensive toolkit to address these six challenges and use the latest methods available to deeply understand your web product.

1.5   Actionable Insights

Actionable insights from this chapter are the following:

- Web products are microcosms of the social universe.

- A gap exists between social processes in a web product and modern data science solutions.

- A web product is an open process or system with millions of possible human behaviors. It's filled with incomplete information, has no defined outcomes, and causal linkages that are difficult to find.

- We need a *counterfactual* to make inferences about causal linkages. Many analysts use predictive validation or correlation between variables to draw incorrect causal linkages.

In the next chapter, we'll start building conceptual models of web products and metrics to test those models.

2

Building a Theory of the Social Universe

In Chapter 1, "Data in Action: A Model of a Dinner Party," there was an example of how user analytics sometimes feels like a game of whack-a-mole, where disparate facts are woven together trying to create a cohesive story that is constantly updated with new information. To help you avoid the problems associated with analyzing data in this way, this chapter will walk you through the process of building testable theories. We'll start off with the dinner party example, but end the chapter with three potential user analytics theories that can be tested. Every time we need to analyze a new social process in a web product, we should start with theory building. It's the necessary foundation to derive actionable insight.

This chapter covers the following topics:

- Building and validating a conceptual model

- Creating metrics from abstract, intangible concepts

- Making inferences about human behavior from data

This chapter is a practical, how-to guide for building conceptual models, testing hypotheses, and creating metrics to test complex theories about user behavior. Having a solid theory is the cornerstone to extracting actionable insight from your web or mobile product.

2.1 Building a Theory

Chapter 1 delved into some of the difficulties of working with behavioral data and modeling social processes. This chapter will help us build theory and define concepts that we can test. For instance, suppose we have a content generation problem in our product. In a content generation problem, users are not generating or sharing enough content in the product, leading to a bare product. It's a common dilemma that makes a product less sticky. To test if this is actually the case, we need to create metrics to quantify the quality and quantity of any content being generated.

It's relatively easy to define quantity. We could do so in this case by counting messages, pictures, and comments. But determining the quality of content means that we need to start thinking about measuring qualitative concepts like "surprising" or "entertaining" content. This chapter will teach you how to go from abstract theories to quantifiable metrics.

2.1.1 Won't Fancy Algorithms Solve All Our Problems?

Building *theory* is vital to improving a web product because we need a framework for understanding what is happening in our product. Otherwise, we're left with a string of unintelligible facts.

I remember meeting an executive who ran one of the core businesses for a large multinational company. He told us he had spent millions of dollars hiring an outside company to run A/B tests in different areas, but he still had no holistic understanding of the product. He knew that under scenario X, users would pick Y, and he knew that a user was moving from product P to Q. But, he had no idea how to fit this information into any kind of broader understanding of the product. Looking back, I wish I would have said, "For *half the price* you paid to those outside consulting companies, I could offer you a better and more holistic view of your product. All you have to do is change your approach to understanding user behavior. *You need to start from the higher level and work your way down to the details, rather than working from the details up.*"

Why were users coming to this executive's product and what were they doing when they got there? He was not sure. He started with no theory, just hypotheses in different unrelated areas that he wanted to test. We could not put that information together in an intelligible way, so the minor pieces of data were useless. The project *failed*. Data is useful, but only when we have a broader context to understand that data—and that's what a theory provides us. We need a holistic picture to organize our ideas. It helps us document what we need to test in our product and where open questions remain.

2.1.2 The Pervasive (and Generally Useless) One-Off Fact

As in the scenario with the executive, in our fast-paced world interesting one-off facts make someone seem more knowledgeable. But this leads to the proliferation of random facts that *obscure*, rather than *enhance*, our understanding.

Suppose you are working as a data scientist for a new company that offers a web streaming platform (basically a Fire TV or Roku-type device where you can stream videos from other sources with social functionality). When you start, your manager tells you the following three facts and asks for your advice: (1) Users of Roku who are Netflix subscribers have declining rates of streaming toward the end of the month; (2) when users are unemployed, they stream Roku at much higher rates; and (3) new users generally wait to receive a message before sending one. He asks you: "What is your advice to enhance user engagement?"

The correct answer from a data analysis point of view is that you have no idea. (Of course, as with all things in this book, just because something makes sense from a statistical or analytical point of view, that does not make it palatable in a work situation.)

To generalize, *in some random case, users do this or that.* You ask yourself, What is actually happening all the other times? More precisely, what happens to usage of non-Netflix subscribers, what is happening to usage when users are employed, and what other types of social interactions—such as passively consuming other people's content, and liking or following other users—are people engaging in? From just hearing these three facts, we actually have no idea what's going on in the rest of the product. Often, people just fill in that vacuum of information with erroneous assumptions—like "non-Netflix users usage grows toward the end of the month." And "after losing a job, users feel depressed and watch Roku." And finally, "new users are not engaging in any other social behavior." But are these assumptions really true? As before, we have no idea—and probably not.

Most people need **context** or background on what is happening before they can accept and understand new facts. Without context, we're left feeling like a lost puppy. We see certain familiar guideposts, but don't know how to get home. That's why having a mental model or theory that is substantiated with data is so useful. It allows us to contextualize how users are behaving in a variety of contexts, and then facts can add to the richness of that understanding.

2.1.3   The Art of the Typology

Categorization, or the practice of putting objects into groups, is a very helpful technique for understanding and generalizing behavior and, in my opinion, is not used nearly enough. *Effectively using typologies can be the difference between deriving an actionable insight from a hypothesis or model and not gaining such insight.*

In one of my first jobs as a data scientist, I was asked to take over a project to quantify social behavior in that product. The company had no social behavior categories. It captured social behavior as the sum of the number of likes, messages, and other interactive content. This led to a very watered-down and useless metric. Simply summing all social behavior, both incoming and outgoing, builds an erroneous indicator. It conflates lots of types of users: (1) users who have a large inbound interaction (meaning messages coming in), (2) users with large outbound interaction (meaning messages going out), and (3) users with varying amounts of inbound and outbound interactions.

This practice suggests that users are one-dimensional people: They either engage in some social interactions or they do not. One also quickly realizes that counting these behaviors often leads to redundant information. For instance, an active social user will generally have lots of both messages and likes—and since those actions are very highly related, little new information is added by summing them. We are also not counting any passive behavior as social engagement. In reality, the first step to commenting or messaging is often passive—reading others' content. Basically, we need to rethink how social behavior works, how different types of social interactions relate to each other, and how we can build indicators that actually reflect meaningful dimensions of social behavior.

Categorization enables us to order and organize lots of data in contextually and meaningful ways. Having categories under "social behavior" helps us to take large numbers of variables and develop a **typology**—that is, ways group subtypes of social behavior that make intuitive sense. For instance, let's say the dimensions that matter for social behavior are active or passive and incoming or outgoing. We can create the typology of social behavior shown in Figure 2.1.

We have four categories:

- **Active out-social:** Out-flowing and active, such as sending messages or liking others' posts.

- **Passive out-social:** Out-flowing and passive, such as reading others' posts or looking at their profiles.

- **Active in-social:** In-flowing and active, such as having someone else sending you a message or comment on a picture.

- **Passive in-social**: In-flowing and passive, such as having someone else read your content.

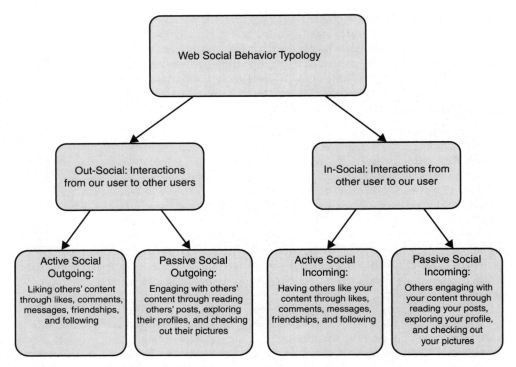

Figure 2.1   Typology of social behavior.

Using this scheme, we can better categorize the behavior that we see and more broadly understand patterns within these different categories of social behavior. We can also identify which behavior is interesting. For instance, we can ask why this person is choosing the passive types of interaction but eschewing active engagement. Also, how does messaging coming in impact messaging going out? Can we enhance messaging by automatically sending a "welcome" message to all new users from an established account?

Without categorizing social behavior, the concept becomes meaningless and we are unable to do anything with it. It may seem like a simple process to build categories (and not the meaty or interesting analytics work), but it's essential. Moreover, without categorization, there often is no actionable insight.

2.1.4 The Project Design Process: Theory Building

The project design process is how one goes from generalizing patterns in user behavior to testing and inference. There are four core aspects of the project design process:

- **Theory development:** Building a general model for how users are behaving in product.

- **Hypothesis generation:** Defining some testable statements that could help validate that theory.

- **Metric creation:** Finding quantifiable measures that represent the desirable quantities.

- **Modeling and inference**: Carrying out experimentation and modeling to make inferences from the original theory.

All of these core aspects of the project design process are needed to fully explore user behavior. The next few sections will explore the first three elements of the project design process.

Figure 2.2 shows the process of moving to model validation.

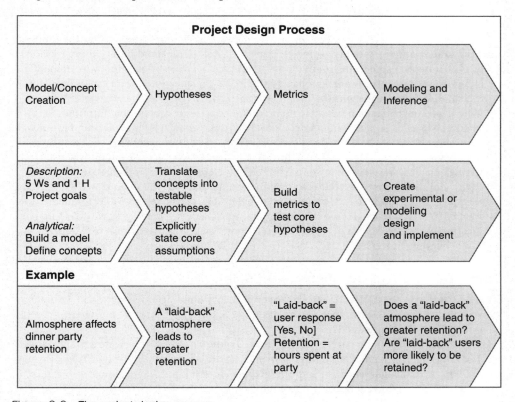

Figure 2.2 The project design process.

2.1.5 Steps to a Good Theory

Before we talk about the important elements of the project design process for theories, let's start by defining a theory.

Theory

A plausible or scientifically acceptable general principle or body of principles offered to explain phenomena.

In this case, the phenomenon we are often trying to explain or predict is human behavior. We are trying to define principles that can explain why people do what they do. A theory has two core building blocks: concepts and principles. **Concepts** are abstract ideas, as we discussed in the previous section. **Principles** are "fundamental truths or propositions that serve as the foundation for a system of beliefs a behavior or for a chain of reasoning." Principles are the connections between ideas in an argument. They set up how different objects or concepts are interrelated. A theory is *not* a hypothesis. A **hypothesis** is an intelligent conjecture that needs to be tested, while a theory is much greater than that. *In essence, a theory is a set of proven or testable factors that explain the phenomenon.*

There are two fundamental reasons why we would want to develop a theory. One is to understand the system, and the other is to predict future behavior. Understanding a system generally means explaining *why* something occurs. Once we can answer the *why* question, we can modify our system. Many executives want actionable insights. By understanding what causes behavior in our system, we can derive insights that will modify behavior in the way that we want.

Predicting future behavior in a system is also useful because we can use that information to make better marketing and investment decisions. For instance, we want to understand *why* people purchase (so we can increase those purchases), or at least what causes them to purchase and whether they will purchase again in the future. A good theory will increase our understanding of purchasing behavior as well as allow us to predict who will likely make a purchase in the future.

When building a theory, we need a few essential components. In this chapter, we'll discuss five unique aspects of a good theory: It needs to be generalizable, objective, verifiable, falsifiable, and reproducible. We'll go through each of these components in detail. But, before we head into our investigation of the ingredients of a good theory, let's consider this question: Where do we start the theory building process?

2.1.6 Description: Questions and Goals

The very first step in the project design process or in theory building is description. If we don't know what we're working with, then we can't assess or analyze anything. We need to first describe the process that we are interested in.

Let's go back to the dinner party example (from Chapter 1). How do we create a simple model to better understand what makes a dinner party *fun*? Before we can determine what's *fun*, we need to know what actually happened at the dinner party and what is *fun*. There are a few core questions that we need to think about and answer.

- What are people actually doing at our dinner party—the *who, what, where, when*, and *how* questions?

- What makes a dinner party fun?

- *Why* are people doing what they are doing?

- What *motivates* our guests to do what they do?

In journalism, a new writer is taught that the core questions to answer for any story are *who, what, where, when, why,* and *how* (called the five *W's* and one *H*). In product analytics, it's similar. We need to understand the core functionality of our product, and by answering these core questions we have a better sense of what we want to understand. What functionality does our web product allow? What are people doing in the product? Who is doing those things and how are they doing them? When and where are they occurring? And last, but not least, why are they occurring?

Let's start this process with our dinner party. First, we need to answer the questions of who came, when, what did they do at the party, and how did they do it. Let's pretend you were a fly on the wall and you watched everything that your guests did. We could generalize and say that your guests partook in three types of activities: (1) socialization, (2) watching the game, and (3) drinking and eating. Every person at your dinner party experienced 1 and 3, but many did not experience 2. The amount of time spent and the level of intensity for all three activities varied by guests. There were also things that your guests did not do at your party, like sleep, spend time reading a book, or doing yard work. These insights are foundational bricks for our theory.

Why is description important? Without assessing what could and does happen, we can't build theories. For a web product, user behavior is often not observable. We need to think about the core functionality of a product and determine what is possible and what it means. For instance, let's say we have a web product where the only social behavior that a user can exhibit is liking a purchase. For instance, Joe purchased a snowmobile, and Martha saw his purchase on his profile and liked it. What does "liking" mean in this context? Who is Martha? Does Martha know Joe in real life? These are all questions that need to be thought about at this point. We need to understand the functionality of a product and, at a high level, what users are doing in the product.

Once, we know what happened, then we must think about the *outcomes*. What are you interested in understanding or explaining? For the dinner party example, we were interested in understanding what a *great* party is. By *great*, we mean our guest had enough *fun* that they would agree to attend a similar party in the future. From there, we can theorize what behaviors or processes are important for that outcome.

2.1.7 Analytical: Theory and Concepts

Next, you should think about the *why*. Why are your users behaving the way they are? What motivates them? Are there any connections or mechanisms that you can think of? We'll go into this process in depth. For right now, let's come up with a theory for our dinner party.

For instance, you could theorize that three things are important to having a *great* party:

- An entertaining social atmosphere
- Good food and drink
- Nice guests

With the right combination of these three things, guests feel at ease, are able to meet their goals of having a relaxing, entertaining evening, and would return for another party in the future.

We have just described what we think is intuitively happening—our hypothesis. That hypothesis could be true, partially true, or false. So, we need to test our model. Right now, though, we don't have the tools to test it. For instance, we don't know how to quantify an *entertaining social atmosphere*. Also, we don't have clear statements from our theory that can be validated. In Section 2.2, "Conceptualization and Measurement," we'll tackle how to conceptualize, measure, and test theory hypotheses. First, we need to understand the components of a good theory.

2.1.8 Qualities of a "Good" Theory

Certain qualities make one theory preferable to another. The five qualities of a good theory are the following:

- *Generalizable*: identifying common phenomenon, behaviors, or incentives
- *Objective*: free from bias
- *Verifiable*: can be tested
- *Falsifiable*: can be proven false
- *Reproducible*: consistent and can be shown in different contexts and examples

This section will discuss these five qualities in detail.

2.1.8.1 Generalization

While theory development is a creative process, we can use some techniques to facilitate this process. The first step is getting a sense of what could happen and what did happen. We explored this process in the previous section in regard to the dinner party. Having a complete understanding of our product and a high-level view of how users are interacting with the product is the first step. With a web product, you should probably avoid collecting any data during the first step. Just observe the behavior of your product, taking a holistic view of what is happening and what functionalities are and are not available. Don't let looking at too much data too early bias your theory.

The next step is to start formulating testable statements—that is, the process of hypothesis generation. To begin this process, we need to focus on the first quality of a good theory, which is that it is adequately generalizable. What does **generalization** mean? It means that we can find a common phenomenon across different people, things, or processes. For instance, we can generalize that people came to the dinner party with the desire to eat dinner, since everyone ate dinner while at the dinner party.

Generalization, even if not always true, is useful for theory development because it allows us to abstract away from individual user behavior, although we have to be very careful with generalization in regard to human behavior. Some outliers will *absolutely not* be described by a given generalized process, and if we develop features for the average user, we might alienate important outliers. Sometimes your best users are your outliers, so it's important to have a good sense of your product and who you are targeting with changes to the product functionality.

Two important statistical concepts that allow us to access the quality of a model or generalization are **Type I** and **Type II** error (Table 2.1). Type I and type II error can sometimes be high enough to force us to scrap our model. Suppose we have identified a relationship between being hungry and eating soon after arriving at the dinner party. Our simple model is that everyone who is hungry eats dinner within 30 minutes of coming to the dinner party. Suppose some people who are hungry do not eat dinner within 30 minutes of coming (maybe they got distracted in a good conversation) and some people eat dinner within 30 minutes even though they are not hungry (maybe they had nothing else to do). Type I error occurs when we classify people as not hungry who are truly hungry, simply because they did not eat in 30 minutes. Type II error occurs when we classify people as hungry who were not hungry, just because they ate within 30 minutes. When we generalize, we will typically have some type I and type II error. How large the type I and II error are indicates how good our theory is at generalizing. A perfect theory will have no type I or type II error.

Table 2.1 **Type I and II Error: Causes and Potential Outcomes**

NULL HYPOTHESIS If you eat dinner within 30 minutes, you were hungry	NULL HYPOTHESIS IS TRUE HUNGRY	NULL HYPOTHESIS IS FALSE NOT HUNGRY
FAIL TO REJECT THE NULL HYPOTHESIS Eat dinner within 30 minutes	TRUE INFERENCE They were HUNGRY and they ate within 30 minutes	TYPE II ERROR (FALSE NEGATIVE) They were NOT hungry, but they ate within 30 minutes
REJECT THE NULL HYPOTHESIS Do not eat dinner within 30 minutes	TYPE I ERROR (FALSE POSITIVE) They were HUNGRY but they did not eat within 30 minutes	TRUE INFERENCE They were NOT hungry and they did not eat within 30 minutes

Recidivism Risk: Type I and Type II Error

A real-world example of where Type I and Type II errors are particularly painful is risk of recidivism in criminals, meaning the probability that a paroled prisoner will commit a new crime. A report of recidivism risk is given to judges at parole hearings based on how the defendant answered 200 questions about lifestyle, past behavior, and other demographic and socioeconomic factors. Then, the model spits out a score indicating how likely the person is to commit another crime.

However, like most models and theories, predictive algorithms have some amount of Type I and Type II error. They fail to predict that certain people will commit crimes and predict that some will commit a crime even though they actually won't. This is a problem because the degree of error can affect whether someone ends up in jail and for how long. The null hypothesis in this example is that the score accurately predicts whether an individual will commit another crime. If the score does not, then we have either Type I or Type II error. Having high Type I error means that people who will not commit another crime are sent to and kept in jail. From a taxpayer's point of view, it results in high costs of housing people who are not a risk to society. Having high Type II error means setting people free who will commit new crimes. This imposes the cost of their misdeeds on society.

How do we balance these two risks? Is one worse than the other? Is having a model worth the effort, given the potential costs? These are the questions that we need to ask for every hypothesis. This is an excellent real-world example because we also have the problem of biased data. For instance, in cases involving nonviolent drug crimes, poor, African American defendants are much more likely to be arrested and prosecuted for low-level drug crimes than are richer, White defendants, even though drug usage among the two groups is often similar. This is one of many biases in the recidivism data. For this reason, it's very important to be cognizant of the cost of Type I and Type II error as well as the quality of the underlying data on which predictive algorithms or models are built. It's also an example of how predictive algorithms can be discriminatory if the model is built on a biased data set.

The next step in generalizing is to look for **connections** between ideas. A connection is a defined relationship between two ideas that were thought to be disparate before. Creativity is often thought of as the process of making disparate connections. Most people filter too heavily. For instance, going back to the dinner party, we might assume that people's conversation topics are unrelated to the layout of the house. But we might miss out on important connections. One potential connection could be that having a smaller house leads to better conversation. In a larger, more spacious house, the topics may be more general and similar to small talk. By comparison, in a smaller, cozy house, they may be more intimate. This difference could also be related to the fact that we might invite more people to a party in a larger house, which then means that the participants know fewer people well. At this point, we're not trying to determine if these connections are true, but rather if they could exist and are interesting.

Another aspect of generalization is trying to answer the *why* question or understand the underlying *causal* process. Thinking analytically about "why" behavior occurs is important. For instance, with our dinner party example, we might hypothesize that dinner party attendees come because they did not have any better activities to do than go to our dinner party. Was there a selection mechanism, such that people who were more popular or had more commitments did not attend? In some natural systems, establishing this kind of relationship may be easier to do since they are a few causal features. As we discussed in Chapter 1, social processes often have thousands of causal variables, and our job is to find the ones that are most important based on the size of the causal effect. We'll discuss in detail how to find these variables and estimate the size of their effect in Chapters 6 and 10-13.

2.1.8.2   Objectivity

Good theories are **objective**. People have biases. Some of those biases are conscious, while others are unconscious. Biases affect how we think and view a web product. People like to confirm what they want to see, a tendency called **confirmation bias**. Biases affect what we will test in our product and how we will assess those tests. We may want to consult outside sources and individuals when building our theory, so we can try to minimize bias and remain as objective as possible. We should also do our best to test and verify that our inferences are correct before we believe them. This step is very important, because human beings face stress or discomfort when new information contradicts currently held beliefs, opinions, and ideas—a condition known as **cognitive dissonance**.

2.1.8.3   Verification

Good theories must be verifiable. What does this mean? First, it means that we must be able to test these theories. **Verificationism** means that only statements that are verifiable through the senses are meaningful, or else they are truths of logic (tautologies). For instance, string theory is a theory of the universe. It states that usually minuscule strings underlie all things, but they are too small to see or even test whether they exist. This theory is cool and interesting and has principles, but it is not currently verifiable.

2.1.8.4   Falsifiability

The last core element of a good theory is being **falsifiable**. Falsifiability is the capacity to prove a theory to be untrue. If the core elements of our theory are false, the theory fails and is proven wrong. For instance, suppose you have the following theory: "American women, on average, are taller than German women solely because the Americans drink more milk in adolescence." You could look at the average height of American and German women to test this theory.

Suppose you find a group of German women are taller. Okay, that does not support your theory. You could then adjust your statement to say that "Midwestern American women are taller than German women because they drink more milk than other American women." You can always come up with ways to make your so-called modified theory become true, but those tweaks are not in line with your original hypothesis. Now let's say Californian women drink less milk than Midwestern women, but more milk than German women in adolescence, but are still shorter than German women. This finding would *disprove* your theory.

Imagine that the only factor that really determines a woman's height is her mother's height. This theory cannot be falsified with adequate testing. In real life, proving a theory is actually very difficult, because showing that a given variable has *no* causal effect is not an easy task. We'll discuss this issue in much more detail in Chapters 6 and 12.

2.1.8.5   Reproducibility

A theory must also be **reproducible**. This simply means that we are able to see a certain type of behavior not just once, but over and over again. For instance, let's say we think smoking causes cancer. To prove this theory, we need to see higher rates of cancer among smokers not just in one cohort, but in most or all cohorts. A reproducible result shows that we are not just dealing with random error or noise, but rather with something real.

We also need to think about the *mechanisms*—in this case, how smoking is related to cancer. Smoking pulls dangerous chemicals in the lungs, leading to mutations in the genes, which leads to lung cancer. The steps to go from smoking to cancer are called the mechanisms. A good theory is able to describe the mechanisms of a phenomenon.

Let's summarize our discussion of the qualities of a good theory. First, a good theory needs to be broad and generalizable. We should be able to describe an interesting process, preferably making novel connections to the elements of interest while still describing the full behavioral process. Second, it needs to be objective. We need to examine our biases and try to avoid doubling down on them. Third, the theory needs to be verifiable and falsifiable. This means that we should be able to test it and show when elements are not true. Moreover, when our ideas are proven untrue, we cannot change the goalposts or theory to match our results. If the key underlying principles are broken, we must drop our theory. Finally, the behavior described in the theory should be reproducible or recurring. The best theories also try to answer the *how* questions, documenting the mechanism for a causal effect or explaining how variables affect one another.

Let's go back to our theory of the dinner party, which states that an entertaining environment, good food, and nice people lead to more people attending a future party. This theory is a generalization of behavior. We're not saying that everyone who perceives our event as having an entertaining environment, good food, and nice people will return, just that it's *more likely* that they will. Our theory is objective. We are trying not to allow our biases to affect our theory. We looked at the descriptive data and came up with a theory. Our theory is verifiable: We can test if our hypotheses are true. It's falsifiable: If our core hypotheses are false, then our theory falls apart. It's reproducible: This relationship would occur at any party—whether it is happening today or ten years in the future.

Now that we have a theory, there are few things we can test. First, we can test if we are accurately describing the phenomenon. Next, we can test whether the hypothesis from our theory holds true. We can also theorize why this phenomenon is happening, and we can devise ways to test that part as well. Finally, if we want to use our theory to predict future behavior, we can test how effective it is at doing that. (Don't worry—all of the testing stuff is covered in later chapters.)

2.2 Conceptualization and Measurement

Answering the initial descriptive questions results in facts that are *observable*. A direct observation is a quantity that is apparent to all and measurable. For instance, the number of people who attended your party is a direct quantity. An indirect quantity is something that is not observable, but still clearly *measurable*. For instance, you could survey your friends on how many hours they slept last night—that quantity is probably not observable to you, but it is *measurable*. Both directly and indirectly measurable quantities are often extensively utilized in user analytics. This section discusses core sociological tools to operationalize qualitative concepts.

2.2.1 Conceptualization

Observable and/or measurable quantities limit us to easily defined objects. We are unable to work with broad, abstract ideas, even though they are easily the most fun and interesting! For instance, consider the idea of *social atmosphere*. Social atmosphere is a **concept** because it's an abstract idea composed of elements that are not indirectly or directly observable and measurable. Most interesting phenomena in web products, such as user incentives and goals, will take some conceptual development. This simply means we'll have to develop and define more complex ideas to capture the most interesting types of behavior. *Conceptualization* is the art of defining abstract ideas and notions. While it is an art, techniques in the social sciences have been developed to improve and streamline the process of concept development and measurement.

Whether the dinner party had an *entertaining* social atmosphere is not easily measurable and not really observable. Social atmosphere, in itself, is a construct; it is a broader idea that must be clearly defined to find ways to measure whether it's *entertaining*. Let's imagine a few social settings with different atmospheres. First, it could be a casual dinner party, with friends strewn about, wine, and a low din from a variety of conversations. Alternatively, a social setting might be a lively park, with playing children and parents talking to one another. The social atmosphere at the park is very different from that at the casual dinner party. This contrast should help you think about what elements should be included in social atmosphere, such as the particularities of the location and types of people.

There are a variety of elements that *might* make up a given social atmosphere. The descriptive elements *could* vary by the person and their preferences. One person could think the social atmosphere is determined by the types of social interaction. Another person could think the social atmosphere is mostly determined by decor and lighting. What does social atmosphere mean to you?

To operationalize an idea and make it useful, we must think about the core attributes of the concept that most people would agree with; this is called construct validity, referring to the process of changing constructs in a hypothesis to measurable quantities in a research study. **Operationalization** is the process of taking a concept and determining how it can be measured. We also need to make sure the definition is reliable and holds in a variety of contexts. While there may be disagreement, we should consider what most people would agree with. A general definition for social atmosphere that many might agree with could be "a general or communal feeling or ambiance of a particular location, environment, and/or grouping of people." Figure 2.3 shows how to go from a concept to measurement.

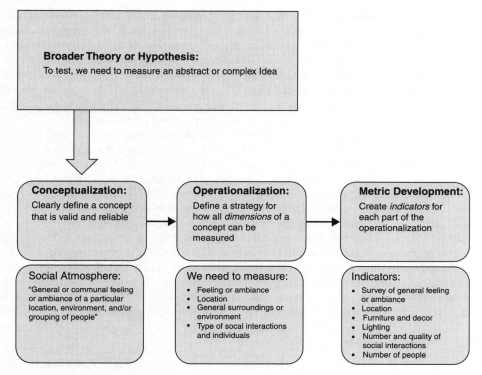

Figure 2.3   Developing metrics.

To get at complex notions or ideas of human behavior, we need to start to define ideas for the sake of measurement. To measure anything, it must be clearly defined. The definition does not necessarily have to include everything, but we need to be able to clearly state what is included in our definition.

Definitions of complex ideas often have *dimensions* or multiple attributes. Dimensions of social atmosphere could vary by culture. For instance, different cultures, countries, or regions could define social atmosphere differently. For instance, some cultures may include dance or dress in a definition. Another dimension may be the age of participants or observers. Older people may describe a social atmosphere in a different way. It's not important to include everything, but we must think about *why* we include certain elements and not others.

We should also consider how others may have defined these concepts in the past. How have others written or thought about social atmosphere? Where has it been important and useful?

Now, that we have a clear (at least thoughtful) definition, we can think of ways to measure the concept. It's not close to a perfect process, and often the depth and nuance of the concept get somewhat lost. However, it's vital because if we are able to quantify even 10% of the *meaningfulness* of a concept, we can find correlations between complex ideas and test aspects of our theory. But be aware that often there is loss in this process.

To operationalize the concept of social atmosphere, we need to find ways to measure the following: (1) the ambiance or general feeling; (2) the location; (3) the surroundings—decor, arrangement, and other qualities; and (4) the types of social interactions. We are saying that social atmosphere has four separate dimensions.

Once a concept has been operationalized, we need to build metrics. Metrics can be composed of a set of **indicators**, which are measurable aspects of a given concept. A survey question about the general feeling could be a measure of the ambiance. The room in the house could be an indicator for location. The degree of brightness of the room might be a measure of the surroundings. The length of a conversation could be an indicator of the type of social interaction. Indicators are often used in survey work, and the examples here are only a few possibilities. In fact, there are lots of potential indicators, so we probably want to start organizing all these indicators in a typology.

Here is another real-world example that is probably used by your healthcare provider and employer. *Well-being* is a complex concept. To define "well-being," Gallup and Healthways developed six dimensions: access to necessities, physical health, healthy behaviors, emotional health, financial health, and life evaluation. Access to necessities is defined as having food and shelter. Physical health is related to current ailments. Healthy behaviors are consistent exercise, eating right, and other practices that are good for the body. Emotional health is the health of one's close relationships, mental stress level, and others. Financial health is related to savings, debt, and meeting financial goals. Finally, life evaluation is how you see your life progressing.

These organizations believed that they needed all six categories to fully encompass the complex idea of wellness. Each dimension was covered by a number of survey questions, which were then aggregated into a score for each category; the scores from all categories were summed to give a wellness score. Such a wellness score allows us to compare two different individuals with different lifestyles and goals on the same well-being scale. Basically, the wellness score allows us to quantify a complex and abstract qualitative concept with indicators of multiple types of wellness.

2.2.2 Measurement

How can we start to measure these conceptual ideas? We'll need to consider the relationships between elements. It's easy if an idea is already quantitative, like the temperature of the house during the dinner party or the amount of alcohol consumed. These are **real-valued** outcomes. However, as we described earlier, lots of interesting ideas lack a clear numeric measurement.

For instance, some ideas are rank-ordered concepts, without any clear measurement of distance, like social class. We know that the upper class is above the middle class, and the middle class is above the lower class. But we do not really know by how much upper class is above middle class, and so forth. The distance between the upper and middle classes could also differ from the distance between the lower and middle classes. Other concepts even lack any type of ordering. For instance, with the concept of relationship status, we can have "single," "married," and so on. There is no clear way to order these categories. Variables that have ordered values are called **ordinal** variables. Variables that have values for which there is no order and that are just categories are called **nominal** variables.

We can also have **count** outcomes, which must be integers. For instance, the number of people who attended and the number of chairs in the living room are count variables. In some measurement classification systems, these sorts of variables are termed **interval** variables.

We may also have **binary** outcomes, which are defined as having only two classes—attended or did not attend, for instance. Table 2.2 presents the types of variables or indicators that can be created to reflect different types of quantities.

Table 2.2 **Variable Types**

Type	Definition
Real-valued	A number from (negative infinity, infinity)
Ordinal	Classes that have an ordering
Nominal	Classes with no ordering
Count	An integer from (0, ∞)
Binary	Boolean, two classes

We can have indicators of all types that describe an abstract concept. For example, for social class, we could have the following indicators: (1) a real-valued variable of household income, (2) an ordinal variable of self-identified class from a survey, (3) a count variable of the number of bedrooms in the home, (4) a nominal variable of whether the person is a renter or owner of the house, and (5) an ordinal variable of level of education completed.

Now that we have created measurable concepts, we can use these concepts to test our hypotheses.

2.2.3 Hypothesis Generation

At this point, we can explicitly state the hypotheses that underlie our theory of dinner parties. First, though, what is a **hypothesis**?

> Hypothesis
>
> A supposition or proposed explanation made on the basis of limited evidence as a starting point for further investigation.

A hypothesis is the first step toward quantifying connections or proposing explanations. At this point, our hypothesis does not have to be right or tested, but should enable us to put our ideas down in writing. A hypothesis is a proposed relationship between two variables or an expectation of change in a variable. For example, we might hypothesize that users who have received a direct message are more likely to feel a personal connection with the product and make a purchase. Or we could develop a hypothesis about changes in the product: Adding a new "like" feature significantly increased retention. We can come up with a few hypotheses that explain behavior.

Going back to our dinner party theory, we have a couple of explicit hypotheses:

1. An *entertaining* social atmosphere makes a guest more likely to return to future parties.

2. Good food makes a guest more likely to return to future parties.

3. Having nice people at a party makes guests more likely to return to future parties.

4. The combination of an *entertaining* atmosphere, good food, and nice guests makes people even more likely to attend compared to these individual factors in isolation.

From these hypotheses, we can explicitly state the core tenets of our theory and start the process of testing them.

Before we move on to the process of finding metrics to test these hypotheses, we should note the two different ways we could define our hypotheses. Let's consider the social atmosphere hypothesis. On the one hand, we could hypothesize that an entertaining social atmosphere leads to a greater likelihood of coming to a future party. To test this, we need data from *many* parties; otherwise, there would be no variation to explore. For all the users at our party, we would have to define the social atmosphere in the same way, so we'd have only one example. We can't generalize from one example.

On the other hand, we could consider the *perception of the social atmosphere*, which would vary by attendees. We could hypothesize that the *perception of an entertaining social atmosphere* makes attendees more likely to return to future parties. When working with theories in product, we need variation in the **independent** variable—that is, the variable that we want to test (here, type of social atmosphere). The outcome variable (here, returning to a future parties), also called the **dependent** variable, should vary as well. Alternatively, we can generally infer that the variation in the independent variable is neither related to nor causing variation in the dependent variable.

2.3   Theories from a Web Product

Now that you have seen how we might measure a theory of a dinner party, let's move to some web analytics examples. This section discusses some theories that are specific to web products. They are simple examples, but could be modified into basic theories for your web product. The first theory is for a simple purchasing site, the next is for the content sharing process, and the third is for a simple social network. We'll go through the tools we learn in this chapter with these three examples.

2.3.1   User Type Purchasing Model

Let's revisit our snowmobile purchasing website. Pretend you are a newly hired data scientist at the snowmobile company and the owner wants to better understand users and increase revenue. Where do you start? First, you pull some of the core metrics from the four areas of the user life cycle: acquisition, retention, engagement, and revenue. (We'll talk more about metrics in Chapter 6, "Why Are My Users Leaving? The Ins and Outs of A/B Testing.") Then you'll want to better understand which users purchase and which do not, so you talk to the owner and some of the founders of the company to understand how they think about users. The owner tells you he isn't quite sure what the categories of users are.

Now you start thinking about what users can do on the site. The site really has pretty limited functionality. It primarily serves the purpose of buying snowmobiles and sharing your purchase on social media. Given this limited functionality, you propose a user type model.

You theorize that three types of users frequent the snowmobile site. The first type is the avid enthusiast. These users know a great deal about snowmobiles. They peruse the latest types, know the competition, and buy multiple snowmobiles. They are rare, but they complete most of our product sales. The second type is the peruser. This type of user is interested in snowmobiles and perhaps even actively searching for one, but is on the fence about a purchase because of cost, space, or uncertainty about usage. Signs of this type of user may be a recurrent visitor who fails to purchase a snowmobile in a timely fashion. The last is the random straggler. These users randomly came to our website. Maybe they were searching for something else and stumbled upon the site. Or maybe they found a link on a social media website. They came and they looked, but their fleeting interest rapidly changed. They are the majority of users who come to the website, and few of them actually make a purchase.

The preceding paragraph described a simple user type model. We described some broader qualitative ideas like "the avid enthusiast." You'll have to use the techniques that we developed in the last section to quantify users of the different types.

Let's explicitly talk about some of the assumptions for this model. The first assumption is that there are three user types, not two or five or ten. This is a pretty strong and probably inaccurate assumption. The next assumption is that for a type to exist, there must be more out-group than in-group variation. This is a very statistical way of saying something simple: The spread should be bigger for random members between groups than within the same group. There is essentially less variation within a group than between groups for your differentiating variables. Finally, you assume that you can at least somewhat measure group membership.

Now you have a theory that is potentially testable. You need to move from theory to testable hypotheses and well-defined metrics. One hypothesis readily falls out of this theory:

> The avid enthusiast, the peruser, and the random straggler have more in common with others in the group than those outside the group on a few dimensions:
>
> i.   retention behavior and
> ii. purchasing behavior.

Let's say the metrics that you use to define these types are based on acquisition and engagement behavior. Then, for this hypothesis to become actionable, you need to define the types of users based on differences in engagement and acquisition behavior and test if these classifications hold for retention and purchasing behavior (the variables that you are most interested in).

Now, you need to take the final step and define metrics for determining membership in each group and testing the usefulness of the group classification for behavior that you are interested in. There are hundreds of potential indicators for these user types, but here we'll go through only a few.

Some metrics you could use to define a type are initial time of first session, creation of a user profile, user recency, frequency of usage, and types of snowmobiles the user searches. Then, some metrics you could use to test this model are time to first purchase, length in product, remain in product until day 3, number of purchases, and the amount of purchase.

Let's say your hypothesis is proven true. You *cannot* say that these indicators of user types or the user typology cause any of the outcome variables—just that they are *correlated*, meaning that some other variable could be pushing both in the same direction. You *can* say that these user behavior typologies are useful for describing and predicting purchasing behavior.

2.3.2   Feed Algorithm Model

Suppose that we have a more complex web product, one that has a feed. What do we mean by a feed? Well, there is a page where social content such as posts and pictures is aggregated from other users. The posts make it to the top of the feed that are posted most recently. This is the most simple feed curation. Our goal is simple here: We need to curate the feed to make the best, most interesting content for an individual rise to the top.

This is a difficult problem for a variety of reasons. What do people actually want to see? There is tons of content from users, with different amounts of popularity. There are also various types of content, such as written and audio. How do we figure out what content is "high quality" and what users want to see? More sophisticated models are even more difficult to implement.

First, we assess the five W's and one H questions about how content feed is viewed and generated: What content, when, where, how, and by whom? We realize that we can see all content, not just our friends. Users can like content actively or passively, by reading content or by "favoriting" content. We do not know exactly how much they're reading, just that they choose to load the next 20 posts. We know precisely if they actively liked content, because they can like or reply. There is no way in the current feed to upvote popular content. New content is prized regardless of quality. Good user-generated content is great, because it costs nothing to create and leads to greater stickiness of the product.

From here, we could generate a theory about how content quality and engagement could be improved. We might assume that users are more likely to like content that other users have liked. Also, that they will likely be interested in content posted by friends whose content they have regularly viewed in the past. A feed can be used to generate more friend connections and social interactions between members who may be connections of connections. They may prefer unique formats like pictures and video over text and audio content. They almost certainly prefer content that is timely and from individuals in their demographic group.

Now we have a theory that is potentially testable. At the point, we need to move from theory to testable hypotheses and well-defined metrics. Our theory has generated a number of hypotheses that we can test:

- Users prefer, on average, content posted by friends.

- Users prefer, on average, more popular content.

- Users prefer more timely content.

- Users prefer videos and pictures to other types of content.

- Users make more friends when they see repeated content of friends of friends' posts.

- Users prefer content from their demographic group.

These are the hypotheses that we can test to validate our model. We then need metrics to validate a qualitative idea of "better." Here we can create two metrics for active and passive consumption.

Next, let's define some metrics of active engagement. We have the number of likes, the number of comments, and the number of shares of a feed item. We could also have the number of clicks for a feed item. These are potential metrics for active engagement.

Capturing passive activity is hard for most web products, because we must try to capture it indirectly. We could capture length of time on the main feed page or number of pages of feed items that a user opens. Overall, we have two metrics of passive engagement: (1) length of time on the feed page and (2) whether a user clicks to load more items. We now have metrics to test our hypotheses.

We can test these hypotheses by looking at a feed algorithm that promotes content of friends over another user's content and see if there is a change in any of our active or passive metrics. We can do this for all our hypotheses.

2.3.3 Middle School Dance Model

Let's consider a social network product—in this case, a social network of tea enthusiasts (of which I definitely am one). The point of this network is to rate new teas and tea shops and to discuss quality teas.

There is a large social component to this application, in that users are creating content by sending messages, rating teas and tea shops, and uploading pictures of tea. Each user can also create a profile and message and post information. You make money by selling ads and recommendations to new tea establishments. However, although there are a lot of people on this social network, you sense that few actually rate any tea establishments. Your goal is to increase the amount of user-generated content. You need a model that can help you do this.

Let's say that the model that you develop is that your product is analogous to a middle school dance in terms of social interaction. A few users are dancing in the middle of the gym; these middle school dance fanatics are the whales. They are the ones who are doing all the rating of the latest tea places, have lots of friends, and send and receive lots of messages.

Meanwhile, hundreds or thousands of wallflowers stand around the gym looking at each other nervously, not dancing and trying to figure out what to do. They are passively consuming content, but really fail to interact socially and generate their own social content. You wonder whether you could pump up the volume of the music, dim the lights, and get some of these wallflowers on the dance floor by making their initial posts or social interactions less intensive, meaningful, and easier. Also, you might wonder if it's worthwhile to have the whales reach out to the wallflowers, and how this might affect the social dynamics of your web product.

You now have the following hypotheses for testing:

1. User behavior varies more between type than within groups (whales and wallflowers).

2. The intensity of usage and the capacity of usage differs by group.

3. Outgoing social interaction of whales-to-whales > whales-to-wallflowers > wallflowers-to-whales > wallflowers-to-wallflowers.

4. The change in active behavior of wallflowers compared to whales is more important to the overall health of the product, demonstrated by the movement of our core metrics.

Now that you've laid out your hypotheses, you need to define some metrics to differentiate the two groups. Let's say it's a friend-based social network, so that would be your social graph. The whales are the most socially connected and central to the social network. You could define them by a number of social network metrics (not discussed in this chapter). For now, let's focus on their network centrality as indicated by number of friend connections and number of connections of friends.

To test hypotheses 1 and 2, you can determine whether retention and engagement metrics vary more between groups than within them. You can use an analysis of variance (ANOVA) to do this analysis (while ANNOVA's are not covered in this text; ANOVA's are discussed in reference text 'Statistical Inference' by George Casella and Roger Berger). For hypothesis 3, you can just check descriptively how much interaction occurs between groups. You can use the average out-going active social interactions (liking, messages, comments, and so on) from whales to whales, whales to wallflowers, wallflowers to whales, and wallflowers to wallflowers. You could pull this measure daily to see how large the variance is for all groups.

Finally, you could force wallflowers in your product to interact more actively (by forcing them to post in during onboarding, for example). You can test the effect of this last hypothesis by running an A/B test to see if forcing social interaction leads to a movement of the core retention, engagement, and revenue metrics described in Chapter 1.

These three examples should have given you an idea of how to carry out the process of theory building in practice. Chapter 4 covers metric development, which will help you measure the qualitative concepts most relevant to your product.

Table 2.3 provides an overview of the three theories that we have developed. It walks through the process from model description to social indicators.

Table 2.3   **Web Products: Three Models**

Mental Model	Simple Model Description	Concepts to Test	Hypotheses	Indicators
Type of user model	Users come in three types: (1) avid enthusiast (motivated purchaser, multiple purchases), (2) peruser (actively searching for product but on the fence), and (3) random straggler (found site with no intent).	We can categorize users into types. We're assuming more out-group than in-group variation. We can test this.	Behavior of members in each group will vary substantially based on our metrics and move in the ways that we predict.	Retention metrics: ■ Total time in product ■ Seconds on homepage ■ Time of first session Revenue metrics: ■ Number of purchases ■ Frequency of purchasing ■ Time to first purchase Behavioral metrics: ■ Click product information ■ Viewed images ■ Click on similar products
Feed algorithm model	Users interact with content that they enjoy, which means content is timely, from individuals in whom they are interested, in unique formats, and liked by other members.	There are some universal truths about quality content. Content that's timely is important. People prefer content that others like. Past behavior is important to future behavior. People like visual content more than written content.	1. Content that is posted more recently is preferable to content posted later. 2. People prefer content that is similar to what they liked in the past. 3. People prefer visual content to written content. 4. People prefer content liked by others.	Feed engagement metrics: ■ Views/exposure ■ Clicks in the feed ■ Time on the feed page

(Continues)

Table 2.3 **(Continued)**

Mental Model	Simple Model Description	Concepts to Test	Hypotheses	Indicators
Middle school model	A few users create most of the content and use the full functionality of the product (the whales). Most users passively consume content and use limited functionality of the product (the wallflowers). Getting the wallflowers off the wall and more integrated into the product defines the success of a product.	Users can fit into types. We're assuming a difference in intensity between passive and active types of content consumption. There is interaction between the whales and the wallflowers.	1. Users of the two types are substantially different based on our metrics. 2. The intensity of usage and the capacity of usage differs by group. 3. The change of behavior of wallflowers over time is important to the overall health of the product (i.e., the movement of our core metrics).	Engagement metrics: ▪ DAU/MAU ▪ Time in average session ▪ Number of events in each session Social metrics: ▪ Outgoing social interaction ▪ Incoming social interaction ▪ Intensity of social interaction Product usage metrics: ▪ Use of full product features ▪ Time to full/half usage Gamification metrics (if they exist): ▪ Reached certain levels (to unlock greater functionality) ▪ Motivated by the game Revenue, retention, and engagement metrics to determine product health

2.4   Actionable Insights

The actionable insights from this chapter are the following:

- Every analysis project has four steps: (1) model building, (2) hypothesis generation, (3) metric creation and (4) statistical analysis and inference.

- We need to build context and background to understand facts about our users. This process takes theory generation. The best theories are generalizable, objective, verifiable, falsifiable, and reproducible.

- Moving from abstract concepts to measurable quantities takes conceptualization, or defining a concept, and operationalization, the process of measuring that concept.

In the next chapter, we'll explore theories of human behavior change, which are integral to causal inference in a web product. Then we'll learn some basic statistical techniques to work and user data (Chapter 4) and discuss some of the most common metrics in user analytics (Chapter 5).

The Coveted Goalpost: How to Change Human Behavior

In Chapter 2, we explored some tools to help us build theories of user behavior. In user analytics, we're often tasked with changing or nudging user behavior. This chapter explores common theories of behavior change, which will help you build more effective theories in your web or mobile product.

In this chapter, we try to answer the following questions: When and how do we change customer behavior? Most importantly, what are the factors that are most likely to change user behavior? Before we jump into behavior change theories, we should discuss how behavior change is related to our goal of deriving actionable insight.

3.1 Understanding Actionable Insight

How does one go from raw data to moving key metrics? This process is more difficult that many people realize. Raw data simply pulled from an application has a whole host of problems. It's messy, it's complex, and there's lots of information tangled together. We must move from structured chaos (raw data) to provable theories. For these reasons, many companies fail to derive actionable insights and often go with an executive's intuition, even if publicly they advocate for "data-driven" decisions. Recall that *actionable* means that a company can take an intelligent business action based on data that has been analyzed. Many of these actionable insights rely on behavioral change.

For instance, suppose we run an A/B test to test the hypothesis that including numbers in the title of promotional materials increases click-through rates (CTR). If including numbers in titles does indeed move CTR, then we should include numbers in titles of future promotional emails—for example, "10 things to do with a new snowmobile"—to increase the likelihood that users will return to the site.

The desired end result in this case is customer behavior change (users are returning to the site). Indeed, for the vast majority of products, many actionable business insights are centered on simple human behavior change actions.

Returning to the project design process diagram that we introduced in Chapter 2, "Building a Theory of the Social Universe," we're now ready to add two extra steps, (1) action and (2) behavior change, as shown in Figure 3.1. *Action* denotes that we take a business action, like adding a purchasing feature on the homepage. *Behavior change* denotes that actions have changed in some way. The goal is to use the insight to move our web metrics in a positive direction. With most web products, to affect the metrics, we usually need to see some user change.

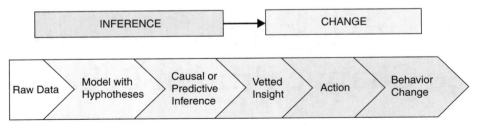

Figure 3.1 The six stages of the process design process, from raw data to the end result of customer behavior change.

To reach the desired result in most cases of customer behavior change, we must go through two main stages. The first stage is inference—basically, how to develop a theory, test it, and generate insights. In later chapters, we'll introduce more sophisticated techniques for inference. The last stage is translating insight into actual user or organizational behavior change (for causal inference-related insights).

In this chapter, we'll touch on both the first stage, developing a theory, and the last stage, translating insight into behavior change. The term "behavior change" is used very liberally here: It could mean a product user behavior change or organizational or other changes needed to implement insights. We'll provide some frameworks for theories about behavior change and some tools for translating insights into the desired change. We'll take a different approach in this chapter: We'll use backward induction—that is, considering our desired result of change and the correct moves to get there. For instance, in checkers or chess, we know how to win by removing all our opponents' pieces or killing the opponent's king. At the current step, what's our best move to get there?

We need to do the same thing with human behavior change. What is the desired change that we seek, and how do we find the best moves to test to get there? Having an understanding of how people behave and why their behavior changes is extremely useful in building theories and hypotheses around the aspects of customer behavior we would like to test. This chapter will help you understand the contemporary theories around human behavior change, discuss strategies to implement change, and provide examples of facilitating change in a web product.

To make any insight actionable, there must be changes within the organization, often at the institutional level. Actionable insight is deeply connected to behavioral change in multiple ways. In this chapter, we'll focus on one type of actionable insight—causal insights, which are directly connected to behavior change. While the other types of insights can lead to behavior change, that is not necessarily an expected or common outcome.

Before we delve deeper into causal insights, let's identify all the different types of insights. Four common types of logic can be actionable:

- Observational

- Comparative

- Causal

- Predictive

Observational insights are simply facts that are coming out of the product. For instance, the insight might be that users are buying X, Y, and Z. The action could be something as simple as making it easier to buy X, Y, and Z by moving those items higher in a given list. Observational insights are cheap (i.e., easy to find), but can be misleading and take a lot of assumptions or often-untested theory to make them actionable.

A comparative insight is based on the comparison between two quantities: X is greater than Y. Often, it's difficult to make this insight actionable, since we do not often know what's causing the difference. Suppose the only difference between the two quantities is a marketing campaign and we can infer causation. We can then operationalize the comparative insight. Comparative insights are harder to find than observational insights, and difficult to make actionable. We need design or context to understand them and make them actionable.

Most of your actionable insights will fall under the observational, causal, or predictive headings. Causal insights are discovered factors that cause your outcome: X caused Y. They are directly actionable, but the most difficult insights to find. A/B tests are often expensive and/or time intensive, and inference from observational data (we'll talk about in later chapters) is HARD. Causal inference is directly related to human behavior. When we understand the factors that *cause* behavior, we can alter them to increase or decrease a given behavior in the aggregate.

Predictive insights are related to predicting the effect of circumstances: Given X, there will be N of Y. Predictive insights are actionable, but often not in relation to user behavioral change. We can use prediction to forecast expenses, prepare for future growth, and anticipate user behavior, but not to change or alter behavior.

Table 3.1 summarizes the four types of inference.

Table 3.1 Types of Insights and How You Can Operationalize Them

Insights	Description	Example
Observational	An insight that is based on description of a phenomenon, environment, or behavior.	Insight: Users spend lots of time on the homepage. Action: Let's make the homepage pretty, navigable, and well organized.
Comparative	An insight related to a comparison between two separate quantities.	Insight: We have seen a significant increase in the population of organic users this month compared to last month. Action: Figure out what caused this increase.
Causal	An insight about a factor that makes another factor happen.	Insight: Seeing a promotion causes users to purchase a handbag. Action: If we show the promotion to more users, we'll see more handbag purchases.
Predictive	An insight related to something that will happen in the future.	Insight: If the population grows at the same rate, we'll need a 5 times larger warehouse by 2020. Action: Plan out the lease/purchase of a larger warehouse.

While other types of inference exist, causal inference is perhaps the most important to actionable insights and human behavior change. In the next section, we'll start exploring human behavior and when and why it changes.

3.2 It's All about Changing "Your" Behavior

The first step in understanding what causes human behavior change is understanding "behavior." A **behavior** is the way in which an individual reacts to a stimulus or situation. For instance, the **stimulus** could be a promotion, and a reaction might be clicking through the email link to buy a product.

Behavior change is more complex than just reacting to a stimulus. It's the idea that we can perform an Action A (we will discuss these actions later in this chapter) that will *cause* a different reaction from the one that would have happened if Action A had never occurred. For instance, a user never returns to the site. However, on one occasion the user responds to an email message by clicking on the return to site link. The user would not have returned had we not sent the email message.

There is a question about semantics here—namely, is this an example of "changing the behavior" or "changing the stimulus"? We'll argue that it's "changing the behavior" since we're explicitly searching for a stimulus in the data (from similar users) to change users' behavior toward what we want them to do. We'll explore this idea in greater detail as we develop more concepts in this domain.

Throughout the technology industry, there is an implicit obsession with human behavior change. You hear it all the time. Organizations ranging from big technology companies to small start-ups make all kinds of claims about human behavior change: "We're revolutionizing the way people do …," "We're driving our users to do …," or "We're improving how …". The list goes on and on. We're changing the way people buy houses, cook meals, drive, monitor their health, and more. Some of the "change" is simply altering the process or the ease of doing certain things. Often, it's more than simply changing the process; it's also about CHANGING human behavior in small ways every time you use a product.

Historically, social scientists studied human behavior (with much less data), and if the results were highly conclusive (think something like "smoking causes cancer"), there would be some policy changes or public campaigns. Those campaigns would take a long time to implement and even longer to alter public consciousness. But today, we have the opportunity to change human behavior immediately and consistently (through frequent and varied app usage) and the ability to study its effects rigorously. The caveat here is that those changes are often small, like clicks and small purchases.

Regardless, this is a significant step forward from the perspective of human history. *Never before have we been able to rigorously study multiple facets of behavior to the precision of a click-stroke.* That fact should give you pause as a user of web products, because all these companies have reams of your data and use it to try to change *your* behavior sometimes explicitly, but more often tacitly. We'll explore those methods in this book. There is a question about whether it is ethical to change user behavior without explicit and consistent consent. Given the controversial nature and the philosophical depth of this topic, it's beyond the scope of this book.

A secondary question, which is very interesting to a data scientist, is what is possible. That is, how much can we change an individual's behavior and how far-reaching will that change be for the general population? The reality is that there is very little research in this area even within web analytics, since it's so new. Many of the best practices in industry are taken from gamification techniques. Many companies use gamification techniques, which are couched in human psychology, to alter user behavior. Most of the academic research in this area is related to behavior modification therapy and health-based behavior change at a population level. Generally, this literature revolves around significant behavior modification programs like smoking cessation and large public awareness campaigns.

We begin our consideration of these issues with the theory around behavior change. How does behavior change happen—that is, what are the underlying psychological processes? What's the difference between short-term and long-term change, and between conscious and unconscious change? After discussing those topics, we'll move to the applications of behavior change in the web analytics space.

First, let's start with the lightest type of user behavior change—the "nudge."

3.2.1 Is It True Behavior Change?

Organ donation absolutely saves lives, but the rates of people who actively choose organ donation are low. We will not delve too deeply into this reluctance, but there are reasons for the low rates, such as the fear of organ harvesting. Basically, when people are forced to think about it, they decide no. However, in places where individuals must opt out of organ donation, many more people choose not to opt out. Maybe they don't think about it, maybe it's too laborious to opt out, or maybe they do not realize they can. Whatever be the reason, this practice leads to high rates of people choosing to donate. Economist Richard Thaler brought out this simple example to argue about the power of the "nudge."

Some examples of nudging in a web product are opting into data sharing (like having a user provide access to information from social media accounts) or encouraging account creation within a web product.

Interestingly, almost all users will react negatively when they are told that they are being nudged. Thaler said, "If people are told that they are being nudged, they will react adversely and resist." The more users know about the underlying thought process behind nudges, the more they resist. In a web product, this means that you must make nudges feel like they are part of the general product flow.

The most interesting aspect of this research is not the power of nudging individual decisions, but the groups that it creates in response. Individuals, when nudged, tend to acquiesce to only those nudges that they agree with (or potentially are indifferent to). Some people will react negatively to nudging. Some users actively resist behavior change, even in regard to the smallest behavior.

We might also want to think about the value of each user that we are "nudging." While "nudging" might encourage the average user toward a particular change, it might also rub a particularly valuable user the wrong way.

The indifferent group, as you can imagine, is generally much larger than the negatively affected group, but the effect on behavior might be much larger and persistent for the negatively affected group. For instance, in the organ donation example, people who react negatively might grow to fear governmental programs and avoid them altogether. In your web product, these turned-off users might never use your product again. They might leave bad reviews. They can hurt your business in a myriad of ways.

The beautiful thing about data science is that we can use techniques to find these users who will react positively and avoid those individuals who will react negatively. We'll talk about this process in detail in Chapter 13 on uplift modeling. Essentially, by using nudging, a particular site architecture, or path dependence, we can encourage user choices. We can then use uplift modeling to mitigate its effects on negatively affected users if we so desire.

This insight is core to the process of designing or structuring a web product. We should consistently be nudging our users toward the behaviors that we desire, with very little emphasis on the fact that it is a "nudge," and we should create obstacles to and highlight behaviors that we do not desire. We can then later modify the product to persuade the users who do not liking the nudging, offering them another path of behavior, and thereby mitigating their negative reactions.

3.2.2 Quitting Smoking: The Herculean Task of Behavioral Change

As we saw in the last section, nudging can be effective for short-term behavior change and tertiary decisions. But what about behavior change that requires substantive, conscious lifestyle changes, like breaking the hold of alcohol addiction? We all know that it's tough to break addictive patterns of behavior.

Quitting smoking is one of the most objectively difficult things to do. It's a behavior that many people would like to change, but are unable to do so. Almost 70% of American smokers want to quit. Smoking increases the risk for heart disease, lung cancer, stroke, and other maladies. It can have deleterious effects on a fetus for pregnant women and on one's children. Yet very few people successfully quit. The average smoker takes between 6 and 30 attempts to successfully quit. The quit rate hovers between 2% and 6% for any quit attempt, without the use of medications.

People often argue that it's difficult to quit smoking for biological reasons. This perception is generally false. Medications can remove most of the biochemical dependence on smoking, and the rate does increase with the use of such medications, but not by that much. Approximately 25% of smokers manage to quit for a period of 6 months with medication. Still, 75% of people fail to quit this health-harming behavior, even when the biochemical dependence factor is removed. That percentage is probably substantially higher than 75% over periods longer than six months. If we believed the problem was primarily chemical dependence, with that factor being removed, we'd expect the rate of smoking cessation to shoot up. But the rate of smoking cessation remains relatively low despite how harmful the behavior is.

Why is the rate of smoking cessation so low, even when we remove the chemical dependency? Because in contrast to the messaging put forth by most technology start-ups, major and sustained human behavior change is incredibly difficult. To get people to make a major life change is a herculean task. There needs to be a collusion of a variety of events: personal motivation to quit, social support, medication, and more, in the case of smoking cessation.

The social environment and support plays a large role in change. Many social regimes have been established to help people try to quit smoking, ranging from phone coaching to support groups. In reality, people rarely reach out for social support to help them quit. In one study, only 6% reached out to a Quitline, a phone support line. At the same time, the added social assistance made medicated treatment much more effective, leading to a 50% to 75% quit rate.

Smoking is not unique. Any major behavior modification is difficult. Even for deleterious behaviors like smoking where the long-term effects are known (e.g., cancer, heart disease, and increased mortality), people struggle to modify their behavior. Chemical dependency, while it may seem like the primary hurdle, is actually a smaller hurdle than intrinsic motivation, internal thoughts, and the social environment.

While most of the behavior change research has been conducted in public health, the results give us insight into behavior change in other domains. Major behavior modification must be driven by internal motivation and social support.

Now let's apply this to the domain of web products. One core aspect of fostering major behavioral change is to have a strong social component. Web communities and social support in those communities are powerful elements; indeed, without social components, you will not see any major behavioral change from your intervention. The elements of a social support community for behavioral change are product specific and must be rigorously tested. For instance, let's say you work for a meal plan company, like Blue Apron, and want to encourage behavioral change, meaning people cooking with your meal boxes weekly. Adding a social component, such as a live stream of users making similar recipes, might lead to greater excitement and interest in the product.

The idea that others are cooking similar things, offering tips, and sharing their day may foster a sense of community and encourage users to remain in a product longer than they would without social features. It might also increase the number of times a day users think about your company, as they are get social responses throughout the day. Eating and some other types of activities may not seem inherently social, but adding a social component can normalize a behavior and increase the excitement and feelings of acceptance/commonality.

For many product features, we'll need to rigorously test the effects. To do so, we first need to understand how to quantitatively measure behavior change.

3.2.3 Measuring Behavior Change

In this section, we'll explore techniques for measurement from applied behavior analysis (ABA). ABA focuses on encouraging behavioral modification for socially aberrant behaviors. While this theory is related to interpersonal behavior change, it can also apply to online behavior in a web environment.

As we noted earlier, a behavior is a response to a stimulus or any inputs, internal or external, conscious or subconscious, and more. The response to a stimulus can be modified by learning, in a process called conditioning. There are two types of behavioral conditioning:

- **Operant conditioning:** Voluntary responses are affected by the consequences. In this process, the behavior is regulated by positive and negative reinforcement. Through this learning process, we make the connection between a behavior and the response (positive or negative) to that behavior.

- **Classical conditioning:** Subconscious responses occur to sensitive stimuli. The best example is Pavlov's dogs. Pavlov would ring a bell every time he fed his dogs. The dogs started to respond not to the food, but to the sound of the bell. Once the bell started ringing, the dogs would salivate, indicating a biological, nonconscious response to a stimulus, in this case the bell.

For now, we'll not delve too deeply into the operant and classical divide, but simply note that behavior can be induced by psychological triggers. However, for measurement in most web applications, operant and classical conditioning are essentially measured in the same way.

Now, how can we measure a behavior? First, we need to assess which qualities of the behavior we are interested in. What constitutes the "behavior"? We can use the tools discussed in Chapter 2 to define and operationalize a particular behavior. Identify the core elements of a behavior, define them, and then figure out how to measure them. For instance, for a user to make a purchase, we might have the following criteria:

- The user makes it through the full user funnel for purchasing.

- The user pays for the purchase.

- The user does not return the purchase within 10 days.

Basically, once a user has satisfied these criteria, then a behavior—"purchasing"—has been achieved.

Once we have defined an interesting behavior to explore, we can then assess other aspects of a given behavior. Table 3.2 provides examples of the four dimensions of behavior that we can measure:

- Repeatability, or how often a behavior occurs

- Temporal extent, or the behavior's duration

- Temporal locus, or the time in between events

- Derivative measures, or other catchall measures

Table 3.2 **Measurement: Types of Behavior**

Concept of Behavior Change Measurement	Description	Examples
Repeatability	How often and the extent of the behavior	Count: total number
		Rate: count of behavior per hour, minute, etc.
		Rate change: how the rate changes over time
Temporal extent	How long a behavior lasts	Duration: the length of time that it takes a behavior to occur
Temporal locus	The time in between behaviors	Response latency: the time from a treatment to the response
		Inter-response time: time from one behavior to the next
Derivative measures	Other measures	Trials to criterion: how many tries it takes to learn a behavior
		Interaction with another behavior: proportional change of one with the other; linear correlation

These four categories of metrics are useful for exploring various dimensions of behavior. Of course, they can be used in measuring not only behavior, but also behavioral change. Change can occur on any of the four dimensions. Many people just focus on whether the behavior occurred or the number of times a behavior occurs, but other aspects such as the time between behaviors and the time it takes to complete a behavior can also be tracked. These can be early signals for behavioral change.

In addition, the ease of learning a behavior or its correlation to other behaviors can be measured and might be interesting in a given context. For example, we can use the metrics to contextualize and track user behavior and behavior change in a web product. In the next chapter, we will begin to understand and analyze metrics for web products; you can then refer back to this section to build your own metrics-related behavior change.

3.3   A Theory about Human Behavioral Change

Every executive wants to know, "How can I get people to buy my product or service?" This is a trillion-dollar question—but as you might suspect, there is no magic bullet. However, some sets of features or factors are more likely to cause people to change their behavior. This section teases out what those factors are.

There could be (and probably are) thousands of potential features in your data set that can *cause* someone to change their behavior. For instance, let's consider the purchasing behavior. We could imagine that the image of the product, the ease of inputting information, the cost of the product, the mood of the user, and the user's purchase preferences could all affect whether a user chooses to make a purchase. Before we consider which factors cause behavior change, ask yourself, how does behavior change occur for you? This section will explore some of the current theories around behavioral change. At the end of the chapter, we'll apply these theories to product settings.

3.3.1   Learning

How do people learn? In many cases, people learn through imitation and reinforcement. Imitation is modeling other people's behavior. Reinforcement is the responses to that behavior that they receive from other people, software, and other factors in the environment. For instance, think of children. They learn new behaviors from watching other kids or adults, imitating them, and receiving a positive or negative response.

A positive response often results in continuing that behavior and applying the learned behavior to more complex situations. If we think about web products, it's useful to teach users how to use new features by providing examples, repetition, and reinforcement to encourage behavior. Repeated behavior can be a very effective tool to increase ease of use, addictiveness, and engagement. It allows users to become adept and use their new skills on harder tasks. (Keep this in mind if you're trying to get a user to complete a harder task. Break it into steps and make it repetitive.)

Now we move to how behavior interacts with the social environment. Human behavior relies on three core tenets and their interacting effects: (1) social imitation and reinforcement, (2) personal thoughts, and (3) behavior. Personal thoughts affect an individual's behavior, and an individual's behavior affects the social environment. The social environment can affect personal thoughts, and thoughts can affect behavior, and so on. All three factors form a cycle in which they interact and adapt to one another. A good model should take into account all three.

While we cannot know what a user's thoughts are, a good assumption about a user's thoughts is that they are driven by self-interest. So ask yourself, if you were that user, what is the driver to engage with your product and complete a given behavior.

The next few models walk through personal thoughts, or the mental tools that human beings use to facilitate behavior.

3.3.2   Cognition

Perception is quite important to behavior and behavior change. How you see yourself and the world affects how you behave. In this chapter, instead of simply focusing on behavior, we'll emphasize behavior change, because it is often what we want to achieve.

As you might imagine, how we think about behavior change matters a great deal to whether we will actually change our behavior. We'll explore a model of how behavior change occurs cognitively.

The Stages of Change model postulates that there are five steps with regard to behavior change:

1. **Precontemplation:** unaware of the problem or the need to change the behavior.

2. **Contemplation:** understanding the problem and thinking about changing behavior.

3. **Preparation:** creating a plan for behavioral change.

4. **Action:** exhibiting the behavior change.

5. **Maintenance:** maintaining that behavior change consistently for more than six months.

These stages allow us to understand the process of moving from understanding and diagnosing a problem to maintaining a consistent behavior change.

What happens during the contemplation and preparation stages? Researchers theorize that they include a **goal-setting** phase and a **goal pursuit** process. In the goal-setting phase, we make promises to ourselves about future behavior; goal pursuit occurs when we try to accomplish those promises. The contemplation and preparation phases are internal and self-regulatory, meaning we assess the efficacy and then change behavior constantly.

In a web product, to promote a large behavioral change, it may be useful to actively set goals for your users and encourage them to hit those goals. Try to do the hard lifting of contemplation and preparation, and "nudge" the users toward the later steps of action and maintenance.

There are two important concepts regarding mental state: self-actualization and self-efficacy. **Self-actualization** is how we see ourselves accomplishing a task (successfully or not). **Self-efficacy** is how we judge our own level of competence based on our own self-perceptions. Perceptions can be "true," arising from success and positive external feedback. Self-efficacy can also come from our own internal psychological state and our own thoughts of persuasion.

During goal setting, a user might consider self-efficacy, including how similar past behaviors went and any potential risks that the user may face. In the goal-pursuit phase, we gain experience related to how well we meet those goals. In preparation, we might self-actualize—that is, we imagine ourselves completing the task—as we plan for behavior change.

In a web product, you can promote self-actualization by showing a user how other users have successfully completed a difficult task or by adding graphics that display completion and the reward expected, like acceptance or encouragement.

3.3.3   Randomized Variable Investment Schedule

Slot machines are extremely addicting to a portion of the population, largely because of the way in which they administer rewards. If wins followed a pattern, such as you will win a dollar every third pull, they would be far less popular, even if they paid out the same amount of money on average. Random rewards are extremely motivating because they are unexpected. People will wait for the next high or the next unexpected reward.

Many companies employ a variable investment schedule to make a product sticky. Psychologist B. F. Skinner found that pigeons respond best when there is a random number of correct responses and those responses occur variably. If they occur according to some pattern, they just weren't as sticky for pigeons or humans.

Online interactions allow us to institute these kinds of intermittent reward schedules because they naturally have repeated interactions. People desire the next high, so having a random component is important to keeping people interested. By employing a randomized reward system, you can increase the likelihood that a user completes an action.

It's important to remember that a reward does not have to be the result of winning something. For example, rewards can be given for completion of a task. If you change the ways in which the product responds to completion, then you can also make that product more addictive.

3.3.4   Outsized Positive Rewards and Mitigated Losses

Another strategy that can be employed to increase the likelihood that a user completes a behavior is to create extremely positive rewards. Use bright colors and flashy graphics to reward a user for completion. When a user fails or faces rejection, mitigate the negative effects of that experience. In short, web products can increase social interactions by extending the positive feelings of acceptance and minimizing the negative feelings of social rejection.

For instance, if you are creating a social network of tea enthusiasts, when two individuals accept each other's friend requests, you can make it a flashy and exciting event. However, if a connection fails to be made, never mention it again and make it difficult to search. Note that this practice can backfire: If your users meet in real life, they might have higher expectations for the interaction.

Outsized positive effects are one of the most effective strategies to successfully grow a large social community. Look at individuals' intrinsic desires and emphasize them in the rewards. If individuals are looking to feel important, emphasize the acceptance dimension in the reward. For example, if a user receives a direct message from another user, add in information about the number of direct messages—for instance, "You received a new message from X. X rarely sends out direct messages." If the sender sends a lot of messages, don't mention it or find some other dimension of "specialness."

3.3.5   Fogg Model of Change

Let's broaden our understanding of human behavior change. It involves more than just cognition; it also includes the external environment. The Fogg model—a very important model in the behavior change literature—argues that behavior change is predicated on three core components:

- Motivation
- Ability
- Triggers

The Fogg model assumes that people, in essence, are lazy. It takes all three components—motivations, ability, and triggers—to get people to do things.

Fogg postulated that there are three types of motivators. The first is pleasure or pain, which produces a powerful, immediate response. The second is hope or fear, which produces a delayed response in anticipation of a positive or negative outcome, respectively. The last is social acceptance, which comprises motivators based on others' perception of us and our perception of others.

The next core component of behavior change is ability. The simpler the behavior or the better we are at the behavior, the more likely we are to change it. The elements that most commonly contribute to the ease of a behavior are time, money, physical effort, cognitive effort, social deviance (not supported by society), and routine. Basically, we consciously or subconsciously assess the difficulty of a behavior before we decide to do it. The more difficult the behavior we're asking our users to do, the lower the likelihood that someone will actually do it.

Suppose we don't know which of the three desired behavior types are motivating our users: pleasure/pain, hope/fear, or social acceptance. We can design A/B tests or experiments to test the most relevant of these motivators. A/B test design is explained in Chapter 6, "Why Are My Users Leaving? The Ins and Outs of A/B Testing," but we'll give an example here. For instance, we could create a step in onboarding where some users see emphasis placed on one motivator, such as the pleasure of "getting a new snowmobile," and others see another motivator based on the "social acceptance" dimension of snowmobiling. That differentiation allows us to better understand which types of user motivators are most likely to sway which types of users.

Generally, you want to break down your A/B testing results by subgroup to best understand their implications for future targeting. People are different and motivations are different, so take into account these subgroup differences when designing your product.

The final aspect of the Fogg behavioral change model consists of triggers. Triggers are reminders, either implicit or explicit, for a behavior. For instance, suppose you've wanted to buy a snowmobile for a long time. A trigger may be seeing your winter jacket in your closet: It reminds you of the fun things that you can do when it snows. Triggers in web products could be a promotion, text message, email, alarm, or other type of messaging.

We can assess the efficacy of a trigger by the user's response and the lag time between a trigger and the corresponding expected behavior. If lots of people click through and immediately complete an action, it's an effective trigger. If it doesn't wear off over time, it's likely not a trigger, but part of some larger behavioral change process. If there is a high click-through rate, but no effect on the expected behavior, it's probably not a good trigger.

The cognition model and the Fogg model can fit together. We can think of the Fogg model as the structural dimensions encouraging behavior change and the cognition model as the internal plan in our heads to bring that behavior change to fruition. To effectively influence behavior change in a web product, it's best to utilize techniques from both models.

3.3.6   ABA Model of Change

Another way of looking at behavior change is that people engage in behavior to achieve a desired result or avoid an undesired result. Carefully observing behavior allows us to access the conditions that might be responsible for that behavior. This can help in our quest for the right causal factors.

Some reasons that an individual would engage in behavior to gain a desired result:

- Access to attention: social support
- Access to tangibles: getting stuff
- Automatic positive reinforcement: a positive response

Some reasons that an individual might engage in behavior to avoid something:

- Avoid social situations or particular tasks (operant)
- Avoid a particular type of stimuli (classical)

The ABA theory allows us to add more depth to our understanding of motivators. If a behavior allows individuals to gain the results that they want or avoid behavior/tasks/stimuli that they do not want, then people will engage in it.

If we are interested in behavior change, we must think about what will motivate our users to act. Also if we don't want our users to complete an action, we must figure out how we can use stimuli to make them avoid a given behavior.

Now that we know that people like positive results and avoid negative results, let's explore how behavior change works in a web product.

3.4   Change in a Web Product

We now have some theories about what causes human behavior change—let's add some insight specific to web products. Web products can support small or large behavior change.

We will use Fogg's idea that humans are lazy and Thaler's idea of nudging to understand how user behavior change works in a web product. Laziness in a web product often means following a structural path or the user funnel. It's the idea of path dependence—that one step leads to the next step. The path-dependent outcome is often following the path of least resistance. For instance, an email provides a link to the homepage, and then the homepage links to the profile, and then the profile links to the messages. This may be a common user pattern because this design is easy, with the next step being the highest click link on the previous web page. Users could take another path, but they might have to scroll down to find it. Following this pattern is easier than meandering off the path. A user in most settings can do:

- Something that is on the path (a nudge behavior)

- Something off the path behavior

What can we do to nudge human behavior change in a web product? We can build it in structurally, so it's the path of least resistance. For small tasks and in the short run, facilitating on-path behavior works well. However, there is no evidence that it will work in the long run.

On-path behavior also could not be behavior change, since it's not always explicit. For instance, suppose we set up a recurring payment system. It automatically deducts a payment for the next month. Have we changed the user's behavior? We really don't know. There are a number of options, but only a couple involve behavioral change:

- Users may never realize a secondary purchase was made (never really changing behavior at all).

- Users might have planned this all along (went through the Stages of Change with the first purchase).

- Users might actively change their mind after the purchase was made (maybe changing future behavior). Before the purchase was made, the users might not have wanted the item, but after the fact might have come to peace with it, either realizing they appreciate the service or deciding it's too laborious to remove.

- Users may try to revoke the purchase (incite a negative reaction from some users). This might also result in behavior change, such as removing themselves from the service or site.

In the next section, we'll go over types of behavior change in a web product. The relevant elements are described in Table 3.3.

Table 3.3 **Types of Causal Change in a Web Product**

Causal Dimension	Description	Example
Structural/on-path	A factor pertaining to a certain setup makes it difficult to avoid path-dependent behaviors	Setting up a recurring payment scheme One-click purchasing
Directed factor	A factor that directly causes a shift in behavior	An exciting promotion or discount A great product/feature change
Marginal change	A factor that matters causes a small active shift off-path (a user who buys diapers now also buys wipes)	A new promotion An email that showcases the latest furniture designs
Outsized change	A factor that causes a massive shift for a user (a user who never purchases now makes a purchase)	A social community that demonizes users with certain types of views, so much so that users change their views over time

There are two dimensions in which we will look at these factors. The first dimension is how these factors appear to the user: (1) Structural factors are on-path factors that can affect behavior at the margins (consciously or subconsciously) and (2) directed factors are factors that change behavior by themselves.

The second dimension is the size of the behavior change produced. The two factors are (1) marginal or small changes in behavior at the margins, such as clicking on a link, and (2) outsized changes or a factor that causes behavior to make a shift, such as a user who never purchases making a purchase.

Built-in path-dependent factors are considered structural in this framework. Structural factors are pernicious in that if we do not watch out for them, they could change users' behavior on the margins. For instance, setting up a recurring payment system removes the extra steps a user must take to reactivate a service, and the laziest users may follow this path-dependent behavior.

Even on-path behaviors can be difficult and conscious. A behavior can be active (needing the user to make a change or click on something) or passive (like the recurring payments, relying on automatic actions). Active on-path behavior can be too onerous for a user. For instance, an initial purchase may require users to enter personal and credit card information. This could be on-path behavior, but it's too onerous for our average user—the easiest course of action is to get off the site. To get users to engage in onerous actions, we need to understand what causes them to behave in such a way. Users may then react negatively to such a change when they realize it's occurring.

The second type of causal factor is directed—that is, something that is directly causal, not circumstantially causal. Theoretically, a structural feature could be directed. If an action will lead to an outcome whether or not it is on-path or off-path, and the action is on-path, then it would be both structural and directed. For instance, a heart-warming message could precede a call to action to support a charity financially. This message is on-path to support a charity as well as convinces a user to financially support the charity.

To cause off-path behavioral change, we need to understand what causes behavior to change. While this is not necessarily the case with structural changes, we generally know that the structural factors are key in behavior change. If we know the directed factors that cause a behavior, we can alter them to change that behavior on average. We may not change the behavior for every user, but we'll change it for a group of users.

Another way to divide causal factors for behavioral change is into marginal change and outsized change. All of the behavior in these two categories is active on the part of the user. A small change in behavior—something on the user path, but requiring an explicit action—is a marginal change. Think about clicking on a link or liking a picture: The costs are low.

Theoretically, the effort to cause this change in behavior should be small if individuals follow the path. For instance, getting a user who buys diapers to buy wipes might not take too much effort, but getting that user to buy expensive jewelry might be much harder. Getting a user who purchases every other Saturday to make a purchase on another day might be a nonmarginal change.

The other end of the spectrum from marginal changes is outsized changes—something that constitutes a substantial reversal in behavior, such as quitting smoking. For an outsized change, the behavioral change is difficult, so much so that it takes a deeper cognitive process such as contemplation and preparation for the shift in behavior. There is a range of possibilities between marginal and outsized changes, and one has to theorize where a potential factor lies on this spectrum.

Your job as an analyst is to build a product in which the structural factors lead to the small behavior changes that you are interested in. In addition, you should be looking to the directed factors that lead to the largest outsized change possible.

You'll find when looking at data there can be hundreds of confounding variables that are hiding in between golden tickets or directed factors. You will need causal inference methods to find these factors.

Obviously, outsized changes in behavior are extremely difficult for clinicians to effect (in regard to smoking or other deleterious behaviors), and similarly difficult for designers of a web product to compel. What should we expect with behavior change? Can we contextualize the results that we see in our product?

3.5 What Are Realistic Expectations for Behavioral Change?

In this section, we'll summarize what we've learned from this chapter and put it into the context of human behavior change in a modern web product.

3.5.1 What Percentage of Users Will See a Real Change in Our Product?

As we have seen with smoking cessation, outsized behavior change is difficult. But can we pin down a numeric ballpark for the proportion of the population for whom we are likely to see some change?

Let me put this question another way: What is a successful A/B test result? We discuss statistical significance in Chapter 6, but here we consider the magnitude of change that is sufficient. To get some numbers here, we consider the results from studies of human behavior change conducted in a variety of domains.

With marginal changes to behavior, like opting in versus opting out for a survey, the way we structure the user funnel can lead to large changes in behavior. The percentage of users opting into a survey can range from the low single digits to 50% to 90%, depending on how it's structured. We saw this with organ donation, and it is an important insight for web products as well. If you want most of your users to do something simple, make it an opt-out behavior, rather than an opt-in behavior. But remember that this can turn off some users; we'll talk about how to find those users in our population in Chapter 13.

Now we move on to outsized behavioral change, such as smoking cessation, downloading an application, making a large in-app purchase, and changing financial habits or self-esteem. The BIG STUFF. We can use smoking cessation and other healthy behaviors to start to contextualize the level of human behavior change that we might see.

Rates of big behavior changes generally stay below 10% (see Table 3.4). That really mirrors what we see in the product. For a major change in behavior, a response rate between 2% and 10% really is great, and more than 10% is highly unlikely and probably not realistic for the vast majority of behaviors. For small changes, such as opt-in in-app behaviors or liking a picture, a successful change can push up behavior change rates substantially higher, but still not usually to more than 30%.

Table 3.4   **Proportion of Population That Succeeds in Making a Behavior Change**

Behavior	% That Experienced Change
Smoking cessation	2–7%
Cessation of alcoholism	3–9%
Dieting success rate	<10%
New Year's resolution success rate	8%
Delete or remove an application (for a variety of web products)	1–5%

Note that most products have already led to some selection within your user population. Users are likely already motivated to accept your core offering if they are on your website, so this is not the rate of conversion of the general population. This may increase your success rates. For instance, suppose you have a dating app: The marriage rates among your users might be higher than those in the general population, because you are selecting for users who are looking to get married soon. However, conversion to purchasing in your app might not be related to getting married, and you may see similar rates of conversion as for other applications.

3.5.2   Are Certain Behaviors Easier to Change?

As analysts, we want to know where the low-hanging fruit is—that is, what behaviors are easiest to change. Let's use our theories about human behavior change and apply it to web products to guess at these behaviors. You can test them within your own web product.

Basically, we can take a few insights from our models of behavior change:

- *Make behavior change as easy as possible.* You want people to purchase, so make purchasing a short and effortless process (you do the work of collating the information).

- *Find triggers that might prime users to change certain behaviors.* Send out a message reminding them to check X.

- *Reinforce positive behavior and negate the effects of potential negative behavior.* Thank users for making a purchase. Avoid telling them how much it cost.

- *Help users visualize a process before going through it.* Show them how easy it is to add a profile picture.

- *Set goals for your users.* Make those goals either explicit or implicit: Spend $30 this month to receive $5 back. Make a first purchase and be entered to win a new Xbox.

- *Think about social acceptance, fear, hope, pleasure, and pain when making a call to action or encouraging a behavior.*

Table 3.5 organizes some of the core insights from the theories on behavior change and provides examples of how you can apply them to your web product.

Table 3.5   **How to Operationalize Human Behavior Theory in a Web Product**

	Description	Web Application Example
Self-actualization/ self-competency	Visualizing yourself completing a task; thinking that you would be good at a task.	Give your users a brief description of the process so they can more easily visualize what they should be doing.
		You could prime some other behavior that they may be good at; make it like a game or a puzzle to complete an action.
Positive/negative reinforcement (learning models)	A response that is positive and reinforces a behavior, or that is negative and causes an adverse reaction to continuing a behavior.	You could award points for completing a task such as writing a post and display points on a leaaderboard.
		You could take away an account if a user acts in a disrespectful way to other users.
Goal setting/goal pursuit (APA)	To achieve behavior change, it takes two phases: setting a goal and then striving to reach that goal.	You could offer up daily goals to improve behavior: "Remember to clean out one of your email spam folders today." Then assess users' achievement of that goal.
Five stages: precontemplation, contemplation, preparation for action, action, and maintenance	Changing behavior takes recognition, understanding how to change, planning for change, making a change, and maintaining that change.	Make your users aware of a behavior: "You have not visited the site recently. We miss you."
		Help users plan how to change by showing them the stages of behavior change.
Motivation: Pain/pleasure Hope/fear Social acceptance/ rejection (Fogg model)	There are different types of motivators. Touching on one of these core motivators can spur behavior.	Users often fear social rejection. Lessen the pain of social rejection by not showing users rejections. Make it difficult for users to see rejected members' profiles.
		Use social support as a tool for conversion. Have reviews or support of a service from friends.
		Determine which triggers are the most powerful for a given user from past behavior. Have you users reacted to call-to-actions that emphasize social acceptance, hope for the future or fear of missing out? Tailor your call-to-actions to what they have responded to.

(Continues)

Table 3.5   **(Continued)**

	Description	Web Application Example
Ability plus triggers (Fogg model)	Always make behaviors as easy as possible from the perspective of time, money, mental and physical effort, etc.	Make it easy to change behavior. For instance, make purchasing quick and easy.
Interaction of the environment, personal thoughts, and behaviors	These three factors interact to create a self-reinforcing process.	Access the nature of your internal social environment—what behaviors it's encouraging and how personal motivation might affect it. Suppose there are a lot of whales and wallflowers in your product. Initially, in your product, all social behavior requires having at least one connection. Most users don't easily make a connection. Maybe having social features be inaccessible initially is reinforcing and increasing the divide between the whales and wallflowers. Assess how initial behavior in your product is setting the scene for later behavior.

3.5.3   Behavioral Change Worksheet

In this section, we provide a worksheet intended to help you run an A/B test with an explicit theory about how uploading a profile picture might lead to behavior change. In this case, the behavior change that interests us is longer retention. The bold questions are the basic questions to ask when testing any causal variable, and the regular text shows my answers for a hypothetical product.

For each potential cause of change, this worksheet will explain how that change occurs within the frameworks that we have learned. It helps guide you toward factors that might be more promising than others.

Sample Worksheet for an A/B Test of Uploading a Profile Picture

What is the feature? Forcing a user to upload a profile picture during onboarding (operant behavior change)

Outcome? Retention—making a user remain in the product longer

Is this a feature that could potentially trigger positive behavior change? Yes

How? (rewards/punishment framework)

Sunk costs fallacy: Users invest in the product more, so they decide to stay longer (main cause)—POSITIVE

Social interaction might increase, in that other users will be more likely to interact with a user with a picture (marginal/secondary cause)—POSITIVE

It could force users to leave the product early by not completing onboarding—NEGATIVE

What will users experience after engaging in this behavior?

Nothing special, maybe a more positive interaction from another user. (It could be that with a profile picture, they get bonus points or it unlocks some gated features.)

Is it an on-path or off-path behavior? Change from off-path to on-path behavior

For which users? New users who must complete onboarding. The bulk of the user base will not have profile pictures.

When? Early in their interaction with the product. They will not be able to interact with any product features yet.

Treatment

How difficult is the behavior for the user in terms of:

Ability

Time? Completion requires taking pictures, uploading them, and pasting them into the prompt. This is hard for older users, and for users without pictures ready.

Money? None

Effort? A lot, depending on if they have a picture ready

Mental exhaustion? Potentially, if they are worried about their picture/how they look

Physical exhaustion? Low

Other? Need to be a little tech savvy

Motivation

Human beings are fundamentally lazy, so what would motivate them to engage in this behavior? Enjoy engaging in this behavior; behavior avoidance

Punishment/reward? Remove access to your product

Triggers feelings of pleasure/pain? None

Triggers feelings of hope/fear? Excited to meet new people/fear of negative interactions

Social acceptance/rejection? Is this the norm in your product? No, because historically users did not do this.

Triggers

Is this treatment a trigger or a cause of behavior change? No

Final Decision: Overall, given that it's on-path behavior, it might lead to a higher rate of uploading profile pictures, but it will likely *not* have a great positive effect on retention. It might even have a potentially negative effect.

Sunk Costs: A negative motivator that may turn some users off and not a positive initial step for your product. Why not some other sunk costs feature—that is, why this one?

The only gain is greater social engagement. Since the number of users having profile pictures is small, these pictures are likely not strong motivators for retention.

3.6   Actionable Insights

In this chapter, you learned that:

- Changing human behavior is very difficult. True rates of behavior change, even with intervention, are probably in the single digits.

- Behavior change is an interactive process involving social environment, internal cognition, and individual behavior. Motivation, ability, and triggers all play roles in behavior change.

- Many factors can cause behavior change. The goal is to find directed factors with an outsized effect.

- Building in structural factors that require users to opt out will lead to behavior change on the margins, also known as "nudging" behavior.

- Using the behavior change framework can help us structure and choose which feature changes are likely to *cause* behavior change.

Behavior change is at the heart of product analytics. Understanding when and why people do what they do is essential for building a successful product. You can use statistics to help you change user behavior (when A/B tests are not available) and predict user behavior when needed. Chapters 4–6 go through basic statistical and demographic tools that can assist you in this effort.

II

Basic Statistical Methods

Distributions in User Analytics

In Part II, we will pivot from qualitative theories and methods toward statistical and demographic methods in user analytics. This section will focus on basic statistical methods. Chapter 4 addresses the basics of metric creation and statistical distributions. Chapter 5 then explores more complicated metric development techniques and common metrics in user analytics. Finally, Chapter 6 delves into A/B testing. The next two sections on predictive and causal methods will build on the chapters in this section.

This chapter is organized in the following way. First, we discuss what metrics are and why they are important. Then, we review some key statistical ideas that underlie metrics such as distributions.

4.1   Why Are Metrics Important?

Intuition alone is seldom adequate for predicting the majority of user behavior in a web product in a consistent way. Metrics, can inform those predictions and make them much more valuable. A metric is a number or quantity of interest that is tracked. If employed correctly, metrics allow us to track and test how changes in our web products affect user behavior.

Suppose we explore the opposite perspective for a moment. One can argue that a lot of business executives make decisions based on *intuition*, rather than on data or metrics. Some companies have built wildly successful products and user campaigns with only limited feedback, through focus groups and user surveys. That was the case for Sony's first-generation PlayStation and Apple's iPod, for example. Sure, some of it's luck, but the reason why many products are so successful probably has to do with an intuitive understanding of the market.

This book is not knocking intuition. Intuition is great if you have it and can rely on it consistently. However, the reality is that many of us are not blessed with an innate ability to see future trends or have an intuitive understanding of our customers. And even if you are, data can help refine that intuitive sense to provide you with feedback on campaigns or new product features.

Intuition also often works until it doesn't. What does this mean? Well, as humans we love to associate wins or any positive outcomes with ourselves. And on the flip side, of course, we attribute all losses and negative outcomes to others. Sure, having intuition may lead to some wins and some losses, but we are far more likely to focus on the wins, leading to a false sense of personal ability. Human beings are all too easily blinded by success, leading to poor long-term choices. For example, when the stock market goes up, some people quit their day jobs to become day traders. With their Warren Buffett–like understanding of the market, they think, how could they lose? Then, a big crash comes along and everyone loses their shirt.

That tendency holds true everywhere, and particularly so in industry. As Count Galeazzo Ciano said, "Victory has a hundred fathers and defeat is an orphan." Time and again, a company may have a great product, a real cash cow. People will often attribute its success to false deities— a great marketing campaign, brand loyalty, and the right spokesperson. Often, times all those elements remain constant over time, yet the product dies anyway. Eventually sales drop precipitously, and we do not fully know *why*. We never put data behind what was *really* driving sales of the product. It's very easy to make the argument that X caused Y, but insanely difficult to prove it.

Metrics can help quantify phenomena. However, not every phenomenon can be quantified. The biggest and most abstract ideas are notoriously difficult to quantify accurately. Even so, we should not abandon metrics. Despite these difficulties, metrics are our tickets to the ballgame. Without metrics, we'll stand outside the baseball stadium imagining what's going on inside. From the crowd's faint cheers and claps, the best among us can probably make a pretty good guess at who's winning and what's happening. But even they will be wrong some of the time with such limited information.

With metrics, it's as if we've gained entry into the stadium. Sure, we're still up in the bleachers and can't fully make out the players or see clearly what's happening on the bench, but we can see some scoreboards. Having the score and seeing some of the action is a huge improvement in itself. Metrics offer the equivalent: some nice aggregated data about our product and some glimpses into users' behavioral patterns.

4.1.1 Statistical Tools for Metric Development

Before we build metrics, we need to start with some core foundational statistical concepts as they relate to web products.

In the next section, we'll cover the statistical distributions that are commonly found in web products. We'll talk about why we choose certain types of measures to aggregate data and how to calculate these measures. In Chapter 5, we'll explore the demographic concepts of age, period, and cohort. These concepts will help us create metrics that are consistent across time and population. We'll also go over some more complex techniques like standardization (in demography) or weighting samples to create metrics that are consistent across different populations or time periods.

If you feel confident in your understanding of basic statistical distributions, skip this chapter and jump right into the higher-level statistical concepts like standardization or common user analytics metrics.

4.1.2 Distributions

We'll start with distributions (*really* statistical distributions). Many of you have encountered them before, even if you might not have realized it. You've probably seen or heard of a bell curve, which is a normal distribution (Figure 4.1). It's pretty intuitive: The idea is that most people exist in the middle of the curve (are average). There are outliers on both extremes of a bell curve, in terms of height or some other feature. The tails of a bell curve are small, meaning that the proportion of very short and very tall people is small. A bell curve is really nice because its symmetrical, meaning there are roughly the same numbers of tall and short people. We explore the normal distribution in Chapter 14, in Listing 14.1.

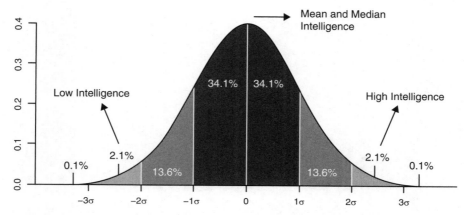

Figure 4.1   The normal distribution.

The next few sections will discuss the intricacies of distributions. First, we'll explore how to define and plot distributions. Next, we'll discuss statistical moments, or how to aggregate distributions into a few key points like the mean, mode, and variance. We'll then explore the exponential distribution and bivariate distributions. The section will give you an overview of key statistical concepts for metric development.

4.1.3   Exploring a Distribution

While you may recognize the shape of a bell curve, these distributions are so common that you've probably worked with them before, even if you have not called them by this name. A **distribution** is simply a listing of all possible values and how often they occur. A **metric** is an aggregated measure representing *one data point or value*, while a distribution represents all potential data points with their frequency. For instance, maybe you've looked at your monthly spending budget in the past. Each monthly spending amount could be ordered by frequency and displayed in a **histogram** (Figure 4.2). (We plot histograms in ggplot and base in Listing 14.6.)

Suppose in the last two years, for three months you spent less than $200; for three months you spent between $200 and $400; for four months you spent between $400 and $600; for two months you spent between $600 and $800; for no months you spent between $800 and $1,000; and for six months you spent $1,000 or more. This data forms a distribution. We can visualize this information and learn about your behavior. For instance, you most frequently spent more than $1,000 per month. The most frequent number is the **mode**. However, the **median** amount spent is between $400 and $600.

Your monthly spending patterns can be plotted as a histogram of ordered values. We can also order the heights of basketball players from shortest to tallest, or we can order the frequency of user purchases. The difficulty with looking at frequency distributions of histograms is that we need to bin the data. Binning the data means putting it into buckets so we can plot it like a bar graph. How big should those buckets be? For instance, should the first three purchases or the first five purchases be in the first bucket?

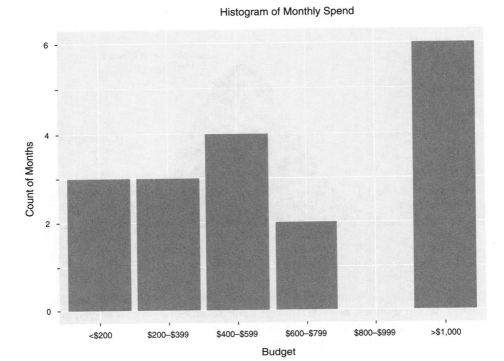

Figure 4.2   A histogram of your monthly spending behavior.

Many computer programs have some default binning formula, but often it's important to vary the binning and see how the histogram changes. If the graph is radically changing so that you're seeing more peaks, your initial binning might have been too wide. If there are vast open spaces in your graph, your binning might have been too narrow (Figure 4.3). We cover binning in R in Listing 14.7.

4.1.4 Mean, Median, and Mode

Why are distributional metrics important? Human beings cannot keep track of hundreds of data points, so we need to focus on a few important ones. For instance, we could look at a distribution of NBA player heights. There could be hundreds of values in our distribution—in other words, a value for each of the players' individual heights. Hundreds of data points are often not useful; we need to aggregate this data into a few points that we can track. The most common ways to aggregate such data are called **statistical moments**. Moments are the numbers that you can calculate that help you categorize the shape or important values of a distribution.

The first important aggregated metric is the **mean**, or the first moment, which is simply the sum of all the data values (here, heights) divided by the number of samples (here, the number of basketball players). Table 4.1 shows the heights of five famous Golden State Warriors.

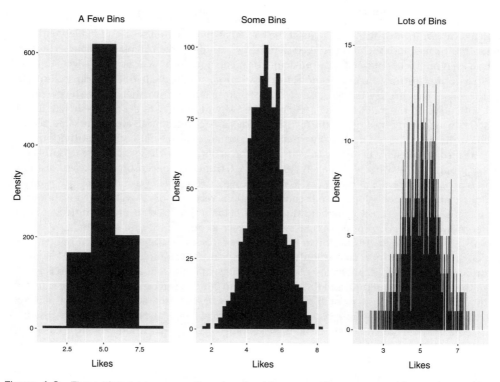

Figure 4.3   Three histograms, one with only a few bins, one with some more bins and one with hundreds of bins. Having more bins leads to a clearer image of the distribution.

Table 4.1   **NBA Golden State Warrior Heights**

Name	Height
Andre Igoudala	6'8" (80 inches)
Steph Curry	6'3" (75 inches)
Kevin Durant	6'9" (81 inches)
Draymond Green	6'7" (79 inches)
Klay Thompson	6'7" (79 inches)

To calculate the mean, we add up the heights in inches: 80 + 75 + 81 + 79 + 79 = 394. Then we divide 394 by 5 because we have five players. That's 6 feet 6.8 inches, or about 6 feet 7 inches.

The mean is useful because it allows us to get a sense of the average player's height. However, the mean is only one value describing a distribution, so it hides information, just as every other single metric does. The mean can be misleading in a number of potential cases where the data is skewed in one direction or is the sum of multiple distributions. We'll go through examples of these cases in the next few paragraphs.

Another potential aggregated metric is the **median**. The median is the middle point in a set of ordered values. So, if we list the heights of the basketball players from shortest to tallest, either the middle one's height or the midpoint between the two middle basketball players' heights (if there are an even number of players) is the median. The median in the NBA example is 6 feet 7 inches.

In a normal distribution or bell curve, the mean is *equal* to the median. The mean is also *equal* to the mode. The **mode** is the most frequently occurring number. In other words, the height of the NBA player in the middle of the list of all players would be equal to the average height for all players. In a normal distribution, the median, mode, and rounded mean are all the same, but the median and mode are not necessarily equal to each other or the mean in other distributions.

The median is often a better measure than the mean because it's less susceptible to outliers. Many problems arise when your data is either skewed, truncated, or censored. A skewed distribution is not symmetrical, but rather pulled more strongly to one side. A truncated distribution is limited above and/or below, often because it contains very high or low values. Truncation is similar to statistical censoring in that values above/below a threshold are often omitted, but it differs from statistical censoring in that we do not keep a count of the omitted values.

With the left-skewed distribution in Figure 4.4, we can see that the median, mode, and mean are all different. In the normal distribution, all three values are around 0.5. In the left-skewed distribution, which looks much closer to what you'll see in product analytics, the mean is around 0.17, the median is about 0.13, and the mode is around 0.01. As you can see, these three values substantially differ in this type of distribution, with the median and mode more clearly reflecting what's happening with the average user than the statistical mean. The mode can be very useful as well, because the mode will be the peak (highest point) of a skewed distribution or the core points of focus in the case of multiple distributions. We cover the mean, median, skew, and kurtosis in Listing 14.3 and Listing 14.5.

Distributions can get more complex, because sometimes they reflect the aggregation of multiple groups or types of behavior. This happens in a few common cases, when the distribution is actually a combination of two or more normal distributions. Suppose we looked at the height of two groups—female gymnasts and male basketball players—together. They are normally distributed. We'd find the mean and median to be around 5 feet 8 inches or 5 feet 9 inches.

The mean and the median are actually not useful in this case because we're aggregating two disparate populations that radically differ on this feature. Instead, we'd want the mean of female gymnasts, which would be about 5 feet 1 inch, and the mean of male basketball players, which is about 6 feet 7 inches. It's important to plot your data to see if looks like an aggregation of two or more groups (Figure 4.5). You can spot this if the data has multiple peaks (bimodal or trimodal) or looks like the aggregation of two or more separate bell curves. The modes of the single distribution would give us the same information; basically, there would be two peaks, at 5 feet 1 inch and 6 feet 7 inches.

You'll also often see multi-peaked data when working with proportions. This kind of distribution, called a beta distribution, is useful for understanding the behavior of proportions. Sometimes we'll see this kind of distribution with proportions of time spent in a product. Many users will be in the 0–20% range and the 80–100% range, but few in the middle (20–80%).

With most distributions, you will want to plot them. Try to figure out what's going on: Is it multimodal, normal, or exponential? Then calculate the mean, median, and mode(s) to measure the distribution.

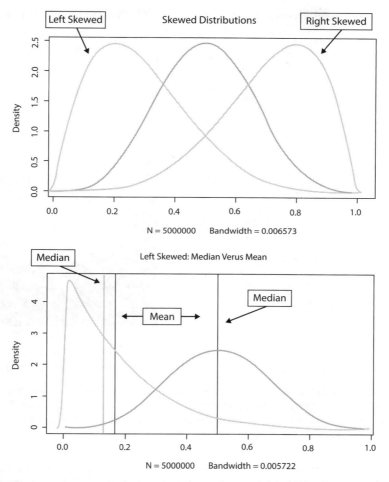

Figure 4.4   The first image shows both a left-skewed distribution and a right-skewed distribution. The second image shows the mean and median for a skewed distribution versus a normal distribution. In the left-skewed distribution, the median is below the mean and the mode is below the median.

4.1.5   Variance

The next aggregated measure of a distribution is **variance**. Variance is a measure of how spread out the data is. It is important because different data sets have different amounts of dispersion.

For instance, if we randomly sampled heights from the world population, there would be a lot of spread from 1 feet to 8 feet. In contrast, top basketball players all tend to be tall (the shortest player is about 5 feet 6 inches), so the spread of heights is much smaller with this group.

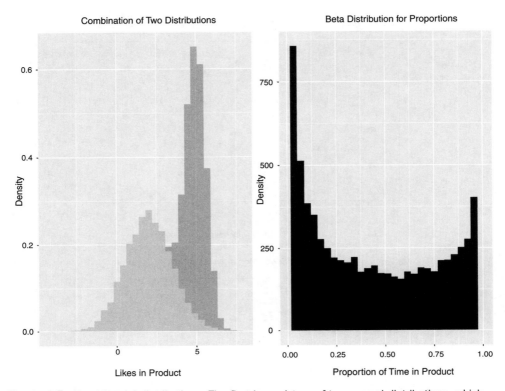

Figure 4.5   Two bimodal distributions. The first is a mixture of two normal distributions, which are shown by the red and green curves and the full distribution with the black curve. The second is the beta distribution and has a bimodal shape at the extremes; such a distribution is commonly encountered when working with ratios.

Another reason that the variance is important is because the tighter the spread around a metric like the mean, the more likely our estimate is to be close to the truth. Conversely, the greater the spread, the more likely that our estimates will be off.

Variance can come from two places: (1) true spread of the distribution and (2) a small sample size as the basis for our estimate. Generally, the smaller our sample size, the greater the variance will be.

The following formula is used to find the variance:

$$\text{Sample Variance} = \frac{\sum_{i=1}^{n}\left(x_i - \mu(x)\right)^2}{n-1}$$

where n is the number of elements in sample x and μ is sample mean

In words, we subtract each element of our sample from the mean, square it, and then sum all of these values. We then divide this number by the number of elements.

The spread of the normal distribution is well known and a good starting point for understanding variance. With a normal distribution, we know that there is a low likelihood of finding a data point at the extreme tails. For instance, it's unlikely that as adults we're taller than 7 feet or shorter than 4 feet. Most values will fall within three standard deviations from the mean. The standard deviation is the square root of the variance; it's just another measure of dispersion. In a normal distribution, we can look at how far away from the mean we are. At 68% of the area under normal distribution, we're about one standard deviation away; at 95% we're two standard deviations away; and at 99.7% we're three standard deviations away. If you have an IQ three standard deviations away from the mean on the upper end, you are really, really smart. If we randomly selected 1,000 people, only three people out of those 1,000 would likely be smarter than you.

Some metrics have a huge dispersion—and that makes them misleading. For instance, an analyst might see that user retention, which is normally around 5 days, increased to 7 days in the latest cohort. He's excited and reports it to the product chief for a small web company, suggesting that it means the latest feature is successful. However, you notice that sample sizes are small and one standard deviation (or the square root of variance) is normally 3 days. From this information, you cannot say with any confidence that there has actually been an increase in retention. Because retention should normally vary by 3 days, this could just be a random difference in retention, not attributable to the feature change.

In a web product, we won't often have all the data, so we'll have to bootstrap to estimate our metrics. Next, we'll consider what a bootstrap sample is and explain how to get a bootstrap sample of variance. We calculate variance in R in Listing 14.5.

4.1.6 Sampling

Let's calculate the sample variance. A sample is a random subset that is used to estimate some characteristic of the full population. Here we'll use a sample to calculate the population variance of our NBA players' heights. We can sample with or without replacement. Replacement means that we can pick values that we have already picked before. For example, suppose we have a hat filled with colored balls—green, yellow, and pink. We pick a pink ball out of the hat. Replacement means that we put it back in and pick again, so with each pick the probability of picking a green, yellow, or pink ball never changes.

We can build a sample by picking from our population each time without regard to our past picks (with replacement). We randomly sampled with replacement five times from a distribution of NBA player heights. We get five players with the following heights: 6 feet 7 inches, 5 feet 11 inches, 7 feet, 6 feet 11 inches, 6 feet 3 inches. The mean for this sample is 6 feet 6 inches.

$$\text{Mean} = \frac{(79+71+84+83+75)}{5} = 78.4 \text{ inches or about } 6'6''$$

To calculate the sample variance, we square the difference between each sample point and the mean, then divide by the number of samples. We can then estimate the variance:

$$\text{Sample Variance} = \frac{(79-78.4)^2 + (71-78.4)^2 + (84-78.4)^2 + (83-78.4)^2 + (75-78.4)^2}{4}$$

The variance of this small sample is 29.8 and the standard deviation is 5.46 inches. We can see that there is quite a bit of variance in this sample.

What's a **bootstrap sample**? It's actually a very simple idea. We sample subsets from our population with replacement many times. Instead of just one small sample of NBA players' heights, we may choose to create 100 small samples and calculate the variance for each sample.

We then find the variance in this example or some other population characteristic for each of our 100 samples. We can use these individual sample estimates to calculate how these estimates vary between samples, also known as the standard error of our population statistic.

The standard error is the standard deviation, or square root of the variance, of a large number of population samples. This may seem confusing: We're calculating the variance for each sample, and then taking the square root of the variance over all samples—but this is how bootstrap sampling would work for a variance metric.

Using bootstrap samples to estimate metrics can be very useful. Often, you do not have the time or the computing power to find a metric for the full population. If you can sample the population and get a reasonably close estimate, then you are in good shape. Random forests (discussed in Chapter 13) also rely on bootstrap resampling.

Our bootstrap estimate of the variance might not be the same as the true variance. Since it's based on lots of small samples and not the full population, an element of randomness is inherent in each sample variance. The amount of wrongness is related to how small each sample of the population is and how many samples we take. The smaller the sample size and the smaller the number of samples, the more likely it is that our estimate will be off in one direction or another, and vice versa. To get more accurate estimates of the variance, we need a large enough sample of the total population or lots of samples.

4.1.7   Other Measures

The mean, median, mode, and variance are the first set of quantities to explore, but lots of other measures of distributions also exist. Here, we'll briefly discuss three of these measures: skew, kurtosis, and slope. Skew quantifies how much the distribution is pulled to one side. Kurtosis is how fat the distribution's tails are or how many points are found at the extreme ends of a distribution (as in Figure 4.6). The higher the kurtosis, the thinner the tails are and the rarer the extreme values are. These measures are more complex to calculate, so we'll revisit skew and kurtosis in Chapter 14, when we calculate them using R.

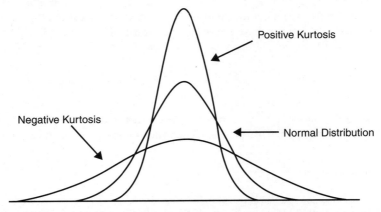

Figure 4.6   Kurtosis is the fatness of the tails of a distribution. The higher the kurtosis, the thinner the tails are and the rarer the extreme values are.

Another measure that is sometimes useful is the slope (the first derivative) or curvature (the second derivative) at certain points in our density plot or smooth histogram. We might want to understand the intricacies of how our density plot is changing over the full interval. You can calculate the slope by calculating the change in two points:

$$m = \frac{y_2 - y_1}{x_2 - x_1}$$

For more information on these statistical concepts, see the bibliography.

4.1.8 The Exponential Distribution

Let's talk about another very important distribution, the exponential, which is common in user data. For instance, views in a content list follow an exponential distribution. Early posts at the top of the page get many more views than later posts. Users view the first few posts and generally ignore the rest. As an example, we can see this type of user behavior in the Apple iTunes store. The top apps in a category get a lot more downloads than the later-appearing apps, even when they are not exponentially better! Number of purchases, time spent in the initial session, number of days a user is active, and many other types of data follow this pattern. Figure 4.7 shows what an exponential distribution looks like.

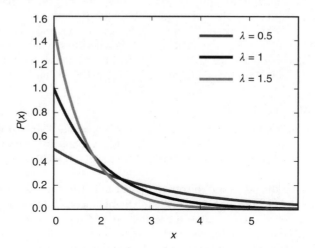

Figure 4.7   The exponential distribution. As the value of lambda increases, the distribution becomes steeper.

It's important to identify whether your data is exponentially distributed. For instance, with purchasing behavior, an exponential distribution suggests that most of your users are buying very little and a few are buying a whole lot. Such a distribution might also show that a few posts are getting a lot of views and most are not.

Mathematically, an exponential distribution is defined in the following way:

$$y = e^{-x}$$

Before you are scared away by this equation, remember from your high school math class, that e^x is an exponential—which means that it grows very quickly. For instance, 2^x grows like this: $2^1 = 2$, $2^2 = 4$, $2^3 = 16$, $2^4 = 32$, $2^5 = 64$, $2^6 = 128$, …. The value doubles at every step. Here e is Euler's number or 2.71, so it's 2.71^1, 2.71^2, …. Since the exponent is negative in e^{-x}, that means the value starts with a large number and rapidly comes down (Figure 2.7). Lambda, λ, is simply how quickly the value decreases. The smaller the value of lambda, the faster it decreases.

It's very important to note that for an exponential distribution, *the mean and the median are not the same*. The mean will be biased toward extreme values, while the median will be a much more reliable indicator.

Let's go back to incomes, which would be an exponential distribution with most people's incomes being the range of \$25,000 to \$125,000 and a few outliers with very high incomes. We want to look at the median because a mean that included the income for Bill Gates, Mark Zuckerberg, or Warren Buffet would be substantially higher than one that did not. Suppose we looked at three people: one making \$50,000, you making \$75,000, and Bill Gates making \$12 billion. The median would be \$75,000, while the mean would be \$4,000,041,666.67.

With the exponential distribution, it's important to calculate both the median and the mode. The mean is equal to $1/\lambda$, so even a slight increase in the value of lambda could represent a huge loss or boon to your business. For instance, suppose it represents the time (in days) between logins. One company initially has a lambda of 2, but it then declines to have a value of 1. That means that users logged in, on average, twice every day initially, but their visits then fell to once every day. Listing 14.2 shows how to sample from an exponential distribution in R.

4.1.9 Bivariate Distribution

The final topic in this section is the bivariate distribution. A bivariate distribution shows how two randomly sampled variables relate to one another. A random variable is a fancy term for a variable that is an outcome of a random drawing. In Chapter 14 section 14.8, we'll show you how to plot a bivariate distribution in R.

We plot one factor on the *x*-axis and the other on the *y*-axis. For instance, suppose we look at NBA players' heights and incomes. Is height related to higher income? By looking at the bivariate distribution, we can tell how these variables are related. In this case, the two variables could be positively related: The taller the NBA player is, the more money he makes. Note that this does not necessarily mean there is a causal link between height and income.

Two variables could also be negatively related, such as school quality and classroom size. "Negatively related" in this example means that the smaller the class size is, the better the quality of the education is. In other words, when one indicator goes up, the other goes down.

Two variables could also be completely unrelated—for example the temperature in Mozambique and a stock's price. In such a case, there is no pattern in how the values in the distribution are placed.

Figure 4.8 summarizes several of these patterns of bivariate distribution. In Listing 14.8, we calculate correlation and plot bivariate relationships in R.

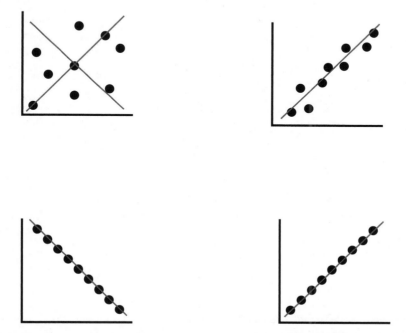

Figure 4.8   These charts show the relationships between two variables. The first is uncorrelated. The others shows positive and negative relationships.

Sometimes, two variables may have some type of nonlinear relationship. For instance, we could look at the relationship between income and amount of mortgage. The very poor will have no mortgage or a small mortgage; likewise, the rich will have no mortgage or a small mortgage (let's assume that they have capital and interest rates are high). In contrast, the middle class will take out a lot of money in mortgages. Hence, there is a U-shape relationship between the size of the mortgage and income, as illustrated in Figure 4.9.

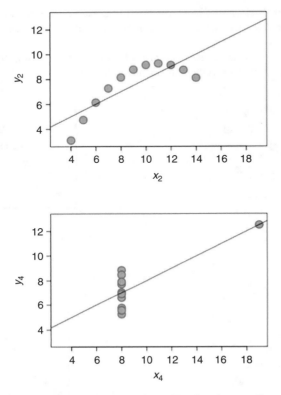

Figure 4.9   Here are two more types of relationships. The first is a nonlinear U-shaped relationship; the second depicts no variance in *x* for all values of *y*.

4.2 Actionable Insights

Now that we have gone through the basics of distributions, and have explored two ubiquitous ones (normal and exponential) and the bivariate distribution, you are in a good place to review what you know. There are a few key takeaways from this chapter that will make working with user data much easier:

- A distribution is a frequency or function that indicates how often each value in a data set appears. A distribution can be plotted with a histogram or density plot.

- Defined distributions are nice, but are not always found in actual user data. Sometimes data does not adhere well to a predefined distribution.

- If you find that your data are exponential or skewed, then the median and the mode will be much more reliable indicators than the mean.

- Variance explains the dispersion of a distribution; the greater the variance, the less reliable the mean or median is as an indicator.

- Bootstrap sampling can be a useful technique to find metrics or data inconsistencies in large data sets.

- Some distributions could be bimodal or aggregate multiple distributions. In such a case, the median or mean of the full distribution will not be a reliable or interesting indicator. Instead, finding the modes or the mean and variance of each normal distribution might be the best path forward.

- Bivariate distributions show how two variables move together.

Throughout the book, we'll build on this knowledge. In Chapter 6, we'll explore some other distributions, such as the chi-squared distribution. We will also use distributions to build metrics (Chapter 5) and make inferences from our A/B tests (Chapter 6).

Retained? Metric Creation and Interpretation

In the last chapter, we discussed some basics of statistical distributions. We'll build on those concepts in this chapter, describing more tools to improve and better understand our metrics.

It's vital for every analyst, data scientist, or business executive interested in working in analytics to effectively use metrics and *key performance indicators* (KPIs)—that is, measures of core business quantities like revenue. Without metrics, we cannot measure what is happening to our product. It's like baking a cake with no kitchen utensils other than the pan. While possible to bake without kitchen utensils, it'll lead to suboptimal results because we can't measure any of the ingredients or mix them outside of the pan. If you are a good cook, you may be able to make an acceptable cake, but most people will be left a mediocre to poor cake, and the worst cakes will be inedible.

This chapter covers the basics of metric development, giving you an intuitive and graphical understanding of how to work with behavioral data. First, we'll discuss the "time" or temporal element in metric development. Second, we'll explore common metrics and how they are calculated for the four core elements of the user life cycle: acquisition, engagement, revenue, and retention. After reading this chapter, you should be able to create metrics for observable quantities such as user days in product and the progression of user purchasing behavior.

5.1 Period, Age, and Cohort

This section considers the time element in metric development. Every metric has an element of time, and we need to understand how to define our population within context.

Demography provides us with a toolkit to do just that. **Demography** is the statistical study of populations. It is very useful when working with user populations in a web product. Central to demography is the relationships among **period**, **age**, and **cohort**.

Because metrics change radically over time as populations change, having a blurred or unclear time element is one of the biggest problems for building useful metrics. An analyst often combines metrics over diverse populations over long time periods, which may lead to incorrect inferences.

We can create better metrics if we understand a few relationships between time and human events. The concepts underlying period, age, and cohort address these relationships.

5.1.1 Period

What is *period*? It's simply a particular time interval. For instance, the 1990s were a period and the first month for your web product is a period. Why are periods important? Because certain elements are present in a period. For instance, the 1990s were a prosperous decade in American history. They featured the first tech bubble, Y2K, the popularization of the Internet, rapid suburbanization, President Bill Clinton, the North American Free Trade Agreement, and so much more. These events affected people living in that time period in a myriad of ways, ranging from cultural mores to layouts of communities. Periods help us define a time interval that has certain characteristics and allows us to compare that time interval to other intervals.

Web products also differ across time. Just think of how Facebook has changed over time—from having a simple address book–type format to now including news feeds, messaging, pictures, and video. The addition of functionality to a web product will often greatly change how people use the product and the type and quality of their interactions. Communities can also grow and develop in a web product over time, so the new user experience can radically change over time.

5.1.2 Age

What is *age*? As the name suggests, it's the length of time that you have been alive. From the standpoint of a web product, "age" refers to the period for which a user has been alive in the product. Users of different ages might have completely different understandings, usage, and feelings about a web product. A user with an age of 1 day might be excited by the novelty of the product interface, while a user at age 3 years might be engaged by the usefulness of the product.

5.1.3 Cohort

What is a *cohort*? The demographic definition of a cohort is a group of users who were born during the same period. For instance, let's say you were born in 1959. Your cohort would be people born from 1950 to 1960. You would have all faced the same events at the same age as other people in your cohort, like the civil rights movement, the women's rights movement, and rapid societal changes and growth of wealth following the end of World War II and reconstruction in Europe. A cohort has no set period; it can be defined as any period you deem important.

Similarly to the demographic definition of cohort, a analog for web products can be developed of cohort membership based on when a user joins a web product. If you joined the product at the same time as another user, you will both experience the feature changes in a similar way. For instance, a cohort of users may have started the product in June 2016.

Let's go back to our snowmobile website example. The website has been around for 10 years. The first few cohorts are nothing like the later cohorts. The initial small user base from the early 2000s consists of young, tech-savvy early adopters of the web version. The cohorts 10 years later have grown 10-fold and include a larger cross-section of the American population, older, more risk-averse, and with half the users on the mobile app rather than the web version.

Suppose we now wanted to calculate some general retention metric for our snowmobile website. Retention is how long a user stays in a web product. We would have to average data across 10 years for many different cohorts and over diverse periods in the product's life, creating essentially a meaningless metric. As this example suggests, having well-defined time variables can be the difference between a good metric and a bad metric.

5.1.4 Lexis Diagram

The three concepts of period, age, and cohort are interrelated. Their relationships are illustrated with a Lexis diagram like that in Figure 5.1. Age is the *y*-axis, and calendar dates are the *x*-axis.

Each line on the Lexis diagram is an individual user from birth to death. A horizontal line represents age across time. Every cohort, when it crosses that horizontal line, becomes that age. The vertical line is a period that represents a single time point in a web product. Thus, a Lexis diagram allows you to visualize age, period, and cohort on the same graph. If you are interested in using Lexis Diagrams to visualize your product population, you can use package 'Epi' and function Lexis.Diagram() to plot Lexis Diagrams in R.

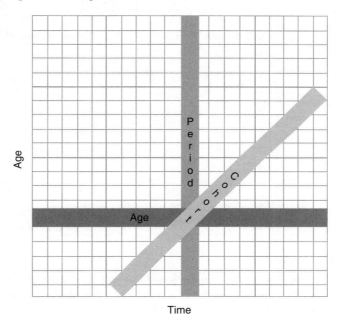

Figure 5.1   A Lexis diagram of a web product shows when users start and when they leave the product.

Age, period, and cohort are so closely related that we only need two of them to know the value of the third. For example, if we know the period and age of a user, we can determine the starting cohort. If we know the cohort and period, we can determine a user's age. Finally, if we know the cohort and age, we can determine the current product period. However, all of these concepts describe slightly different aspects of our population over time.

5.1.5   Period versus Cohort?

Most metrics or measures are either cohort or period measures. A cohort measure uses a given cohort as the base population. For instance, you can calculate the lifetime value of the cohort that started in May 2013.

A period measure aggregates data from all living cohorts over a selected period. Most period metrics look at the full life of the product. For instance, if your product is available from March 2013 to July 2017, most period metrics will use that full data set. We can also calculate period metrics over a shorter length of time. For instance, we could calculate the period metric for average days in the product for March 2014 to March 2015.

These two types of metrics can give you substantially different views of your product. But both period and cohort measures can also be *wrong* in the sense that neither alone will give you a full view of your product. Table 5.1 presents fictitious user days in product based on whether users started on the first, second, or third day that a product was launched. In this example, the maximum number of days the product has been available is 13. Every user is in the product a minimum of 1 day.

Table 5.1   **All Users and Their Number of Days in a Web Product**

User Number	User Days of Entry	Days in Product
1	1	2
2	1	5
3	1	1
4	2	1
5	2	8
6	2	Still in product
7	2	3
8	2	5
9	3	1
10	3	Still in product

5.1.6   Cohort Retention

Now let's calculate retention—the expectation from day 0 or the average days in product for all users when they start in the product. It's the sum of the user's days in product for all users in cohort Y divided by the total number of users in cohort Y.

$$Cohort\ expectation\ at\ day\ 0 = \frac{Sum\ user\ days\ in\ product\ of\ cohort\ Y}{Total\ number\ of\ users\ in\ cohort\ Y}$$

From Table 5.2, we can tell that the days in product varies widely depending on when a user started. Cohort I stayed in the product on average 2.6 days, cohort II stayed in the product 5.6 days, and cohort III stayed in the product 5.5 days. The cohort sizes can also vary. Part of the variation in length could be attributable to the sample size.

Table 5.2   **Calculation of Cohort Retention for Each Cohort of Users***

Day	Calculating Retention	Cohort Retention
Day 1	$= \frac{(2 + 5 + 1)}{3}$	2.6 Days
Day 2	$= \frac{(1 + 8 + 11 + 3 + 5)}{5}$	5.6 Days
Day 3	$= \frac{(1 + 10)}{2}$	5.5 Days

*Assuming the maximum number of days in the product is 12, although the user can continue in product.

However, for many web products, this variation could also be attributable to product changes over time. With such a small sample size, we can't really make any inferences about our web products. We'll talk about the sample sizes needed to make inferences about changes in retention in subsequent chapters.

Just for fun, let's assume that the sample sizes here were larger, large enough for us to generally believe these numbers and for variance to be very low. This tells us that the cohorts have drastically different retention. Perhaps something happened between day 1 and day 3 that led to this drastic increase in retention. We'd want to see if this trend of longer days in the product continues through day 4 and day 5 and so on.

5.1.7   Period Retention

Now, let's calculate the simple period measure of retention. The period measure of retention is the sum of days the user spent in the product divided by the total number of users.

$$Period\ retention\ expectation\ at\ day\ 0 = \frac{Sum\ user\ days\ in\ product\ in\ period\ Y}{Total\ number\ of\ users\ in\ period\ Y}$$

$$Period\ retention = \frac{(2+5+1+1+8+11+3+5+1+10)}{10}$$
$$= 4.7\ days$$

The period retention metric tells us that the average number of days in the product at day 0 is 4.7. This value differs from our cohort retention statistic. We can tell that this number is in between the smaller and larger cohort numbers. Since the sample period measure does not take into account how many people are in each cohort, it disproportionately weights the metric toward larger cohorts. In this example, cohort II is larger than the other two cohorts. This kind of difference is not always good; for instance, you might have had a bug on day 2 that did not allow users to remain in the product that's skewing your results.

We could reweight this metric to make each cohort equally proportioned; we'll do this in the next section on standardization. For now, we point out that the period measures weight your data based on the size of the cohorts that are included in them. Often, cohorts in web products are radically different. We should understand what is going on at the cohort level before we blindly accept any period measure.

Listing 14.9 provides an example of calculating period and cohort retention in R. Table 5.3 identifies the pros and cons of using period and cohort measures. Every metric is either a period or cohort measure. We'll see that period measures can have nasty denominator problems. Often, cohort measures are the way to go, but not always.

Table 5.3   **Use of Cohort versus Period Measures**

Measure	Pros and Cons
Cohort	Pros:
	■ Looks at the same population over time (no need to consider weighting)
	■ Considers changes across an indicator over time—how retention changes as the product matures
	■ Easy to understand

(Continues)

Table 5.3   **(Continued)**

Measure	Pros and Cons
	Cons: - Truncated, especially if the product is young (meaning the metrics are not accurate) - Cohorts could differ not just by time, but also by other types of user segmentation (e.g., organic versus purchased, male versus female)
Period	Pros: - Most commonly used measures - Useful when cohorts are evenly sized (or weighted approximately the same) - Useful when data is sparse Cons: - Confusing aggregation of cohorts makes the metric sometimes meaningless - Often biased toward earlier cohorts (if retention in the product is increasing over time, the simple period measure will be biased downward)

Note that both period and cohort measures of retention are truncated because you still have users in the product. It's best to get retention measures from early cohorts for which there are few users still left in product. The only caveat with this approach is that early cohorts are at least somewhat reflective of later cohorts. Otherwise, there are ways to adjust these measures to include some projections of life for users still in the product. You can find more information on this topic in the advanced readings.

In the next section, we'll go through simple standardization procedures for metrics. This step is important because it allows us to compare the same standardized populations over time, remove bad data, and explore how our metrics can change if the underlying populations change.

5.1.8   Standardization

Demographers call reweighting based on user characteristics, such as age and **standardization** (this term is used in many disciplines to mean different things, but here it simply means reweighting to make sure metrics are comparable). Theoretically, if you are the manager of a web product, you'll probably want to look at your metrics over time—for instance, if you are interested in knowing whether purchasing has gone up over time or whether your users are staying longer in the product. To do so, you need to have a measure that is consistent and reveals if users are purchasing more or staying longer.

However, as we saw in the last section, period measures are biased toward the size of a given cohort. We might want to reweight these metrics to make sure that we are comparing the right two quantities. Alternatively, if you want an understandable measure of retention that is not biased toward the size of a given cohort, you can use standardization to create this measure of retention.

In the last section, we saw that there were different numbers of users in different cohorts. In that case, the period measure that we calculated was biased toward our largest cohort, cohort 2. Now, we want a measure that weights each cohort equally. We'll use weights to standardize our population so cohorts are evenly weighted.

Standardization is a simple procedure. In this example, to standardize the data, we multiply our retention metric by ⅓, since there are three cohorts, and sum the reweighted rates. By doing so, we get a smaller number of user days, as expected. Our unweighted measure compared to our weighted measure is smaller because we are down-weighting day 2 and up-weighting the other two cohorts with lower levels of retention. The retention metric is 4.7 days for our simple period measure versus 4.58 days for our standardized period measure (Table 5.4).

Table 5.4   **Standardized Measure of Retention with All Cohorts Equally Weighted**

Day (Cohort)	Weighting	Retention	Total
Day 1	$\frac{1}{3}$	2.6 days	$\frac{8}{9}$
Day 2	$\frac{1}{3}$	5.6 days	$\frac{28}{15}$
Day 3	$\frac{1}{3}$	5.5 days	$\frac{11}{6}$
			$= \frac{8}{9} + \frac{28}{15} + \frac{11}{6}$
			$= 4.58$ days

We can use a variety of weights to standardize a population, but the weights must always sum to 1. Let's say we wanted to reweight by some measure of population quality, which was 0.6, 0.2, and 0.2 for the three cohorts, respectively. In this case, there was a bug on day 2, so we could reweight to ½, 0, and ½ to remove the bug's effect on retention. Again, we simply multiply the weights and our calculated cohort metric and then sum to get the reweighted metric.

We can calculate rates for a wide range of things, such as age and gender, and reweight our population along those lines. Suppose we have a very weird cohort that's 80% male and 20% female when our usual population split is 50-50. We could reweight our retention metrics to see if the difference in population proportion is driving the difference in retention rates. To do so, we just calculate rates by feature. In the preceding example, we would replace the cohort with gender groups, calculate the metric for each gender, and multiply by the correct weight.

Standardization is quite useful and not too difficult to implement. I've found it particularly useful in web products when you want to remove unevenly sized and later cohorts because they have not reached product milestones that you're interested in measuring.

5.2   Metric Development

Now that we have explored some important statistical and demographical tools, let's jump back into web analytics. As we discussed in Chapter 2, you have a snowmobile website where you sell some of the newest models on the market. You're a novice—not with snowmobiles, that is, but with web analytics. This is your *first* website. You're not sure what types of behavior you should be capturing or even what types of metrics that other web products care about. This portion of the chapter will help you build some introductory metrics for your website.

Even with your simple purchasing site, a user could participate in numerous potential behaviors, such as clicking on the email links or different pages, products, and images; registering and sharing purchasing information; completing a purchase; and following up with customer support. The site could have recurring customers, and customers could link your products to their social media accounts. All of these behaviors could take place on one day or over a period of a few months, meaning there is a time element to every user action. Each customer is also part of our user base and could be included in a metric's given population. Thus, in addition to a time element, every metric has a defined population, which could be small (a single user) or large (our entire user base).

5.2.1 Conceptualization

There are many interesting behaviors and complex patterns of behaviors. How can we potentially filter out what's important? Well, that's where conceptualization comes in handy. **Conceptualization** means taking concepts and turning them into things we can measure. Some of the heavy lifting has already been done for you—there are four key concepts that are essential to every web product:

- **Acquisition**: the process of a user entering or joining a web product.

- **Retention**: how long a user stays or remains active in a web product.

- **Engagement**: how interactive the user is in the product.

- **Revenue**: the money exchanged or total receipts.

These core concepts can help us understand which behaviors we should watch closely. While we may miss some important behavior, they enable us to filter out a lot of the less interesting behavior that is occurring. Think of exploring these concepts as your first pass at understanding user behavior. Also think back to the behavior change: We can develop behavior change metrics for these four aspects of user behavior.

First, let's think of a common user cycle in our product. Joe is a snowmobile enthusiast and wants to buy a snowmobile. He searched for "snowmobile 2017 model" on Google and comes to your homepage. This is the first step, *acquisition*, which means how a new user comes to your product. Since Joe did not come from a paid source (like a Facebook ad), he is an *organic* user. Joe sees that your website is great, so he decides that he needs to be a member and get your weekly email newsletter.

Joe signs up for an account that gives him a profile on your site, and you send him weekly emails with information and promotional offers. Joe occasionally clicks on these email links and comes back to your site. All of his behavior interacting with your site, messages, and content is considered *engagement* with the product.

Joe eventually takes the leap and purchases a snowmobile. He clicks on a few snowmobile thumbnails to find out more about each one's specs. Eventually, he settles on a model that's currently on sale and he buys it through PayPal. His behavior around this purchase relates to the concept of *revenue*.

After the purchase, Joe receives the snowmobile and never clicks on any of the other promotional emails. A year passes, and finally he clicks on the link again for a "snowmobile turbo 2000," but he does not purchase the snowmobile. Another year passes, and you essentially consider him a dead user. Being active in product for a time period is considered Joe's *retention* in product.

But when is the user life cycle really over? This is actually one of the hardest questions to answer with modern web products, because account reactivation or re-engagement with the website can be as easy as clicking an email link. We'll discuss this topic in more detail. When do we consider a user dead versus inactive, and at what cost can we revive a user? How long has he remained in the product and will he ever return? These are all questions related to a user's *retention*.

These four metrics will take you through the life cycle and the important behaviors of most users. Next, we'll examine most of the core metrics that you see on your first day of work at this web company as a user analyst. Each section includes a table with common metrics for each of these concepts, and it describes how each metric is calculated and includes a simple example.

Our goal in this chapter is to teach you how to create metrics to answer basic or descriptive questions about your web product: How are users coming to your product? How long are they staying? How engaged are they? and How much revenue are they generating while there?

To create generalizable metrics across web products, we need to remain at a relatively high level. Note that most of the metrics covered in this chapter are part of the first stage of data analysis or descriptive inference. To test our hypothesis, we might need to create more specialized metrics for our particular question, whether it is comparative or causal inference. When we are creating those specialized metrics, it's often important to take the demographic techniques outlined in this chapter and the human behavior change measurement tools (from Chapter 3) into account.

5.2.2 Acquisition

As discussed in the prior section, acquisition metrics are related to how users find and enter your product. They can also be related to completion of product onboarding.

Onboarding is simply the process users experience the first time they sign on or join a web product. Joe, the snowmobile aficionado, might come to your homepage to see a few snowmobiles that he's interested in purchasing. A pop-up may ask him if he would like to register or sign in. Joe decides to join and is sent to a registration page. These initial steps of registering and integrating a new user into a web product can vary in intensity and importance depending on the product. Onboarding for some websites is intensive, including surveys and credit card information; for others, it's as easy as clicking on a link. Completion of these activities is generally included within the acquisition process.

User acquisition is often a more complex process than just figuring out where your users come from. User acquisition can also include a user's intrinsic motivation to join your product. Why are users coming to your product, and what drives them there? This, of course, is a very difficult question to answer and one probably best answered with A/B testing and survey research. Nevertheless, where users are coming from as well as demographic and socioeconomic information may help us find patterns in user behavior or commonalities among users.

The next few sections explore some of the most common types of acquisition metrics: ratio-based metrics and funnel-based metrics. At the end of the section, we provide a table summarizing the most commonly employed acquisition-based metrics.

5.2.3 Ratio-Based Metrics

The most common types of user analytics metrics are often ratio-based. These are simple metrics, and ones that you have probably encountered before. What proportion of your users are returning after day 1, and so on? There are ratio-based metrics for acquisition, but also for the other three types of user behavior. We'll talk about more ratio-based metrics in later sections.

Ratios reveal observational information about what's happening in our product, but they do not identify causal relationships between behaviors.

For instance, say you have a health website, a social community related to jogging. You find that most of your acquired users are women older than age 50. You can start your analysis by asking yourself: Why is my site disproportionately popular with that community? The answer could be as simple as the fact that your first users were women older than 50 and the product is better known in those circles, or that something intrinsic about your product appeals to this particular demographic. A ratio-based metric helps us find these interesting facts, although we cannot say being age 50 and female *causes* someone to join your community.

Most of the acquisition metrics related to where users are coming from take the form of ratios. A ratio is a part or share of a composite whole. For instance, we could be interested in understanding what portion of new users are coming from traditional channels, such as Google or Facebook. Another way to look at this issue is to determine the proportion coming from a web search based on certain keywords, such as "snowmobiles buy" versus "snowmobiles speed." Ratio-based metrics for acquisition are calculated as the number of users coming from a particular channel divided by the total number of acquired users.

$$Acquisition\ from\ channel\ X\ in\ period\ Y = \frac{Total\ number\ of\ users\ from\ channel\ X\ starting\ in\ period\ Y}{Total\ number\ of\ users\ starting\ in\ period\ Y}$$

Like every metric, a ratio-based metric needs to be defined over a time period and for a given population. We can define a time period of any length of time, from seconds to years. In this example, we will define the period as the month of June. We could then define a population for this metric, such as acquired users in the month of June. The total number of these users is placed in the denominator. The numerator is the number of acquired users in the month of June.

On a side note, we acknowledge that we have not really defined "acquired." Does "acquired" include users who stay on the landing page for at least one second, who lingered for one minute, or who simply entered the product? We could change this definition of "acquired" depending on what we think best captures the concept we intend. For some websites, an acquired user may be one who stays in the product for 30 minutes after joining, while for another site the definition might be simply coming to the landing page. Think through your definitions and how much your population might change if the key definitions changed.

Demographic and socioeconomic information about your acquired users can be actionable. Demographics of your acquired users include age, gender, and location. Socioeconomic information includes social class, interests, and income. For instance, we can look at the proportion of Google acquired users who are younger than age 20. This is simply a proportion of a proportion. Our denominator is the number of those Google acquired users who are younger 20 divided by all new users acquired from Google. This kind of metric can be useful if our site disproportionately caters to one age group.

Next, we can look at the cost of gaining a user. Online marketing is a very important tool to acquire new users. To determine the cost of acquisition, we simply add up all the costs of gaining new users in a given period. Then, we divide that by the total number of acquired new users who joined in a given period. If you're running your own personal website, you might calculate the time spent acquiring users divided by the total number of new acquired users.

$$Cost\ of\ acquisition = \frac{Sum\ of\ acquisition\ costs\ over\ period\ Y}{Total\ number\ of\ users\ starting\ in\ period\ Y}$$

5.2.3.1 User Funnel

Initial behavior on a platform is very predictive of the quality of a user. However, we need to capture a series of behaviors rather than one. With the previously described metrics, we focused on only one action. Now we want a way to keep track of a stream of user actions or a customer journey. The customer journey is the complete sum of experiences a user has when interacting with your company. We need a more sophisticated way of keeping track of a user's interactions with our product.

For instance, clicking through from an email, logging onto the product, and viewing the product homepage may be the full user experience with your product. How do we visualize and track those behaviors together, rather than as singular interactions?

User Funnel Diagram

One of the best tools to understand a user's journey, especially if it's short, is a user funnel. A **user funnel** is a diagram showing a series of user steps and the proportions of users who are moving through those steps. It enables us to see how users progress, where users are dropping off, and what the rate of progression is. A user funnel can be used to understand path dependence or the behaviors that lead to subsequent behaviors in your product. Utilizing path dependence, as discussed in Chapter 3, is the best way to nudge user behavior in your web product.

The key metrics for user funnels are user completion ratios, referring to the proportion of users who complete a given action. Figure 5.2 is a diagram of a simple web product user funnel. It shows the user progression from loading the landing page to onboarding completion. We can see that each step of the user funnel has equal or fewer numbers of users as in the previous step.

If we see a dramatic drop-off at a step, then we can investigate why users are falling off on that step. The slope of the funnel also tells us how fast the user drop-off is. The steeper the funnel becomes, the more quickly users are leaving the funnel. It's important to find the earliest step in the funnel where there is a dramatic drop-off and target that step first.

Figure 5.2 shows a user funnel from email opening to purchasing on your snowmobile website. We can see users' progression ratios at each step. We notice a large drop-off at the fourth step, putting the item into the cart. There is only a 50% progression at that stage, and we need to ask why. We might have been thinking that the bulk of drop-off was actually at the fifth step, payment, if we did not draw this information out, but our analysis reveals that assumption is incorrect.

Once people put an item in cart, 95% progress to payment, so putting an item in the cart is the real blocker, not actually paying. If we can increase the proportion of people who complete that step, we can potentially increase the numbers later on in the funnel. Please note, this is just a descriptive inference, not causal inference, so this may very well not change customer purchasing behavior. However, its a good candidate to consider for a causal effect. For instance, even if the progression for step 5 is 100%, we know that this rate can never surpass 31% of the user base, so improving progression in the earlier steps is more important than tweaking the later steps. User funnels can be useful for other event streams as well. When a user logs on to a product and stays in that product for a period of time, that span of activity is called a **session**. In a session, a user can do a number of things, and often these follow a certain path. For instance, to use a website, users must first log in; after logging on, they are taken to a feed; in the feed, they click on a feed element; then they are taken to a page with a given feed element; and there they click to purchase. This is one particular stream of user events. There is an element of path dependence in this sequence: To purchase, a user must complete the prior steps. However, if 50% of users are not completing the login, they can never reach the purchasing stage—so you have a major drop-off problem. You can also include more funnel diagrams that cover the user path only after key steps (high drop-off steps) to show what users are doing if they pursue the off-path behavior.

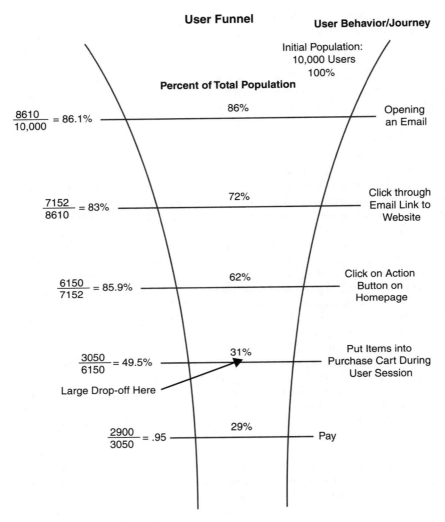

Figure 5.2   A simple user funnel diagram.

Difficulties arise with getting valuable information from user funnels when you have too many paths. For instance, one user might log on and then go to the profile page and update the profile, while another user might log on and go to the home page and click on an ad and purchase a snowmobile. If there are too many paths, funnel diagrams become less useful. Some amount of path dependence is essential to having a good user funnel. Most websites and applications have very clear paths, especially with today's emphasis on mobile apps first, which makes web funnels more important today than in the past.

The last important acquisition metric is time spent in the first session for newly acquired users. Time is a real-valued variable that can be used to understand a user's interest in a given website. Time spent in the first session will result in a distribution. Table 5.5 summarizes the acquisition metrics.

Table 5.5 **Some of the Most Useful Metrics for Acquisition**

Metrics	Type	Example
Acquired source	Proportion	$\dfrac{\text{User acquired FROM source X}}{\text{Total number of acquired users}}$ Total users: 40 Google: 25 $= \dfrac{25}{40}$ $= \dfrac{5}{8}$
Cost of acquisition	Average/ median	$\dfrac{\text{Cost of acquiring users}}{\text{Total number of users acquired}}$ $= \$ \dfrac{100}{40}$ $= \$2.50$ per user
User completion ratios (user onboarding funnel)	Ratio	Number of users who completed onboarding: Number of users who visit the landing page
Time of initial session	Distribution	Time on the landing page

Acquisition metrics are important for understanding how people are coming to your site, how long they are staying there, and how they are initially interacting with content. They also allow us to track how the user population changes over time with growth in the product. Your initial user population may be small and high quality because they heard about your product, joined early, and became die-hard fans. As your product grows, the population will probably get diluted with less enthusiastic and interested users. Purchased users through marketing channels are also oftentimes different in important ways from organic users. It's important to track changes in the acquired population so you can understand and respond to the changing needs of your population.

Similarly to how demographers may project population, you may also need to foresee changes that may become necessary in your product based on underlying changes in the population. Acquisition metrics can be useful for projection methods, which are described in Chapter 9.

5.2.4 Retention

While acquisition metrics help us understand how to bring new users into our product, we also need metrics to understand how long our members stay. Retention is a measure of how long your users stay in your product. Retention allows us to think about product "stickiness." Generally, the better you are at retaining your customers, the more face time that you have with your customers. Joe, our fictitious snowmobile enthusiast, was active until he purchased his snowmobile. Then he became inactive. However, a year later, he again logged onto the site. Was he retained for only a few months or for a year and a few months? While this seems like an easy concept to define, we will see throughout this book that retention is actually a multidimensional process. It's often hard to tell if "inactive" users are truly gone from a web product.

On a side note, there is often a trade-off between very high user retention rates and new user acquisition. Very close-knit social networks will often have high retention, but will be difficult for new users to join; hence they will have low levels of new user acquisition. Conversely, products with a lot of acquired new users can have low levels of retention, since there's always a constant stream of new people in the product and it has little continuity for existing users.

To better understand the community and different rates of retention for different user segments, it is useful to capture some product retention metrics. The easiest to define and most used retention metric is average days in product. It is probably the most widely used metric in industry.

$$\textit{Period retention expectation at day } 0 = \frac{\textit{Sum of user days in product over period Y}}{\textit{Total number of unique users in product over period Y}}$$

$$\textit{Cohort retention expectation at day } 0 = \frac{\textit{Sum of user days in product for cohort starting in period Y}}{\textit{Total number of users in cohort starting over period Y}}$$

This metric is simply the sum of the days in product divided by the total population of users in whom we are interested; it is often called the expectation of life in product at day 0. We can also have expectations of life from day 3, where we disregard the population who did not make it to day 3 when calculating the average.

Let's say there are six users on day 0 who have the following days in the product: 1, 5, 0, 7, 3, 20. For simplicity, we'll calculate the period metric since we don't have information on the cohort. (We already saw an example of calculating a cohort metric in section 5.1.6.) The expectation at day 0 is sum of user days ($1 + 5 + 0 + 7 + 3 + 20 = 36$) which we divide by the number of users, 6, to give an average of 6 days. That's pretty straightforward.

Likewise, we can calculate expectations for later days, such as expectation at day 2 or day 3. This allows us to get a sense of user drop-off in the first three days. Often, the first three days in any web product, we'll see the highest user drop-off.

For instance, the expectation at day 3 is defined as the average days for users who make it to day 3. We sum the days in product for users who make it to day 3 and divide this by the number of those users: $5 + 7 + 3 + 20 = 35/4 = 8.5$ days. As we can see, when we remove users who drop off early, by definition our metric has to either stay the same or increase. The degree by which it increases is very important. If it goes up dramatically, we can tell that our product has a lot of early churn (users who join and leave), but has good "stickiness" for users who remain. However, if it goes up only a little, we have low initial churn and our retention number at day 0 is consistent with our general product retention.

Another type of retention metrics commonly used in industry are Booleans (TRUE or FALSE variables). An example is whether a user makes it to day 3 in the product. These aggregated Booleans become proportions. A variable could be defined based on our past user set of users who make it to day 3, {F, T, F, T, T, T}; the proportion of users who make it to day 3 would be 4/6, or 66%.

Another common retention metric is customer churn rate. The churn rate is the total number of customers who started on day x who leave the product divided by the total number of customers who begin on day x. This is a ratio-based metric. Suppose we are interested in the total number of customers who churn by day 10. In this case, 5/6 customers churn by day 10, so our churn rate is about 83%.

$$\textit{Cohort X customer churn rate} = \frac{\textit{Total number of users who leave in period X and started in period Y}}{\textit{Total number of unique users who started in period Y}}$$

5.2.4.1 Undefined Denominators

A common problem with period metrics is including the same population in the numerator and denominator. Understanding your population is vital to building good metrics. Every metric has a population that we are focused on; thus, deciding which "population" you want to focus on is vital to building a metric.

For cohort metrics, defining a population is straightforward: The numerator and denominator populations are the same. The population for a cohort metric, for instance, is the population that started in the product during the chosen interval. With period metrics, however, it's not so straightforward.

Let's consider the period customer churn rate, for which the equation was just given. With the churn rate, we're trying to figure out how many users leave in a given period. It's clear what the numerator should be: the total number of users who leave a product in period Y.

But it's not so clear what the denominator should be. It should be some measure of the total population, but from what time point? The total population measured at the beginning of a period, the end of the period, or a midpoint? We might get completely different estimates of the total population if we chose the beginning, middle, or end of a period.

We might miss some users who join and leave during the period if we chose the beginning or the end. In an extreme case, all our users might leave before the end of the period. There are many different scenarios of churn that would lead us to choose one time point over another, but at the end of the day, we must pick one or find some other way to get an accurate measure of population. This is the heart of the denominator problem with period metrics.

Some customers who are active might be less likely to churn than less active or inactive customers. We could add in a predictive or a probability component to our churn metric.

$$Period\ customer\ churn\ rate = \frac{Total\ number\ of\ users\ who\ leave\ in\ period\ Y}{What?}$$

There is no right answer here, and different companies will calculate the churn metric differently. But it's important to consider exactly who is your target population and what you want to do with this metric. We will see this problem crop up with a whole host of period metrics. If your population is relatively stable, the beginning of a period or a midpoint from the prior period is usually fine. However, if you have lots of new users and churn, you may need to develop a predictive metric or to shorten your window to a day or an hour.

Another example of the numerator and denominator problem arises with feed item views. It's difficult to figure out how many feed items a user may have passively viewed. Suppose we want to capture the click-through rate on feed items; to do so, we need some measure of exposure. Let's say that we just capture whether the user clicked a button after 20 items. Basically, we don't have an accurate measure of views, our denominator, which will make our metric much less accurate.

Table 5.6 provides an overview of the retention metrics discussed in this section and examples of how to calculate them. Overall, retention metrics are useful and commonplace in most web analytics frameworks. Most are easy to calculate, but they have their shortcomings. Retention, as we discussed earlier, is a process rather than a simple action, and we'll talk about some of its complexities in Chapter 9 on population forecasting.

Table 5.6 **The Most Useful Metrics for Retention**

Metrics	Type	Example
Average time in product from day X	Average/median	Total days in product from X $\overline{\text{Total users in product}}$ $$= \frac{(6+10+15+4+0+2)}{6}$$ $$= \frac{37}{6}$$
Proportion to day X	Proportion	$\dfrac{\text{Total number of users who make it to day}}{\text{Total users}}$ $$= (T, F, F, T)$$ $$= \frac{2}{4}$$ $$= 50\%$$
Customer churn rate	Proportion/ratio	$\dfrac{\text{Users who leave in Y}}{\text{Total number of unique users}}$ $$= \frac{3}{12}$$ $$= \frac{1}{4}$$
Predicted retention to day X	Probability	We'll see an example of this later in the book.

5.2.5 Engagement

While retention metrics inform us about user length in product, we also need metrics to help us understand how users are engaging with the product. Engagement is a measure of how active a user is on a given website. Joe, the snowmobile aficionado, did a lot of different things on your website. He logged on and signed up for the weekly emails. He clicked through from the email and looked at inventory on the site. He may have even read some of the information that you provided about snowmobiles.

Websites have different levels of natural engagement. For Facebook, a very active user might check the site multiple times a day, while a less active user might check the site weekly. In contrast, on the snowmobile sales site, an active user might check monthly, while a not-so-active user might return yearly. It's good to understand your engagement baseline, meaning what should be classified as active on your particular site.

The most common industry metrics for engagement are *monthly active users* (MAU) and *daily active users* (DAU). MAU is usually defined as all the users who touched the product in the last month divided by all the users in the product (sometimes divided by all the active users in a product).

$$\textit{Monthly active users}\,(\textit{MAU}) = \frac{\textit{Total number of users who touched the product in month Y}}{\textit{Total number of users in product}}$$

DAU is also defined in a similar way: the number of users who touched the product in a day divided by active users in a product.

$$Daily\ active\ users\ (MAU) = \frac{Total\ number\ of\ users\ who\ touched\ the\ product\ on\ day\ Y}{Total\ number\ of\ users\ in\ product}$$

Note that DAU and MAU can be **rolling metrics**, such as some monthly metrics. A rolling metric is defined over a window that moves. For instance, MAU could be defined from September 3 to November 3, and then recalculated for the period of September 4 to November 4, and so on. Even though there are 12 months, MAU could be recalculated 365 times. With this metric, there is overlap in the underlying population for 29 days in the past and future.

Another very common metric in web analytics is the *net promoter score* (NPS). The NPS is a survey question: "How likely are you to recommend this product to other users?" It gives the user a scale of numbers such as 1–10 to choose from. A high NPS suggests that the customer is happy with the product and demonstrates high brand loyalty, whereas a low NPS suggests the exact opposite—that the user is unhappy with the product and shows little to no brand loyalty. In fact, the reasoning that individuals and groups of users employ when assigning an NPS of 7 versus 3, for example, can be quite complex, encompassing the functionality of the product, the community, pricing, and a myriad of other features.

Other common metric types include visitor frequency, recency, engagement with product features, and median length of session. Visitor frequency can be as simple as how many times users touched the product in the last three months. Visitor recency is the last time that they touched the product.

Some metrics for engagement are defined by the functionality of the product. For instance, you may have **gated** features. "Gated" means that they need to be unlocked by the user reaching some milestone or paying for something. What proportion of the users are engaging with the gated functionalities? This is another measure of engagement.

The average length of a user's session can be another metric. This is often a first-pass metric because it conflates two types of users: users who touch often with a short session time and users who rarely touch with a long session time. The first type of user could be a good user. Usually combining this variable with another variable such as visitor recency might better highlight types of user engagement.

One metric that is particularly useful for engagement is scroll depth on the homepage or feed page. Scroll depth is how far a user goes down a webpage. Some pages have a button to click to retrieve more information, comments, or content. It's a measure of passive engagement.

Web products generally have two types of engagement: active and passive. **Passive engagement** is viewing content without interacting with it. For instance, if a user sees a friend's picture or reads a product review, that is a passive activity. In contrast, if a user sends the friend a message or writes a product review, that is **active engagement**.

Active engagement is more difficult to achieve than passive engagement. Active engagement helps to create content and improve your product, while passive engagement has minimal effect on the community and content.

Finding metrics for passive engagement is often more challenging, as we can't always tell if a user is passively engaged. This leads us to the problematic question: Are users looking at content or do they just have their browser open and scroll down? What is the level of engagement with the content—are they avidly reading or just browsing?

Overall, engagement metrics are important for getting a complete picture of what your users are actually doing: how often they come, how deep they go, and how much they use your product. Table 5.7 shows the metrics for engagement discussed in this section, along with examples of how to calculate them.

Table 5.7   **Some of the Most Useful Metrics for Engagement**

Metrics	Type	Example
MAU/DAU	Proportion	$= \dfrac{\text{Total number of users who touched last month}}{\text{Total number of active users}}$
NPS	Average	Would you recommend this product to a friend or family member? Answer: [1–10]
Frequency of usage/ user recency	Distribution	Date of last visit
Use of functionality/ scroll depth	Distribution	Number of clicks or down scrolls to view additional content
Session time	Distribution	Length of time of the session

5.2.6   Revenue

Revenue metrics are useful for understanding the purchasing behavior of your customer base. Profit is the measure of how much money you made after subtracting costs; it's equal to revenue minus costs.

A number of revenue metrics are commonly used in web analytics. The first is *average revenue per user* (ARPU), calculated as the total revenue divided by the full user base.

$$Average\ revenue\ per\ user\ (ARPU) = \frac{Total\ revenue}{Total\ number\ of\ users\ in\ product}$$

Note that ARPU is traditionally an average, although a median here may be more useful. This is likely an exponential or skewed normal distribution, so the median and mode are actually better indicators.

The next set of metrics deals with purchasing behavior. The purchase conversion is the proportion of your population that you have converted; it's calculated as the number of users who made a purchase divided by the total users. If you have 12 users and 6 have made a purchase, your purchase conversion rate is 50%. Time to first purchase is also another useful metric. Generally, the shorter the time to first purchase, the better. Beware: It's important to consider what proportion of your user base is actually making it to the first purchase when you consider this metric. Some web products will have a short length of time to first purchase, because such a small number of users are actually making purchases.

The final useful basic revenue metric is *customer lifetime value*, which is the total profit derived from customers over their full life in the product.

$$Cohort\ customer\ lifetime\ value = \frac{Total\ profit\ from\ cohort\ X}{Total\ number\ of\ users\ in\ cohort\ X}$$

Customer lifetime value can be calculated for users who have left the product and predicted for users who are still in the product.

A product for which the measure of customer lifetime value makes sense is a product that has been around for a while. In this case, it's best to use the cohort measure of lifetime value for some of your earlier cohorts.

5.2.7 Progression Ratios

Progression ratios are useful because they tell us how addictive a behavior is; they are particularly useful to get a handle on some kind of continued behavior in a population, such as purchasing. *Purchasing progression ratios* consider the rate of purchasing from the second to the third purchase, third to the fourth purchase, and so on. If purchasing is "sticky," these ratios should approach 1 for larger numbers of purchases.

For instance, when looking at purchasing, people often look at first or second purchase metrics and then neglect higher numbers. Is purchase 3, 4, or 5 important? Purchasing progression ratios will tell you that.

A progression ratio is defined as follows:

$$Progression\ ratio = \frac{Total\ number\ of\ users\ who\ make\ it\ AT\ LEAST\ to\ n+1\ purchases}{Total\ number\ of\ users\ who\ make\ it\ AT\ LEAST\ to\ purchase\ n}$$

We order our data by the number of people who purchase at least x times. For instance, first we consider every user who makes zero purchases or more. That's all users—in this example, 10,000 users. Then, we look at all the users who made at least one purchase—that's 7,800. We create a table with all the users who make it at least to purchase n. We then calculate the ratio between those who make it to n and those who make it to $n + 1$ (Table 5.8). Then we're done.

Table 5.8 **Parity Progression Ratios for Progressing to the $n + 1$ Purchase**

Purchase Number (AT LEAST)	Total Number of Users	Progression Ratios
0	10,000	
1	7,800	$= \dfrac{7,800}{10,000} = 0.78$
2	3,560	$= \dfrac{3,560}{7,800} = 0.46$
3	2,875	$= \dfrac{2,875}{3,560} = 0.81$
4	2,000	$= \dfrac{2,000}{2,875} = 0.70$
5	1,876	$= \dfrac{1,876}{2,000} = 0.94$

(Continues)

Table 5.8   **(Continued)**

Purchase Number (AT LEAST)	Total Number of Users	Progression Ratios
6	1,450	$= \dfrac{1,450}{1,876} = 0.77$
7	1,000	$= \dfrac{1,000}{1,450} = 0.69$
8	543	$= \dfrac{543}{1,000} = 0.54$
9	500	$= \dfrac{500}{543} = 0.92$
10	450	$= \dfrac{450}{500} = 0.90$
11	425	$= \dfrac{425}{450} = 0.94$
11+	410	$= \dfrac{410}{425} = 0.96$

We can plot the results and see how the ratio changes with each purchase. Figure 5.3 displays the plot of the progression ratios for purchasing in this example. We can see that as the number of purchases increases, the ratio also increases. This is very normal behavior. Basically, purchasing gets more sticky as the number of purchases grows. We can also see blockages in purchases. It seems as if it's difficult to progress from one to two purchases, and from seven to eight purchases. In Listing 14.10, we calculate the parity progression ratio for this example and plot it in R.

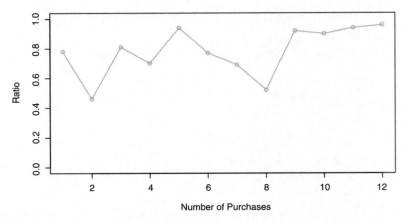

Figure 5.3   Plot of the progression ratio for each purchase.

Progression ratios come in handy when want users to progress to higher and higher levels. We want to know at what level the behavior is very sticky (more than 0.95 progression ratio). We also want to know if there are stopgaps where users are failing to progress, such as from purchase 1 to 2 and from purchase 7 to 8 in this example.

Overall, revenue metrics are pretty standard and useful for understanding purchasing behavior and discovering how lucrative a product is. While many more potential revenue metrics exist, the metrics summarized in Table 5.9 are the building blocks and simple, first-pass metrics. Chapter 9 will enable us to build better metrics by delving more deeply into the time and population elements of good metrics.

Table 5.9   **Some of the Most Useful Metrics for Revenue**

Metrics	Type	Example
Average revenue per user	Average But consider using the median or mode	$\dfrac{\text{Total revenue}}{\text{Total number of users}}$ $= \dfrac{300 \text{ million}}{100 \text{ million users}}$ $= \$3 \text{ per user}$
Purchase conversion	Ratio	$\dfrac{\text{Number of users with at least one purchase}}{\text{Total number of users}}$ $= \dfrac{1,000}{10,000}$ $= 10\%$
Time to first purchase	Distribution	This is a distribution, so we can take the median, mean or mode. Plot and decide.
Purchase progression ratios	Ratios	Total number of users who make it AT LEAST to n+1 purchases/Total number of users who make it AT LEAST to n purchases $= \dfrac{500}{1000}$ $= 50\%$
Customer lifetime value	Ratio	$\dfrac{\textit{Total profit from cohort X}}{\textit{Total number of users in cohort X}}$ $= \dfrac{10 \text{ million}}{1 \text{ million}}$ $= \$10 \text{ per user}$

5.3   Actionable Insights

In this chapter, you learned that:

- Metrics help us quantify an observable phenomenon accurately.

- There is a difference between period and cohort metrics. Cohort metrics aggregate different periods, whereas period metrics aggregate different cohorts.

- The most useful metrics for analyzing acquisition, retention, engagement, and revenue are averages, medians, ratios, and proportions.

Metrics are vital to measuring behavior in a web product. The tools in this chapter can be used with the measurement techniques in Chapter 4 to operationalize and quantify abstract ideas around user behavior. These simple techniques are the core building blocks to work with user behavior.

Chapter 6 will delve into A/B testing. Metrics are the key outcome variables for an A/B test, and we will continue to encounter metrics in every remaining chapter of the book. We will build on the statistical tools that we learned in this chapter to carry out more sophisticated statistical analyses and tests in those chapters.

Why Are My Users Leaving? The Ins and Outs of A/B Testing

In the prior chapters, we discussed theory development and the process of metrics creation and development. All of the tools we learned in prior chapters are used in conjunction to further our understanding of user behavior. To test our theories, we need to establish hypotheses and test them. We use conceptualization to create quantitative metrics to measure qualitative concepts and test our hypotheses. Then, we use the results of these tests to either falsify or confirm our theories.

In this chapter, we focus on the process of testing our hypotheses. We assume that you have built a theory with an eye toward behavior change, used the metrics creation techniques to develop sound/interesting outcome metrics, and picked interesting treatments to test.

This chapter provides a practitioner's how-to guide to A/B testing. Metrics are often our outcome variables for A/B tests. This chapter covers the following topics:

- The differences between causal inference and correlation

- The nuts and bolts of A/B testing

- Building statistical tests to test our hypotheses

The first part of this chapter explains the need for A/B testing by exploring the difficulty of inferring *why* something happens from everyday data. The second part is a how-to guide to A/B tests, including conducting statistical tests to determine the effects of an intervention or treatment. The third part discusses common errors that occur with user data and how to avoid these in practice.

6.1 An A/B Test

We will start by defining an A/B test. An A/B test, also known as a split test, involves randomly picking some users for the first variant (usually the control) and some users for the second variant (the treatment).

For instance, in a medical setting, we randomly divide a group of subjects into two subgroups: one group will get the new drug (the treated group), and the other will get a placebo or sugar pill (the control group). In this setting, the A/B test is generally called a *randomized controlled* trial (RCT), but it is based on a similar statistical design as is applied in nonmedical settings. Next we provide some helpful definitions for treatment and control groups, which will be used throughout this chapter. We will build on these ideas in the section focused on advanced causal inference techniques.

In a medical setting, there are often strict guidelines placed on testing, since you are working with human subjects. In contrast, in the world of user analytics, the guidelines are relatively slim. Instead, the core problem in user analytics is selection. Selection means that the users coming to your site are nonrandom. Medical trials are often randomized, and many medical studies actively try to increase the sample representativeness. In A/B testing, you often have a strongly selected population to begin with. It is hard to get a representative sample of the general population in such a case.

When an A/B test takes place in a web context, that setting allows for more flexibility, repeated testing, and more variations. However, there is often limited follow-up compared to a medical trial.

- **Treatment:** Some element, action, or feature that could have a causal effect on something else. It could be a change to our website, a behavioral action, a medication, or something else.

- **Treated group:** A random group of participants who are given the treatment.

- **Control group:** A random group of participants who do not receive the treatment. They do not know that they did not receive treatment and often are given a placebo to prevent them from inferring that they did not receive the treatment. In the world of user analytics, it's easier to get away with no placebo, because you do not have to inform users that they are being tested.

We want all the conditions to be the same for both the treatment and the control, except for the treatment variable. In this case, we will change the cancer drug that we give to study participants.

We also need an outcome or some metric, which we can use to determine our treatment effect. In our medical trial, the outcome is life expectancy and the treatment effect is how much longer our cancer patients live based on receiving the new drug versus the placebo.

In a web context, suppose we want to test the effect of a new algorithm. We could add an algorithm to suggest friends to users in our snowmobile site. The random users assigned to the treatment will see the new algorithm's results. The users assigned to the control do not see the new algorithm's results.

We then consider the effect of viewing the results of the algorithm on retention. In this case, one outcome we may consider is the difference in average retention between the group who saw the new algorithm's results and the group who did not.

To make sure that our theories are indeed correct, they often need to be tested. This is not always readily apparent, so we'll spend some time in the next two subsections exploring why and when A/B testing is needed. The introductory sections will also help you recognize incorrect inferences from nonexperimental data.

6.2   The Curious Case of Free Weekly Events

Before we jump into A/B testing, let's explore why it's difficult to understand *why* something happens from regular "observational" data. **Observational data** is simply the data that we collect on what customers do. We don't need any special setup to collect this data. How, then, does observational data lead us astray? We'll explore a common example.

Angry Dodo Birds: The Sand Saga, a mobile gaming company, hires you as a data consultant. This company runs special events monthly to help bolster engagement in its product. The events allow free access to the gated web features such as higher, more complex levels.

The product managers think weekly events *cause* more purchasing because they find users who took part in these weekends buy more stuff on their site—free dodo treats and shiny weapons. Since the leadership team identifies these events as causing more purchasing, they want to increase the number of these free events and the number of users who have access to those events to drive more purchasing. Of course, this comes at a cost, so they ask you: Will this work?

SpellBook, another well-known mobile product, also needs your consulting wisdom. SpellBook is a social network that hosts weekly spelling competitions between users. Users can compete against other users for perks. Users who participate in these competitions make more purchases in the product, such as spelling bee videos and Scrabble games. Again, the executives think that greater engagement in these competitions *causes* greater purchasing. Due to this perceived causal relationship, they want to increase the number of competitions and randomly place new users into these competitions. They also ask you: Will this work?

Do you think that these strategies were successful? Basically, if the executives are right and either the special events or competitions *cause* greater purchasing, then these strategies of expanding access would greatly increase their revenue.

However, neither company could tell from the data that either of these events actually causes greater purchasing in their product. Just because two variables are highly related, this does not mean that one **caused** the other.

The examples described here are true stories (though obviously different company names and products were used), and this scenario happens often in industry. An A/B test was run at both companies, and executives at Angry Dodo Birds were right: Monthly special events had a **huge causal effect** on purchasing. In contrast, the executives at SpellBook made an erroneous assumption: In fact, greater engagement in these competitions did not lead to more purchasing. There was almost **no causal effect** of the competitions, only a strong correlation.

With the data currently available to either Angry Dodo Birds and SpellBook, there is no way for you to know as the data consultant if there is a causal effect of either the greater access on weekends or the spelling competitions on purchasing. *We need to either run an experiment (an A/B test or other type) or try to use statistical techniques to properly assess causality from observational (nonrandomized) data.*

This example shows us that a "relationship" between two variables need not be causal. Two variables could, indeed, just be related, without one causing the other.

To better understand noncausal relationships, we need to understand the concept of correlation. Correlation is the directionless relationship between two things. An example is the gross domestic product (GDP) and employment. As the GDP increases, the population employment rate also goes up; conversely, as the population employment rate goes up, GDP increases. Measures of these two economic ideas are related. We don't know if there is a causal relationship, but we know that they generally move together.

The next section discusses why making conclusions from observed data often doesn't result in inferences that are causal, but rather those that are correlative in nature. In later sections, we'll explore what we need to make causal inferences.

To understand how a relationship can be solely correlative, we'll discuss spurious correlation (a correlation driven by an outside variable), selection bias (patterns in nonrandomized data that make inferences difficult), and randomness (data devoid of built-in patterns). These concepts will help us understand the need for A/B testing.

6.2.1 Spurious Correlation

Let's start with the concept of spurious correlation. A **spurious correlation** is a relationship between two variables driven by a third outside variable.

Most people struggle to understand the concept of spurious correlation when they first see it. It's absolutely *not intuitive*. Consider the following thought experiment. Figure 6.1 is the number of "likes" for a popular movie and the number of downloads of that movie on a company's website. Do you think that the number of movie "likes" causes the number of downloads, based on looking at Figure 6.1?

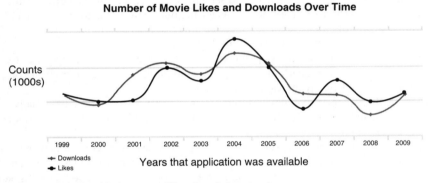

Figure 6.1   The relationship between "likes" and downloads.

When asked this question in workshops, participants will often say, "Yes, of course—don't you see the relationship?" The follow-up question is then, What is the mechanism? A mechanism is how one factor causes the outcome through any mitigating or intermediate variables. *Why do you think "likes" cause more downloads?* Think about your answer. There are lots of potential explanations. Here are some common ones: "Likes" lead others to think the movie is good, so more people download it. "Likes" lead to more people viewing the movie page. Since items with more views come up in more feeds, that leads more people to view the movie and download. The reasoning goes on and on.

Figure 6.2 shows the real names for two variables: the number of people killed by venomous spiders and the number of letters in the winning word at the Scripps National Spelling Bee. How many people would think the number of letters in the winning word *caused* venomous spiders to attack? None, of course.

Lots of variables can be related (in this case, letters and spider killings are highly correlated) even if one did not cause the other. *Correlation is a linear relationship between two variables. It does not imply that one causes the other.*

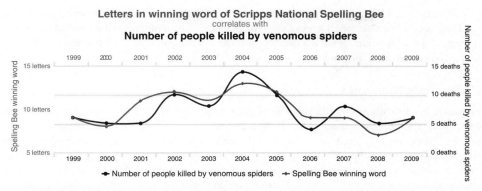

Figure 6.2   The relationship between spelling bees and venomous spider deaths.

The variables that you care about in a web product are more likely to be causally related than letters and spider bites, or windstorms in the Sahara and the stock market. Even so, that doesn't mean that thinking a causal relationship exists without empirical support is any less false.

Regarding whether "likes" *cause* more downloads in our movie example, there could be a spurious relationship with page views. Page views can cause more "likes" of the movie, since people need to see the movie page to "like" it. Page views can also cause more downloads of the movie, as people need to see a movie to download it. More people viewed the movie, and therefore more people got interested and downloaded it. The number of likes had no effect on the number of downloads. Perhaps users never even noticed the "like" icon.

Many correlations in your product are driven by **spurious relationships**. A spurious relationship between B and C occurs when some variable A is causing B and C to go up. When you see B and C go up, you might assume that they are causally related. However, B and C are only related through A, so your inference about a relationship between B and C is incorrect. In Figure 6.3, we can see a visual representation of this idea. If we only look at B and C, we incorrectly assume a causal relationship between them. However, if we widen the view, we notice that A causes both.

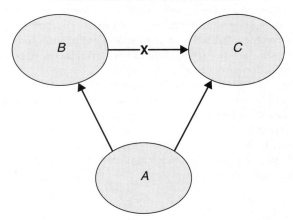

Figure 6.3   Spurious relationship. A causes B and C. However, one could mistakenly think B causes C.

To flesh out the idea of spurious correlation, we need to understand another concept, selection bias. Selection bias occurs when a set of data has preset selection patterns that prevent us from making valid causal inferences. It's related to spurious correlation because it prevents us from differentiating between spurious and causal relationships in real data.

6.2.2 Selection Bias

The reason it's difficult to identify spurious relationships is because of selection bias. **Selection bias** occurs when people self-select (or are nonrandomly selected) into certain behavioral patterns. An example will help us understand this definition. Suppose your company puts you in charge of analyzing the data from historical health awareness days. The managers ask you, Does having a company health awareness day increase company retention? During the annual health awareness day, your company holds a 5K run for employees and their families. A small number of employees sign up and do the 5K run. Those who do sign up to stay at the company two years longer, on average, than those that do not.

When the company managers see this data, they argue that everyone should be forced to do a 5K run on the next health awareness day. The CEO agrees, and you analyze the data again and find that the retention number does not go up. In fact, it goes down. Why? The effect that you see on retention could be selection bias, meaning that there is no causal relationship between the run and retention.

Selection bias arises when users are not randomly picked from the population, but are selected by some other force. In this example, those more invested in the company are more likely to run the 5K race when it's optional. The fact that employees who run the 5K race are more invested than the average employee is driving the lower turnover of these employees. Company interest is our hidden A variable driving the correlation between our participation in the 5K run and higher retention. We can see that the selection bias is the nonrandom way in which employees are selecting into the 5K run; it is driving the difference in retention. The treatment of running the 5K run is not causing the increase in retention.

The key to understanding why we cannot make inferences from this data is to understand how observational data differs from randomized data. Randomness is like rainbows. This metaphor might seem over the top, but it's really not. Randomness to a statistician is like rainbows to a small child: It will brighten your day.

Of course, you don't believe me yet, so let's go back and reframe our example. Let's say that instead of letting anyone sign up for the company's 5K run, we randomly assigned participants. Judy from accounting was included, while Steve in billing had to cheer Judy on from the sidelines. Now, we find the same result: Participation in the 5K run increased company retention. Well, that's it, folks, we're done. We can all go home now.

Really, it's that simple. When the B variable we're interested is randomized, we can assume that the effect is causal. Why? Because randomness eliminates the spurious relationships. So, you can tell Jim, the CEO, to have more health awareness days and encourage everyone to run a 5K. It will have a positive causal effect.

Since it's much easier to determine correlation than causation, in the next section, we'll nail down the technical definition of correlation. It's important not only to understand the concept, but also how it's traditionally measured.

6.3   But It's Correlated …

We need to discuss how to quantify "relationships" between variables. The following are two very common ways that people talk about relationships between variables. The first is the simple proportional approach, which is comparing how two groups differ in outcome. The other is the linear correlation coefficient, which is how two variables move together or apart linearly. Both of these concepts are limited and often lead to incorrect inferences. Each subsection here discusses common errors in inference.

We'll consider the proportional comparison first. From entry-level employees to executives, incorrect conclusions from proportional comparisons are extremely common.

6.3.1   Proportional Comparisons

With proportional comparisons, we compare two quantities against each other, usually one of which is categorical. Suppose we have two variables: participation in the 5K race (categorical—did or did not) and retention. We can compare retention to participation in the 5K race. We could also compare salary to participation in the 5K race. These are proportional relationships. In Table 6.1, it's apparent that there is a substantial difference in the median retention and salary of the two groups. Median retention is 1.79 years longer and median salary is $19,580 higher for participants in the 5K run.

Table 6.1   **Proportional Comparisons**

	Retention (Median)	Salary (Median)
5K Participants	5.35 years	$85,560
5K Nonparticipants	3.56 years	$65,980

Differences in outcomes between these two groups are often used to justify "causation." I've heard hundreds of times the false attribution of causation to a proportional difference. In other words, since participants in the 5K have higher salaries, we might think that we can infer that participation *causes* a raise in salary. In reality, all we can say is that *we do not know if they are causally related*. There could be a selection effect in which those employees with higher salaries are more likely to run a 5K race, and their self-selection boosts the salary number.

This relationship could also involve **reverse causality**, in which a higher salary *causes* greater retention. *Notice that correlation is undirected; however, causation has an implied direction.* X causes Y, but Y does not cause X. On the other hand, X is correlated with Y, and Y is correlated with X. Again, we absolutely do not know based on proportional comparisons whether this relationship is spurious or causality in one direction or the other. In reality, a large proportional difference might mean that something interesting is going on and this effect may be a good candidate for an A/B test. Other than that, the proportional comparison is not especially useful for drawing insights. Many features or behaviors in web products will be proportionally related.

We'll probably find an apple under every apple tree, so to speak. If there is a very large change in the secondary variable or a corresponding linear or exponential unit change (called a dosage effect), that relationship might be interesting. We'll explore these types of special cases, in which proportional differences might denote a causal relationship, in Chapter 12.

6.3.2   Linear Correlations

As discussed in the prior section, the most common way I've seen variables compared is through proportional relationships. The other way that people typically show a relationship between two variables is through a **linear correlation coefficient**. The linear correlation coefficient measures the strength of a linear relationship between two variables. It implies *no causal relationship*. We explored this idea in Chapter 5 when we looked at bivariate graphing.

We looked for positive and negative correlations between variables. Variables that are positively correlated are basically equal to the *x* = *y* line. Negatively correlated values create a triangle with the *x*- and *y*-axes. Figure 6.5 illustrates the different types of correlative relationships and their corresponding correlation coefficient values. A correlation coefficient of –1 is a perfect negative correlation, +1 is a perfect positive correlation, and 0 is no linear correlation. On a practical level, a high linear correlation is greater than 0.7, a moderate correlation is in the range of 0.3 to 0.7 and a low correlation is less than 0.3.

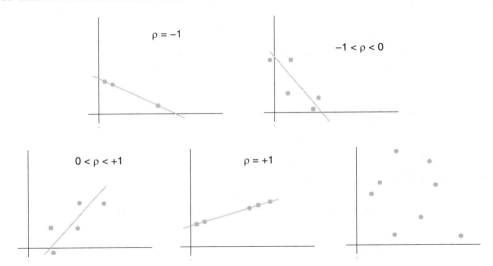

Figure 6.4   The correlation coefficient with different data patterns. As explained in Chapter 3, *p* is the correlation coefficient.

How do we calculate linear correlation? In Chapter 5, we discussed variance, which is the spread of a set of variables. Linear correlation is related to the idea of covariance, or how the spreads of the two distributions relate to each other. The correlation coefficient is then adjusted by dividing the covariance by the standard deviation to create a metric that ranges from –1 to +1.

In Table 6.2, we calculate the correlation coefficient for a hypothetical example of 10 users' spend and retention data. From this example, we can see how this metric is calculated. The numerator is how *X* and *Y* vary together, and the denominator is how each varies on its own. The correlation coefficient is 0.76, in this case meaning that retention and spending are highly positively correlated. This means spending longer in the product is linearly related to spending more. We cannot make any causal claims, however.

Table 6.2   **Calculating the Correlation Between Retention and Spending**

Observation Number	Retention	Spend	X * Y	X^2	Y^2
1	3	0	0	9	0
2	5	10	50	25	100
3	7	15	105	49	225
4	1	2	2	1	4
5	12	17	204	144	289
6	16	3	48	256	9
7	34	52	1,768	1,156	2,704
8	18	1	18	324	1
9	1	0	0	1	0
10	24	16	384	576	256
SUM	121	116	2,579	2,541	3,588

6.3.2.1   Calculating Correlation

From Table 6.2, we can get the following summary quantities:

$$N = 10$$

$$\sum X*Y = 2,579$$

(Here we sum the column of $X*Y$.)

$$\sum X = 121$$

(This is the sum of the retention column.)

$$\sum Y = 116$$

(This is the sum of the spending column.)

$$\sum X^2 = 2,541$$

(This is the sum of the X^2 column.)

$$\sum Y^2 = 3,588$$

(This is the sum of the Y^2 column.)

To get the numerator, we need to calculate the following equation:

$$Numerator = N * \sum X*Y - \sum X * \sum Y$$

This is equivalent to calculating the covariance of X and Y. We calculated all these values above. Using the values in Table 6.2, this calculation is:

$$= 10*(2,579)-(121*116)$$

$$= 11,754$$

Then, we can calculate the denominator from the following equation:

$$Denominator = \sqrt{\left(N*\sum X^2 - \sum X^2\right)*\left(N*\sum Y^2 - \sum Y^2\right)}$$

$$= \sqrt{(10*2,541-121^2)*(10*3,588-116^2)}$$

$$= \sqrt{10,769*22,424}$$

$$= 15,540$$

The denominator denotes how each X and Y vary separately. Next, we divide the numerator by the denominator to get our correlation coefficient:

$$= \frac{11,754}{15,540}$$

$$= 0.76$$

(High correlation)

6.3.3 Nonlinear Relationships

What happens when there is a nonlinear relationship, like $y = x^2$? In this case, the correlation coefficient is 0. This does not mean that x and y are independent, because clearly they are not. The correlation coefficient is not useful for denoting correlation in nonlinear functions.

Let's consider another nonlinear relationship. What if you have a sin x and cos x function? Of course, these are very similar functions: sin x is the shifted cos x function. These functions are plotted in Figure 6.6. However, the correlation coefficient is again 0. We might think that these were two time-dependent variables, one shifted and the other not. However, the correlation coefficient will tell you that they are not related at all.

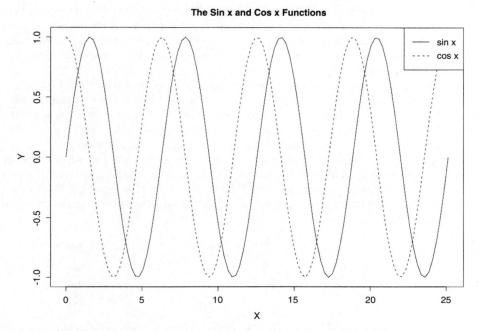

Figure 6.5   The sin x and cos x distributions. The correlation coefficient is 0.

There are other methods to consider nonlinear relationships between variables. In fact, there is a whole area of statistics focused on time-dependent variables; we'll introduce time series modeling techniques in Chapter 12. We can explore the relationship between time-dependent variables with the use of lags and other methods.

Correlation is a useful tool that helps us create a metric for linear relationships. Correlation shows us when variables are positively or negatively linearly related. However, it does not work for nonlinear relationships, so be very careful when using it. Correlation also does not imply causation.

Now that we have found the inferential difficulties for correlation, how do we get to infer causal relationships? For that we need generally randomness. In the next section, we'll delve deeper into the concept of randomness.

6.4   Why Randomness?

Randomness is absolutely one of the most difficult concepts to explain. It's why many people find statistics so difficult. Most people like to think in terms of **determinism**. Think about the idea of fate, that there is a drawn-out path for your life. Fate is deterministic or predetermined, meaning there is no possibility that some random perturbation can pull you off the path. It's like turning on a light. On a superficial level, when you turn the switch, electric current runs through the cord and the light bulb lights. It's easy to imagine, understand, and predict the deterministic process. In contrast, it's very difficult to imagine randomness.

For example, if we have a blue, red, or yellow ball in a hat, which will I pick out? Which event in a series of events will occur, and how does that event affect the next events? The most difficult realization is that there are patterns to randomness. In other words, if you draw a blue ball from a hat (and replace it) a thousand, a million, or a billion times, the number of blue balls drawn will tend toward the true probability of picking a blue ball.

One of the best ways to comprehend or imagine randomness is to see it in the form of simulation. Suppose that we draw enough numbers from a distribution so that we can see the shape of the distribution. This allows us to determine whether there is an order or pattern to the randomness—that yes, each individual choice may be random, but over time they tend to follow a certain pattern or distribution. Randomness is integral to the A/B testing process.

Figure 6.6 depicts a simulation of a quarter circle. Here, we're randomly drawing from a point within the circle. As we draw more and more samples, the circle gets filled in, and we can see that we are drawing a quarter circle. If we looked at only a few points, we could not discern this information, but after a large enough sample the pattern becomes clear to us even though we are randomly sampling.

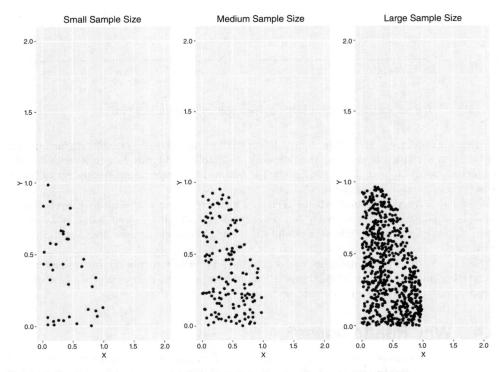

Figure 6.6   As we draw more and more samples, the quarter circle gets filled in.

Randomness is the key to A/B testing. According to Ronald Fisher, the father of modern-day statistics, "randomness is the only reasoned basis for inference." If we are to have an experiment that is believable, we need to operationalize randomness. We can operationalize the probability of an event occurring. If it's very unlikely to happen randomly but happens anyway, we can generally assume that it happened due to the mechanism we are testing. To properly design an A/B test, we need to think about how to operationalize randomness.

Now that we have a better understanding of why we need randomness and what randomness is, let's explore the process of carrying out an A/B test.

6.5   The Nuts and Bolts of an A/B Test

This section walks through the basics of A/B testing with examples from web products. As we discussed in the introduction to this chapter, a simple A/B test is an experiment run on two groups of randomized users, one group that receives the treatment and one group that does not. We use A/B testing to understand how features, behaviors, and other potential treatments will affect outcomes for our users. It's extremely useful in understanding cause-and-effect relationships and getting clear feedback on what works and what doesn't. A/B testing gets its name from its function. There are two variants, and group A gets one and group B gets another.

Why is A/B testing important?

- It helps us solve the problems that we mentioned earlier—spurious relationships and selection bias.

- It allows us to assess causal relationships between variables.

- It's relatively easy to implement in a web application.

The next few subsections show how to set up an A/B test, interpret it, understand the randomization process, and implement basic hypothesis testing and power analysis.

6.5.1   A/B Test Process

Before we dive into the details, let's consider the big-picture view of the A/B testing process. Figure 6.7 shows the three phases of A/B testing.

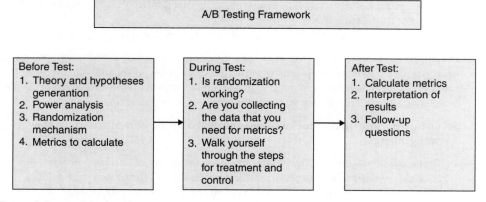

Figure 6.7   A/B testing diagram.

Phase one is pre-test set-up. We need to build a theory and identify a hypothesis to test (discussed in Chapter 2), find the sample size for our test, create a randomization mechanism, and finally determine the metrics that we want to capture for our treatment effect.

Phase two is when the test is running. We need to keep track of a few things. First, we need to know whether users in treatment and control can actually see the treatment or control elements. Second, we need to ensure that the randomness mechanism is working as expected. Finally, we need to check that we are accurately collecting user data. In practice, there is often at least one error in the setup and data collection process.

Finally, phase three occurs after the test has completed and we have collected all data. After we have collected all the data, we need to analyze and interpret the results of the A/B test. Is the effect size large enough for all our metrics and in the direction we hypothesized? Did we accept or reject our initial hypotheses? Is there agreement among all of our metrics?

In the next section, we'll explore the pre-test phase in more detail.

6.5.2 The Setup

In this section, we'll discuss each individual part of the pre-test, set-up process for a well-designed A/B test. An A/B test, or split test, is based on a simple idea: We split users into multiple subgroups in which they are given (treatment) or not given (control) the intervention. All conditions need to be the same for the treated and control groups, except for the treatment variable. In other words, those who do and don't receive the treatment should receive similar medical care, have similar medical histories, and so on. We need randomness to ensure this consistency across groups.

We also need an outcome, or some metric, that we can use to determine the **treatment effect**. In medical trials, the outcome is often life expectancy. In our case, we will compare the average life span of cancer patients who take the new drug with the life span of those given the placebo.

We want to make sure the **magnitude** of the effect is sufficiently large. In other words, what is the size of the treatment effect? Will the medication increase life expectancy by 2 days or by 10 years for the average participant? If the effect is large enough, we can use **significance testing** to then see if the effect is statistically significant (meaning that it is likely not a random effect, but rather the effect of the treatment).

The following are the steps needed to conduct an A/B test (pre-test):

1. Determine the sample size for the treatment and control groups by performing a **power analysis**. Often in large web products, we do not need to use power analysis since the number of users needed to conduct an A/B test is relatively small. In our medical case, this is an issue, and we'll discuss a simple example at the end of the section.

2. Set up the **randomization mechanism** and design the experiment. Consider the following questions:

   ▪ *What is our sample and which users are included in the selection?* This becomes complex quickly if we want to test something later in a user funnel. In the web page color example we'll use in this chapter, if users must complete a few steps before they even reach the page with the purple background, we must ask ourselves, What types of selection of users is occurring before the randomization? Basically, the earlier in the user funnel or user session history that selection occurs, the better and more generalizable the results will be.

- *When and how will the users be put into randomized groups?* Ideally, this assignment should occur very close to when they are receiving treatment. Otherwise, other factors might bias the results.

- *What is the treatment?* We're looking for the Goldilocks "just right" middle. The treatment should not be too complicated or we won't be able to understand the causal pathways. It can't be too simple, such as a simple font change on the web page's title, or it likely will have a marginal or no effect. (We'll talk about this more in the interpretation section.) The stage and resources of the company might also determine the complexity of the treatment. If you work for a large tech company, you have the resources to test extensively. If you work for a small company, you will have to use A/B testing sparingly to some degree.

3. Determine the outcome metric or metrics to identify an effect. We encountered metric creation and operationalization in Chapter 5. From a given metric, we can identify the distribution and statistical test. We'll see examples of this later in this section.

For our web product example, let's say we want to test changing the background color from blue to purple for our website. How can we set up an A/B test to test the effect of this change? One approach would be to send our treated group to the purple background while the control group gets the original blue background. Suppose our outcome is click-through rates (CTR) to the site. We want to find the effect of the change of background color on CTR to a purchasing page. We do a simple power analysis, or an analysis to determine sample size, and find 1,000 users are enough to determine if there is a 5% effect. We'll discuss power analysis at the end of this section.

First, though, we'll analyze a hypothetical result. Suppose that 1,000 people are randomly sent to the blue background and 1,000 people are sent to the purple background. Table 6.3 is the result of that A/B test.

Table 6.3   **The results of our banner A/B test on click-through rates.**

	Click	**No Click**	
Blue (control)	175	825	
Purple (treatment)	225	775	5% increase

We can see that more people clicked through when the page had a purple background. As denoted in Table 6.3, there was a 5% increase between those who received the treatment versus those in the control group. We now need to decide if the magnitude of this effect is large and significant. First, let's consider the magnitude. If we have 1 million users, 5% might be large—it's equal to 50,000 users. If we have 1,000 users, though, 5% is only 50 users. Does it matter since it's only 50 people? It's important that you assess the magnitude based on your unique web product's size or your particular outcome variable. This consideration is called *practical significance*. Depending on the behavior, we can also assess the efficacy of our intervention. If you remember from Chapter 3, for a large scale behavior change a response of less than 10% is still a good result. For smaller changes, a rate closer to 30% might be a good result.

The next step is to determine whether this difference is just a random perturbation or is really meaningful. This consideration is called *statistical significance*. We'll tackle this question in the section on hypothesis testing. The next section will help us understand why setting up the random mechanism correctly is integral to the accuracy of our test.

6.5.3 Randomization

We'll skip step one, power analysis, for now, as it's often not needed in a web context—usually our sample sizes are large enough. We'll revisit power analysis in section 6.5.5.1. In this subsection, we'll jump right to step two, randomization. As discussed earlier, randomization is a difficult concept. We *need* randomization to define the treated and control groups appropriately. Without randomization, there is no A/B test.

We can vary treatments or outcomes and still have an A/B test, but when we remove randomization our A/B test fails to provide us with results. *Randomization creates two similar groups* by selecting similar proportions of users on all features. With randomized selection of groups, the average proportion in both the treatment and the control conditions will be approximately equal on every feature (i.e., every nontreated feature).

Let's unpack this idea about "similar" groups a little more. Suppose we know that gender is important for a certain behavior we want to test, but we are not interested in the effect of gender but rather some other factor. We're running a dating website and we want to A/B test whether adding a "Like" button to a profile increases the probability of a message being sent. We think that men are more likely to use a "Like" button (click it) and/or respond to "Like" by sending a message.

If we run an A/B test and randomly sample the user population, we should, on average, get similar proportions of men and women in each group. Let's say 40% of our user population is female and 60% is male. Both the treatment and control groups for the A/B test should be about 40% female and 60% male.

On the other hand, if we just captured behavior that naturally occurred, we might see a selection bias. Perhaps men are more likely to actively use the "Like" button and message another member, or our sample group is 85% male and 15% female.

Randomness allows us to make inferences, because it removes **selection bias**. Eliminating selection bias from a potential test allows us to assume there is no confounding A variable, since the treatment and control groups have equal shares of users with the A attribute. In this case, there is no selection of active male users in the product (our sample would be about 40% female and 60% male based on the demographics of the site); we're getting the same cross-section of the population of the dating site in both the treatment and control groups. We can also look at just male or just female users in treatment and control to estimate the treatment effect in each subpopulation. This allows us to attribute all the difference in outcome to the variation or the treatment variable. It might sound confusing, but the idea is really simple: *Randomness allows us to create similar populations, without understanding all the thousands of potentially confounding characteristics of those populations.*

The lack of randomization is why social science and medical research is often so hard to conduct. For instance, we could ask the question, does having a single parent *cause* you to earn less money? We can't easily run an A/B test to answer this question because *we can't randomly make some people single parents and others not.* So we really don't know the causal effect. We can use other methods to try and get at it, but they will never be as good as a clear-cut A/B test.

The inability to randomize is a huge problem that crops up in lots of complex path-dependent or contextual settings. We'll see that it's also a problem when asking big social questions in a web product, but for now let's revel in the wonderfulness of A/B testing for answering simple questions about social behavior in a web product.

A/B testing is a very powerful tool and makes causal inference possible by solving the selection problem. Randomization creates simpler populations for the treatment and control conditions so we can isolate and test the effect of just one feature.

6.5.4 Hypothesis Testing

Now that we have discussed A/B testing setup and randomization, we should have all the tools we need to run an A/B test. Suppose we run an A/B test with the setup described in the earlier section and collect some data. How do we analyze and interpret the results?

Our first step is to calculate the average treatment effect (ATE). The ATE is the average difference in our chosen metric between our treated and control groups. Let's return to our purple background A/B test example, where we saw a 5% increase in CTR for our treated population versus our control population. Great, but how do we know that this difference is not due to random chance? Suppose we randomly draw out members of our treated and control populations. There is a small chance that they could be extremely different even if we are drawing from the same distribution. We need to calculate how unlikely it is that we would obtain this result.

This brings us to the topic of statistical significance testing. Such testing tells us whether a causal effect is a random perturbation or *a real effect*. We want to be able to differentiate numbers that are important from meaningless variations.

Statisticians have devised a way to accomplish exactly that: They use randomness to determine whether some number is likely an aberration. As mentioned earlier in the chapter, Ronald Fisher, the father of modern statistics, said that "randomization is the basis of all inference." We've seen that on a larger level with A/B testing, but we'll rely on the same idea to determine if our results are real. Significance testing operationalizes randomness to find values that are unlikely to be attributable to chance. To do this kind of testing, we need to talk about a few concepts, the first of which is the test statistic.

A **test statistic** is a standardized value, like the mean, that we can use to create a null hypothesis. As we discussed in Chapter 3, the null hypothesis is the baseline hypothesis that there is no effect or no relationship between two quantities. For instance, in web analytics, we want to determine if there was a shift in the mean between the treatment and control groups. Our test statistic is the mean and the null hypothesis is that the mean CTR is the same for both the treatment and control groups.

Once we have a test statistic, we need to identify the distribution that is used to test it. If we cannot identify the right distribution, we can use statistical tests that do not require a defined distribution. CTRs generally follow a chi-squared distribution. Table 6.5 found later in this chapter, summarizes the metrics, test statistics, and distributional assumptions for common web analytics metrics.

Finally, we need to calculate the test statistic and compare it to the distribution for our statistic distribution to determine the probability that this outcome could occur by chance. The goal of the test is to determine whether the probability that this result could occur randomly is low enough that our result is the true effect.

In this section, we'll go through three numeric examples. To carry out statistical testing in R, please refer to Chapter 15 and Listings 15.1–15.7. Here are the three examples that we will examine:

- Click-through rates using the chi-squared distribution

- Difference in means using a *t*-test

- Two survival curves using the log-rank test

Of course, these three examples will not exhaust the types of statistical testing that we can do. At the end of the section, Table 6.5 identifies common problems that arise with user analytics, test statistics, statistical tests, and distributions. In Chapter 15, we'll discuss some other A/B testing examples in R to more comprehensively cover this topic.

6.5.4.1 CTR with Chi-Squared Test

Suppose we want to make a change to a promotion banner on our website (new banner: "Snowmobile Sale: 50% off" versus old banner: "Snowmobile Deals: 5% off") and we want to know if the CTR increased. We have an outcome, which is the number of users who clicked through with the new versus the old banner. Suppose that all of these users are new to the site and randomly selected. How do we tell if there has been a change in CTR due to the banner change?

Our null hypothesis, or our baseline outcome, is that there has been no change to CTR with a banner change. A null hypothesis is the default position that there is no relationship between two phenomena. Great, we have a hypothesis! Our metric is the CTR—that is, the proportion of users who click through on the banner.

Okay, now we are on to the test component. Suppose 45 out of 856 users clicked through on the old banner and 99 out of 1,298 clicked through on the new banner. We can assume that these two groups are randomly selected populations. How can we tell if the promotion was successful? We can use the Pearson chi-squared test since our response variable is categorical: clicked through or did not click through. A categorical variable is one that has a non-numeric response; it results in two or more categories, such as a gender of "male," "female," or "unknown."

The Pearson chi-squared test is a statistical test applied to categorical data to determine whether the observed distribution of clicks arose by chance. The null hypothesis for this test in our example is that the CTR does *not* depend on the promotional banner that each user saw. In other words, regardless of the promo, the same proportion of users would have clicked through. We then compare the rate calculated from the expected proportions clicking through to the actual rate calculated from our test. We capture the probability of getting that test statistic from the chi-squared distribution table.

Chi-Squared Calculations

In this section, we'll work through an example of how to carry out the Chi-Squared test.

To carry out the chi-squared test for the CTR example, we will use a two-by-two contingency table, shown in Table 6.4. While this table shows all the calculated values, in this section we'll show you how these values are derived.

The initial number is the observed number, the number in the brackets [ ] is the expected number, and the number in the parentheses ( ) is the test statistic for that value in the contingency table. We need to calculate this test statistic for each square of the 2×2 contingency table.

Table 6.4 Two-by-Two Contingency Table to Calculate the Chi-Squared Test Statistic*

	Before Promo	After Promo	Row Totals
Clicked Through	45 [57.23] (2.61)	99 [86.77] (1.72)	144
Did Not Click Through	811 [789.77] (0.19)	1,199 [1,211.23] (.12)	2,010
Column Totals	856	1,298	2,154

*Degrees of freedom = $(2 - 1) * (2 - 1) = 1$.

First, we must calculate the expected rate for each entry of the contingency table. For the box in the top left, Clicked Through Before Promo, we calculate the average CTR regardless of the promo and multiply it by the total users before promo. The average CTR is 45 + 99 or 144 divided by the sum of all users, or 2,154. We then multiply this number by the number of users before the promo, or 856 users.

$$= 856 * \frac{144}{2,154}$$

$$= 57.23$$

This number, 57.23, is the expected CTR if the promo did not matter.

Next, we take the observed value, minus the expected value squared, divided by the expected value to calculate the test statistic. The test statistic for the top left-hand box is

$$= \frac{(45 - 57.23)^2}{57.23}$$

$$= 2.61$$

We can carry this out for each value of the contingency table. See if you can calculate the expected value and test statistic for the other three positions in the contingency table.

If we add all the test statistics in the contingency table, we get the full test statistic, which is 4.64. Now we can use the Chi-squared distribution to calculate the probability of getting this test statistic.

Now that we have calculated the test statistic for the full contingency table, we need to determine the degrees of freedom. Degrees of freedom is the number of independent values in a calculation that are allowed to vary. This example has 1 degree of freedom. The degrees of freedom calculation appears in the table note (we subtract 1 from each row of the contingency table and multiply the result to get one degree of freedom for this example).

Chi-Squared Significance Test

We can use the chi-squared table in Figure 6.8 to determine the probability of this test statistic occurring based on the first row, which give the probabilities for one degree of freedom. The value we want is at the end of the first row between 3.84 and 6.63 for one degree of freedom. We have only one control group. We know that the probability is between 5% and 1%. Given the exact p value for this result (0.031147) and the fact that we have only one independent test, it's likely sufficient to reject the null hypothesis: That is, the banner likely had an effect on CTR. In 1 out of 32 times, this outcome would occur from random chance—a probability that is likely sufficient to reject the null.

Significance Table for the Chi-Squared Distribution

Degrees of Freedom	Probability of a Larger Value of x^2								
	0.99	0.95	0.90	0.75	0.50	0.25	0.10	0.05	0.01
1	0.000	0.004	0.016	0.102	0.455	1.32	2.71	3.84	6.63
2	0.020	0.103	0.211	0.575	1.386	2.77	4.61	5.99	9.21
3	0.115	0.352	0.584	1.212	2.366	4.11	6.25	7.81	11.34
4	0.297	0.711	1.064	1.923	3.357	5.39	7.78	9.49	13.28
5	0.554	1.145	1.610	2.675	4.351	6.63	9.24	11.07	15.09
6	0.872	1.635	2.204	3.455	5.348	7.84	10.64	12.59	16.81
7	1.239	2.167	2.833	4.255	6.346	9.04	12.02	14.07	18.48
8	1.647	2.733	3.490	5.071	7.344	10.22	13.36	15.51	20.09
9	2.088	3.325	4.168	5.899	8.343	11.39	14.68	16.92	21.67
10	2.558	3.940	4.865	6.737	9.342	12.55	15.99	18.31	23.21
11	3.053	4.575	5.578	7.584	10.341	13.70	17.28	19.68	24.72
12	3.571	5.226	6.304	8.438	11.340	14.85	18.55	21.03	6.22
13	4.107	5.892	7.042	9.299	12.340	15.98	19.81	22.36	27.69
14	4.660	6.571	7.790	10.165	13.339	17.12	21.06	23.68	29.14
15	5.229	7.261	8.547	11.037	14.339	18.25	22.31	25.00	30.58
16	5.812	7.962	9.312	11.912	15.338	19.37	23.54	26.30	32.00
17	6.408	8.672	10.085	12.792	16.338	20.49	24.77	27.59	33.41
18	7.015	9.390	10.865	13.675	17.338	21.60	25.99	28.87	34.80
19	7.633	10.117	11.651	14.562	18.338	22.72	27.20	30.14	36.19
20	8.260	10.851	12.443	15.452	19.337	23.83	28.41	31.41	37.57
22	9.542	12.338	14.041	17.240	21.337	26.04	30.81	33.92	40.29
24	10.856	13.848	15.659	19.037	23.337	28.24	33.20	36.42	42.98
26	12.198	15.379	17.292	20.843	25.336	30.43	35.56	38.89	45.64
28	13.565	16.928	18.939	22.657	27.336	32.62	37.92	41.34	48.28
30	14.953	18.493	20.599	24.478	29.336	34.80	40.26	43.77	50.89
40	22.164	26.509	29.051	33.660	39.335	45.62	51.80	55.76	63.69
50	27.707	34.764	37.689	42.942	49.335	56.33	63.17	67.50	76.15
60	37.485	43.188	46.459	52.294	59.335	66.98	74.40	79.08	88.38

Significance for This Statistical Test Is between These Two Values

Figure 6.8 A chi-squared distribution table with the circled entry for our promotion example. The rows denote the degrees of freedom, and the columns are the probabilities for the test statistic values in the table.

As we saw in this example, we need two things to perform a significance test: a **test statistic** and a **probability distribution** (which may be a hypothetical distribution like the normal distribution). In this case, the test statistic was CTR and the distribution assumed was the chi-squared distribution.

Let's now generalize the process that we used for the last example. There are five steps:

1. Determine the test statistic.

2. Explicitly write out the null hypothesis for the statistical hypothesis test.

3. Determine the statistical test we want to use.

4. Calculate the applicable test statistic.

5. Determine if the null hypothesis can be rejected.

Table 6.5 is an aggregation of common tests of metrics for a web product. You can use it to help you run similar tests in your own product. In this section, we carried out this testing by hand, but it's much easier to calculate the test statistic in R, as we'll see in Chapter 15.

Table 6.5 **Statistical Test Choice by Metric**

Analytics Example	Test Statistic	Distribution	Comments
Differences in clicks (engagement)	CTR	Chi-squared distribution; chi-squared test	Can also use Fisher's exact test or the Barnard test for small numbers of users (based on a binomial distribution)
Revenue	(Mean) Revenue	Normal or Gaussian distribution; t-test	Be careful: Often, revenue is not normally distributed.
Time between events	(Mean) Number of purchases in a session	Exponential distribution; F-test; Poisson distribution; Poisson test	Depending on the underlying assumptions
Retention (population)	Survival curve or Kaplan–Meier curve	Survival distribution, log-rank test	How long a user has taken from one event to the next
Difference between the two distributions (purchasing)	Two distributions	No distribution assumption; Mann–Whitney U test	
Difference between two distributions	Two distributions	No distribution assumption; KS-test	
Count outcome	Number of transactions	E-test	

The most commonly used A/B test is Welch's t-test (a two-sample test with unequal variances) for an assumed normal distribution. It's often the go-to statistical test for analysts, but it may not necessarily be the right test for your data. We'll see an example of Student's t-test, a simplified version of Welch's t-test in the next subsection.

First, though, let's consider some examples of other types of statistical tests that can be run. Another test that can be useful is the F-test. It might be used in the following scenario: We decide to alter the purchasing process on an online website and are interested in a purchasing metric like number of purchases in a session. Purchases in a session is often exponentially distributed. We could use an F-test (underlying F-distribution) to test if the mean purchases of two distributions are the same.

In statistics, we can distinguish between parametric and nonparametric tests. With parametric tests, we know the underlying distribution; with nonparametric tests, we do not know the underlying distribution. In the latter case, we can use the Mann–Whitney U test or the KS-test to test whether the distributions are similar.

6.5.4.2 *t*-Test Example for Average Revenue

Now that we have worked through a Pearson chi-squared test example and seen the table of metrics, tests, and distributions, we'll work through another simple statistical testing example to see if we can apply what we have learned. Let's start with step one, which is determining the metric. We will be analyzing the average amount spent in the product. Looking at the Table 6.5, can you determine which statistical test we will need?

If you guessed a t-test, then you would be correct. To use a t-test, we must assume that our variable of interest follows a normal distribution. In this chapter, we'll calculate the simple Student's t-test, because Welch's t-test is a more numerically complex example. In practice, you generally want to use Welch's t-test. Figure 6.9 shows you the formula to calculate the test statistic for a t-test. We need three quantities to calculate the t-test test statistic: the mean, the standard deviation, and the sample size for each of our samples.

$$t = \frac{\mu_1 - \mu_2}{\sqrt{\dfrac{\sigma_1^2}{N_1} - \dfrac{\sigma_2^2}{N_1}}}$$

where μ is the means, σ is the standard deviation, and N is the sample size for each sample, respectively

Figure 6.9 t-Test equation.

Let's say that the means of spending for our samples are 5.25 and 7.89, respectively, and the standard deviations are 2.3 and 2.5, respectively. We have 1,000 observations in each sample. Now, take some time and calculate the test statistic. We'll do it together in the next section.

t-Test Calculations

First, let's start with the numerator. The numerator is 7.89 – 5.25 = 2.64.

The denominator is

$$= \sqrt{\frac{2.3^2}{1,000} + \frac{2.5^2}{1,000}}$$

$$= .107$$

$$= \frac{2.64}{0.107}$$

$$\approx 24$$

Now, we have to look up the p value for this t statistic. The p value in this case is less than 0.01%. We can reject the null hypothesis that these two samples have the same mean value.

6.5.4.3 Survival Curves

Now that we have seen examples of testing the CTR with the Pearson chi-squared value and testing revenue with Student's t-test, the next metric that we need to test is retention. Retention is a generally a harder metric to consider because we like to look at the full distribution. We're not generally interested in users' mean time in product, but rather the proportion surviving past each time point.

Considering user survival in a product leads us to work with survival curves, like the one shown in Figure 6.10. A survival curve illustrates the probability of surviving over time. It is calculated by looking at the proportion of the population that has survived at each time interval. The survival curve over discrete time intervals is called a Kaplan–Meier (KM) curve. For instance, if only 90% of the population starting January 1 survives to day 10, then that's the value of the KM curve at day 10 for that cohort. If 20% survive to day 400, then that's the value at day 400.

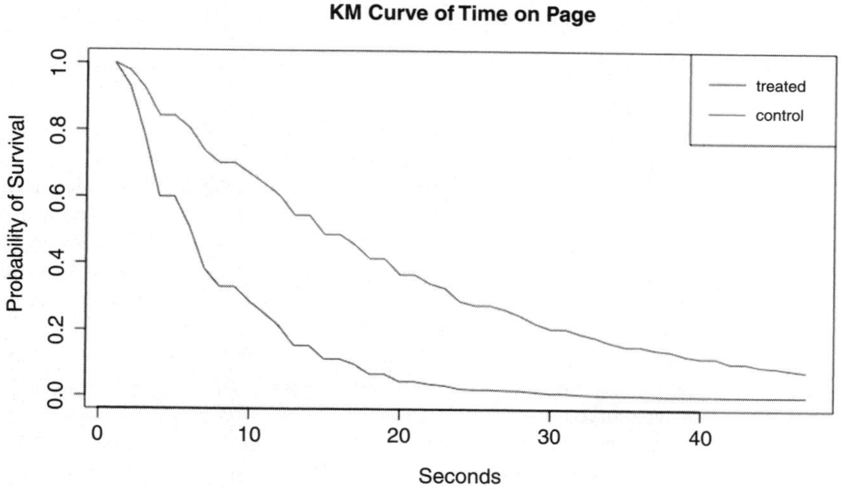

KM Curve of Time on Page

Figure 6.10   Kaplan–Meier curve of Survival curve for user time on a web page.

KM curves are useful for looking at the effects on retention in a product after an intervention (in our case, a treatment). As we have done with other test statistics, we can compare the two KM curves for the treatment and control groups to tell whether the treated population has a different probability of survival.

In this section and in R Listing 15.3, we focus on the more general version, the survival curve. The x-axis is time measured in some units, and the y-axis is the percentage of the population. In our A/B testing example, we will have two groups with different survival curves, starting at 100%; all 1,000 users exist at the start of the A/B test. We'll explore how these two different groups decline over time.

Survival curves are the basis of survival analysis, a set of tools that's primarily used in demography and public health. The scope of their application is much wider than the example provided in this chapter might suggest. A great resource for investigating survival analysis further is *Applied Survival Analysis* by David Hosmer and Stanley Lemeshow.

The sidebar describes the log-rank test—that is, the hypothesis test used to determine if two survival curves are the same. In Chapter 15, Listing 15.5, we'll go over how to calculate the log-rank test using R and determine whether two KM curves are the same.

Survival Curve: Log-Rank Test Example

In this subsection on survival curves, we're interested in determining if the treatment (i.e., seeing a promotional banner) has affected user retention. We're defining user retention as the cohort survival curve shown in Figure 6.10.

More precisely:

- Outcome variable: Time on banner or placebo web page with click-to-purchase button

- Treatment: Seeing the banner or promotion

The test statistic here is the survival curve itself.

Our null hypothesis in this case is that both survival curves are the same. In other words, for users, seeing the banner did not affect retention.

The log-rank test is complicated to calculate by hand, so we'll leave out the technical details in this example. Instead, we'll explain the general idea. We look at how many users reach the endpoint (leaving the page) at a set of discrete time intervals. We do some calculations similar to those for the chi-squared test. We calculate the average rates of treatment and control group members who make it to certain discrete time points. We compare the actual rate of leaving the page in the treated group to the expected failure rate if we took the average between the treatment and control groups. If the expected rate is drastically different from the observed rate, once divided by the standard deviation, then we can say that the two survival curves are likely different.

We can tell the survival curves are vastly different in our example. The median time on the page is 0.47 second for the treated group and 1.35 seconds for the control group. If we calculate the log rank-test using the example data given earlier, the p value is essentially zero. Refer to Chapter 15, Listing 15.5, for a discussion of performing the log-rank test in R.

6.5.5 Power Analysis

The final topic presented here for A/B testing setup is power analysis. **Statistical power** is simply the ability for a test to detect an effect of a certain size if one exists. If the statistical power is high, then we have a good test. If not, then we need to increase the sample size to determine an effect.

In a constrained environment, power analysis is a useful tool because it helps us determine precisely the minimum sample size that we need to run a hypothesis test. Power analysis will determine sample size for a specific statistical test.

Earlier in this chapter, we discussed examples of statistical significance and magnitude. In this section, we'll work backward from a good result (i.e., we can show that the test had an effect) to the sample size needed to obtain that result. Ideally, you should run this analysis before moving forward with an A/B test.

In essence, statistical power is your test's ability to detect an effect. As discussed in Chapter 2, it's inversely related to Type II error, or rejecting a null hypothesis that is not true.

We need a test with a high statistical power, but we're limited by sample size. How do we determine the minimum sample size needed to run our test?

First, we need to determine how much statistical power we need. A statistical power around 0.99 means that in 1 out of 100 cases where there is an effect, we will not detect it. The standard power is 90%. Okay, now let's determine the sample size that we need for this test. The power to detect small effects like 1% will be different from the power needed to detect large effects (more than 10%). As part of calculating the sample size, we must determine how large an effect we need to see for the treatment to be considered effective.

In this section, we assume that our data is normal. Our hypothesis test is Welch's t-test, and our metric for Welch's t-test is the mean of the distribution. We need to calculate the t statistic and the p value to find the level of significance of this test.

To determine statistical power, we need to use the following equation:

$$Sample\ size = \frac{\sigma^2 * (Z_1 + Z_2)^2}{\mu_{diff}^2}$$

where σ^2 is the variance, μ_{diff} is the size of the effect, Z_1 is the Z – score of the level of

statistical significance for the test and

Z_1 is the Z – score for the power of the hypothesis test

6.5.5.1 Calculation Statistical Power

We'll work through an example to better understand how to calculate sample size based on a hypothesis test of the results. Suppose you're put in charge of running a promotional campaign to determine if offering a $5 credit will increase revenue. Given the cost of the promotion, you are given a hard limit of 1,000 users. Will you have an adequate sample size to run your test?

1. Users' mean spending is currently $5.25. Your manager would like to see at least a $0.50 difference in spending (increase, preferred!) for the change to be considered meaningful.

2. The standard deviation of your current distribution is equal to $1.

3. We want a high level of statistical significance for our result—let's say less than 0.01%.

4. We're looking to see a high level of power for our test, 90%.

To calculate the number of observations needed, we multiply the numerator, the variance, by the sum of our squared Z-scores for statistical significance and test power. The Z-score is the value of our test statistic for a t-test. Here the standard deviation is 1, and 1 squared is 1. We then multiply 1 by the two measures of power. We want the Z-score for a p value of 0.01 for our test's significance. The Z-value for a 0.01% p value is 2.33. Next, we want the Z-value for our power level, here 0.90, which is 1.28. We need to square these two numbers. The numerator is equal to about 13.02.

The denominator is the difference we're looking for: $5.75 – $5.25 = $0.50, where 0.5^2 or .25.

The total sample size that we need for this test is more than 53 observations (or 106 observations between the control and treatment group). Yay, we can run our test and find out the effect of this promotional banner for substantially less than we thought! We carry out this process in R in Chapter 15, Listing 15.8.

6.6   Pitfalls in A/B testing

So far, we've gone through the following topics: A/B testing set-up, randomization, hypothesis testing, and power analysis. In this section, we address common errors when running A/B tests. These include general pitfalls, a lack of randomness, differing patterns between segments, and different patterns between short- and long-run effects.

6.6.1   General Pitfalls

Finding a good treatment to test is often difficult. With A/B testing, you must tread a fine line between not having treatments that are too complex, yet still having treatments that may have a large effect. Minuscule treatments may not create a large-enough effect to make it worthwhile to test. For instance, testing background colors for a homepage button may not be worthwhile. Another problem with such tiny treatments is that there are just too many of them to test. It's like searching for a needle in a haystack. Testing every small variation of a web page from color to formatting is just too costly, unless you have an A/B testing platform and billions of users.

At the same time, more complex treatments make it difficult to discern what's responsible for a change. Complex treatments can be impossible to interpret because they have too many untested pieces or too many variants. Let's say we wanted to explore the effect of a seven-day workout regimen on health. There are lots of pieces to this regimen: healthy eating, a daily run, a phone call from a health coach, and more. We find a huge effect from this regimen. For instance, participants live an average of two years longer. Yippee, everyone should do this regimen!

In reality, we cannot tell what piece or combination of pieces of the workout regimen led to the huge effect on health. If our treatment is too complicated, it really negates the usefulness and replicability of our test. Ideally, with any A/B test, you want something that is a big enough change that it can potentially have a large effect, but not too complicated so it doesn't have lots of pieces.

In general, *too many useless things get A/B tested and many complicated A/B tests are useless*. A/B testing is a great tool for certain types of questions, but not all. These questions include, but are not limited to:

- Simple feature changes, such as changing buttons or positioning of content
- Some larger feature changes with a clear impact, such as removal of the user bio page
- Clear algorithm changes, such as building out a recommendation algorithm
- Changes in a user funnel or onboarding process
- Email, texting, or other types of user messaging
- Sets of very closely related behavioral interventions, such as the addition of a chat feature to a product

A/B tests will not answer every type of question. An A/B test will not search the product space for the best potential feature change. It will only test a predefined feature change. If we don't know what to test, an A/B test will not help us.

Suppose we are testing features that don't make sense in our product. For instance, suppose we are building a function for uploading pictures in a social network of older people that is primarily web based, or gamifying a purchasing feature of the product that is rarely used. An A/B test will never highlight this kind of discrepancy or inform us why this is the wrong direction. We need to create a thoughtful cohesive model to help us organize and prioritize the most impactful changes to a web product, as discussed in Chapter 2.

More Complex Treatments

Let's say our treatment does have a few pieces. How do we work with this? If we want to make lots of changes, the complexity of the A/B testing setup grows quickly. There are a number of ways in which a test can become more complex. The first is by adding more variants to the original test. Let's say we want to vary the color of our website's background; the possibilities will be red, green, blue, and purple. Now there are four groups, with the original control being the blue background.

Or we could vary different elements that were dependent on one another. For instance, let's say that we want to make three changes: change the color, change the location of an action button, and change the content of the promotional banner. We would have to run eight different variants of the test. We'd have to vary each combination to see the best combination of elements.

In the following example, A stands for color and varies between 1 and 2, B stands for location and varies between 1 and 2, and C stands for change of content and varies between 1 and 2. The following are the eight combinations that we will need to test:

A1, B1, C1

A2, B1, C1

A1, B2, C1

A2, B2, C1

A1, B1, C2

A2, B1, C2

A1, B2, C2

A2, B2, C2

It is clear that testing of multiple pieces of a treatment can grow in complexity very fast.

Having two A/B tests that follow in a user funnel can lead to difficult problems of interpretation. What do I mean by this? Each A/B test must be independent of the other tests, meaning that the outcome of one test cannot affect the selection of users into the next test. We could have an A/B test that causes nonrandomness of another A/B test.

A/B testing will become very complex with even a few variants. This is why it's imperative to have a general theory before beginning this process. A general theory helps us build the right hypotheses to test. We need theory to organize our thoughts and contextual insights. If we make decisions based on random facts, we may end up running useless A/B tests. This is akin to wandering around a city without a map or any major landmarks to guide us, just the occasional street name. To avoid this problem, one of the first steps in user analytics is theory building. We need a map or major landmarks to determine where to go and what to test.

When we have multiple hypotheses that we want to test simultaneously, that situation can alter the level of significance that we need for our results. Since we might not be able to assume that each test is significant, the bar for having a significant result increases. We will not discuss this method here, but we can use the Bonferroni correction to find the p value that we should use to determine significant results.

6.6.2   No Randomness

Sometimes users are not selected randomly, but we may think their selection is random. Do you have any doubts that your sampling may not be correct?

Under a condition of randomness, the mean, median, and distributions of the treatment and control groups on a variety of features (not including the outcome variable) should be equal. If the means are significantly different, it's potentially evidence of nonrandomness. You should go back and determine whether there is evidence of selection on multiple features (explained in detail in Chapter 12). Randomness ensures that every element has an equal probability of being chosen, and that the distributions of the treatment and control groups on every feature (except the outcome) are similar. It's a good way to quickly identify an error in your A/B testing methodology.

Once randomness is assured, we can use an A/A test or a placebo test, where we send both groups—treatment and control—to the same banner or give all users a placebo and see if there is an effect. If it does have an effect, then you know that your setup is not working correctly.

6.6.3   Differing Patterns Between Groups

Another common pitfall with A/B tests is the presence of differing patterns within subgroups, such as by gender or age. An A/B test metric will estimate the average treatment effect. This means that individuals or subgroups could have vastly different treatment effects than the average.

To see how this works, let's return to the SpellBook example. Women may respond differently to spelling competitions than men do. Let's assume that female users prefer competitions to a greater extent than male users do. Thus, male and female users may have different reactions to the treatment, but we might not see that difference in the outcome of the A/B test.

The effects of treatment might not be discernible when we find the average treatment effect for two subgroups:

- False no effect. We see no effect or a small effect, since the effect on one subgroup counteracts the other.

- Small effect, hiding the magnitude of the effect. We only see a small effect, since it disproportionately helps one subgroup over another, creating a skewed effect size.

- True no effect. The effect does not occur in either group.

- True small, moderate, or large effect, which affects both groups similarly.

As you can see, there are cases where the general effect that you see with your primary metric can be deceptive. There are two steps you can take to avoid these problems:

- It's important to have more than one metric. If those metrics are moving in different directions, or if they don't make sense with your general "theory," it's probably a case of differing subpopulation behavior.

- It's important to do a post-treatment analysis and separate the treatment effects out by subpopulation. If your sample size is large enough, you can divide your population on important behavioral and demographic features, such as number of purchases, gender, or age, and examine the outcome metric to see if the effect sizes vary.

If you know that there will be varying effects by group before you run your A/B test, then you can use blocking. With **blocking**, you create randomized subgroups within your treatment and control populations. For instance, suppose you know that women have a different response in general to a given treatment, but you're not interested in the effect of gender. You can then block on gender by creating separate groups for male users and female users and then in each group randomly assigning users into treatment and control groups. In this setup, there will be a female treatment and control group and a male treatment and control group. Blocking will reduce the variation in the treatment effect, making your estimate more precise. We will not go into detail about it here, but know that it's a good technique to use in cases where you expect a lot of variability between groups, but are not too interested in the blocking variable.

6.6.4 Differing Patterns in Long- and Short-Run Effects

Since A/B testing does not generally clarify the mechanism for "why" something is happening, it makes understanding what's actually happening difficult. We sometimes see conflicting results.

For instance, suppose we have a short-run indicator that moves in one direction and a long-run indicator that moves the other direction. If we vary the background color, we could see that people click through at a higher rate, but then stay on the next page for a shorter amount of time. We don't know why seeing a different color banner had an effect on CTR.

Suppose that purple is a relaxing color and it made users want to click through; or suppose users thought the purple color was ugly and knew the main homepage was prettier, so they clicked through. We don't actually know the underlying mechanisms that are creating the effect, so we need to do some post hoc analysis to see what's driving it.

Perhaps short-term indicators, like average time spent in the next session, go up for the treated group, but retention goes down in the product. Do these findings mean that the change was successful? There is no clear solution to this problem. It must be analyzed case by case. We have to develop a hypothesis for why this may be happening and test it. We can also use user research, following up with the control and treated groups with questions that try to highlight the mechanism.

Going back to the website background case, our follow-up analysis might be determining whether users clicked through because the page's color was so relaxing or so ugly. We might want to check how long they spent on the purple versus blue background before they clicked through, and how long they then spent on the next page.

As stated in Chapter 3, an A/B test or any other statistical method will not generate a theory or hypotheses for us. We need to already have these in place before we move forward with an A/B test. If we find outcomes that we don't understand, we need to go back to our theory and create further hypotheses to test other dimensions.

6.7 Actionable Insights

In this chapter, the takeaways are the following:

- Selection bias is a huge problem that plagues nonrandom, observational data.

- Correlation does not indicate nonlinear or causal relationships.

- A/B testing is the best way to find causal relationships for clear, well-defined features.

- To complete an A/B test, we need to determine sample size using power analysis, specify metrics, and carry out a statistical test to determine if there was an effect.

- There are two components of an effect: the magnitude or size of the effect and the statistical significance or likelihood of the effect.

Using A/B testing is vital to improving any web product. It's the only clear way of removing selection bias and drawing clear causal inferences. But A/B testing is also limited, in that we need to have small changes to products, or the testing can get very complex very quickly. We also need to have a clear idea of what to test in our product, or we will spend every waking moment A/B testing.

All in all, A/B testing is a powerful tool when used correctly. In Chapter 13 on Uplift Modeling we'll use predictive modeling to extract more information from our A/B testing results. Predictive modeling techniques, when combined with an A/B test, can be used to determine subgroup population effects, instead of average effects as with an A/B test.

III

Predictive Methods

Modeling the User Space: *k*-Means and PCA

In the last section, we covered distributions, metrics, and A/B testing. These techniques are important for us to operationalize concepts. In this chapter, we'll be learning tools to group similar variables, which can be very useful when we want to create metrics to represent a broad conceptual idea. Clustering can also be used to narrow down a large set of variables or group similar observations together.

In this section, we will expand our toolkit to include clustering and predictive algorithms. The first two chapters will focus on machine learning tools, and the last chapter will discuss demographic prediction (projection) techniques. This chapter is intended for business practitioners new to clustering methods. Chapter 8 is a primer of predictive methods for practitioners. If you have a strong background in predictive modeling, you can move ahead to Chapter 9, which focuses on demographic population projection methods.

Before we explore clustering, we'll go through some basic machine learning concepts and definitions that we will use throughout Chapters 7 and 8. In this chapter, we will focus on two clustering algorithms: *k*-means and principal components analysis. While these methods will not help us with human behavior *change*, they can help us select important variables, operationalize concepts, and create categories for analysis. Chapter 8 is an extension of the ideas from this chapter and covers predictive algorithms such as linear and logistic regressions, decision trees, and support vector machines.

7.1   What Is a Model?

In this section, we define introductory concepts that are important to understanding any learning algorithm. First, let's start with the definition of algorithm. **Algorithms** are rules or instructions given to a computer to solve a problem.

Machine learning algorithms generally fall into two categories: (1) unsupervised and (2) supervised learning algorithms. **Unsupervised learning algorithms** or explanatory algorithms search for relationships among your variables. These algorithms have no outcome variable, which is called a label in machine learning terminology. In this chapter, we'll cover two unsupervised learning algorithms, *k*-means and principal components analysis.

Supervised learning algorithms forecast a future result or classify an outcome. These algorithms go through a set of instructions to predict future outcomes or new cases. In machine learning terms, supervised learning models have labels, meaning that one can build a model using past data and labels to predict future labels. In Chapter 8, we'll cover a few different supervised learning algorithms—namely, linear and logistic regression, decision trees, and support vector machines.

In supervised learning, there are two basic types of models: classification and regression. Classification models have outcomes that are binary or have multiple discrete groups. Regression models have numeric outcomes. For instance, we might try to predict what type of snowmobile a user might buy; this would be a classification problem. For a regression model, we might want to predict the revenue for the next quarter or the average spend for users in the following month.

A **model** in the context of an unsupervised learning algorithm is generally built on the full set of data to organize, categorize, or better understand our data. Unsupervised or supervised machine learning models have **features**, also known as **variables**, that find relationships among those variables. The term "feature" is used frequently in the machine learning community, while the term "variable" is used more often in other disciplines, such as statistics and the social sciences. We'll generally use "variable" throughout the text.

In the social sciences, one often has one or a few key variables of interest. In this case, our key variables are called **independent variables** and our label for a supervised learning model is called a **dependent variable**. In this chapter, we refer to a row of data as an observation. **Confounding variables** are a set of variables that we think could drive spurious relationships between our independent variables and outcome.

A model in the context of a supervised learning algorithm is built with a training data set and validated with your test data set. **Training data** is data that we use to build our model. By "building our model," we mean determining the correct parameters for our data, given the structure of a given algorithm. We'll see an example in the discussion of ordinary least squares (OLS) in Chapter 8. Once we have built the model, we then run this model on **test data**, or data set aside to assess the quality of this model.

Now that we have explained the basics of models and their components, we'll start exploring the unsupervised learning technique of clustering.

7.2 Clustering Techniques

Clustering is a large part of the unsupervised learning toolkit. With clustering, there are no defined labels, meaning that we are not predicting or classifying an outcome. Instead, we are trying to glean information about how our variables relate and/or break users up into meaningful groups.

Clustering algorithms focus on building groups of observations that share similarities. Clustering is not a specific algorithm, but rather a set of algorithms that solve a defined problem—that is, the problem of finding groups of observations that share commonalities.

Next, we will investigate two clustering algorithms that are very useful in modeling user behavior:

- *k*-Means
- Principal components analysis (PCA)

7.2.1 Segmenting Users, Novice Users, and Unsupervised Learning

We can use clustering in a couple of different ways to understand user behavior. First, we can use clustering to operationalize qualitative concepts. In Chapter 2, we discussed how to operationalize qualitative concepts. As we noted there, we often need to find different metrics that measure the components of a qualitative concept. Clustering, particularly PCA, is a tool that enables you to understand which metrics to include, and not to include, to encapsulate a qualitative concept. Many metrics measure the same thing. PCA will help you determine metrics that are in practice measuring different dimensions of a particular concept. This will help you create new qualitative metrics to track in your web product. Clustering techniques can also be used in variable selection which is out of the scope of this book. Variable selection will lightly touched on in later chapters such as in the Chapter 8 Lasso Regression sidebar and in Chapter 13 on Uplift Modelling.

Second, we can use clustering to create user types for targeting/marketing and behavioral analysis. User typing in practice is difficult since there are many potential ways to break up a user population. Often, there is no easy way to validate that your user typing is correct. In user clustering, we break users into groups that share similarities (meaningful or not). Sometimes, our analysis may yield unintelligible results or groups that are too broad or too narrow. If we use clustering to find groups, understanding why an algorithm created certain clusters can also be difficult.

Historically, this problem was solved in a completely different way. In user analytics and marketing, analysts create user segments based on demographic factors. User segmentation differs from clustering in that we are creating groups of customers based on similarities. Data science has upended the segmentation process. Instead of starting with groups, clustering finds similarities between users, so they can be grouped. It's also widened the set of factors to group by including complex, sometimes real-time, behavioral variables. This represents a major change in the way we think about grouping our users.

While clustering techniques are very interesting, they have limited application without a theory and testing. We need a theory to determine what grouping might be actionable. Then, we can examine what segments stand out in the data. In this section, we'll explore a common clustering example (T-shirts). Then, we'll explore k-means and PCA when testing the whale and wallflower theory from Chapter 2.

7.2.1.1 T-Shirt Sizes: Are Real-Life Products This Easy?

A real-world example of clustering is looking at a user's height, weight and body mass index (BMI) to discern T-shirt size. This is clearly a clustering problem, because we know how many T-shirt sizes are available and whether those T-shirts fit an individual.

Suppose a T-shirt company makes three sizes of shirts: small, medium, and large. Great, this is a huge help because we know how many groups there ought to be. Then, we can employ some algorithm to start grouping users into these three categories, based on weight, height, and BMI. We'll discuss some of those algorithms in the next section. Finally, we can check if the users fit into the shirts and access our model's quality. This example fits well in the clustering framework.

Unfortunately, most problems in user analytics lack external criteria such as the number of groups we need and/or feedback regarding the accuracy of our clustering choice. This makes clustering less helpful and makes it hard to derive actionable insights. For instance, how many user groups are there in our snowmobile product? Without a theory, we have no idea what makes sense. Most algorithms have statistical methods that can help users determine the correct number or do not require the user to determine the number of clusters. While this can be helpful, without a theory in place, it's still difficult to make sense of these results. Many analysts try to make sense of the grouping after the fact, but that can lead us astray.

If we carry out user research to define the number of meaningful groups, the resulting clustering can be much more useful. For instance, we could survey our users on their general personalities, what they like about snowmobiles, and their favorite outdoor equipment and sports, and then apply a clustering algorithm to find users who answered many of the questions in the same way. With surveys, it's important to get a representative product population to draw inferences. The best way to do this is to randomly assign users to your survey. It's also important to survey the full conceptual idea that you want to operationalize (see Chapter 2) and preferably to have a sufficient number of questions for each component. We did not carry this out in this example because of complexity, but the combination of a well-developed, methodologically sound survey in conjunction with clustering algorithms can be particularly useful for user typing. We also need to have a theory of how those answers are related to purchasing behavior for snowmobiles. Then, we can test that hypothesis.

In Chapter 2, we talked about the theory about the whales and wallflowers. We determined there were two meaningful groups in that case. We'll use that example to explore *k*-means and PCA.

7.2.1.2   *k*-Means

k-Means partitions *your* observations into *a chosen number of* clusters, in which each observation belongs to the cluster with the nearest mean. In Chapter 16, Listing 16.9, *k*-means is applied in R.

Continuing with the T-shirt example, suppose we want to determine users' sizes based on height, weight, and BMI information. In this example, we cannot meet the participants and have to just rely on their data.

We need to set three random mean values (because there are three T-shirt sizes) for our three variables of height, weight, and BMI. Then, we calculate the distance of every point to the means chosen. Next, we assign each point to its closest mean. We then recalculate the mean with all the observations assigned to that mean. We do this process over and over again until we have stable means and groups.

The process of finding the mean of each group (small, medium, large) in terms of height, weight, and BMI demonstrates how *k*-means work. Here is the formalized *k*-means algorithm:

***k*-Means Algorithm**   Let's assume there are m groups and n points. Create m buckets ($B_0 \ldots B_m$) for each group to save the points assigned to a group. Start with no points in the buckets.

1. Randomly choose a mean for each group in (G_0 , ... , G_{m-1}).

2. For each point X_i in the set (X_0 , ... , X_{n-1}).

   a. For each mean M_j in (M_0 ,..., M_m) compute the distance (e.g., Euclidean) from the point X_i to the mean M_j.

   b. Assign X_i to the nearest mean and save it in bucket B_j.

3. With new assignments in the buckets, compute a new mean for each bucket.

4. Repeat steps 1 through 3 until stable groups are formed.

Now let's step back and examine how the *k*-means algorithm works. The first assignment step randomly places the means in three locations. Then, the algorithm determines the distance from each point to each mean and assigns each point to the closest mean. Next, it recalculates the mean for the new cluster of points assigned to a given mean, and then it reassigns points to that mean. It repeats these steps until the mean is stable (does not move) for the groupings.

You might surmise that the initial random placement determines where the centers of the clusters eventually end up. The initial placement does affect the end result in some cases, but less often than you might think. The key is to run *k*-means a large number of times and see how often you find the same results.

Let's explore a numeric example. We'll use the whales and wallflowers example from Chapter 2. Recall that whales are the users who produce content and engage actively in the product. Wallflowers are the users who passively consume content and represent the majority of your users. Table 7.1 has the first five observations of the whales and wallflower data. The actual data set, which is available on the book website, consists of 20 users or observations with four variables:

1. Social behavior: A Boolean indicating whether the user engages in higher-level social engagement.

2. Profile description length: A numeric variable denoting the character length of the user's profile description.

3. Achieve level two (first day): Another Boolean indicating whether the user reached the second level on the same day as joining.

4. User friends: A count variable for the number of friends.

In our theory, some are whales and some are wallflowers. Which ones would you classify as whales and which as wallflowers?

Table 7.1   Whales and Wallflowers: First Five Example Users

User	Social Behavior	Profile Description Length	Reaching Level 2 on First Day	User Friends	Whale or Wallflower? (You Guess)
1	1	121	1	2	
2	1	54	0	17	
3	1	16	1	3	
4	1	87	1	43	
5	1	291	1	5	

For the sake of validity, let's assume these are the most important features in dividing whales and wallflowers. We use *k*-means to create two groups; see Table 7.2 for the results for the first five users. We cover k-means in R in Listing 15.9 in Chapter 15. Which groups does *k*-means create? The *k*-means column indicates membership in the two groups with a 1 and 2.

Table 7.2   *k*-Means (Two-Groups) Classification of Whales and Wallflowers

User	Social Behavior	Profile Description Length	Reaching Level 2 on First Day	User Friends	*k*-Means
1	1	121	1	2	1
2	1	54	0	17	2
3	1	16	1	3	2
4	1	87	1	43	2
5	1	291	1	5	1

Now, we have also calculated the means of those groups. Table 7.3 shows the centers based on the means for the two groups defined by *k*-means. Notice that Group 1 has significantly better outcomes than Group 2.

Table 7.3 ***k*-Means Examples Centers**

	Social Behavior	Profile Description	Reaching Level 2 on First Day	User Friends
1	0.50	163.25	0.62	6.62
2	0.25	21.33	0.42	2.67

Group 1 are the whales. As we can see from Table 7.4, they have about 3 times as many friends, have 8 times as many characters in their description, are much more likely to reach level 2, and have a greater likelihood of complex social behavior. This makes Group 2 the wallflowers. Do you agree with these clusters? Do you feel that user 4 is correctly classified?

k-Means is not always perfect. We can end up with different results depending on our initial placement of the means. However, *k*-means is often a good first step toward defining user clusters for a specified number of groups. Although methods exist to determine the number of initial means, we will not explore them here.

k-Means often fails if we have no clear theory for the user groups. In such a case, we be unsure how many groups are represented in our data and what groupings *k*-means is finding. It's then difficult to make the results from *k*-means *actionable*.

The key to using *k*-means in practice is to have a clear theory in place with a sense of the number of groupings and an understanding of your set of user attributes. Then use *k*-means to determine if that pans out in the actual data. Is your data actually best explained by four groups, but you had only three user types in your theory? Are the means far apart on the set of attributes that you predicted, and closer on another set of attributes that you predicted?

7.2.1.3 Principal Components Analysis

PCA is commonly used in a variety of fields under many different names: singular value decomposition (SVD) in linear algebra, the Hotelling transform in image processing, proper orthogonal decomposition (POD) in mechanical engineering, and many more. PCA is a very versatile technique. We'll only discuss PCA within the context of user analytics, where it is used for different applications than you might see in other domains.

Let's return to the T-shirt example. Each factor—height, weight, and BMI—might explain some of the same variation. Variation here means the variety of body shapes and sizes in each T-shirt size. However, these three factors might also have some overlap. For instance, a tall person might also be heavyset and have a high BMI. All of these variables are correlated with one another, so it can be clunky to define T-shirt sizes by three metrics. Instead, we might want to just rely on one variable score to determine what size each participant will get—that is, small, medium, or large. PCA will allow us to find an observant score. It may also help us understand that BMI and height are highly correlated, but the variable weight is not correlated with either. It will help us understand how our variables relate to one another. The first component will describe the most variation and generally be an unbalanced combination of the variables (in this case height, weight, and BMI).

   PCA is a transformation that converts correlated variables into linearly uncorrelated vectors called **principal components**. These vectors are a weighted combination of the variables. In PCA, the principal components are orthogonal vectors (or at a right angle), meaning that each vector is facing a different direction and there is no overlap. You can think of PCA as rotating the *x-y-z* axes into the direction with the most variation for our data set. The first component explains the most variation. Then, the next vector, the second component, has the second most variation and so on. Each vector is uncorrelated and orthogonal (at a right angle) to the others. The calculation of PCA is complex. See the sidebar, "The Linear Algebra and Mathematics Behind PCA," for a numerical example of PCA calculation.

Linear Algebra and Mathematics Behind PCA

Linear algebra is a framework that uses matrices to represent linear equations. It's useful because we can define high dimensional spaces with simple equations. Linear algebra also allows us to invert these equations and calculate important values based on a set of equations, rather than just one or two. This sidebar is mathematically intensive and only for those with an interest in exploring PCA with an calculated example.

   Principal components analysis is based on eigenvectors, a core concept in linear algebra. In this sidebar, we will go through a simple example of calculating eigenvectors. We'll see eigenvectors/values come up again in Chapter 9 in examples of population projection.

   The following will be a two-dimensional example of calculating eigenvectors and values. From the eigenvectors, we'll calculate the component size and rotation.

   We'll start with a simple example. We are measuring the height and width of various flowers in our backyard. We are able to measure the height and width of 6 flowers. These measurements are represented in the following matrix:

$$x = \begin{pmatrix} 3 & 8 \\ 6 & 1 \\ 2 & 5 \\ 7 & 6 \\ 2 & 1 \\ 8 & 2 \end{pmatrix}$$

   The first step is to calculate the covariance matrix. Covariance is a measure of correlation between two variables. When there are multiple variables, the dependency between the variables is represented by a covariance matrix. For a vector of size n, the covariance matrix is of size $n \times n$, the element $[i, j]$ of the covariance matrix represents the covariance between ith and jth element of the vector.

   We went through an example of calculating the covariance coefficient in Chapter 6. We will not repeat this calculation here, instead we will use R to calculate the covariance matrix for our two-dimensional example. The size of the covariance matrix in this case is 2×2 as shown here:

$$A = \begin{pmatrix} 6.967 & -.067 \\ -.067 & 9.067 \end{pmatrix}$$

Then, the next step is to calculate the eigenvectors and eigenvalue. The idea behind an eigenvector is to find a scalar or number that corresponds to a matrix. It's a little complex to find this as you can imagine. It's based on this equation:

$$Av = \lambda v,$$

where A is a matrix with certain properties, v is a matrix with eigenvectors, and lambda is the eigenvalue or numerical value or scalar.

Then the characteristic polynomial:

$$|A - \lambda I| = 0 \text{ where } I \text{ is the identity matrix}$$

We calculate the eigenvectors for our characteristic polynomial for this two-dimensional covariance matrix:

$$|A - \lambda I| = \begin{pmatrix} 6.967 - \lambda & .067 \\ .067 & 9.067 - \lambda \end{pmatrix}$$

$$= (6.967 - \lambda)(9.067 - \lambda) - -.067^2$$

$$= 63.1653 - 16.034\lambda - \lambda^2$$

Then, we can solve for the roots of this quadratic equation. We get eigenvalues of 9.07 and 6.96. We can then take the square root and sum them which 5.65. We divide it by the square root of each to get components equal to 53% and 47% respectively. This is the size of the first component (53%) and second component (47%). Now that we have component sizes, we can calculate the rotations. To do that we need to solve for the eigenvectors:

We need to solve the following equations for the *x*'s =

$$A - 6.96\lambda = \begin{bmatrix} .002 & -.067 \\ -.067 & 2.102 \end{bmatrix} * \begin{pmatrix} x1 \\ x2 \end{pmatrix} = 0 \tag{1}$$

$$= \begin{bmatrix} -.999 \\ -.032 \end{bmatrix} \tag{2}$$

A brief note, the eigenvectors are 31.531 and 1, but to get eigenvectors that are unit length for the PCA rotation we must divide by the euclidean length to get this solution.

$$A - 9.07\lambda = \begin{bmatrix} -2.102 & -.067 \\ -.067 & -.002 \end{bmatrix} * \begin{pmatrix} x1 \\ x2 \end{pmatrix} = 0 \tag{3}$$

$$= \begin{bmatrix} -.032 \\ -.999 \end{bmatrix} \tag{4}$$

The two eigenvectors give us the composition of the components. The first eigenvector is the first component and the second eigenvector is the second component, which are primarily in the direction of each feature. This is because the components are pretty uncorrelated (we can see that from the correlation matrix). Hopefully, this gives a little insight into PCA.

In user analytics, PCA is commonly used in two ways: dimension reduction and clustering. Dimension reduction is about limiting the number of features that we have. Some problems have a large number of variables, but clearly not every variable is useful in predicting an outcome—so how do we remove some of the redundancy? PCA can help us achieve this goal by creating a weighted combination of variables that explain more variation than the original variables explain individually. Clustering helps us understand how the observations relate to one another. We'll return to the whale and wallflowers example to help further explore this use case.

PCA can also be explained graphically (see Figure 7.1). PCA creates principal components, which are vectors made up of a combination of features. A vector has a magnitude and a direction, and is usually represented as a directed line segment. Vectors that are orthogonal never intersect and pass each other at a 90-degree angle. We can think of PCA as rotating our orthogonal graphical axes or vectors (x, y, and y) toward the directions in which most of the variation is explained. The magnitude of each vector is the size of each component, so unlike in our axes example the size of each directed line segment will likely vary.

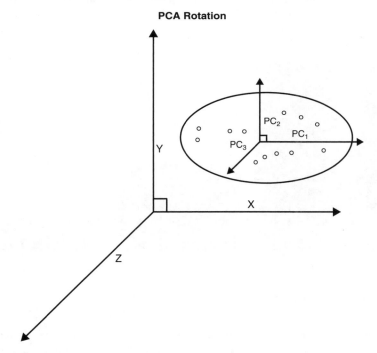

Figure 7.1   PCA rotation.

PCA only works well with numeric variables. We'll add in one more numeric variable so that we have three in our web product example: retention, profile length, and friends. Retention is a count variable equal to days in product.

PCA will help us better understand our data in a variety of ways. Here is what should we look for with PCA:

1. *The size of the components:* The larger the components, the more variation they explain.

2. *The rotations of the vectors:* The size and direction of the coefficients for each of the vectors tell us about the composition of that component. The larger the coefficient, generally the more important the variable is.

3. *Clustering of the data:* We can tell how our observations compare to each other.

First, we can assess the size of each component, which is analogous to the amount of variation explained. Figure 7.2 shows the component number against its proportion of explanation. We can see that the first component explains most of the variation, about 60%. The second component explains about 30% of the total variation, and the last component explains about 10%. You can see an example of how to calculate this in the sidebar, "The Linear Algebra and Mathematics Behind PCA." In Chapter 15, Listing 15.10, we will use R to apply PCA to this example.

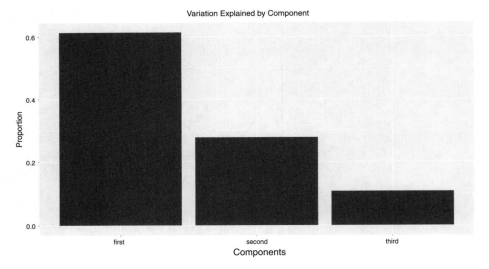

Figure 7.2   Variation explained by component.

Now, let's consider the rotation of each component. Remember that we are considering three variables: retention, profile length, and number of friends. After carrying out PCA, we get the composition of the components. Table 7.4 is the PCA axis rotation for the whales and wallflowers example. From Table 7.4, we can see that the first component is a combination of all three, weighted most heavily toward profile length and most lightly toward retention. The second component is primarily retention and number of friends.

Table 7.4   **PCA Components for Whales and Wallflowers**

	PC1	PC2	PC3
profile_len	−0.6659015	0.07732564	0.7420215
friends	−0.5780273	0.5753324	−0.05786856
retention	−0.4716563	−0.8142463	−0.3384184

Now that we've explored the variation and explained and the composition of the components, we need to explore how PCA clusters users. One way to visualize PCA results is to create a biplot. A biplot uses both points and vectors to represent data. In our example, the vectors are the features, the points are the individual users, and the x- and y-axes are the first two components. A biplot can help us better visualize these three components in two dimensions. Recall that two dimensions in this example explain almost 90% of the variation.

Figure 7.3 is a biplot of the first two components for the whales and wallflowers example. The whales are primarily on the right side of the plot—namely, observations 6, 7, 11, 13, 15, 16, and 20. The whales are well separated by the features that we picked. To the left, the rest are the wallflowers that we are not separating well with the features that we picked.

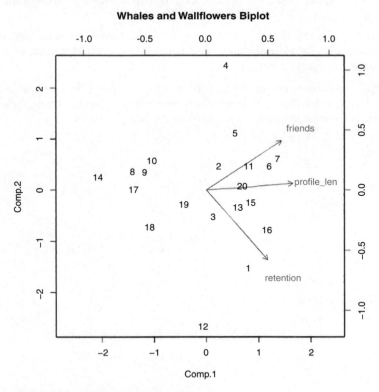

Figure 7.3   Whales and wallflowers biplot of PCA results.

With PCA, we are relying on a few assumptions, including that the data is normally distributed and real-valued. In cases in which these assumptions do not hold, we can use other methods of analysis, such as independent component analysis (ICA) and multiple correspondence analysis (MCA). However, those methods are outside the scope of this text.

PCA is useful to understand how our independent variables relate to one another. We can use it to create a set of metrics for measuring qualitative concepts; in fact, this is one of the most actionable uses of PCA in product analytics. PCA results can also help us better understand the relationships between our prime confounding variables and our outcome. A confounding variable is one that might be driving the relationship between the variable of interest and the outcome.

Both PCA and *k*-means explore the variables or features, sometimes described as the X space or feature space. Clustering algorithms help us group observations based on similarities that we might not recognize simply by looking at the data. Clustering can be useful for seeing how numeric variables relate to broader conceptualizations and theory.

7.3 Actionable Insights

The actionable insights from this chapter are the following:

- Clustering methods like *k*-means and PCA can help us explore our variables and test our theories.

- Supervised learning is used to predict and classify data. Unsupervised learning is exploratory and used to understand relationships between variables and operationalize qualitative concepts like user types.

In this chapter, we covered clustering algorithms, which are part of the unsupervised learning toolkit. In the next chapter, we'll cover a few supervised learning algorithms, including least squares, logistic regression, decision trees, and support vector machines.

Predicting User Behavior: Regression, Decision Trees, and Support Vector Machines

In the last chapter, we discussed the basics of clustering algorithms, which are exploratory algorithms without defined outcomes or labels. In this chapter, we'll explore predictive algorithms, which are algorithms that use historical data to predict new outcomes. Predictive algorithms have defined outcomes or labels; they are also called supervised learning algorithms. These algorithms are particularly useful when trying to predict user behavior or distributional needs.

This chapter examines some predictive models that should be in every analyst's toolkit:

- k-Nearest neighbor
- Ordinary least squares (OLS)
- Logistic regression
- Decision trees
- Support vector machines (SVM)

This chapter is foundational, as the techniques explained in this chapter will be expanded in later chapters. If you have a good understanding of predictive inference and OLS, logistic regression, and decision trees, you can skip this chapter and move on to demographic projection methods.

8.1 Predictive Inference

It has become popular for companies to show off their novel applications of prediction, such as recommendation systems for movie selection or apparel choice. Some of these models can predict user behaviors ranging from purchasing to user churn. Other models can identify fraud in user reports and remove disruptive or illicit video content.

Initially, you might think that prediction can be applied everywhere. However, when working with user behavior, the result is most actionable when prediction itself is the desired outcome. Many actionable insights are either observational or causal; far fewer are solely predictive.

That does not mean that prediction cannot be used for particular cases or to better understand the relationship between variables. Prediction can be validated, which is useful when dealing with observational data. As we saw from Chapter 6 on A/B testing, causal insights can *only* be validated by randomization in the experimental design. This makes any post-event, nonrandomized analysis very difficult, and perhaps even impossible, to validate from a causal perspective. In the next in the next subtopic on causal inference, we'll explore some tools to find causal relationships in observational data and you'll see just how much more difficult it is. Observational insights, while sometimes useful, suffer from selection problems that invalidate most inference.

Predictive modeling has some nice properties. With predicted inference, we can easily assess how good we are at it, compared to past tries. One simple way to do this is to divide your data into a training set and a test set. You can then assess how good you are at predicting your test set. You can try out different models and compare how "good" each one is.

Note that you don't always have the "true" or acceptable error rate. It's difficult to know if your error rate is too high, compared to what a user might assume to be "too high." For instance, let's say you force users to see "Recommended Snowmobiles" every time they enter your site. Most of these recommendations are unhelpful to your users; however, a given model was most predictive among comparable models, so it was added.

Prediction offers easy validation, but it's often imperative we validate it against important baselines. For instance, Fearon's (2003) famous paper in the social sciences realm applied a regression model to predict civil war. However, error rates of the model were higher than just guessing the simple null hypothesis of no civil war. With prediction, we need real, meaningful conceptual baselines (preferably based on the input of a human expert). Without these human baselines, you might find yourself comparing poor models, where one fits only marginally better than the alternatives.

In well-defined systems (e.g., a light switch turning on a light), predictive insight is equivalent to causal insight. However, in any system with randomness (e.g., human behavior), this is simply not true. That's why we need more than just prediction to understand "why" something is occurring.

8.2   Much Ado about Prediction?

In this section, we'll discuss what's unique about prediction, what some of its problems are, and where it is best applied.

The problem with using prediction to understand or alter human behavior is that it's confusing. It leads to the "black box" problem. Human beings need to understand *why* something is happening. Without understanding the causal relationships, it's easy to get confused about what's happening.

You also can't justify to your users, for instance, that you're not being discriminatory. You can never be sure that your models are not relying on a user's demographic characteristics, such as gender or race, to make predictive insights (for instance, if you remove gender, there might still be problems if other variables could be a proxy for gender). You also cannot justify to your users why something is happening. For instance, suppose you have a model to predict the credit quality of a person. You predict low credit quality, but when a user inquires "Why?", you do not know.

Prediction can anger customers when they feel wrongly "typed" or are subject to inconsistent or seemingly arbitrary behavior of a complex, learned algorithm. Getting incorrect recommendations can be frustrating for your users. For instance, if a user watches one horror movie, then every movie recommended to that user is a horror movie. Then the user watches another horror movie, validating your model, but gets tired of seeing the same thing and leaves your product.

It's difficult to understand how users are actually reacting to a predictive algorithm and how it's affecting behavior, both positively and negatively, in both the short and long run. True "actionable" predictive outcomes are rare in the world of user analytics. Most "actionable" insights beg for causal inference.

At a *Fortune* 500 company, an analyst made a presentation about predicting individual users' retention. The presentation showed which features were essential to predicting retention and the error rates of the model. It indicated that adding a profile picture was highly predictive of retention. One of the first questions that was asked at the end of the presentation was "Why does adding a profile picture *cause* users to be retained?"

That was an excellent question, but there is no good response to it. Adding a profile picture didn't *cause* retention, but it is *correlated* with retention. Then, the presenter went on to explain spurious relationships. The same person who asked the earlier question now inquired, "Then what's the usefulness of this model?" In this case, there wasn't a good reason to predict retention, since at this point the company was interested in what it could do to foster retention. When we drill down into the reasons for why we want to predict something, there aren't always good reasons other than it's a relatively straightforward application.

We definitely want to understand *why* someone is retained (causal inference). We also want to observe the conditions when they are retained (observational insights). In addition, we want to target those users who are most likely to be reclaimed (by our win-back campaign) before they leave (elements of prediction and causal inference). None of these is quite the same thing as predicting who will leave. It's not as easily actionable in the context of user behavior, though it is often applied in that setting.

8.2.1   Applications of Predictive Algorithms

There are many applications of predictive algorithms. But before we indiscriminately apply these algorithms, we should always ask whether what we are trying to model fits within a predictive framework.

What are some good uses of predictive modeling?

- Forecasting revenue/inventory to help make better decisions

- Predicting user behavior to make long-term investment plans

- Recommendation algorithms or website add-ons (these should also be A/B tested with short- and long-term metrics)

- Smart systems which aid users in making decisions

- Fraud prevention

- Targeting certain groups for promotional campaigns, though we can improve these models with uplift modeling (causal + predictive modeling, discussed in Chapter 9)

- Understanding correlative relationships between interesting variables

The reason that predictive methods have taken the world by storm is the ease of application and validation. Predictive tools are useful to have for clear classification or prediction applications. Predictive algorithms also form the building blocks of other types of methodologies for causal inference.

Relying on prediction to answer causal questions, however, will lead us astray. Sometimes with clearly predictive questions, especially in the context of user behavior, there is often a behavioral component that craves causal inference.

8.2.2 Prediction in Behavioral Contexts Is Rarely Just Prediction

One of the hardest problems that data scientists can face is to build algorithms related to determining *goals* for users. As we discussed in Chapter 3, *goal setting* is core to any major behavior change regime.

Suppose we build pedometers and want to determine the number of steps a user will take tomorrow, so we can set achievable goals for the user. It's truly a predictive problem in that we want to *predict* the number of steps a user will take the next day. Prediction, check. This is a difficult predictive problem because of *data limitations and complexity*. You have some data on steps, weather, geolocation and walkability, but no real social data about a user. User walking patterns vary tremendously. Some users are marathon walkers, whereas others may have just had leg surgery: You just don't know very much about their personal situation.

On top of that, *a human element* is involved in determining what makes a good goal. This problem entails more than just predicting the number of steps users will take tomorrow; it also requires figuring out a "good" personalized goal for users. A good goal is pushing a user to walk more, but to an achievable extent, something that the user doesn't regard as too hard. Goal setting is a skill, and a difficult one at that. Then how can an algorithm know this for me? There could be tremendous variation between users.

Many predictive problems are like the goal prediction example, where there is an element of user behavior baked in. Humanness and fuzziness get added to the problem, making it much harder, and we crave some causal inference. What step goals *cause* people to walk more? From empirical research, we know that step goals cause people to walk more. But different types of goals and user types have not been thoroughly tested (with experiments).

This question suggests how prediction often needs to be paired with causal inference when it is applied to human behavior. This is what makes it quite difficult to personalize and build out the right model without A/B testing. Even with A/B testing, it can be hard to access individual effects (we'll discuss this topic in detail in Chapter 13). For instance, in the walking example, we can set a low goal that everyone achieves and *causes* the average person to walk more. But that goal is not really a challenge for marathon walker Sally, and she slowly drops out of our product.

In general, it's best practice to use both A/B testing, predictive modeling and personalization to better tune algorithms to our users' needs. Now that we have explored why we might need predictive modeling, let's explore some popular modeling techniques.

8.3 Predictive Modeling

Predictive modeling is core to the data science toolkit. Many of these algorithms, like OLS and SVM, were developed more than a half century ago. The huge growth in data and data processing has led to a modern renaissance in predictive or supervised learning methods, as these algorithms are now being applied to a whole host of new problems in user analytics.

We'll see that predictive methods underlie many of the causal inference methods discussed in later chapters. Many of those methodologies are design-driven, allowing for causal inference from predictive methods in the right circumstances.

8.3.1 Simple Explanation: Methods

In this chapter, we'll examine five different predictive modeling techniques. The first technique is *k*-nearest neighbor, a simple classification technique based on proximity. Then, we'll explore linear regression, which is one of the most important predictive algorithms. Next, we'll touch upon logistic regression, a technique to predict a class outcome such as "yes" or "no", or "whale" or "wallflower." Then, we'll go over two nonlinear methods: decision tree models and support vector machines. Both of these nonlinear methods are extremely useful techniques that generally achieve good results in practice.

The goal of this section is not to provide a rigorous mathematical introduction to these methods, but rather to present a simple, clear practitioner's guide to applying them to business use cases.

8.3.1.1 *k*-Nearest Neighbor

We'll revisit the T-shirt example from Chapter 7 on clustering to explain the *k*-nearest neighbor method. Suppose we wanted to find the correct shirt size (small, medium, large) for 500 volunteers quickly. This would be considered a classification problem. Our volunteer coordinator told us it must be done in 10 minutes or less. Suppose we have one advantage: We already have a bunch of volunteers (say 20 or so) who wear each T-shirt size. How would you go about solving this problem?

One method we could use is to ask the volunteers who wear each T-shirt size to stand in a separate section of the gym. The large-size wearers could stand by the bleachers, the medium-size wearers by the lockers, and the small-size wearers by the basketball hoops. Then, we could ask each person as he or she enters the gym to find the group of people closest to their general stature. This is kind of like how *k*-nearest neighbor works. We expect that "birds of a feather" will "flock together"—that is, similar people will gather around each other. Then, we assess their "class" from the majority around them. If someone chooses a group with a majority of small T-shirt wearers, we assume they wear a small size, and so on.

The *k*-nearest neighbor method depends on this assumption—that observations that look similar will group together such that the majority class is a good prediction for the observation. Here are the steps of *k*-nearest neighbor:

1. Gather a training set of data that has been classified.

2. Determine the surrounding group around a training observation.

3. Find the majority class in that group, which is our prediction for the observation.

The difficulty with *k*-nearest neighbor is defining the nearest neighbors. How should we define similarity or closeness of a group? In the preceding example, the members of the groups have a similar stature, so we could use height, weight, and body mass index (BMI). We could measure how close individual group members are to each other on those three dimensions. There will likely be some gray areas, as some individuals could be in either the medium or the large group, or in either the medium and small group.

If we are too liberal with our definition of "closeness," maybe it's not a good group; for example, perhaps it has too many mediums classified as smalls. If our definition of "closeness" is too narrow, it may not result in a representative group. For example, perhaps the small group fails to capture all the smalls, with some being erroneously typed as larges and mediums. We can use test data sets to refine the parameters needed to describe a group—that is, similarity measures.

One important similarity measure used in clustering techniques is "distance," which defines "closeness" between two data points. There are many distance measures available to create clusters. The simplest and easiest to compute is the Euclidean distance, which, as you may recall from your high school geometry class, is the length of the line between two points. In our T-shirt example, we can use Euclidean distance to measure how far each person in the large group is in terms of height and weight from the volunteers in the large group. To calculate one person's distance from a large volunteer, we subtract their height from the height of the volunteer and square it. Next, we subtract their weight from the weight of the volunteer and square it. Finally, we add both squared quantities together and take the square root; that result is our measurement of how close those two points are. Once we have this information, we can determine if that is the closest group for them or the best label for them. For a detailed discussion on distance metrics, refer to Hastie et al. (2009).

Now that we have covered k-nearest neighbor (a simple classification technique), we'll move on to one of the most popular regression models, linear regression. In classification, we predict a class or label (e.g., "small," "medium," and "large" for T-shirt size). In regression, we will be predicting a real-valued outcome, such as income.

8.3.1.2 Linear Regression

A key piece of artillery in the predictive toolkit is linear regression. There are many aspects of linear regression, and we'll just go over the simplest elements in this basic introduction. Most introductory statistics classes teach regression with mathematical proofs. However, this book will focus on an intuitive and visual understanding of regression.

Many statistical texts begin the discussion of regression with the assumptions needed to derive OLS. It's useful to explore the assumptions once you have understood the method; these assumptions of OLS are covered in Appendix 8-1. OLS assumptions may not hold in practice. OLS can still be validated through prediction, instead of internally by proving the validity of assumptions. If the model predictions are accurate and generalize over the test data set, then we can still use the model. We'll discuss how to validate our models in Section 8.4, "Validation of Supervised Learning Models."

Linear regression is sometimes called ordinary least squares (OLS) since OLS is the most common method used to estimate a linear regression. These terms are interchangeable throughout this text. First, let's just understand the concept of a linear regression from a two-dimensional perspective. Suppose we have data that we would like to generalize in a meaningful way.

With regression, we explicitly assume that we want to use a line (it's also possible to model more complex curves with regression by transforming your x variables by, for example, squaring or cubing them). Use of a line is an important assumption here, because this is not the only way to model data.

In linear regression, we want a line that best fits the data. How do we ensure this? We assume that we need to find the line that minimizes error.

How do we define error? Error is the Euclidean or squared distance between the line and the actual observation. Note that this is also not the only definition of error, and some other regression methods use different measures of error (e.g., lasso).

Figure 8.1 is a good example of a linear model applied to a set of data. The data appears to be linear and well explained by this approach. To minimize error, we want to minimize the distance between our line and the actual observations. The line with the lowest mean squared error is the solution, the best-fitting line. Refer to the plot in Figure 8.2.

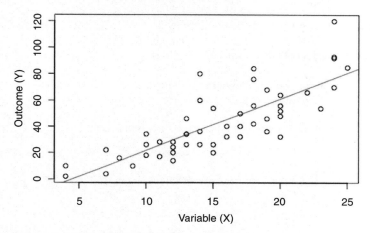

Figure 8.1   Linear regression in two dimensions.

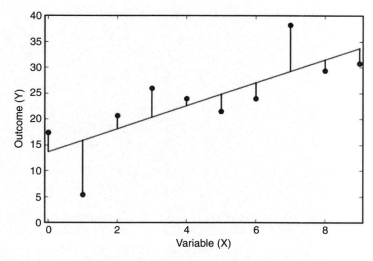

Figure 8.2   Visualization of the distance between our data points and the line (residuals).

Now that we have seen what this data set looks like in two dimensions, let's calculate OLS for this example. The equation for a line is expressed as follows:

$$y = Ax + B$$

Let's say we have five points: (3, 4), (5, 8), (2, 3), (7, 13), (6, 10).

How do we calculate the optimal line in the two-dimensional case? First, we need to calculate the means for both the x's and y's.

The mean of the x's is $3 + 5 + 2 + 7 + 6 = \dfrac{23}{5} = 4.6$.

The mean of the y's is $4 + 8 + 3 + 13 + 10 = \dfrac{38}{5} = 7.6$.

We need to calculate a few quantities which are shown in Table 8.1 to determine the slope A and intercept B in the equation above.

Table 8.1   **Calculating the Slope of the Example Regression Line**

	x	x − x-mean	y	y − y-mean	(x-mean)(y-mean)	(x-mean)^2
1	3	3 − 4.6 = −1.6	4	4 − 7.6 = −3.6	5.76	2.56
2	5	5 − 4.6 = 0.4	8	8 − 7.6 = 0.4	0.16	0.16
3	2	2 − 4.6 = −2.6	3	3 − 7.6 = −4.6	11.96	6.76
4	7	7 − 4.6 = 2.4	13	13 − 7.6 = 5.4	12.96	5.76
5	6	6 − 4.6 = 1.4	10	10 − 7.6 = 2.4	3.36	1.96
Total					34.2	17.2

Next, we need to calculate the slope of the line, which is calculated as shown in Table 8.1. The slope is 34.2/17.2 = 1.9884.

$$A = \frac{34.2}{17.2}$$

$$A = 1.9884$$

Then we can solve for the intercept, by plugging the means into the equation with the calculated slope, so y minus the mean of x multiplied by the slope, 1.9884.

$$7.6 - (1.9884) * 4.6 = B$$

$$-1.5465 = B$$

Our regression line for this simple example is this:

$$y = 1.9884 * x - 1.5465$$

Now, let's see how it predicts future points. Let's say we have a new x-value equal to 9. What is the predicted y value? It's 16.35, which is 1.9884 * (9) − 1.5465. Note, this is not necessarily the true y value, rather the predicted value based on this model.

In this case, we are trying to summarize the complexity of a data set with a formula, which defines a line. There are a few things that we have to interpret in a linear regression. First, we need the coefficient(s); here, there is only one. Since it's only one variable, we can easily visualize the coefficient as the slope of our line. For instance, we could have a formula, $y = 3x + 5$. The 3 is the slope or coefficient value from our regression; it indicates that a 1-unit increase in x results in a 3-unit increase in y.

Then there is a constant, which is 5. It means when x is zero, y takes the value of the constant, 5. Suppose this equation summarizes earnings (in thousands) by age for our population. Earnings for an 18-year-old would be calculated as 18 * 3 + 5 = $59,000. For a 32-year-old, the calculation would be 32 * 3 + 5 = $101,000. Interpretation of linear coefficients is not more complex; it's just that there can be many x's, so there are also lots of coefficients. It's harder to visualize in multiple dimensions.

The other piece of interpretation is whether the coefficient is zero, which means there is no relationship with the outcome variable. This is our null hypothesis for our statistical test—the default position of no relationship between x and y. Our model can include more complex variables, but the simplest version assumes that the slope is zero.

Just as we tested whether our A/B test results were significant in Chapter 6, we can test for significance using the regression coefficients. Statistical significance in this context means that if the coefficient for the x variable is correlated with the y variable or outcome, it's unlikely due to randomness.

We can get some other important pieces of information from a regression:

- **Coefficient**: The rate of change in the outcome as a function of changes in the independent variable or variable of interest while holding the other independent variables constant. As discussed in the beginning of the chapter, an independent variable is a feature in our regression.

- **Statistical significance**: Whether these coefficients are significantly different from zero.

- **Standard error**: An estimate of the standard deviation of the coefficient; in other words, an estimate of how much the coefficient varies over many different cases.

- **t Statistic**: The coefficient value divided by its standard error; the value of the t statistic used to compare to the **Student's t distribution** to determine the p value.

- **p Value**: A high p value means that changes in the predictor are not related to changes in the outcome. The p value reflects the probability of an equal or more extreme outcome occurring, when the null hypothesis is true. In layman's terms, if the p value is high, this result is very likely to occur and your results are likely a mere coincidence. On the other hand, if it's low (< 0.05), your results are likely real and unlikely to happen randomly.

- **Constant**: The value of the outcome when independent variables are equal to zero.

- **Predictions**: Predicted values of the outcome based on observed values for the independent variables.

- **Goodness-of-fit measures**: These measures, which indicate how well the model fits the data, can validate our models when we do not use predictive validation. In the context of a linear regression, one commonly used goodness-of-fit measure is R-squared, which indicates the size of the difference between the expected value from the model coefficient(s) and the value found in the data. Generally, the larger the R-squared value, the better the model fit, though this value will increase whenever another variable is added, even if that variable does not make sense for the model. To account for this possibility, we often use adjusted R-squared, which takes a number of variables into account. However, this measure can still be problematic as it can be high even in nonsensical models as long as the variables are highly correlated.

Now that we can interpret the results of a linear regression, let's explore these ideas in an example. Returning to our whales and wallflowers example, suppose we are trying to predict user retention in days (outcome) with our independent variables: social behavior, profile length, reaching level 2 on the first day, and number of friends.

We will run this regression in R and display the output in Table 8.2. The regression is fit in R in Chapter 15, Listing 15.12.

Table 8.2 **Regression Output**

Variables	Estimate	Std. Error	t Value	Pr(> |t|)
(Intercept)	0.80194	0.39157	2.048	0.0585
Social behavior	−0.22654	0.47011	−0.482	0.6368
Log (profile description + 1)	0.23126	0.11789	1.962	0.0686
Reaching_level_2_first.day	−0.11218	0.41212	−0.272	0.7892
Log (user friends + 1)	−0.07531	0.31632	−0.238	0.815
Residual standard error: 0.8202 on 15 degrees of freedom				
Multiple R-squared: 0.2292				
Adjusted R-squared: 0.02361				
F statistic: 1.115 on 4 and 15 DF, p value: 0.386				

The first element in Table 8.2 is a distributional summary of the residuals. As we noted earlier, residuals are the differences between the sample outcomes and the predicted outcomes. This summary more or less shows us how much the model error varies.

Next, Table 8.2 shows the estimates, standard error, t value, and p value, which we explained earlier in the section. We'll interpret them later for this particular model.

Finally, at the bottom of Table 8.2, we see the R-squared and adjusted R-squared values for the regression. Again, we'll interpret the results for this example later.

Now, let's interpret the coefficients and p values from this model. While it's easier to interpret non-logged variables, the best practice is to log variables, if logging them will result in a distribution that resembles a normal distribution. Since we already interpreted the coefficients for income in the simple model at the beginning of this section, we'll walk you through the best practices for interpreting logged coefficients, which are very common in user analytics.

If the variables are normally distributed, we'll see a better fit with our models. If both our outcome and our dependent variables are not logged, the interpretation is that a 1-unit increase in x leads to a coefficient-sized increase in y, just as in the simple income example we calculated earlier. In this case, our outcome is a log of product days, which means that a 1-unit increase in x leads to a coefficient-sized percentage change in y.

First, let's interpret the coefficients. Our dummy or Boolean variables are "social behavior" and "reaching level 2 on the first day." First, we must take the exponential of our coefficient value, or exp(−0.22654). Then, we calculate 1 − exp(−0.22652) = −0.21. Thus, a 1-unit increase in social behavior leads to a 21% decline in days in product. Similarly, a 1-unit increase in reaching level 2 can be interpreted as 1 − exp(−0.11218), or an 11% decline in user days in product.

When the x variable is also a log, then it's interpreted as indicating that a 1-unit percentage change in x leads to a percentage change in y. For instance, suppose we look at length of a profile description, the only variable that is positive and might be significant. The coefficient is 0.23. Thus, a 10% change in the profile description leads to approximately a 2.3% increase in days in product, and a 1% change leads to a 0.23% increase in days in product. We can interpret "user friends" similarly.

Next, let's consider the statistical significance of the regression coefficients. We can tell that the log of profile description is significantly correlated to days in product at less than the 10% level. "Less than the 10% level" refers to the p value, which is 0.07 in this case. Statistical significance, as we discussed in Chapter 6, means that this outcome is unlikely to occur randomly and would occur in only one in 10 times. The lower the p value, the more likely it is that the correlation is nonrandom. The rest of the variables are not significant.

The adjusted R-squared value is very low at 2%, meaning that we are not really explaining a lot of the variation with this regression. This model may not be a good fit for our data.

A good way to understand what our model is doing is to examine its predictions. In Chapter 15, Listing 15.13, we calculate the model's prediction for each of our users. There are also more formalized and rigorous methods of model quality. However, as a first pass, it's often useful to see what our model predicts well or fails to predict. This model predicts user 4 will spend 10 days in product, and the user actually spent 0 days. For user 7, we predict 11 days in product, but she actually spent 5 days in product.

Our model's prediction in this case is mediocre. Perhaps the variables are not good at explaining the outcome, or the model does not fit the data well, or both. In this case, the poor performance of the model is due to both.

Lasso Regression

Lasso regression is a variant of linear regression and can be very useful in practice. Lasso regressions perform feature selection—that is, removing redundant or unnecessary variables without sacrificing predictive power. A huge problem for linear regression is multicollinearity or high correlation, where more than one variable basically explains the same variation. Perfect or near-perfect correlation will cause OLS to break and the estimates to be wrong. Lasso regression allows us to find and remove redundant features or variables that model the same variation. With user analytics, many variables will have multicollinearity problems. Thus, it's important to be introduced to this technique.

With the lasso regression, we use regularization and the L1 norm to improve OLS accuracy and interpretation. In regularization, we impose a cost for model complexity. Regularization helps to limit overfitting. Overfitting occurs when the model developed is not generalizable, meaning that the model fits the training data set, but is not accurate on data that it has never "seen."

In addition to regularization, we use the L1 norm distance metric. What's a distance metric? It's how we measure how far apart two points are. There are many ways to define the distance between two points. The most common distance measurement is Euclidean distance, which is equal to sqrt($x^2 + y^2$). We use the Euclidean distance metric in OLS. In OLS, we minimize error by using the sum of squared error. The Euclidean distance metric is based on the L2 norm. However, if we use a different distance measurement—here, the L1 norm, which is abs(x) with a regression model—we get a different result. Using the L1 norm, the regression model forces the absolute value of the regression coefficients of highly correlated variables to be less than a fixed value, which forces them to be set to zero, thereby removing variables from the model. By this process, it helps us select the variables with the most variability.

Lasso regressions are often discussed in connection with ridge regression and ElasticNet, but a more technical discussion of these models is beyond the scope of this book. Please refer to *The Elements of Statistical Learning* by Hastie et al. for an overview of these methods.

What Is Normalization?

In normalization, we adjust variables measured on different scales to the same scale. For instance, if we include lots of variables that vary from [1, 5] and some that vary from [1,000,000, 5,000,000], many models will wrongly assume that the larger variables are more important. Thus, if we normalize them, we'll get better results.

To normalize, we can use this simple equation:

$$[x - \text{Min}(x)]/[\text{Max}(x) - \text{min}(x)]$$

Also, when we have data on more than one level, as is the case for our motivation variable (i.e., low, medium, and high), it's often better to turn that variable into a binary [0, 1] variable. For instance, we could turn our motivation variable into two dummy variables: high or not, and medium or not. That technique will lead to a better-fitting model.

8.3.1.3 Logistic Regression

The logistic regression has a similar form to the linear regression, and is used for a binary outcome variable. A logistic regression is estimated through maximum likelihood estimation (which we will not discuss here). Maximum likelihood estimation is a fundamental concept in statistical pattern recognition and should be explored in more detail if you are mathematically inclined. Please refer to Hastie et al.'s (2009) *The Elements of Statistical Learning* for a more in-depth discussion.

To fully interpret a logistic regression, we must understand the concept of an odds ratio. In this section, we'll first go over how to interpret the odds ratio, and then we'll explore how to interpret it within the context of a logistic regression. First, the odds of an event is the probability that an event occurs. **Probability** represents how likely an event is to happen. The **odds** is the probability of an event divided by the probability of a non-event.

The **odds ratio** is the probability of an event given a condition A divided by the probability of an event with no condition A. A simple example of an odds ratio is the number of male users who "like" a celebrity post and the number of female users who "like" a celebrity post. For example, 60 male users "like" a celebrity post out of 100, while only 30 female users "like" that celebrity post out of 100. The odds that a man "likes" the post is 60:40 or 3:2, because 60 "liked" the post and 40 did not. The odds that a female user "likes" the post is 3:7, because 30 "liked" the post and 70 did not. Then the odds ratio is the ratio of the odds for men and women: 3:2/3:7 or 0.6/0.4 * 0.3/0.7 = (0.6 * 0.7)/(0.4 * 0.3) = 3.5. Men are 3.5 times more likely to "like" a post than are female users.

The **log odds** is simply the log of the odds ratio. It is a very important concept to understand when working with a logistic regression, because the coefficients are log odds, not probabilities. We will have to convert them to probabilities to interpret them as such.

Now that we have discussed the odds ratio, let's go back to discussing the logistic regression. The outcome variable for a logistic regression is binary. The output produced can be interpreted (once converted) as the probability of achieving an outcome.

We can use the logistic regression to assess the odds of a given event occurring. For instance, let's say we are trying to predict whether users send a message on our platform based on whether they reach level 2 on the first day (not reaching level 2 on the first day is the baseline model). The logistic regression coefficient would be the log odds of sending a message given that users reached level 2 versus users did not reach level 2. Then, the regression coefficient itself can be understood as the odds ratio when we take the $e^{coefficient}$.

Suppose we are interested in the probabilities, not the log odds. We can calculate the probabilities of the baseline model by using equation 8.1, with the coefficient being the coefficient on the intercept. Then, we can get the probabilities for the other coefficients in the same way, also solving equation 8.1:

$$Probabilities = \frac{e^{coefficient}}{1 + e^{coefficient}}$$

(8.1)

In Chapter 15, Listing 15.14 implements this probability function in R. Let's explore this calculation with the whales and wallflowers example. First, the outcome variable in this model must be binary. In this example, it's sending a message. We'll include a few variables such as reaching level 2 on the first day, days in product or retention, profile description length, and number of friends.

Table 8.3 shows the logistic regression output. The estimates are our coefficients, which are log odds. The log odds of sending a message given a user reached level 2 in this example is 1.98. We finds this value of 1.98 by finding the exponentiation of the coefficient, $e^{0.6835}$. This means that the odds that someone who reached level 2 on the first day will send a message are 98% higher than the odds for someone who did not. That's a large difference!

Table 8.3   **Logistic Regression Output**

Coefficients:	Estimates	Std. Error	Z Value	Pr(> |z|)
(Intercept)	−4.3374	2.507	−1.73	0.0836
Reaching_level_2_first_day	0.6835	1.2259	0.558	0.5771
Log (days_in_product)	−0.2366	0.9624	−0.246	0.8058
Log (profile description)	0.3386	0.484	0.7	0.4842
Log (user_friends)	1.5497	1.2408	1.249	0.2117
Null deviance: 25.898 on 19 dof				
Residual deviance: 17.674 on 15 dof				
AIC: 27.674				
Number of Fisher scoring iterations: 5				

Now, let's calculate probabilities. The probability of sending a message (not to be confused with the p value, which is also a probability) based on the intercept or baseline model is 0.0129. We get this estimate by using the coefficient for the intercept (–4.34) and deriving the probability based on equation 8.1. This is actually an important value because it represents our baseline model. In our baseline model, we assume that a user did not reach level 2 on the first day, spent zero days in product, did not write a profile description, and has zero friends. In the baseline model, the probability of sending a message is slightly more than 1%.

Now, let's try to understand the effect of varying some of the confounder variables. If we assume that a user reached level 2 on the first day, the probability of this person sending a message increases to 2.5%. We get this by adding (0.68 + –4.34) and then solving equation 8.1 for the probability.

Let's assume that a user has 15 friends. How does this affect the probability of sending a message? If we reevaluate the model with a user who meets the baseline criteria but has 15 friends, the probability jumps to a 66% chance of sending a message. To get this value, we multiply the friends coefficient by 15, then add the intercept, and finally solve equation 8.1 for the probability.

We can see from this example that the model is a little more complex to interpret than the linear regression and that we have to deal with odds ratios and probabilities. Unlike with linear regression, the baseline model for a logistic regression is very important for interpretation because our comparison is always made against the baseline. We can vary characteristics, but we use the baseline model to compare how those characteristics affect the odds or change the probability.

Here are the main results that we can get from a logistic regression:

- **Coefficients**: They can be converted into the log odds by $e^{coefficient}$. It can be converted into a probability by equation 8.1.

- **Null hypothesis:** There is no relationship between the independent variable and the outcome. The null is zero again, since $\log(1) = 0$. A log of 1 implies no relationship between the variable and the outcome.

- **Z statistic:** The coefficient divided by the standard error; in layman's terms, the coefficient divided by how much it varies. We then compare this statistic to the chi-squared distribution to get the p value, similar to our click-through rate example in Chapter 6.

- **p value:** This is similar to our linear regression results. The p value reflects the probability of an equal or more extreme outcome occurring, when the null hypothesis is true. On the one hand, if the p value is high, this result is very likely to occur and your results are likely just a coincidence. On the other hand, if it's low (< 0.05), your results are likely real and unlikely to happen randomly.

- **Constant**: Reflects the baseline model, assuming a zero for all other coefficients.

- **Predictions**: Predicted values for each of the observations, or future observations based on their values for x.

- **Goodness-of-fit measures**: Similar to OLS, these measures show how well our models fit the data. This book will not go into detail about these measures, but you can see the further readings for more information, particularly Daniel Powers and Yu Xie's (2000) *Statistical Methods for Categorical Analysis*.

Just as for OLS, we use these measures for logistic regression to interpret the effect of confounders on the outcome, predict the outcome for future cases, and assess the quality of the model fit. Logistic regressions are used often as the first pass in many causal inference methods. We'll see more examples of logistic regressions in later chapters. A general note on application of logistic regression if you are working with small sample sizes and rare events, i.e. few occurrences in one of the classes, then logistic regression is generally not the best choice. This will become important in our causal inference applications of logistic regression, as those are generally smaller data sets and often unproportional. In addition, a tip to get better fit with logistic regression and other classifiers with rare event outcomes is to increase the proportion of rare event observations by copying those observations with minor modifications, like dropping the value of one variable randomly, and adding them to the data set.

Another popular technique is decision trees, which we cover in the next section.

8.3.1.4 Decision Trees

In this section, we'll provide a brief introduction to decision tree models. In Chapter 13 section 13.5 on uplift modeling, we'll explore decision trees models in greater depth.

A decision tree is a straightforward, yet powerful algorithm. In essence, this algorithm uses a set of rules to divide and classify data. A decision tree can be seen as similar to a game of "Twenty Questions," where the algorithm classifies data based on responses to questions.

Let's explore how a game of Twenty Questions works and consider how this relates to decision trees' selection rules. Suppose we are trying to guess a friend's favorite country in the game Twenty Questions. A possible question is whether GDP per capita is higher than \$30,000. This is a good question because it would exclude a substantial proportion of potential countries. Our best strategy is to ask questions that would divide the data in as close to half as possible, and then repeat this process until we have only one country left to guess. A particularly poor first question is whether the country is America, because it does not eliminate enough possibilities. If the answer is false, then you still have all the countries, except the United States, to still search.

This same intuition holds for decision trees. They want to find the "best" questions to classify the data and the best questions divide the data in as close to half as possible. This increases the amount of information by the greatest factor. How we assess the quality of the data divisions is at the heart of forming a decision tree and can greatly change our results. There are multiple ways in which decision trees find the best questions or make splits. The idea of information gain and other methods to assess our divisions are formalized and explained in Chapter 13 section 13.5.5.

In this section, we'll just go over the basic idea and structure of a decision tree, then we'll explore an example. Each decision tree starts out with nodes and branches. At each node, a decision rule is applied to observations that make it down that path. Users who meet the rule would move to the branch on the right, whereas users who do not would move to the left. The final output is the users grouped in terminal or final nodes based on their responses to the decision rules.

Applying this process to an example often helps to elucidate this tree structure more, so let's investigate the decision tree for our whales and wallflowers example. We'll use a decision tree to predict whether a user is a whale or a wallflower, which is a binary outcome. We'll use the same whales and wallflower data set from Chapter 7. We use all the variables, except social behavior, including retention, profile length, number of friends, and reaching level 2 on the first day.

Figure 8.3 shows the result from Chapter 15, Listing 15.15, which implements the decision tree in R. It's a simple one-node decision tree where the decision rule is applied to divide the population into two groups, whales and wallflowers. The only rule for classifying social behavior here is whether the character length is greater than 43 characters or $e^{3.781}$ or 48; if it is, we classify the user as a whale rather than a wallflower. We have to exponentiate the result in Figure 8.3 because of we logged profile description length before including that variable in the model. In other words, if a user has a profile description longer than 43 characters, they are a whale; otherwise, they are a wallflower. We can assess the quality of this prediction using the precision and recall metrics described in the sidebar in Section 8.4, "Validation of Supervised Learning Models"; an R implementation is provided in Chapter 15 Listing 15.16.

We can calculate the success rate at each node in a decision tree. This can help us determine how good each question is at classifying observations and the usefulness of each independent variable. Decision trees can incorporate many different types of data—such as binary and nonbinary—as well as different data sources in the same tree, or data with missing observations for important variables.

Finally, decision trees simplify testing our classification strategy and the parameters in the model. We can test our rate of error in classification or prediction by selecting different learning parameters through cross-validation and improve our prediction.

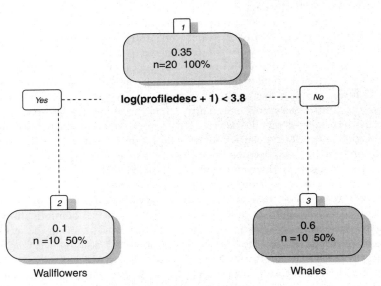

**Decision Tree to
Predict Whale and Wallflower Example**

Figure 8.3   A decision tree model of the whales and wallflowers.

Decision trees provide us with a great example of overfitting. If we have one observation in each bucket at the bottom of a decision tree, this is an archetypical example of overfitting. Overfitting will lead to high classification error on the test set; we might not be able to classify many future observations correctly. If we have a few splits, this could lead to "underfitting," where classification error can be lowered by adding additional splits to classify data. See the sidebar on overfitting and underfitting at the end of this section for an overview.

We can use cross-validation to prune the tree—this means finding the number of nodes (depth of the tree) that does not overfit or underfit the model. Overfitting leads to bad out-of-sample prediction, whereas underfitting suggests that a more accurate prediction is possible. Pruning a decision tree is very important for improving model fit.

Similar to linear regression and logistic regression, decision trees yield causal relationships only under limited circumstances. Graphical tree models can allow for causal inference if the researcher can verify that the structure of the tree has certain attributes. Graphical causal models and causal-inference trees show that there are ways of determining causes using a tree-based method. However, we will not delve deeper into these methods in this book.

This section provides just a quick introduction to decision trees. A model that combines many decision tree models into a singular model is called a random forest. One class of uplift models is based on random forests and causal conditional inference forests. Chapter 13 explores decision trees, random forests, and causal conditional inference forests in greater detail.

In the next section, we'll explore our last predictive technique, support vector machines. Similar to decision trees, SVM is an innovative nonlinear technique to divide data into categories. Note that these methods were initially created as classification techniques, but now have regression analogs. Recall that classification refers to a binary or multiclass outcome, while regression refers to a real or numeric outcome. The regression analogs are out of scope of this text.

Overfitting and Underfitting

Two core concepts in data science are overfitting and underfitting. We overfit a model when we apply a model too closely to the training data set, such that we are modeling noise rather than the true signal. Such a model will not perform well on the test data set or in production. It does not generalize beyond the training data set. The most extreme example of overfitting is fitting a model to every data point. Although we get our training set 100% correct, our test set is not well predicted.

Underfitting is the opposite, and leads to a model that could be improved to increase prediction. With this problem, we fail to model the full signal. In an underfit model that we improve, error rates will decline on both the training and test sets with better models. An example of underfitting is a very basic model (say, a linear model for a polynomial data set) that poorly predicts both training and test data.

As you can see from these examples, comparing the training and test sets is very important to diagnosing overfitting and underfitting. Our training and test set can be used to set parameters and determine the right number of parameters for a given model.

8.3.1.5 Support Vector Machines

The final predictive modeling method that we'll discuss is the support vector machine (SVM). SVM is a very popular, but a relatively complex technique, so we'll only go over the motivation, general idea, and tuning parameters for SVM. We will not go through a full mathematical derivation of SVM. Please check out Hastie et al's (2009) *The Elements of Statistical Learning,* for an introduction to SVM. In this section, we'll go a little deeper into applying SVM for practical situations, like tuning, because we will not come back to this technique in later chapters of the book. We fit an SVM in Listing 15.17 in Chapter 15.

Nuts and Bolts of SVM

Similar to logistic regression, SVM was developed as a classifier (although an algorithm for SVM regression does exist). For instance, SVM can be used to predict whether a user is a "whale" or "wallflower" or whether an image shows an 8 or a 6.

To understand the basic concept of an SVM, it's best to start with the two-dimensional example where data has an x value and a y value. The two-dimensional example was called a perceptron machine. This data is labeled, meaning that it has a specified class. In Figure 8.4, it's the black and white classes. The goal of the perceptron is to find the line that best separates the two classes or maximizes the margin between the two classes. Many lines could be defined to divide the two classes: See the central line. The goal of the perceptron algorithm is to maximize that margin, so the separating line is the one with the largest margin between the classes.

In the analog to the two-dimensional example, in higher dimensions we build a higher dimensional hyperplane (the analog of the line in higher dimensions) to separate classes and maximize the margin (sometimes called the functional margin). We can separate more than two classes by building SVMs with one class and all the others. For instance, suppose we have blue, red, and purple classes. We can build a hyperplane between the blue class and the other two classes, then between the red class and the other two classes, and finally between the purple class and the other two classes.

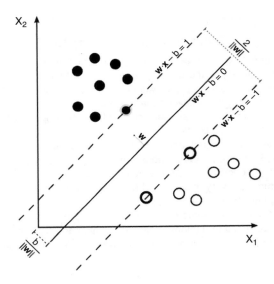

Figure 8.4   A perceptron machine.

Parameters for Tuning an SVM

SVMs can be tuned or we can better fit this general algorithm to specific problems. There are a few parameters that we can use to tune. Tuning a model is similar to tuning a musical instrument. In **tuning**, we slightly adapt our model for better performance or, in the case of an instrument, for better sound. However, tuning can be done by using cross-validation—that is, building models on training data and applying those models to estimate error on our test data set. We then select parameters with the lowest rates of error.

The primary tuning parameters for an SVM are the following:

- Kernel function, or the function used to specify how to build a hyperplane

- Cost parameters, or the soft margin

A linear hyperplane may not be sufficient to divide classes, so with an SVM, there is a kernel function. We can define a special kernel function to better divide our data. There are a number of popular kernels: radial basis kernel (RBF), Gaussian (or normal), polynomial, linear, and Laplacian.

One of the most popular is the RBF, which relies on a measure of cosine similarity or the trigonometric cosine angle between two vectors. We won't go into the use of kernels in depth, as finding the correct kernel is problem specific and labor intensive—generally we build models with different kernels and then test these models on our test set. Kernels can also have their own tuning parameters. In this case, the RBF kernel has a tuning parameter called the "gamma" parameter. We will not discuss it in depth here, but it's good to know that kernels can also be tuned.

The next parameter that we can select is the cost parameter. The cost parameter puts a weight on misclassifying examples. By doing so, it creates a soft margin. There is sometimes a trade-off between how well an SVM classifies points and how thick the margin is. For a high value of C, we'll see a smaller margin hyperplane if there is a trade-off between classification and thickness of the margin. Conversely, for a low value of C, we'll see a thicker margin hyperplane even if the trade-off is misclassifying more points.

The R section of Chapter 15 will apply SVM to a small user analytics data set to classify users' social behavior. We'll also explore SVM in Listing 15.17, including how tuning works in practice on this larger simulated data set.

In the next section, we'll discuss model validation for OLS, logistic regression, decision tree, and SVM models.

8.4   Validation of Supervised Learning Models

Now that we have explored some supervised modeling techniques, let's discuss the validation process for these models. In this section, we go through a number of ways to pick our best models.

The simplest approach is to break our data set into two parts, a test set and a training set. We can fit a model on the training data, then check our prediction against the test data.

Looking at the error rate on our test data is the simplest way to validate a predictive algorithm. We can fit the training data on a different predictive model to see which algorithm best predicts the outcomes. We can continue this process until we find a sufficient model. In the next section, we'll discuss another popular way to validate our models, known as k-fold cross-validation.

8.4.1   *k*-Fold Cross-Validation

k-Fold cross-validation is another validation technique in which data is randomly divided into k equal sets. One set is removed for testing, and the rest is used as the training set. This allows for k different testing examples.

For instance, we can divide the data into three sets, known as 3-folds. We leave out the first fold for testing, and then we train on folds 2 and 3. Next, we leave out the second fold for testing and train on folds 1 and 3. Finally, we leave out the third fold for testing and train on folds 1 and 2. We can then average the error rates of the three trials to calculate our model error. We'll see an example of this approach using R in Listing 15.18.

8.4.2 Leave-One-Out Cross-Validation

Leave-one-out cross-validation is another validation technique. With this method, we take k-fold cross-validation to the extreme by leaving out all the data except for one observation or one row of our data set. Here are the steps for leave-one-out cross-validation:

Step 1: Randomly select (without replacement) one test example or row to leave out. As discussed in Chapter 4, "without replacement" means that after we select the observation, we do not return it to the pool; thus, that it cannot be picked again in the future. (This means that we will select every observation in the data set.)

Step 2: Train our model on our entire data set except for the observation selected.

Step 3: Run our model on the row that we have left out.

Step 4: Repeat the previous three steps for every observation in our data set.

Step 5: Take the average error as our model's error rate.

We generalize leave-one-out cross-validation to become leave-N-out cross-validation, but we will not explore that in detail here. Listing 15.18 shows an example of implementing leave-one-out cross-validation in R.

Now that we have explored some validation techniques, out next topic is how do we determine whether our model is predicting an outcome well. Prediction has a clear outcome in the simplest sense: Can we predict future outcomes? There are a number of metrics to assess the quality of prediction in terms of how useful or hard it is to predict certain examples, but in essence it's about getting future examples correct.

The simplest metrics to validate models are how many observations you got wrong (classification) or the distance from the true results to the predicted results (regression). More complex metrics for validation are also available (see the sidebar "Precision, Recall, and the $F1$ Score"). Consult William Green's (2003) *Econometric Analysis* and Seymour Geisser's (1993) *Predictive Inference* for more information about model validation.

8.4.3 Precision, Recall, and the *F1*-Score

In the section "Validation of Supervised Learning Models," we discussed techniques for structuring our training and test data sets. But what metrics should we use to compare models?

First, we can just determine how much error we have. To do so, we can divide the number of observations we predicted correctly by the total number of observations. Alternatively, in a regression problem, we can figure out how close our predictions are to the correct numeric outcome. These two metrics are pretty straightforward. However, some better metrics are available for classification error or predicting a class outcome—for instance, whether a user purchases a snowmobile or not. The error rate based solely on whether we made the right prediction can mask some important aspects of how good our model is. Now let's consider the quality of our model.

Table 8.4 shows how to calculate two important classification metrics, precision and recall. The columns represent the true outcome—for example, whether the user purchased a snowmobile or not. The rows represent the prediction from our model—that is, whether we predicted that the user would purchase a snowmobile or not. Both metrics are closely related to Type I and Type II error, which were discussed in Chapter 2.

Table 8.4   **Precision and Recall**

		True Condition		
		1	**0**	
	1	True Positive	False Positive (Type I error)	Precision = True Positive/ Predicted Condition Positive
Predicted Condition	**0**	False Negative (Type II error)	True Negative	
		Recall = True Positive/ True Condition Positive		

The precision metric provides a measure of how relevant our classification choices are. We calculate this metric by looking at how many items we predicted positively and are truly positive over the population of predicted positive. For instance, how many users were predicted to purchase snowmobiles and actually did so is our numerator. Our denominator is again how many users we predicted to buy a snowmobile. If the value of the metric is low, we are not correctly identifying those users who will buy (there are lots of false positives and a high Type I error; we are misclassifying lots of people as purchasers). The following equation defines the precision calculation:

$$Precision = \frac{True\ positive}{Predicted\ conditional\ positive}$$

The recall metric provides a measure of how many relevant choices are selected from the population of true choices. The value of the recall metric is the number of predicted users who purchased divided by the total population of users who purchased a product. We can see that if recall is low, then we are not doing a good job at finding purchasers within the full population of purchasers (lots of false negatives and high Type II error; we are missing lots of potential purchasers). Here is how we calculate recall:

$$Recall = \frac{True\ positive}{True\ condition\ positive}$$

The *F*1 score is a popular weighted measure of the precision and recall metrics that can be used to compare different classification algorithms. Here is the equation for *F*1 score:

$$F1\ score = \frac{2}{\dfrac{1}{Recall} + \dfrac{1}{Precision}}$$

Another way to think about and visualize classification error is as the receiver operating characteristic curve (ROC), which will not be discussed in detail in this book. Nevertheless, ROC curves are a good place to start if you are interested in learning more about these ideas. Listing 15.16 has an example of calculating precision, recall, and the *F*1 score in R.

Now that we have covered ways to validate these models, it's time to start applying these techniques to predicting and validating models on some data sets of your choice.

8.5   Actionable Insights

The actionable insights from this chapter are the following:

- OLS is an useful algorithm and is often the first-pass choice.

- Decision trees and SVM are useful for classification/regression problems.

- Tuning helps to improve model fit for most algorithms, and quality tuning can greatly improve models. Scaling data and changing multiclass variables to Boolean variables can also improve model fit.

This chapter was a primer on a few of the most useful predictive algorithms. We will touch on these algorithms again throughout the book. But before we move on to causal inference methods, in Chapter 9 we'll learn population forecasting techniques from demography that we can use to project population changes in a web or mobile product. It's a completely different approach to prediction.

Appendix

The following core assumptions should be met when using OLS, as the accuracy of the estimates will be negatively impacted if they are not:

- *Linearity holds.* There must be a linear relationship between the independent variables and the outcome variable. With OLS, we're not able to model nonlinearity very well.

- *Variables are not perfectly related (no multicollinearity).* Variables that are highly correlated with each other will create problems for our model.

- *There is no heteroscedasticity or auto-correlation.* Heteroscedasticity is defined by errors that vary in size at different places. For instance, suppose we have a set of basketball players' heights and weights. We could have a great deal of variance at higher heights, but much lower variance at lower heights. Tall players could be huge like Shaquille O'Neal or thin like Michael Jordan, while small players are all thin. This would break the "no heteroscedasticity" assumption. This is actually relatively easy to correct. Refer to Jeffrey Wooldridge's (2013) *Introductory Econometrics* for a review of robust standard errors and two-stage least squares. Auto-correlation is the correlation of a variable with a delayed copy of itself as a function of delay. This is denoting correlation with a variable and itself with a time lag. We'll discuss autocorrelation in more depth in Chapter 11.

- *We have random sampling of observations.* This is often an assumption broken in practice. If we have randomized, experimental data, that's great, but it's rare.

- *Error terms are orthogonal to the independent variables and have a conditional mean of zero.* This is a core assumption related to the derivation of OLS. In the derivation of OLS, we are assuming that the independent variables and the error terms are uncorrelated. In a graphical sense, this means that the error term is orthogonal or at a right angle to the independent variables or X's. No matter what value we choose for X's or the independent variable, we assume that the average value of the distribution of error terms is zero.

- *Errors are normally distributed.* If you are interested in a more thorough examination of the assumptions, two texts worth reading are Orley Ashenfelter, Phillip Levine, and David Zimmerman's (2006) *Statistics and Econometrics* and Michael Oakes's (1986) *Statistical Inference.* The second book adopts a proof-based approach.

Forecasting Population Changes in Product: Demographic Projections

This chapter examines what happens from launch to death of a web product. When working with web products, it's important to understand where your product is in the underlying life cycle and what the prior stages of the product looked like. As we will see with uplift modeling in Chapter 13, this understanding can be the difference between a successful and unsuccessful marketing campaign. Understanding the life cycle can also be useful when you start projecting future population needs. In addition, this chapter will help you think about product retention as a multidimensional process and model subpopulation changes in a more sophisticated way.

In Chapter 2, we discussed how many practitioners fail to recognize that behavior is a social process when building key metrics. In Chapter 8, we discussed a common subset of machine learning models used to predict user behavior. This chapter offers a different set of forecasting tools from demography that you can use to model social processes, predict population growth, and access future business costs.

This chapter covers the following topics:

- The life cycle of a web product

- Modeling retention as a multidimensional process

- Reviewing multistate models and transition probabilities

- Demographic population prediction applied to web applications

This chapter is more dense than prior chapters because we cover a lot of material quickly, so we can apply these tools to real-world problems. The section "Different Models of Retention" is more rigorous, and can be skipped if you are not interested in modeling user behavior as a process. The section "The Art of Population Projection" is also rigorous, but will teach you the nuts and bolts of population projection.

The best way to read these sections is to try to understand the assumptions and then derive the examples yourself. Demography itself is a very hands-on art. Initially, we start with a set of assumptions and then project outcomes based on those assumptions. A thorough understanding of which assumptions are being made and how the population projection process works is needed to apply these methods.

The final sections on population baselines, momentum, and oscillation are advanced topics that we will briefly introduce here. These topics hint at the reach and power of demographic projection models and can help you better apply these methods to contemporary web products.

If you are not interested in demographic projection methods, this chapter can be skipped, as no other chapters in this book are reliant on this material.

9.1   Why Should We Spend Time on the Product Life Cycle?

Social communities change over time. They can gain new members and lose others, the social environment can flourish or wane, the goals of members can solidify or change. Web communities are no different. The numbers and types of users will change the vibrancy and interactions of a community. Despite their many unique characteristics, there are some commonalities in terms of how communities, products, and web networks grow. We'll explore some of the interesting qualitative and quantitative aspects of community growth.

Many companies are interested in how user populations change and grow. For instance, a very popular set of questions concerns the right time to release new features or products. Do you wait until late in the product's life (with a video game, for example) because the new product will siphon users from your old one? Do you release the new product early to drum up interest and increase your revenue and market share?

Another set of questions concerns future inventory needs. How much inventory should we buy for next year? The answer depends on the population and where we are in the population life cycle. Is the user space saturated? Are we late in the game, or will we see exponential growth in the number of users and run out of inventory?

Another set of questions is related to social networks and the spread of information by word of mouth or social media. How does information about our product spread through the population? How do we grow a new product?

These are all interesting questions—especially the last about how information spreads—but are very difficult to answer. The tools offered in this chapter are useful for understanding general trends in your user population. For that reason, this book devotes an entire chapter to demographic projection models.

Unlike machine learning models, demographers shy away from saying their models are truly predictive. They'll call such models *projection* because they have been proven wrong often (e.g., demographers did not predict the 1960s Baby Boom). However, demographers have the best track record on predicting human behavior of any academic discipline. This chapter does not discuss growth strategies, but instead focuses on quantification and projection of growth going forward based on your current trajectory.

9.2   Birth, Death, and the Full Life Cycle

Before jumping into modeling population, let's discuss the life cycle of a product. When we're working with web products, products can be considered "living communities." In turn, we see many of the same types of elements as occur with natural organisms, including birth, growth, vibrancy, and death of a community. This section will develop a simple product life-cycle model based on the innovation adoption life cycle.

The fact that these web communities are not physical (and sometimes in real-time) hides the large and nuanced effects that these online communities can have on users. For users, an online group can be as powerful as a real physical community and sometimes more encompassing than a real community.

People can come to a web community to get validation, to make friends, or for voyeuristic purposes. Many unique driving factors can push individuals to join a web community, and when they come together individuals can create something greater than themselves. The goals and desires of these users may vary by when they come to the product and their background.

In this section, we'll explore how users vary by *cohort*. We discussed cohorts in Chapter 5. Recall that a cohort is a group of users who started in the product in the same period. We'll use the basic types from Everett Rogers's bell curve of user types (see Figure 9.1). See his book *Diffusions of Innovations* (2003) for more on Rogers's bell curve and theory of diffusion. Here is a list of user types:

- *Innovators*: These individuals first develop the idea. The spread of the idea depends on the innovation itself, time, and the communication channels. It's also related to how connected and central innovators are, as this affects the speed and diffusion of an idea, innovation, or product.

- *Early adopters*: These people like new innovations and are willing to try them out. They often pay a cost in terms of quality for newness of the product.

- *Early majority*: These people join when the idea starts to take off or we see exponential growth in the product usage.

- *Late majority*: These people come after the product has peaked.

- *Laggards*: These latecomers to the product keep the product alive until it dies.

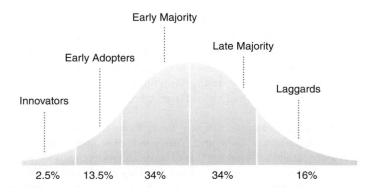

Figure 9.1   Rogers's bell curve of user types in the life cycle of innovation adoption.

Rogers's curve assumes that the innovation catches on eventually. It would look very different for an innovation that dies soon after inception. We're assuming the same thing for our web product—that it grows exponentially.

However, there are some crucial differences in the lifecycle of a web product compared to Rogers's bell curve of adoption. For a web product, user death is rarer, so the distribution is often not quite a bell curve. Different web products may also have different distributions. We'll consider one example with a distribution common to many web products. Figure 9.2 shows a potential web adaptation of Rogers's curve. For web products, inactivity is common, so it is essential to add a dimension of active and inactive (we can see this addition in Figure 9.2).

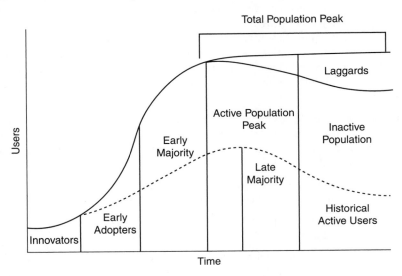

Figure 9.2   Life cycle of a web product.

In Figure 9.2, there is not much of a bell curve because the user death rate is very low, and individuals can and do come back. Web products that see massive growth start in a similar way, with innovators, early adopters, and the early majority. Then, they build a large shadow user base that can return anytime between when they become inactive until product death. After they peak, they continue to pick up the late majority and laggards (growing slowly in total size toward the end). Even though total user numbers can be high, the active base can be very small (especially in the late stages of the life cycle).

Take our snowmobile website example. The early adopters are the snowmobile enthusiasts who heard about the website through word of mouth. Their behavior is often unlike the behavior of later users. They are early adopters, technology enthusiasts, or product enthusiasts. Generally, you do not want to build your product for these users, but they are the only users whom you can observe in the early days. They'll be very committed users, so as you add other user types who lack the same proclivity for remaining in product, your retention rate and other metrics may decrease.

The early majority hears about your website through word of mouth or magazine articles written by early adopters. Then, your website gains acclaim and the late majority follows. Your total user population peaks with this late majority, and their participation marks when your community is most vibrant. Later, the community starts to have dead segments due to user inactivity. Laggards, who are late adopters and not up on new trends, join your snowmobile site before the product dies or floats into oblivion. Through these different periods, the community can be substantially different, even though the product features have not changed.

Rapidly changing communities can be one reason that scaling a web product is hard. The community changes, and changes rapidly, making it difficult to keep up. At some point, if your web product catches on, you may see exponential growth in the population and the community gets diluted. With a rapidly growing product, there are lots of short-term active users. They are not as committed as your early users before your high growth. The mid-peak of the short-term active users can last for a long time, with new cohorts moving through the product quickly.

In the snowmobile site, we can think of this pattern occurring when the site is named as a top site for snowmobiles in an outdoor magazine and website. Then, more information about the site is spread by word of mouth, and users start pouring in.

Over time, these users will likely get tired of your product. They're not whales and may lose their foothold in the community or find a new site that attracts them more. For some reason that you may or may not know, they drop off the map. Other users see the attrition and follow suit. As your web product starts to die, you'll find lots of inactive users who dilute your pool. Your community will go back to a small number of diehard users who won't leave and lots of inactive or occasionally active users. For example, in this stage, we have lots of people on our snowmobile listserv, but very few users click through. Many have blocked your messages or put them in a spam folder.

It's important to know where you are in terms of product life cycle so that you can better understand and analyze your product. Let's make this discussion a little more technical. As an example, we'll create a simple web product with a user population and see how population changes over time. We'll talk about some important population ideas like exponential growth and stable and stationary populations in the next section.

Note that we'll investigate the process for a successful web product. Lots of web products never see exponential growth (or the exponential growth is short-lived) of their user base. We'll use demographic models in this chapter to look at what kinds of growth rates that you want to see in your product and how you can understand and model exponential growth.

9.3 Different Models of Retention

Every company has its own idiosyncratic metrics for retention. Most retention metrics can be improved. This chapter will focus on retention, but the lessons learned here can also be applied to engagement, revenue, and acquisition metrics. How can retention metrics be improved? Two types of inferential errors are extremely common with retention metrics. First, retention metrics often fail to capture the retention *process*. Second, as discussed in Chapter 5, retention metrics often aggregate cohorts of users over many different product periods into one metric. These accumulative metrics mask important information.

Retention is a great example of a complicated concept, which is often boiled down to a simple, sometimes meaningless, metric. In Chapter 5, we discussed traditional ways to measure retention. One popular option is simply the average number of user days (expectation at day 0 or average days in product from day 0) in product. Other commonly cited retention metrics include those such as the last touch or the number of users who made it to day 3. Many companies rely heavily on those early metrics, often regardless of their quality, because of historical path dependence. It takes effort and time to deeply revisit and revise them.

Why are these metrics not capturing the nuances of user retention?

- The multidimensional process (since retention is a social process, as described in Chapter 1) is collapsed into two states: an active state and a dead state. In reality, there could be many states in between active and dead accounts.

- There are often more than two states in the user trajectory. These earlier movements between states can affect time to the end state. For instance, how long does it take for a new user to become a paying user or a daily active user? This can affect how long users stay in the product.

- We assume that the end state is stable. We are assuming in this case that once users delete their account, they will never create a new account. We are also assuming that they do not have multiple accounts and that the deleted account is their only account on the site.

- We assume that multiple groups will see similar retention rates, implying that aggregating them is an acceptable approach.

Simply put, we're taking a complex social process and boiling it down to a simple two-state problem. We're also assuming that we can aggregate many different groups of users into one metric. As you can see, a lot of (potentially incorrect) assumptions are made for common retention metrics.

For instance, organic and paid users might have very different patterns of retention. Our paid users may come into the product for the sole purpose of checking out the product and then leave when that incentive is gone. In contrast, organic users may like our product and progress more normally through states. It's important to break users into core subgroups.

We also need to think about why we care about retention. Are we using retention to predict which users might leave the product? Are we using it to predict how the population will change over time? Our goals should also drive our determination of metric.

For instance, suppose we are interested in finding users who are about to become inactive. What *causes* a user to go from active to inactive? If the user has previously been an active user, becoming inactive is a major change in behavior. People do not normally take the initiative to change something that is working. There must be something (a cause, whether internal to the product or external in the user's life) that is causing this person to change her/his behavior.

Often, users show signs of fading away before complete disengagement occurs. Most active users will not just "ghost" or leave unexpectedly; instead, they will leave clues for the analysts. There might even be a clear triggering event—the proverbial straw that broke the camel's back. It could be one too many emails or an annoying onboarding step. We need to find out where these bottlenecks are occurring. We need a metric more fluid and richer than average days in product.

9.3.1 The Transition Matrix

Now that we have introduced a different way to think about retention, let's model retention by using a multistate model. To create a multistate model, we need a few elements:

1. A model of the states that users can progress through. We will calculate the transition probabilities between states or how likely users will progress from a state in period 1 to a state in period 2 (which can include the same state). Any state that a user cannot progress to has a transition probability of 0.

2. A matrix with the population of users in each state in the first period. We can call this the population matrix. We'll use these initial population numbers as denominators to calculate the transition probabilities.

3. A transition matrix with the transition probabilities or probabilities of transitioning between states.

The cornerstone of population projection—or more broadly, modeling population in states—is the transition matrix. A transition matrix is a matrix of probabilities defined for movement from any state in an initial period to another state in the next period. The transition matrix is a square matrix with the columns and rows with all the states of the model. *When modeling a population in a transition matrix, users start in a column state and move into the row state. This means that we read the transition matrix as the user's probability of moving from the column state to the row state.* This can be a little confusing, as it might differ from other applications of multistate modeling.

9.3.2   Snowmobile Transition Example

Consider our snowmobile website, where users can enter into or exit from a number of different states. We have five states in this simple model: new users, active users, paying users, lost users, and dead users.

Figure 9.3 is a multistate diagram for our snowmobile website, which enables us to see how users can move between states. A new user can become an active user or a lost user, but not a paying or dead user. An active user can move to all the states, except new user. Likewise, an active, paying or lost user can also move to any of the states, except new user. In all states except new user, a user can remain in the same state from period 1 to period 2. From here, we can calculate the transition probabilities between states—that is, the probability of moving from one state to the next.

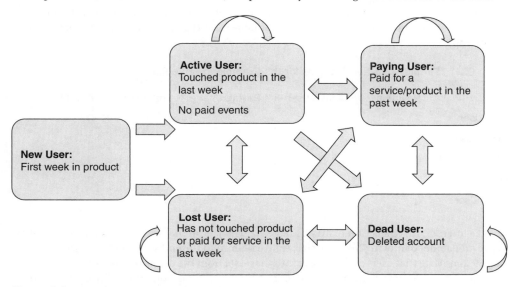

Figure 9.3   A multistate model of retention.

Table 9.1 shows a contrived example of a population matrix or the initial user populations in period 1. These values will be our denominators for our transition probability calculations. We'll assume that in our snowmobile example, each state initially has 1,000 people. Our population matrix has our initial population in the first period, but will be updated in each period with the new subgroup numbers.

Table 9.1   **Example of the Initial Population in a Web Product**

	Initial Population
New users	1,000
Active users	1,000
Paying users	1,000
Inactive users	1,000
Dead users	1,000

Now that we have set initial population numbers, it's useful to understand how users are progressing and moving between states. In a real web product, you would just look at the population numbers from the last period.

Note that the concept of a period is flexible. In demographic population projections, a period is often defined as 5 years, but that would not make sense for many web products. As discussed in Chapter 5, a period is a set amount of time. You can define a period as a day, a month, or a year. Ideally, a period should be a length of time relevant to or sufficient to estimate the transition states within your product.

Now, we'll create a transition matrix. For a visualization of the transition matrix without calculated transition probabilities, see Figure 9.3. Table 9.2 is the potential transition matrix for this example.

Table 9.2   **Simple Transition Matrices for the Example in Table 9.1**

	New User	Active User	Paying User	Lost User	Dead User
New User	X	O	O	O	O
Active User	X	X	X	X	O
Paying User	O	X	X	X	O
Lost User	X	X	X	X	O
Dead User	O	X	X	X	X

Let's interpret this transition matrix in Table 9.2. First, recall that we read the transition matrix as the probability of moving from the start state (column) to the end state (row). The zeros in Table 9.2 indicate that users cannot move into that state from the column state. For instance, a new user cannot become a paying or dead user, so we have a transition probability of zero in this case. Note that these zeros reflect our assumptions. For instance, if we assumed that users can move to any state from any state, then there would be no zeros in our transition matrix.

The X's indicate the numbers we need to calculate, and the zeros represent that users cannot move into that row state from the column state. We can find the state of our users in period 2, then calculate the transition probabilities as shown in Table 9.3.

Table 9.3   **A Potential Transition Matrix Based on the State Transitions in This Web Product over One Period**

	New User	Active User	Paying User	Lost User	Dead User
New User	1.25 (1,250/1,000)	0	0	0	0
Active User	0.5 (500/1,000)	0.5 (500/1,000)	0.4 (400/1,000)	0.05 (50/1,000)	0
Paying User	0	0.2 (200/1,000)	0.1 (100/1,000)	0.05 (50/1,000)	0
Lost User	0.5 (500/1,000)	0.25 (250/1,000)	0.5 (500/1,000)	0.8 (800/1,000)	0
Dead User	0	0.05 (50/1,000)	0 (0/1,000)	0.1 (100/1,000)	1

We know that there are 1,000 users in each state in period 1. How are these users moving through the states? We can follow these estimates in Table 9.3. There are 1,250 new users coming in period 2. Dividing this value by the initial 1,000 users in the new user category in period 1 gives the first row, first column entry in Table 9.3 of 1.25. We'd estimate this number in a real web product in the same way.

We calculate the transition probabilities by looking at the movement of users from the first to the second period. For instance, we start with 1,000 new users in period 1 and all of those users transition to another state: 500 to active users and 500 to lost users. Thus, the transition probabilities for the first column are [1.25, 0.5, 0, 0.5, 0].

For active users, none can move back to being a new user, 500 remain active, 200 transition to paying users, 250 transition to lost users, and 50 transition to dead users, so the second column is [0, 0.5, 0.2, 0.25, 0.05]. For paying users, again none can move back to being a new user, 400 move back to active users, 100 remain as paying users, 500 move to lost users, and 0 move to dead users. The third column is then [0, 0.4, 0.1, 0.5, 0]. For lost users, again none can move back to new users, 50 move to active users, 50 move to paying users, 800 remain lost, and 100 move to the dead state. Thus, the fourth column is [0, 0.05, 0.05, 0.8, 0.1]. Finally, dead users cannot move to any of the other states, so all the users stay dead. The fifth column is then [0, 0, 0, 0, 1].

We can sum the rows to find the largest groups in period 2: 2,050 lost users and 1,450 active users in our web products.

In Figure 9.4, the multistate diagram includes the transition probabilities that we calculated from the population flows between period 1 and 2. We can visualize these numbers in terms of how the users are moving through the states within the product.

Why is it useful to model transition probabilities? Transition probabilities are powerful metrics that help us do the following:

- Solve some of the problems with the traditional retention metric. We can track users through multiple states, we can keep track of the time between states, and we can potentially find bottlenecks or the "straw that breaks the camel's back." Note that this last task is much harder and probably requires more work and collection of more data than just transition probabilities.

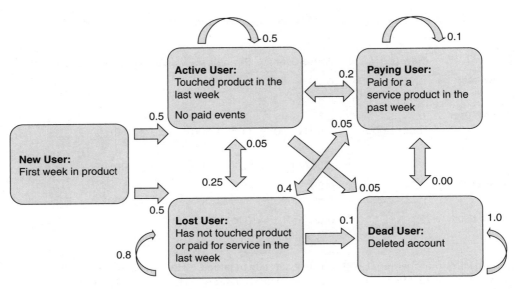

Figure 9.4   Multistate retention model.

- Keep track of many different states/or subpopulations and identify where probabilities change the most over time.

- Project populations based on our current rates and see how close those population projections are to the truth (see Figure 9.5).

- Estimate of the growth rate that we need to maintain our user base. (We'll see how to do this in the following sections.) Our retention metric now maps directly to our product population now and in the future.

We have a model of our key states—exactly what we want to track in our product—and we can calculate how people are moving through these key states. Multistate models are flexible and can be adjusted to the needs of your product.

To summarize, we can develop the following insights for our simple snowmobile model:

- *Population projections.* This is calculated by multiplying the transition matrix and the population matrix. (You don't need to understand the mechanics of this example, as we'll discuss projection in much more depth in the following sections.) In our example, period 1 has a total population of 5,000. In period 2, the total population is 5,250. In period 3, it's 6,662, and so on. We can tell that this product will see exponential growth because the rate for the only reproducing cell (new users) is greater than 1—specifically, 1.25. We'll talk more about how to determine if the total population is growing, declining, or remaining stable in more complex models in later sections.

- *Comparison of proportional sizes of groups.* We can also tell from this model that although the number of paying users is growing at a fast rate, they will never be a large proportion of our users because the bulk of users are moving to and remaining in other states. Even though we started with equal proportions, the populations are rapidly moving toward a very unequal distribution that could make this web product unstable in the long run.

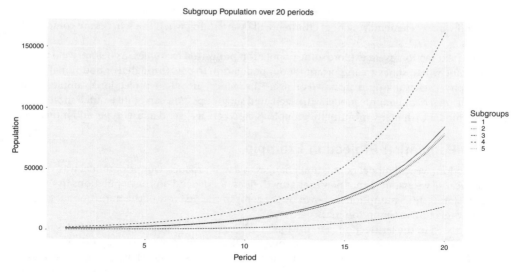

Figure 9.5   Population subgroup growth in a state model.

- *Bottlenecks*. Where are users moving and why are they moving toward certain states? Are users getting stuck in a given state? Many times, you might find that users are getting stuck in the active state and not progressing to paying users. Looking at your data in this way can help you find points where progression is stalling. A transition matrix is like a multidimensional version of a user funnel.

Calculations of these insights using R appear in Chapter 15, Listing 15.19.

In demographic population projection, a transition matrix that has some auxiliary assumptions (discussed in later sections) is called a **Leslie matrix**. Usually in a transition matrix, all values must be between 0 and 1. A key difference between the traditional multistate transition matrix and the Leslie matrix is that the top row of a Leslie matrix is not probabilities and can be greater than 1, as we are projecting population growth over time.

In the snowmobile example, we'll use a general population projection matrix. In the next section, we'll construct a Leslie matrix and show an example of traditional population projection. The snowmobile example in this section is expanded to show you how to apply these concepts to more general ideas than just pure population projection.

9.4   The Art of Population Prediction

Demography has developed useful tools for working with populations that apply to web analytics. Demographers make population *projections*. While these are "predictions" about population, they are also mathematical models based on general assumptions about how populations grow. Validation is based on design and model, rather than prediction. Note that you can add predictive validation techniques like cross-validation to improve your projection models, as we discussed in Chapter 8.

Population projections or resource projections are important because governments or businesses need to make investments to meet the needs of or monetize different populations. Projecting how populations will grow and change is helpful in making future investments.

For instance, to determine how many new elementary schools a city needs, it is essential to project how many elementary school children will be attending when the schools are completed in 5 years.

In the next section, we'll explore some population projection examples. As before, we'll need to determine which states are important for our population to pass through. For traditional demography, these subgroups are based on age. This section includes a projection example based on a traditional demographic model with age-based subgroups. You can build a much more complex model with many meaningful groupings based on age, gender, user type, and more.

9.4.1   Population Projection Example

In this section, we will model population changes in a web product. Our prior model was very simple because we assumed that new user growth does not depend on the populations in the different states (this assumption is shown by the zeros in the first row of the transition matrix). We'll now relax this assumption in this section.

As discussed in the last section, a transition matrix to project population that includes *some auxiliary assumptions* (discussed in later sections) is called a Leslie matrix. The top row of a Leslie matrix is used to project future populations and can have values greater than 1. We'll see examples of this in this section.

Demographers use Leslie matrices to project populations in localities. Leslie matrices have a very particular structure in which all users move from one state to the preceding state or the end state, but to no other state. Our example in "Different Models of Retention" would not fit in this paradigm since a user could move from one to multiple states, such as from being an active user to either a paying, inactive, or dead state. Although we will not cover this topic here, we can modify these demographic methods to apply to our earlier model.

(As a side note for those readers who are familiar with Markov chain modeling, demographic population projection is different from a traditional Markov chain multistate model, since we are projecting populations instead of probabilities.)

We also need to decide the duration of each state. In this example, the period will be one month. We'll assume that we just launched a new snowmobile social network, and our goal is to project the number of users for the product in 5 months.

Table 9.4 presents the Leslie matrix for the model. There are two core assumptions: (1) that all users are alive for 3 months or less and (2) that new users come into the product by word of mouth (meaning the size of the active groups at each time point affects future population size). We'll also assume that word of mouth varies by the length of time users have been in the product. Unlike in the prior model, since the new model is based on user age, users must move to the next state (i.e., the next month or die).

Table 9.4   **Leslie Matrix for the Word-of-Mouth Model**

	User (1 Month)	User (2 Months)	User (3 Months)
User (1 Month)	New users (word of mouth)	New users (word of mouth)	New users (word of mouth)
User (2 Months)	User death from 1 to 2	0	0
User (3 Months)	0	User death from 2 to 3	0

In Table 9.4, similar to the example in the last section, we read the column as the user's start state and the row as the user's end state. The first row includes the new users who come into the product by word-of-mouth. Since individuals must progress to the next state, there are structural 0s. For instance, a user at 2 months cannot progress to 2 months; she must either move to 3 months or leave the product. Similar to our last example, these zeros are the state movements that cannot exist. Here they cannot exist because they are time-based and users cannot go forward or back in time.

9.4.2 User Death by a Thousand Cuts

We will go through an example of population projection in this section and calculate a number of auxiliary metrics related to how our population is changing. We'll go over age-specific growth rates, survivorship and calculation of Leslie matrix elements, population projection, Leslie matrix eigenvectors, growth rates, and the net replacement ratio.

9.4.2.1 Surviving Population and Age-Specific Growth Rates

First, we need to estimate a few quantities directly from our web product. In particular, we need to estimate the proportion of the population surviving or remaining to the end of each period. (This is similar to the survival curve that we estimated in Chapter 6.) In this example, the periods are defined by months in our web product.

We need to find the proportion of users remaining in product at the end of each state. We are assuming that at month 0, all users exist, so the proportion surviving at month 0 is 1. At month 1, only 70% of the users remain, so the proportion surviving is 0.7; at month 2, only 40% of the original users exist, so the proportion surviving is 0.4. That's the first column in Table 9.5.

Table 9.5 **Assumptions for the Word-of-Mouth Model: Example 1**

	Proportion Surviving	Word-of-Mouth Growth Rate
User Month 0	1.0	NA
User Month 1	0.7	0.08
User Month 2	0.4	0.20
User Month 3	0.0	0.40

The other quantity that we need to find is how many new people each user is bringing into the product. (We could add growth rates from other channels as well, but for simplicity's sake, we'll assume that our primary growth is through word-of-mouth.) The word-of-mouth rate is how many people, on average, hear about the product and join. For instance, between month 0 and month 1, 8 out of 100 people talk about the product to friends and family and they join. Between month 1 and month 2, 20 people recommend the product to friends and family and they join. Between months 2 and 3, 40 users out of 100 recommended users join the product. That's the second column in Table 9.5. We'll explain these concepts in detail in later sections.

Let's consider the word-of-mouth rates and define a few concepts. The word-of-mouth rate can be thought of as an age-specific metric, since it is dependent on user age. The older users are, the more likely they are to invite people who actually join the application.

The age-specific word-of-mouth rate (based on the age-specific fertility rates for demographic population projection) is important because it can tell us a lot about how the population is growing. The age-specific population rate for 1 month is 0.08, for 2 months is 0.2, and for 3 months is 0.4, as seen in Table 9.5.

The total word-of-mouth rate is the sum of all age-specific word-of-mouth rates, which is 0.68. This is analogous to the demographic concept of the total fertility rate, which is the sum of the various age-specific fertility rates. It can be interpreted as saying that the average user going through the product at the current rates can be expected to invite 0.68 new users over the course of the user's life in product (3 months).

9.4.2.2 Constructing the Leslie Matrix

Now that we have calculated the total and age-specific word-of-mouth rates, we can use these rates when we construct our Leslie matrix. The Leslie Matrix is similar to the transition matrix, except that it has a special structure that will allow us to more easily project the population into the future.

Since the Leslie transition matrix has time-based states, users can only move to the next time based state (they cannot move back or skip states). Thus, a user cannot move in the following directions:

1. From period 1 to period 3

2. From period 2 back to period 1

3. From period 3 back to period 1

4. From period 3 back to period 2

This insight means that all rows of our Leslie matrix, except the first, will have zeros for all values, except for the off-diagonals—that is, [2, 1] and [3, 2] in Table 9.4. We'll come back to the first row later in this section, as this row estimates growth rates. We'll calculate the growth rates based on the age-specific word-of-mouth rates that we estimated in the last section.

Let's calculate the off-diagonal values for [2, 1] and [3, 2] first. The off-diagonal values in Table 9.5 are survivorship rates. Survivorship rates are estimates of the proportion of the population that remains from the first period to the second period. Unlike the multistate model, in which we were purposely vague about the period (i.e., when a period starts and ends), here we use a specific formula that calculates the surviving population from the middle of the prior period to the middle of the next period.

We calculate survivorship by taking the ratio of the proportion surviving to the middle of period 2 to the proportion surviving to the middle of period 1. In this example, we need to calculate the survivorship rates for users moving from the middle of month 1 to the middle of month 2 [2, 1], and for users moving from the middle of month 2 to the middle of month 3 [3, 2]. We average the surviving proportion from the two periods to calculate the proportion surviving to mid-period.

Survivorship at month 4 is zero, meaning all users leave the product after month 3. We'll assume this for simplicity.

> ### Note
>
> It's always a problem to decide how to count user survivorship. Some users may join at the beginning of the period and some at the end. We will do this by averaging and considering that average as the population at mid-period.

Let's calculate survivorship from month 1 to month 2. We do this by determining the proportion in product at mid-month 2 divided by the proportion in product at mid-month 1.

$$Survivorship_1 = \frac{(Surviving_1 + Surviving_2)}{(Surviving_0 + Surviving_1)}$$

The proportion surviving at month 0 is 1, at month 1 is 0.7, and at month 2 is 0.4. Then, we can estimate the population at month 0.5 to be 0.85. We can estimate population at month 1.5 to be 0.55. Then, 0.55/.85, which is equal to about 0.65, gives us the value [2, 1].

$$\text{Leslie matrix } [2,1] = \frac{\left[\frac{(0.7+0.4)}{2}\right]}{\left[\frac{(1+0.7)}{2}\right]} = \frac{(0.7+0.4)}{(1+0.7)} = 0.65$$

Let's calculate survivorship from month 2 to month 3 in the same way as above. This gives us the value 0.36.

$$\text{Leslie matrix } [3,2] = \frac{(0.4+0)}{(0.7+0.4)} = 0.36$$

These survivorship values will go into our off-diagonal in our constructed Leslie matrix. See Table 9.6 for the input values.

Table 9.6   Leslie Matrix for the Word-of-Mouth Model: Example 1

	User (1 Month)	User (2 Months)	User (3 Months)
User (1 Month)	0.85/2 * [0.08 + 0.2 * (0.65)] = **0.09**	0.85/2 * [0.2 + 0.3 * (0.36)] = **0.13**	0.85/2 * (0.3 + 0) = **0.13**
User (2 Months)	(0.7 + 0.4)/(1 + 0.7) = **0.65**	0	0
User (3 Months)	0	(0.4 + 0)/(0.7 + 0.4) = **0.36**	0

Great! We have calculated the off-diagonal values from row 2 to the last row. In the next section, we'll calculate the first row of our Leslie matrix.

9.4.2.3 Calculating Product Growth: First Row of the Leslie Matrix

Calculating product growth—that is, the first row of the Leslie matrix—is a little more complicated than calculating the survivorship, because we must take survivorship into account when estimating product growth in the later period. Why? Because the population that has left the product will likely not invite more new users to the product. This may not be the case in reality, but it is an assumption we will use here to simplify the calculation.

To calculate the first row or the growth rates, we need to multiply the population mid-period by the growth and survivorship rates in both periods. We'll break up the calculation into parts. First, we need to calculate the proportion of the population remaining mid-period or at ½ of a month. The population at month ½ is 0.85.

$$Pop1 = \frac{(Time\ interval)}{2} * (Population\ month\ 0-1) = \frac{1}{2} * (1 + 0.7) = 0.85$$

Now, we need to go back to our age-specific word-of-mouth rates, as those are our product growth rates. As you might remember from the past section, the age-specific growth rates were 0.08 at month 1, 0.2 at month 2, and 0.4 at month 3.

To calculate product growth, we need to multiply growth by survivorship. For instance, we cannot just average the growth of period 1 (0.08) and the growth of period 2 (0.20). The reason is that some users leave; that is, the survivorship proportion at month 0 is 1 and at month 1 is 0.65. We then multiply our age-specific growth rates by survivorship. For instance, at month 0, we multiply our age-specific rate of 0.08 by the survivorship ratio of 1, since no one has left the product at the beginning of the period.

In month 1, we must multiply our month 2 age-specific growth rate of 0.2 by the proportion of our user population who survived to month 2 of 0.65, which is 0.13. We then sum these two values: 0.08 + 0.13 = 0.21. We average the two values by dividing the sum by 2, giving a value of 0.105. Finally, we multiply the growth rates by our population, which is 0.85, which gives us 0.09—the Leslie matrix value [1, 1].

The following equation will help us calculate growth rates for the space in the first row and first column of the Leslie matrix or user growth from month 0 to month 1.

$$Leslie\ matrix\ [1, 1] = \frac{(Pop1)}{2} * (growth1 + growth2 * survivorship2)$$

$$= \frac{0.85}{2} * (0.08*1 + 0.2*0.65) = 0.09$$

User growth is attributed to users moving from month 1 to month 2. This is the number in the first row, second column of the Leslie matrix. We calculate [1, 2] and [1, 3] in the same way in which we calculated [1, 1].

$$Leslie\ matrix\ [1, 2] = \frac{(Pop1)}{2} * (growth2 + growth3 * survivorship3)$$

$$= \frac{0.85}{2} * (0.2*1 + 0.3*0.36) = 0.13$$

User growth is attributed to users moving from month 2 to month 3. Note that survivorship and growth in the fourth period in this example is zero.

$$\text{Leslie matrix } [1,\ 3] = \frac{(Pop1)}{2} * \left(growth3 + growth4 * survivorship4\right)$$

$$= \frac{0.85}{2} * (0.3 * 1 + 0) = 0.13$$

Now, we can input all of these values into our Leslie matrix, as shown in Table 9.6. The Leslie matrix is key to projecting populations in our product and learning about how our product will change over time. In the next few sections, we'll project the population over five periods and calculate a number of metrics directly or indirectly related to the Leslie matrix.

9.4.2.4   Projection Population

In the last section, we calculated the values for the demographic cornerstone of population projection, the Leslie matrix. After doing all that work, we want to see some dividends. In this section, we'll use this Leslie matrix (Table 9.6) to project the population over five periods. First, as in our example for the multistate model, we need a population matrix. Our initial population matrix, shown in Table 9.7, is based on the user's age in product. It holds the number of users in each category in period 1.

Table 9.7   **Initial Population Matrix for Word-of-Mouth Model: Example 1**

	Initial Population
User 1 Month	100,000
User 2 Months	50,000
User 3 Months	25,000

In this example, there are 100,000 users in month 1, 50,0000 users in month 2, and 25,000 users in month 3. We want to find the number of users in each state in the next period. To get this result, we must multiply our Leslie matrix by our initial population matrix. We have rounded all the values of the Leslie Matrix to make the calculations easier.

We can see this process in Figure 9.6. Note that this process involves matrix multiplication. Let's examine in more detail how it works.

$$\begin{bmatrix} 0.09 & 0.13 & 0.13 \\ 0.65 & 0 & 0 \\ 0 & 0.36 & 0 \end{bmatrix} \times \begin{bmatrix} 100{,}000 \\ 50{,}000 \\ 25{,}000 \end{bmatrix} = \begin{bmatrix} 18{,}750 \\ 65{,}000 \\ 18{,}000 \end{bmatrix}$$

Figure 9.6   Matrix multiplication for population projection.

As see in Figure 9.6, we multiply these populations by our transition probabilities to get the population in the next period. The first row of the transition matrix is growth. To get growth in our product, we multiply the initial population by the first row of the transition matrix. For instance, in the first period, new user growth is 100,000 * 0.09 + 50,000 * 0.13 + 25,000 * 0.13 = 18,750 new users.

Now, we need to calculate the surviving users from the cohort moving from month 1 to 2 and the cohort moving from month 2 to 3. We multiply 100,000 * 0.65 + 50,000 * 0 + 25,000 * 0 to get 65,000 users remaining from cohort 1. We lost 35,000 users between month 1 and 2. Next, we calculate the users surviving from month 2 to month 3. We multiply 100,000 * 0 + 50,000 * 0.36 + 0 * 25,000 to get 18,000 users who survive from month 2 to month 3. We sum 18,750 + 65,000 + 18,000 to get the population in the next period. The total population in the next period is 101,750, down from 175,000 users initially.

Our new population matrix for period 2 shows 18,750 users in month 1, 65,000 users in month 2, and 18,000 users in month 3. We can continue to multiply these new population matrices by our Leslie matrix to project changes in the population over time.

By period 5, the result would look like Figure 9.7. We can see that the population rapidly declines. This means that our growth rate is not high enough to sustain the current population that we have. We cover this calculation in R Listing 15.20.

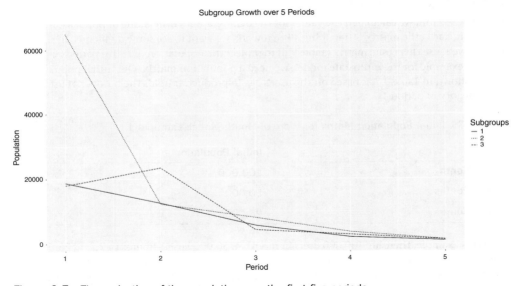

Figure 9.7   The projection of the population over the first five periods.

9.4.2.5   Exponential Growth or Decay

Next, we will calculate a few important population quantities. The first indicates whether the population is growing, staying the same, or declining. We can find this information directly from the Leslie matrix, by calculating the first eigenvector.

(You do not have to know the process to calculate eigenvectors, just how to interpret them. You can use the eigen() function in R to calculate these from the Leslie matrix. The sidebar in Chapter 7 explains how to calculate eigenvectors and eigenvalues. This section just discusses how to interpret eigenvalues based on this Leslie matrix. In Chapter 15, Listings 15.20–15.22, we calculate values and graph this example.)

The eigenvectors for this Leslie matrix are as follows:

$$\lambda = [0.44, -0.17 + 0.2i, -0.17 - 0.2i]$$

Since the first eigenvector is less than 1 (0.44), this population will decline exponentially. If the eigenvector is greater than 1, the population will grow exponentially.

9.4.2.6   Growth Rate/Doubling

If a population grows or declines exponentially, that means that it can double or shrink quickly, respectively. This trend can be either good or bad for your web product. In this section, we'll calculate a very important metric, your population growth rate. We do not need the Leslie matrix calculations to calculate these rates.

Let's calculate the short-term growth rate. What's the growth rate? It is a measure of how fast the population is growing overall.

The growth rate is calculated based on the exponential distribution, which we saw in Chapter 5. Here is the formula for the exponential distribution at a single point: $K(T\_1) = K(T\_0) e^{-rt}$. We divide both sides of the formula by $K(T\_0)$, take the natural log, and then divide by T to get a formula for our growth rate.

The following equation is a typical growth rate formula:

$$r = \left(\frac{1}{T}\right) * ln\left(\frac{K(t+1)}{K(t)}\right)$$

Here is the calculation of the short-term growth rate in our example. Remember that period 2 had a population of 101,750 users, as we calculated in our population projection. The initial population was 175,000. The time period is 1, so T equals 1. Then, we just take the natural log of the population in period 2 over the population in period 1:

$$r_s = 1 * ln\left(\frac{101,750}{175,000}\right) = -0.54$$

Yikes! You probably want to do something to prevent this population loss. We can calculate how long it takes the population to decline by half. We calculate half-life by dividing the natural log of 2 by the short-term growth rate. Given this equation, we can approximate doubling by using the half-life equation, ln (2)/r. It enables us to calculate how quickly our population will double or shrink by half.

$$Half\text{-}life = \frac{ln\ (2)}{-0.54} = -1.28\ \text{periods}$$

In about 1 month, your web population has been halved. This is an extreme case of a dying product. Most product populations will not decline this fast.

9.4.2.7   Net Replacement Rate

We can also approximate whether the population is replenishing itself by calculating the net replacement rate (NRR). The NRR tells us about our rate of renewal and is not period specific. We'll alter this definition for product analytics.

In demography, the NRR is the expected number of newborn daughters per prospective mother. In this book, NRR is the number of new users per prospective user. Note though our definition of NRR differs from the demographic definition because in demography we must multiply the rate by the proportion of female babies at birth. Clearly, in product analytics, gender does not matter.

In Table 9.8, we assume that there are 1,000 people in each of the three cohorts at mid-period. We calculate the NRR by summing the new users (342) invited by each cohort and divide that by the hypothetical cohort size, which is 1,000. The NRR in this example is $= \frac{342}{1,000} = 0.34$. The replacement rate is the speed at which the population is replacing itself when NRR = 1. Our population NRR is far below the replacement rate.

Table 9.8   **Calculating the NRR**

	Survivorship (Mid-Period)	Growth Rate	New Users
Month 1	(1 + 0.7)/2 = 0.85 * 1,000 = 850	0.08	68
Month 2	(0.7 + 0.4)/(1 + 0.7) = 0.65 * 1,000 = 650	0.20	130
Month 3	(0.4 + 0)/(0.7 + 0.4) = 0.36 * 1,000 = 360	0.40	144
		= 0.08 + 0.20 + 0.40 = 0.68	= 68 + 130 + 144 = 342

The NRR is important because it's not based on population totals, but rather on the numbers needed to maintain the population from generation to generation. We could quickly surmise from the NRR that our population will not remain consistent over time. The NRR is a great web metric to track if you're trying to maintain a consistent population.

If we choose to calculate only the NRR, we can also use it to approximate the growth rate. We'll go through an example of calculating the NRR and the approximate growth rate.

$$r \approx \frac{log\ (NRR)}{Average\ age\ at\ word\text{-}of\text{-}mouth\ reference}$$

The numerator is the log of the net replacement rate. The denominator is calculated as follows in this example. We calculate the average age for a new user by multiplying the age at each interval: 68 * 1 + 130 * 2 + 144 * 3 = 760. Then, we divide the total new users by the average new user's age. The average age of new users is the denominator of this approximation:

$$r \approx \frac{ln\ (0.34)}{\dfrac{760}{342}} = -0.48$$

The approximate growth rate is close to the true short-term growth rate (–0.54), but not quite there (–0.48). This is another useful approximation when we want to calculate growth rates quickly or if we want to approximate the growth rate for a future period.

9.4.3 Exponential Growth Example

Now that we've seen an example of population decay or rapid decline, in this section we'll examine an example of exponential growth. We'll keep our survival rates unchanged, but modify the word-of-mouth growth rates. In this example, our product is much more popular and information about it is spreading quickly through the general population.

With this example, we'll see why every product tries to get you to invite your friends or update your contacts list. In Chapter 15, Listings 15.23–15.25, we calculate this example in R.

We will not describe the process of calculating these values in detail, as it's analogous to the last example in terms of process. Please try to calculate the core values on your own for this web example to see if you have understood the basic concepts.

The age-specific word-of-mouth rates are given in Table 9.9. Total word-of-mouth rates are 7 in this example, which is substantially higher than in our previous example. Basically, a user will invite seven people over the life of the product.

Table 9.9   **Assumptions for the Exponential Growth Example**

	Proportion Surviving	**Word-of-Mouth Growth Rate**
User Month 0	1.0	1
User Month 1	0.7	3
User Month 2	0.4	4
User Month 3	0.0	0

We use the same process to solve for the Leslie matrix (Table 9.10) as in the prior example. We will not go through the calculation of this Matrix, but see if you can solve for the values of this matrix yourself.

Table 9.10   **Leslie Matrix for Word-of-Mouth Model: Example 2**

	User (1 Month)	**User (2 Months)**	**User (3 Months)**
User (1 Month)	1.66	1.89	1.7
User (2 Months)	(0.7 + 0.4)/(1 + 0.7) = 0.65	0	0
User (3 Months)	0	(0.4 + 0)/(0.7 + 0.4) = 0.36	0

As we explained earlier, the survival proportions have stayed the same, but the rate of growth for new users has changed. We're assuming a radically different word-of-mouth rate of growth. For every user who comes in at 1 month, that user brings at least one user with them. At 3 months, a user has brought seven users with them, on average. These numbers are clearly large, but they help demonstrate the idea.

After we calculate the Leslie matrix, the next step is to solve for the eigenvectors. The following are the eigenvectors computed for this matrix: $[2.3, -0.31 + 0.28i, -0.31 - 28i]$.

We can tell from the first eigenvector that there is exponential growth, because the first eigenvector, 2.3, is greater than 1. Next, we'll calculate the short-term and long-term growth rates.

We went through an explanation of the short-term growth rates in the prior example. Here is the calculated short-term growth rate:

$$r_s = 1 * ln\left(\frac{368,000}{175,000}\right) = 0.74$$

We can calculate how long it takes the population to double in this example.

$$Pop\_double = \frac{ln\,(2)}{-0.24} = 0.93 \text{ period}$$

So, in about 1 month, your web population has been doubled. This is an extreme case of a rapidly growing product, with number of users doubling every period. Most product populations will not grow this fast.

Next, let's calculate the NRR for this example. In Table 9.11, we assume that there are 1,000 people in each of the three cohorts. The NRR in this example is $\frac{4,240}{1,000} = 4.24$. The replacement rate is NRR = 1. Clearly, our user population is growing much faster than the replacement rate (i.e., the rate at which the population would stay the same over time).

Table 9.11   **Calculating the NRR for Example 2**

	Survivorship	Growth Rate	New Users
1	(1 + 0.7)/2 = 0.85 * 1,000 = 850	1	850
2	(0.7 + 0.4)/(1 + 0.7) = 0.65 * 1,000 = 650	3	1,950
3	(0.4 + 0)/(0.7 + 0.4) = 0.36 * 1,000 = 360	4	1,440
		= 1 + 3 + 4 = 7	= 850 + 1,950 + 1,440 = 4,240

We can calculate our growth rate estimate based on the NNR. Again, it's close to the earlier growth rate, but not exactly the same: 0.68 versus 0.74.

$$r \approx \frac{ln(4.24)}{\frac{9,070}{4,240}} = 0.68$$

Referring to the plot in Figure 9.8, we can see that the population is rapidly growing, rather than declining as in the user death example.

Were you able to calculate all of these values correctly? If not, spend a little time to understand these calculations, as we will build on these concepts in the next few sections.

In the next section, we'll cover some core population concepts related to how a population grows. We'll discuss stationary and stable populations, population momentum. and oscillations.

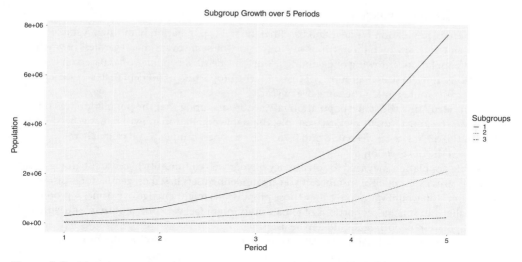

Figure 9.8 Plot of the population from the example 2 word-of-mouth model projected out five periods.

9.4.3.1 Stationary Population

We just looked at two population examples that were relatively extreme. Most products fall somewhere in between these extremes. How do we know whether population growth rates are acceptable, when they are extreme? We need some population baselines to use as guidance. This section on stationary population and the next section on stable populations will provide us with just these kinds of key population baselines that you can use to compare your product's growth.

Consider the case when our growth rate is 0, which means that the population is neither growing nor declining. That's called a stationary population. In other words, the population of a web product stays the same over time regardless of the rates at which new users join and old users leave.

To demonstrate the stationary population case, consider an example where we have 10 million users, with a growth of 2 million users per year and a death rate of 2 million users per year. Here, the rates of growth and death are similar. Although this can seem simple on the surface, calculating stationary properties can be very complex owing to subpopulation differences in growth and death rates.

An especially useful aspect of the concept of stationary population is the stationary population equation. It's a simple heuristic for what it takes to maintain a stationary population.

$$1 = growth\_rate_{newuser} * retention_0$$

Suppose we have a web product with average new user retention of 45 days. This means $1/45 * 1,000 = 22$ users per 1,000 need to join each day to offset the drop-off in the retained population. This is a very useful heuristic with which to quickly get a sense of your product's population.

9.4.3.2   Stable Population

The stationary population is one useful baseline; the stable population is another. A stable population is one in which proportions of groups stay the same over time, regardless of whether the total population is growing or declining. Note that the stable population is based on the proportions, not the sizes of groups. For instance, the proportion of users in first, second, and third months would remain the same over a year.

When calculating the stable population rate, we are assuming that the population remains stable over the long term. In the first example, the stable population growth rate was between −0.57 and −0.58; it was between 0.75 and 0.76 in the second example. We'll calculate these numbers in the next section.

A stable population may lead to consistency of your web community because subgroups maintain their sizes over time. For instance, if you are modeling users based on gender for a dating application, you would want to see how those proportions might change over time. A product with smaller and smaller proportions of female users might feel very different than one with a stable population of both male and female users.

Why do we care about stable populations? It's because they confer some nice properties.

- Growth rates become fixed over time.

- Growth rates are independent of population sizes.

- Proportions of groups become fixed over time.

- Proportions of groups become independent of initial populations.

- Stable population growth rates are a long-term baseline or scenario against which you can compare your actual growth rates.

It's nice to use stable population theory as a potential scenario of what's happening in your web product over time. Stable population rates are likely not what's happening in your web product, but they allow you to identify which groups are not growing as fast.

It's very simple to assess if our actual population is even close to a stable population. Table 9.12 depicts three different cohorts, at 1, 2, and 3 months. To check whether this is a stable population, we can calculate how much they increase or decrease in the next period. If these factors are the same, then it's a stable population. As we can see from Table 9.12, this is not true. The factor by which they increase differs wildly by cohort. At 1 month, the population is growing rapidly; at 2 months, it is declining. *This is not a stable population!* Your product is going to change radically over time.

Table 9.12   **Unequal Subgroup Population Growth Rates**

	Initial Population	At T1	Factor Increase
1 month	100,000	350,250	$\frac{350,250}{100,000} = 3.5$
2 months	75,000	65,000	$\frac{65,000}{75,000} = 0.87$
3 months	25,000	27,000	$\frac{27,000}{25,000} = 1.08$

Stable Growth Rate

The stable population is a great baseline; we can compare our growth rates with the stable population growth rate. In this sidebar, we'll explain how to calculate the stable population growth rate—that is, the growth rate needed to maintain a stable population (as defined in the previous section). (This section is mathematically complex and dense, so please skip it if you aren't interested in using the stable population as a baseline in your product.)

The stable growth rate is a good long-term growth rate to hit for a web population that's growing, but with groups remaining proportionally similar over time. This is called Lokta's R. The R refers to the growth rate.

Table 9.13 shows how to calculate the components for Lokta's R. The first column is survivorship, whose calculation is shown in Table 9.5. The second column is growth, which we assumed. The third column is the product, which is the product of survivorship and growth. The product is what we need to approximate the long-term growth rate. Note that the long-run growth rate (Lokta's R) may not make sense in our user death example since the population is declining so quickly. However, we'll go through the process of calculating it to show how it's done.

Lokta's R is defined in the following way. We'll call the growth rate here, r_{stable}:

$$1 = \sum \left(Survivorship * Growth \right) * e^{-r_{stable} * x}$$

Table 9.13 **Calculating Lokta's R**

	Survivorship	Growth	Product
1	$\dfrac{(1 + 0.7)}{2} = 0.85$	0.08	0.68
2	$\dfrac{(0.7 + 0.4)}{(1 + 0.7)} = 0.65$	0.20	0.13
3	$\dfrac{(0.4 + 0)}{(0.7 + 0.4)} = 0.36$	0.40	0.14

Using the example shown in Table 9.13, we will calculate the coefficients to approximate the long-term growth rate, r_stable. To do so, we'll need the product numbers from Table 9.13 and the first column of the Lexis diagram (Table 9.6).

The first term of Lokta's equation is:

$$\left[\frac{(0.0680 + 0.13)}{2} \right] * e^{-r} = 0.099 \; e^{-r}$$

We use the average of the product values for periods 1 and 2 and multiply that by $e^{-x * r}$.

On the other side of the equation, we take the first transition probability and multiply it by $e^{-x * r}$, where x is the length of time.

$$\left[\frac{(Product\_1 + Product\_2)}{2} \right] * e^{(-1 * r)}$$

$$= \left[\frac{(0.0680 + 0.13)}{2} \right] * e^{-r} = 0.099 \ e^{-r}$$

We'll do the same with the average product values for periods 2 and 3. The next term is:

$$= \left[\frac{(0.13 + 0.14)}{2} \right] * e^{(-2 * r)} = 0.135 * e^{(-2 * r)}$$

The final term is:

$$= \left[\frac{(0.14 + 0)}{2} \right] * e^{(-3 * r)} = 0.07 * \cdots e^{(-3 * r)}$$

These terms should add to 1, the point at which we have a stationary (nonchanging) population.

We can add all these terms into the following equation (based on the Lokta's R equation):

$$1 = 0.099e^{-r} + 0.135 * e^{-2} + 0.07 * e^{-3}$$

There is no easy way to solve this analytically: We need to use R. Refer to Chapter 15, Listings 15.22 and 15.25, for an implementation in R. When we solve this equation, Lokta's growth rate is between −0.57 and −0.58. This means that the population of the product is rapidly hemorrhaging at a rate of $1 - r$ or about 430 to 440 per 1,000 users per month. This drop-off rate is higher than our short-term growth, so we do not have a stable population.

Now let's calculate the product matrix and the long-run stable population growth rate based on these numbers (see Table 9.14).

Table 9.14 **Calculation of Lokta's R, the Stationary Population Growth Rate**

	Survivorship	Growth	Product
1	$\frac{(1 + 0.7)}{2} = 0.85$	1	0.85
2	$\frac{(0.7 + 0.4)}{(1 + 0.7)} = 0.65$	3	1.95
3	$\frac{(0.4 + 0)}{(0.7 + 0.4)} = 0.36$	4	1.44

By the same process as used earlier, this is Lokta's equation for the exemplary example:

$$1 = 0.85 * e^{-r} + 1.95 * e^{-2r} + 1.44 * e^{-3r}$$

Here r is equal to about 0.75, which means we're gaining about 750 users per 1,000, a rapid growth rate. The stable population growth rate is higher than our growth rate of 0.74, but in practice this is very close to a stable population. Compare this example with your own product, as it involves a product with phenomenal growth and subpopulation stability (basically what everyone is looking for in a web product).

Everything is the same in this example in terms of survivorship as in the last example. That is, people are staying just as long, but the rapid word-of-mouth rate (or growth rates) allows for crazy growth in the product. Growth rates are often more important than survivorship, so you may want to emphasize growth over retention. If growth is petering out, that's when retention becomes a key consideration.

9.4.3.3   Population Momentum

Population momentum is based on the idea that it takes time to turn around a growing population. It's like the *Titanic*: The ship did not sink immediately, but slowly and surely. Web populations will not change immediately, because of built-up population momentum. How do we determine how much built-up momentum is there is to move population forward on its current trajectory?

A very common scenario for a popular web product is bad press or some unforeseen event, which causes the rate of population growth to drop by some factor to the replacement rate (a nongrowing population based on new user acquisition). In this case, we assume it moves from one stable population growth rate to a new stable population.

Based on NRR = 1, the population should be stationary, but there is population pressure from a rapidly growing population from the prior periods. What will the new stationary population size be, based on the old growth rates, NRR, and initial population? Although this is a specific example, it's a common scenario that demonstrates the underlying population momentum.

What happens in this scenario is complex. The population will oscillate until it finally reaches a stable population. The older high growth rates have brought in a lot of users. Even though current growth rates are down, we'll still see a lot of population growth when those users invite new users, and then those users invite even more new users. We'll see smaller and smaller echo booms that mirror the original high growth rate, until the population settles down to the ultimate stationary population.

The complexity of these calculations stems from the fact that population has some underlying momentum, like a hurtling object. Once the population has grown, it'll take some time to bring its size back down. We'll explore this phenomenon with the help of an example.

Facebook's Cambridge Analytica scandal is an example of how an event can affect population momentum. Even after the Cambridge Analytica scandal, Facebook's population was still growing, and it continues to grow, albeit at a much lower rate. This seems counterintuitive at face value. However, you should recognize that Facebook has a huge population and that friends are still inviting friends to join them on this website. Thus, you're unlikely to see the full effect of the scandal immediately, and the population might oscillate until it settles on a stationary long-term growth rate.

This describes the Keyfitz scenario, in which a population that has been steadily increasing for a long time evolves into a stable population. Some external shock lowers the word-of-mouth effect substantially (here, a domestic scandal), which then kills any growth in the product. The NRR falls to close to 1.

We can use Keyfitz's approximation to estimate the new stable population after the population settles. The following equation is the Keyfitz's approximation:

$$\text{Keyfitz's approximation: } K(new\_stable) = K(old\_stable) * \frac{Growth\ rate * e\_0}{\sqrt{NRR}}$$

Now, let's explore a numeric example with our snowmobile website. Suppose this site has been growing well, but it received some bad press about one of the popular snowmobiles and user growth plummets. The population for this website is now at the replacement rate.

In the period before the bad press occurred, the number of users of this site grew from 1 million to 1.05 million in a month, for a growth rate of 0.07. User retention is about 20 months, on average, in product.

We estimate the NRR to be 1.5, above the replacement rate, before the scandal. If this same growth rate held, then the population would be about 1.5 million after 5 periods, which is greater than the Keyfitz long-term stationary population of 1.2 million. We can see that the population will increase by 150,000 users under the Keyfitz scenario, solely due to population momentum. However, this increase is less than it would be if the high growth rates continued even for a few more periods.

Ultimately, due to this scandal, population will settle on:

$$K(t) \approx 1,050,000 * \frac{0.07 * 20}{\sqrt{1.5}} \approx 1.2 \text{ million} \qquad \text{\textit{Keyfitz scenario}}$$

$$K(t) \approx K(0) * e^{-rt} = 1,050,000 * e^{0.07*5} = 1.49 \text{ million} \qquad \text{Normal, 5 periods}$$

More Information from the Leslie Matrix: Population Oscillation and Eigenvectors

We can accurately project population oscillations, just as we saw with the Keyfitz scenario. After World War II, there was a large increase in the number of babies born when the soldiers returned home. The population in that cohort was so large that when they hit reproductive age in the 1980s and 1990s, there was an echo boom. Population ebbs and flows with the variations in cohorts, creating long-term gyrations in the population.

To predict how a population will oscillate, we can use the eigenvectors from the Leslie matrix. As we saw in our earlier example, the second and third eigenvectors are complex, which means that they are representing population oscillations. While we will not discuss the details here, but Chapter 15 will show how we can translate those eigenvectors into x and y coordinates and plot the oscillations.

We can tell from the second and third eigenvalues from the two examples that each oscillation is much smaller than the preceding oscillation. We can see from Figure 9.9 that the first oscillation for example 2 is larger than that for example 1. Figure 9.10 and Figure 9.11 show the smaller oscillations in the later periods that are not visible in Figure 9.8 because they are much smaller.

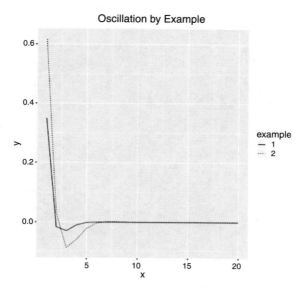

Figure 9.9   Image of the population oscillations for example 1 and example 2 over 20 periods.

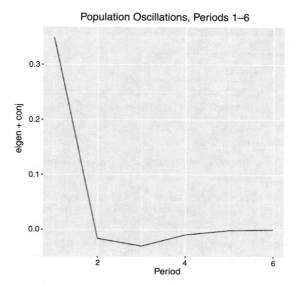

Figure 9.10   The smaller oscillations in the first four periods and the next four periods for example 1.

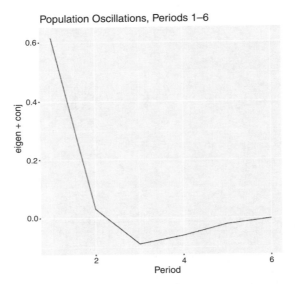

Figure 9.11   Oscillations in the first four periods and the next four periods for example 2.

How do we get information about the oscillations from just looking at the eigenvectors? Table 9.15 shows how to read all the eigenvectors of a Leslie matrix.

Table 9.15   **The Meaning of Different Values of the Eigenvectors for Population Patterns over Time**

Eigenvalue	Outcome
> 0	▪ If eigenvalue > 1, then exponential growth ▪ If eigenvalue < 1, then exponential decay
−1 < eigenvalue < 0	▪ Damped oscillations toward a stationary population with period equal to 2
< −1	▪ Diverging oscillations with period 2; moving from a stationary population to a diverging population
Complex values	▪ See Chapter 15 on how to translate eigenvalues into projections of oscillations

If you are interested in a more mathematical approach to population projection, refer to Nathan Keyfitz and Hal Caswell's (2005) *Applied Mathematical Demography*.

This chapter has explored the following questions. Are there common patterns that define the life of web products? How do web products grow or die? The life cycle of a web product is very important to how we should build theories, define metrics, and explore behavior. This chapter provided tools that you can use to analyze web products at different stages of that cycle.

9.5   Actionable Insights

Actionable insights from this chapter are the following:

- Understanding the product life cycle is imperative to the success of any campaign; different strategies should be used at points early versus late in the user life cycle (because of user types).

- The life cycle of a product is characterized by different user types: innovators, early adopters, early majority, late majority, and laggards.

- Transition probabilities can be used as metrics and to project population changes in product. The quality of this metric depends on how well the underlying state model represents user behavior in your product.

- Population projection can help you predict future total population (as well as subgroup populations). It helps you understand how your product community will change over time. In addition, it helps you project future population needs so you can make the necessary investments.

- Stable population theory gives us a baseline against which to compare product changes.

In this chapter, we learned some techniques for modeling retention and discovering how populations change over time. We used simplified state models to understand how populations can move through states of a product, which can be used to model retention or other social processes.

In the next section, we'll explore causal inference methods. We covered A/B testing in Chapter 6. When we don't have experimental data, we need to produce causal insights from observational data—something that is generally difficult. The next three chapters will work through methods to achieve this goal.

IV

Causal Inference Methods

In Pursuit of the Experiment: Natural Experiments and Difference-in-Difference Modeling

In the last section on predictive methods, we covered both machine learning and demographic forecasting models. These models help us predict user behavior and forecast subpopulation changes and business needs. While predictive insights are useful, they cannot help us change user behavior.

In this section, we'll examine causal inference methods. Causal inference is an exploration of factors that determine an outcome. Understanding causation will allow us to run better campaigns, build better products, and alter user behavior.

As discussed in Chapter 6 on A/B testing, randomness is the reasoned basis of inference according to Ronald Fisher the father of modern statistics and experimental designs are the gold standard of causal inference. A well-designed experiment allows us to operationalize randomization to estimate causal effects or the effect of a desired treatment on an outcome. However, almost all data in this world is observational, meaning that it doesn't come from a well-defined experiment.

How do we use observational data to derive causal insights? For example, using product data, how can you determine what *causes* changes in purchasing, retention, or other user behavior? Chapters 10, 11, and 12 will cover causal inference from real-world, nonexperimental data. Chapter 13, on uplift modeling, discusses a technique to tease out more information from experimental data.

There are two approaches to finding causal insights that we will cover here. The first is the **natural experiment**, in which assignment of a population into treatment and control groups occurs due to some random process. The second approach is a **quasi-experiment**, in which there is no random assignment of a population into treatment and control groups. In most quasi-experimental designs, the researcher controls the process of user assignment into these groups.

Chapter 10 focuses on techniques to analyze natural experiments. Chapters 11 and 12 examine two quasi-experimental design techniques, regression discontinuity and statistical matching. All of these methods are best applied on small, well-chosen data sets, which is contrary to the expectations of predictive methods.

Causal inference techniques are very applicable to real-world problems, but are not widely used due to a lack of knowledge about the methodology, design requirements, and sometimes the analytical rigor of these techniques.

Please note this section is more technically rigorous than almost any previous section of the book, particularly Chapters 12, 13, and 14. It might be useful to understand the concepts, even if you do not understand the mathematical tools. Refer to Chapter 16 for information on the implementation and interpretation of these methods in R.

Before we delve into natural experiments, let's explore the topic of causal inference from observational data in more depth. We covered predictive inference and its use cases. Now, we'll see some examples of causal inference from observational data and take a bird's-eye view of the differences between causal and predictive inference.

10.1 Why Causal Inference?

The question "Why causal inference?" is a little funny on its face, since we're asking why we should be trying to infer *why*. But let's explore how causal inference differs from prediction when relying on observational data. The example we'll consider is the relationship between smoking and cancer. While this is not a product analytics example, it effectively communicates the benefits and difficulties of inferring causation from observational data.

For nearly 20 years, the proof that smoking *causes* cancer eluded statisticians and biostatisticians. This link was long suspected because studies showed a much higher prevalence of lung cancer in smokers. The cancer risk was substantial. However, there were no randomized controlled trials to prove that smoking *caused* cancer, since researchers could not assign some people to smoke considering there could be deleterious side effects. Researchers also could not assume that smoking *caused* cancer, as some other variable(s) might be driving the effect. Inferring causality is vital to developing actionable insights and policy prescriptions. Without understanding the causal impact, we cannot make policies that will change outcomes or behaviors.

For instance, if the Centers for Disease Control and Prevention (CDC) could definitively say that smoking caused cancer, it could create guidelines and health campaigns and inform medical professionals of the risk. But before researchers were able to show the causal link, smoking was just correlated to (or predicted) lung cancer, and as such organizational bodies could not make any definitive policy prescriptions.

Likewise, in user analytics, causal insights are the gold standard for developing actionable prescriptions. Without causal inferences, it's hard to improve your product or change user behavior. Many of the most important causal relationships must be found by obtaining and analyzing observational data because of the inability to randomize assignment of individuals to treatment.

10.2 Causal Inference versus Prediction

For the last hundred years, causal thinking has become the norm. We like to ask the question, "Why is *something* happening?" We like simple cause-and-effect chains. "I'm living longer, because I drink red wine once a week."

Social processes are rarely simple, with thousands, and potentially millions, of causal factors existing that might influence any outcome. Causal chains can be long with many intervening variables. How long you live is based on genetic factors, the environment (from infancy through old age), relationships, attitudes, and how all these complex factors interact.

Predicting how long you will live, while it might be interesting and useful for actuarial purposes, will not tell you *what* to change to live longer. The reason is that while variables can be correlated and good predictors, they may not be causally related. Predicting how long you will live is also much easier than understanding all of the causes of *why* you live 83.6 years. That's the crux of the difference between prediction and causal inference. Causation, even though more difficult to pin down, is *actionable*, meaning we can understand why something is happening and change it. Prediction is about forecasting the future based on the current world. We can put everything into our model and predict something spectacular, but we never really know *why*. If we change anything, our models might not be relevant.

In some cases, prediction is very useful, but in most cases, prediction becomes a proxy for causal relationships, which is very misleading. In user analytics, we generally want to understand *why* our customers are purchasing, engaging, being retained, or some other metric. We want to move these metrics by changing behavior. To change behavior, we generally need to understand *why*.

Currently, data science (AI/machine learning) is primarily focused on prediction, while social science methodology has been primarily focused on causal inference. While prediction gets better with more data, causal inference generally does not. This is the first time in history we have been able to collect large amounts of precisely measured data on human behavior.

Justifiably, prediction is seeing a renaissance—but causal inference is not, even though it's integral to insight. With the rapid growth and massive amounts of behavioral data available, the gap between data science (generally predictive) and social science (causal and ethnographic) approaches to understanding human behavior is expanding. In the space of user analytics, this split is readily apparent because of overreliance on predictive methods for insight.

Table 10.1 shows the core differences between prediction and causal inference. The language in the table is broad, and something that is generally true is not always true in every context. There are six dimensions of comparison: (1) internal and external validation, (2) addition of more data, (3) generalizability, (4) core application, (5) discriminatory, and (6) when does it fail?

Table 10.1 **Core Differences between Causal Inference and Prediction**

Criterion	Prediction	Causal Inference
Internal and external validity	External validation can be granted through testing with a test set. (Easier) Internal validation is not granted, but could hold in some contexts.	Internal validation is granted by design. It is harder to implement or design. External validation is possible by further testing. (Much harder)
Addition of more data	Improves with data.	Unless data is what is needed for design and has a clear counterfactual (or an inferred counterfactual can be generated), inference does not improve.
Generalizable	More likely to be generalizable to other data sets, contexts, and groups given the much larger samples used in creation of models. The degree of generalizability is related to the representativeness and size of the sample.	Often cannot be easily generalizable to other data sets, contexts, and groups. The degree of generalizability is dependent on the representativeness and size of the sample.

(Continues)

Table 10.1   **(Continued)**

Criterion	Prediction	Causal Inference
Core application	Most useful in predicting human behavior. While one can try to use predictive or correlative models to find causal relationships, it is not guaranteed and correlation can lead to erroneous "causal linkages." See Chapter 6 for an explanation as to why.	Useful in understanding and altering human behavior. Key to changing human behavior is understanding what causes human behavior change. Chapter 3 discusses how causation relates to human behavior change.
Discriminatory	Can be discriminatory; black box; confusing results for nonpredictive outcomes.	If design and implementation are done correctly (with mechanisms or connections between causal variables and outcomes), not easily discriminatory because of the reasoning or mechanisms involved; results are clear, actionable, and defensible. The causal impact can differ based on demographic factors.
When does it fail?	Failure to predict aberrant behavior; potentially limits to prediction of human behavior. Prediction is time-dependent. The further away from the event we are, the harder it is to predict. Some outcomes might not be predictable, given the data that we have, or due to randomness in the process. Recent studies show the inability to predict children's long-run trajectories based on childhood factors.	Failure to quantify the treatment effect for outliers; limits to the understanding of the full causes of an outcome. Statistical methods of causal inference are generally centered on average effects (individual treatment effects are harder or impossible to determine). See Chapter 13 for a review of individual treatment effects.

Internal validity is how well an experimental or model design can rule out alternative explanations for its findings. **External validity** is the ability to apply findings from a particular study or model to a context outside of the one studied.

Causal inference and prediction are useful for different types of applications. The core takeaway from Table 10.1 is that causal inference relies on the validity of the design (or internal validity) for support. More data without context does not generally help improve causal inference.

Causal inference generalizability depends on the size and representativeness of the sample. The primary use-case of causal inference is to determine "why" something happens and how to change behavior. Causal inference is much more defensible against discrimination claims because of its use of mechanisms and understanding of "why" an outcome occurs.

Causal inference methods generally fail to detect individual treatment effects. However, work is being done to remedy this blind spot. Uplift modeling is an approach for estimating subgroup treatment effects—that is, a proxy of the individual treatment effect. This topic is discussed in Chapter 13.

Now that we have an understanding of how causal inference differs from prediction and why it's useful, let's explore situations where A/B testing does not work.

10.3   When A/B Testing Doesn't Work

Before we delve into tools for causal inference from observational data, let's explore why A/B testing does not always work. This understanding allows us to recognize situations in which we'll need to rely on other tools—namely, natural experiments and quasi-experimental methods.

A/B testing fails when the treatment is broader, more complex, historical, or when the organization lacks the infrastructure to support A/B testing. This happens often.

Often, data scientists or analysts are responding to decisions already made by executives, product owners, or user experts. Executives and other decision makers frequently rely on intuition or on past experience with similar products to make decisions. They might reach out to you, the data scientist, to provide some evidence as to whether their decisions were good. Since the decisions were already made, you cannot A/B test historical data, unless the design was used during implementation.

What can you do to show that their observations are, in fact, true? All you have is observational data, which often suffers from selection bias and spurious correlations, to draw your inferences. As a reminder, selection bias occurs when non-random differences exist between treatment and hypothetical control groups.

For example, let's review the example in Chapter 6. You run a dating website and you're trying to figure out why some users click "like" on another's profile, while others do not. Say you're interested in testing whether a new feature you built increases "likes." Perhaps that feature could be a modal that prompts a user to "like" a profile if the user has remained on the profile for more than 10 seconds. However, male users disproportionately "like," so your treatment population is 90% male, while your control population is only 60% male. A spurious correlation occurs when a third (unknown) variable actually drives the relationship between two test variables. In this case, it's difficult to test your feature, since gender may be driving a portion of the effect. We don't know how to find members in the control group who look like the treated population on a variety of factors. In this case, gender is an obvious factor, but there could be others we aren't thinking of.

You can't A/B test this feature change because it's already rolled out and all users already see it. Instead, you'll need to use some other techniques to judge its efficacy.

10.3.1   Broader Social Phenomena

We cannot use A/B testing for broader social phenomena, as some types of phenomena are difficult to test. The first type of treatment is one that is too complex. It's hard to create an experiment for more complex treatments like having a physical trainer or using Facebook.

For instance, in Chapter 6 on A/B testing, we discussed the case of a health coach to help an individual quit smoking. If the health coach interacts with a person often and in varying ways, it's very difficult to ascertain which parts of treatment are causing the effect. We might need to run hundreds, and maybe thousands, of A/B tests to really pin down which health coach behaviors cause users to quit. For many organizations, running thousands of A/B tests is impractical. Observational data may help guide us toward what health coach behaviors are the most likely to cause users to change their behavior. A good technique that can be used in this case is statistical matching (discussed in Chapter 12) to limit the number of potential mechanisms to test.

Another type of phenomenon that cannot be easily tested is treatments that are not easily randomized, because of how or when they occur or because they involve harmful impacts to the user. For instance, we cannot ask half our participants to start smoking. It's impossible to use a traditional split test to estimate the effect of smoking on lung cancer for this reason.

More complex social phenomena are difficult to test because there is no comparable counterfactual and we cannot build one. We can't create the same household with smokers and nonsmokers, so no perfect counterfactual exists.

Another example is user motivation; it's impossible to randomly assign motivation to users. Demographic factors also fall into this category. Suppose we want to consider the effect of marriage on a user's purchase of photo albums. We think married couples purchase more of these products, but we cannot assign marriage randomly to some couples and not others. With demographic factors, it might be best to look at the effects of factors by subgroup—that is, the effect of a treatment on married users and then the effect of a treatment on unmarried users.

Another example of phenomena that we cannot easily A/B test are phenomena with very small sample sizes. A political example makes this point extremely clearly. Suppose we were interested in theorizing what would be the effect on defense policy if Hillary Clinton were president instead of Donald Trump. There is no way to test or validate such a theory because there is no comparable counterfactual. The best we might be able to do is compare the U.S. election to that in another country where we assume a Hillary-like candidate won and show the effect on defense policy. This argument will likely fall apart because another country might differ from the United States in many ways that may affect defense policy. For instance, it will not be the world's primary superpower.

With broad social phenomenon, we can never fully understand all the causal factors, but the goal is to at least understand the main factors. With some phenomena, such as the U.S. presidency, for which there's very little comparability, we might not be able to infer very much at all with traditional statistical methods. There may be other qualitative tools that we could use to guess what would happen. For example, we could identify the structural limits to the job. What is the president allowed to do and what are current norms for presidents around defense policy? We could also ask political pundits or Hillary Clinton's friends what she might do in that position. They may be able to make educated guesses at what she would do as president, but we will never be able to validate those guesses. Hillary Clinton herself probably cannot imagine or know exactly what she would do in conflict situations that might arise.

10.3.2   Historical Action

Often, we are interested in using historical data to validate our inferences. Many companies have only recently set up an A/B testing framework. In this case, you're left with only observational data.

10.3.3   No Infrastructure

Building an A/B testing infrastructure is often expensive and takes political will, so many organizations do not have the capability to test most user behavior. This leaves you with the same problems as cited earlier: You're stuck trying to infer from observational data.

Now, that we have reviewed some of the situations when A/B testing does not work, we can discuss some of the potential tools we have at our disposal to infer causation in these situations.

When we do not have actual experiments, we can often find sort-of experiments, or natural situations that are similar to experimental setups. Similar to the case with experiments *design* is extremely important with sort-of experiments, because internal validity drives the results. Recall that internal validity is how well an experimental or model design can rule out alternative explanations for its findings.

In the next section, we'll discuss some of the situations when natural experiments or sort-of experimental designs might be appropriate. Then, we'll discuss some of the most popular designs in the context of a web product.

10.4   Nuts and Bolts of Causal Inference from Real-World Data

This section includes the nuts and bolts of causal inference in practice. We will refer to the terms presented here throughout the rest of this chapter and in the next three chapters of the book.

10.4.1   Causal Inference Terminology

We'll discuss treatment effects in the next few chapters. Treatment effects in the context of observational data are analogous to the "causal effect" of a variable on an outcome. The use of the *treatment effects* terminology is a legacy of the statistical tradition from which these methods originate. Many of these methods were developed to "look and feel" like experimental results, as experiments are the gold standard of causal inference.

The causal framework in the observational case is more complex than just one estimate of the "treatment" or "causal" effect, because we often have to use statistical methods to reproduce the counterfactual or control group. This framework is bulky, but we promise that if you put the work in to understand the basics, it will make the rest of this section much easier to digest.

The following are a few important terms/concepts to define before we explore these techniques:

- **Average treatment effect on the treated (ATT):** This is the expected treatment effect on those who experienced the treatment. One can think of this as the effect of treatment on the population that looks like the treated group.

- **Average treatment effect on the controls (ATC):** This is the expected treatment effect on those in the control group. One can think of this as the effect of treatment on the population that looks like the controls.

- **Average treatment effect (ATE):** This is the treatment effect on the full population, both treated and controls. It is analogous to the causal or treatment effect from an experiment or A/B test.

In an A/B test or experiment, we have just one focus, the ATE. That's because we have valid controls that we can compare to our treated population. However, when trying to infer causation from observational data, we need more concepts because the treatment and control groups might belong to entirely different subgroups.

The ATT is one such concept. The underlying need for the ATT is based on the fact that treated and control groups in observational data could be very different because of selection bias. We could have highly motivated users in the treatment group versus generally less motivated users in the control group. Then, it would be like comparing oranges to tangerines. The ATT helps us with this. We want to know the treatment effect for people who look like the treated members. We calculate this by estimating the difference between the treated users and those controls who look like the treated users. In this example, we seek out a similar proportion of highly motivated members of the control group to compare to highly motivated members of the treated group. The ATC is the treatment effect for the control group based on the treated group members who look like the controls.

The ATT and ATC are not easily understood concepts, so let's explore another example. For instance, we can generally assume that men are more likely to "like" a woman's picture than the converse. Your treatment is having your profile picture "liked." Our control group is 50% female, while our treated group is 20% female. Are we going to have a problem here?

As we explained earlier, this would be a case where our ATT and ATC would likely be different. Our ATC is likely to be lower than our ATT just based on the demographic composition of the groups. We also need to decide if we are interested in the ATT, ATC, or ATE. If we are only interested in users who look like the treated group, then we'd be interested in the ATT. If we are interested in the general population, we probably want to calculate the ATE. We'll use these concepts intermittently in the next few sections. For more on these concepts, see *Matched Sampling for Causal Effects* by Donald Rubin (2006).

The next section discusses how to find natural experiments that are useful for inferring causality in a web product.

10.4.2   Natural Experiments

Now that we understand the core concepts of causal inference from observational data, we can explore situations where experimental conditions occur in the real world. Natural experiments are where we try to operationalize real-world randomness to find the causal effects of a factor on an outcome of interest. We'll explore techniques to analyze natural experiments in the rest of this chapter.

10.4.2.1   Assumptions of a Natural Experiment

The core assumption of a natural experiment is the as-if random assumption. In web analytics, another assumption is also needed to procure good results, the early-behavior assumption:

- **As-if random assumption:** A process is randomly placing users in the treatment and control groups. It's analogous to an A/B test randomly assigning members to one group or another. This allows us to use randomization to infer the effects of a treatment.

- **Early-behavior assumption:** Randomization must happen early in the user funnel. As described in Chapter 5, the user funnel is the series of events starting from the beginning of a user session or user onboarding. If randomization happens too late in the user funnel, it can lead to a small group that is poorly selected for inference. While the validity inside the experiment would hold, it would be hard to draw inferences for the general product. This assumption allows us to make valid causal inferences over the largest product population possible.

As noted early, it's important for causal inference to rely on a *valid counterfactual*. A counterfactual is a situation in which the treatment condition did not occur, but everything else is the same. For instance, in a medical trial, it would be giving a participant a placebo instead of the treatment pill. When we look for natural experiments, we are essentially trying to find a valid counterfactual or group of people who received the placebo. This means that we will need randomization.

As noted in Chapter 6, Ronald Fisher, the father of modern statistics, described randomization as "the reasoned basis for inference." How do we find randomization in real life? We need to find some mechanism or phenomenon that randomly divides users into groups.

Here the counterfactual stems from random sorting that occurs in the real world, essentially mimicking the creation of treatment and control groups. This random assignment is the key to making a natural experiment work and the first assumption. You might think randomness almost never happens in the real world. While this is generally true, there are some very nice cases that we can find and take advantage of.

The second assumption is that the process occurs early enough in the user funnel. If it happens too late in the user funnel, the external validity decreases tremendously and the prescriptive power of the results declines with it. For instance, if we have a very small group of preselected users who experience the treatment, we might estimate a causal effect of an outcome for them. We may never be able to make it actionable, since we cannot re-create that group or its beliefs from the results for the rest of the user population.

Next, let's look at an example involving as-if random design to assess its validity—in this case, a famous social science example. Researchers wanted to understand the causal effect on women's earnings of the addition of a child to a family. The problem is that the decision to have a child is not random, so having a child in and of itself cannot be used as a natural experiment to infer the effect on earnings of having a child.

However, having a third child might have an element of randomness. Many parents want to have at least one boy and one girl, so families who have two children of one gender are more likely to have a third child. They assume that the gender of the first and second children is random. The treatment group defined in the example comprises individuals who had a third child after having two children of the same gender, and the control group consists of users who had no third child after having two children of different genders. If this is truly random, then it would be a great as-if random design.

First, let's recap what we know so far: The variable that we are interested in having an *additional* (read third) child and our outcome variable is future earnings for women. We're looking for a randomization mechanism and we're assuming it's the gender of the second child (randomly male or female).

How do we assess if this is a good design? We need to compare it to our core assumptions. This could be a poor selection of an as-if random mechanism for the following two reasons:

- **Breaking as-if random assumption:** Having a third child is *not* solely determined by the sex of the second child; there are other nonrandom factors involved. For instance, we can make an assumption that more educated parents are less likely to have a third child regardless of the child's sex. In this case, parents' education could have an effect on the mother's earnings. In fact, it probably does, meaning that this would fail to produce a valid experiment. There are ways around this problem, potentially by using instrumental variables. We'll discuss this more in the Instrumental Variables sidebar later in this chapter.

- **Breaking the early-behavior assumption:** We will assume that the first as-if random assumption holds. Even if that is the case, another problem you face is how much selection occurred prior to the event. For instance, suppose we're interested in the general insights about women. It is a known fact that only 40% of the population has two or more children. Since we are looking at the effect of a third child on earnings, our analysis would apply only to those women who had 2 or more children, or about 40% of the female population of reproductive age. It's important to note that it's not a random 40% of the population. Rather, we actually have selection, meaning that women who might value their careers highly are more likely to not have children or have one child. Women who value their careers more are also more likely to have higher earnings. By progressing to higher numbers of children, we're applying our analysis to fewer and fewer women and we're probably missing major causal factors early in the funnel. Our analysis would not be wrong, but it would apply to just a small subsection of women who would not be representative of the general population.

10.4.2.2 Examples of Natural Experiments

Let's explore a few more examples to help clarify this idea. Here are some fun examples from academic papers:

- **Natural disaster on political stability:** The design in this case includes an earthquake. The as-if random assumption is that an earthquake is random, so if we compare similar regions, one with an earthquake and one without, it would lead to inference about the effects of earthquakes on, say, political stability. (See Omelicheva's [2011] paper, "Natural Disasters: Triggers of Political Instability?")

- **Miscarriage and teen pregnancy:** The design for this pseudo-experiment involves miscarriage. The assumption is that having a miscarriage is a biological phenomenon and in most cases is random in young mothers. The treatment group is teen mothers who had a baby and the controls are those who had a miscarriage. We could then look at the effects of teen pregnancy on a host of outcomes. (See Ashcraft et al.'s [2013] "The Consequences of Teenage Childbearing.")

Here are some product analytics examples:

- **Marketing campaigns in a designated market area:** Another great example found in the product analytics space is a redrawn boundary, geographic or other. Suppose a region historically received a specialized campaign, but no longer does because the region was redrawn for unrelated reasons. The redrawn boundary could be seen as random. The control group would be users on the edge of the redrawn boundary who no longer receive the treatment. The treatment group would be users on the boundary who continue to receive the same old treatment.

- **Score and progression to a new level:** This is an example in which we have leveling or gated features in which users have to get a certain score to pass—for instance, get less than 50 and they progress versus get more than 50 and they fail to pass. We could look at users who got 49 points and 51 points in terms of retention in the product. We'd assume that the skill level is pretty equal at 49 and 51 points, but randomness helps one group pass and the other group fail. Other attributes are randomly distributed. However, we should be wary if there are other mechanisms for passage, such as all paid users progress regardless of score. (We'll discuss this quasi-experimental design in more depth in Chapter 11 on regression discontinuity.)

Sometimes a better way to understand is to explore the anti-patterns or when the natural experiment framework fails to hold. Here are some bad natural experiment designs from the product analytics space:

- **An extra post in a news feed is random:** The idea is that one extra post, comment, or "like" can be used as a randomizer. For instance, the treatment group could be defined as users who posted pictures three times versus users who posted twice. The number of pictures posted is seen as random. The problem is that there could be selection on a variety of factors other than just one extra post. Users who post an extra item could have more friends, have more "likes," join on a different day, and so on. Since there is a clear behavior in which users are engaging, it's hard to justify that this behavior is indeed random.

- **Cohort analysis:** It's hard to justify that different cohorts are really random. Different people often join products on different days and times. For instance, younger users might join during the afternoon, while users who work during the day might not. When we find selection on demographics, behavior, and other factors, it breaks the as-if random assumption.

10.4.2.3 Analyzing a Natural Experiment

Similar to the process in a regular experiment, in a natural experiment we use our natural random assignment to calculate the effects. *We then calculate the difference in our outcomes for the treatment and controls just as we would do in a real experiment.*

Since we thoroughly explored the A/B testing toolkit in Chapter 6, we will not go over these basic methods in this chapter, but will extend upon them by exploring a difference-in-difference design. Refer to Chapter 6 for an overview of how to calculate the treatment effect, check for statistical significance, and assess the magnitude of the effect size in an experiment.

In addition to the experimental design, we should check whether our as-if random assumption is correct. For our natural experiment to work, we need to show balance (or no selection bias) on our confounding variables, unless we are sure that our assignment is random. Refer to Chapter 12 on statistical matching for information on how to calculate balance.

The next section explores a natural experiment with a difference-in-difference framework. Why can't we just use an A/B testing framework for natural experiments? The reason is that most natural experiments do not have random mechanisms that allow for randomization on the individual level.

In cases where randomization is at the group level, such as with the earthquake and boundary examples, it is best to use a difference-in-difference design. The problem is that post-intervention trends could bias our results over time; it's best to use a difference-in-difference design to correct for these issues.

Instrumental Variables

When you don't have a clear-cut as-if random variable, you can use instrumental variables to determine the ATE. This version of the least squares regression (when the regression model is completed in two stages) is appropriate if a secondary variable is related to the independent variable of interest, but not the dependent variable. In the case of the Angrist example of women's fertility on earnings, the sex of the first two children has an effect on having a third child, but should not have an effect on earnings.

Let's examine the Angrist example of the sex of the first two children as a random instrument in more detail. The problem with using a regression to find a "causal effect" in this case is that earnings can affect having a third child or children can affect earnings, and we are unable to isolate the latter to determine if there is an effect of an additional child on earnings. The instrument in this example is the sex of the first two children. The idea is that women have a third child not because of wanting a third child, but because of randomness regarding the gender of their first two children. The gender of their first two children can be used as an instrument to determine the effect of an additional child on earnings. You can then use an "as-if" random variable as an instrument, including some of the other confounders in the regression to try to mitigate the nonrandom components of the treatment variable.

Two-stage least squares is relatively easy to carry out in practice. Here, we'll go over the process to use instrumental variables in R to estimate the causal effect of a treatment, when you find an instrument, capturing some randomness in the direction that you're interested in. In this case, we're explaining how an additional child affects earnings, not how earnings affect having an additional child. Note that if the treatment was completely random, no instrument would be needed. In this example, if having children was completely random, we would not need an instrument.

We need OLS to estimate the effect of our instrument. We regress our confounders and our instrumental variable on earnings. In this case, our confounders could be women's education, prior earnings, marital status, sex of the first and second children, and more. The instrumental variable would be a dummy variable for the first two children having the same gender. The data set would include only women with two or three children.

To carry this out in R, we get the fitted values from our simple regression model, similarly to how we carried out a regression in Chapter 8. We would run the first regression: regression_object = lm(confounders + instrument). Then we would find the fitted values from the first regression: fitted_values = fitted.values(regression_object).

Finally, we regress those fitted values to get our output: output = lm(confounders+fitted_values). We can then look at the summary of the final output to determine the coefficient on fitted_values. This single coefficient on the fitted_values variable is the estimate of the effect of the treatment.

For a more in-depth exploration of the methodology, including when it fails, see *Introductory Econometrics* by Jeffery Wooldridge (2013).

10.4.3   Operationalizing Geographic Space: Difference-in-Difference Modeling

As we learned in the last section, to employ these techniques we generally need to mimic an experiment. Now, let's cover an application of a natural experiment that is very common. Often in industry we have situations where one group is exposed to treatment, somewhat randomly, and another group is not. In this case, we do not see individual random assignment. We want a method that can remove the permanent differences between the groups. **Difference-in-difference (DID)** will also remove post-treatment biases in the data, like national secular trends that affect both the treatment and control groups.

One case often encountered in industry is marketing campaigns that are launched in two very similar regions, with one randomly getting the treatment, usually a promotional campaign. For example, the campaign could be a TV commercial. It's hard to run a randomized TV campaign. The focus of TV commercials' targeting is often demographic, and it's often difficult to convince organizations to randomize commercials, because they are expensive. However, there could also be peculiarities about how regions are targeted that can be operationalized easily.

We want to explore the effects of a promotional TV campaign in one designated market area (DMA) versus another, but we are unable to randomize the viewers. A DMA is a market or a geographic region that receives the same TV offerings. The counterfactual in this case is that a viewer would be equally likely to live in one DMA as in another.

10.4.3.1 Experimental Example

Individual users essentially randomly chose to live in one DMA over another. For instance, users may be given a random assignment into a subdivision on one side or the other side of the border of a DMA, due to a housing lottery. If this is the case and randomness holds, then we could design this like an experiment (or an as-if random design). Then it's straightforward to assess the efficacy of a campaign. It's the ATT minus the ATC, which equals the ATE. See the example in Table 10.2.

Table 10.2 **Pseudo-Experimental Example**

Treatment	After Commercial	Difference (ATE)
DMA 1 (treated)	4,230 downloads	
DMA 2 (control)	3,548 downloads	
	Treatment effect:	682 downloads (ATE)

Suppose it's not so straightforward to assess the efficacy of a campaign. Obviously, there are reasons that the DMAs are not randomly chosen. Better schools or jobs in a DMA, for instance, might be reasons that two DMAs are not completely equal. If better schools separate two DMAs, this suggests that the treatment and control groups are not the same; that is, selection is occurring. If the groups are substantially different from each other in ways that are relevant to our treatment and outcome, then that may invalidate our design.

10.4.3.2 Difference-in-Difference Assumptions

For DID estimation to work, we need to rely on the following assumptions:

- **Parallel trends:** The two groups show the same general trends. Graphing this is the best approach to show the effects for two both groups pre and post treatment. (See Figure 10.1 for an example.)

- **Composition of groups is stable over time:** The two groups cannot change composition during the experimental period or be subject to any other promotions or events that might explain the difference.

- **No spillover effects:** The causal effect in one DMA cannot affect the other DMA in any way.

- **No other major confounding factor:** All kinds of things can happen that affect user behavior—for example, an ongoing bug that prevents user sign-up, other promotions, and more. Watch out for other potential causal variables that might occur during the same period.

- **Regression assumptions:** We must assume the regression assumptions hold. These assumptions include linearity, random sampling, no multicollinearity, and more. (Refer to Chapter 6 for more details.)

Now, let's consider an example of the DID design (Figure 10.1). Let's say our promotional campaign ran in North and South Dakota and these states are pretty similar in the case of our product sales and for our particular demographic.

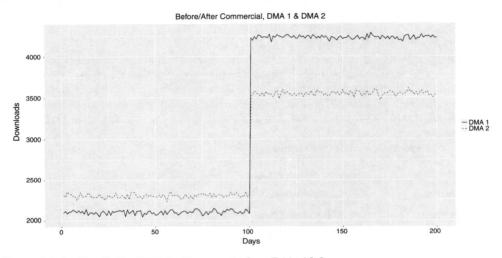

Figure 10.1   Hypothetical DID design example from Table 10.2

10.4.3.3   Difference-in-Difference Modeling

DID relies on linear regression and all the linear regression assumptions hold, as well as the parallel trend assumption that we talked about. However, the ATE can be estimated simply by the average effect on the treated group minus the average effect on the control group. This is analogous to the ordinary least squares (OLS) estimate discussed in Chapter 6.

Table 10.3 provides an example showing the difference-in-difference ATT estimate for the commercial. We cannot find the ATE with this method.

Table 10.3   **DID Table for ATT Calculation**

Treatment	Before Commercial	After Commercial	Difference
DMA 1 (treated)	2,100 downloads	4,230 downloads	2,130
DMA 2 (control)	2,300 downloads	3,548 downloads	1,248
	−200	682	882 (ATT)

10.4.3.4   Estimation with OLS to Get Standard Errors (Retention)

We can use a regression (OLS) to find out if the ATT for the DID model is statistically significant. If the effect is statistically significant, that suggests it's substantially larger than would likely occur due to random chance.

We went over linear regression in Chapter 8. The y variable is downloads, similar to the example in the last section. This is the setup for the linear regression where we add in variables for time, treatment, and their interaction. Both treatment and time are dummy variables for whether an observation is in the treatment or control group and whether it's pre or post treatment. Note that these variables do not rely on the unit of time. In Chapter 16, Listing 16.1, we implement this DID model in R.

$$y = \text{inter} + b1*\text{time} + b2*\text{treatment} + b3*(\text{time} * \text{treatment}) + \varepsilon$$

Here, inter is the intercept; $b1$ and $b2$ are the coefficients on treatment and time, respectively; $b3$ is the ATT estimate from Table 10.3; and treated:time is the interaction or treatment variable. We can use the t statistic to tell if significant.

Table 10.4 shows the regression output from R. We cover this in Chapter 16 R Listing 16.2.

Table 10.4   **Difference-in-Difference Regression Results**

Coefficients	Estimate	Std. Error	t Value	Pr(> $|t|$)
(Intercept)	2,298.95	2.42	949.9	<2e-16 ***
treated	−199.88	3.423	−58.4	<2e-16 ***
time	1,248.413	3.423	364.7	<2e-16 ***
treated:time	882.568	4.841	182.3	<2e-16 ***

10.4.3.5   Interpretation of Regression Results

We can see that in this example the coefficients of the regressions mirror the values calculated in the DID table. The reason that we run a regression is to get the standard errors, t statistic, and p values from the regression results. In this case, every coefficient in this model is significant. We're most interested in the treated:time variable, as this is the estimated ATT, which is the estimate of the causal effect of the commercial on downloads. In this case, the time:treated variable is large (882 downloads) and significant, suggesting a large causal effect of this commercial campaign.

Let's say we see a statistically significant effect. In practice, this means that our estimated ATT from our regression has a p value less than 1%. That does not show that our causal estimate is correct, but it adds credence to our argument that this feature *likely caused the effect*.

The causal estimate in this case is 882 downloads. We can interpret this in the following way: *Our promotion caused 882 more downloads than would have occurred without the promotion*. This is an extremely strong and prescriptive result, it tells us that we should have more promotions: Our campaign was very effective in causing our desired result of more downloads.

Of course, since this is not a real experiment, we can never be 100% sure that the promotion was responsible for the full effect and not some other factor. The reason we can never be sure is because the counterfactual is close, but not exactly the same (as with true randomization). However, in this example, the effect is very large, clear, and likely causal.

If the effect is indeed causal, that relationship is often made very clear with this type of design, or by focusing on key subgroups. It's key to look for subgroups who will be most affected by the treatment, such as users who watch many hours of TV, have multiple TVs in their homes, and the like. If the effect is even more pronounced among these subgroups, then you have a strong case for a causal effect. (We'll discuss this in the next chapter on regression discontinuity designs. We'll also discuss how to remove seasonality from time-series data, which can make the effect more clear and pronounced.)

10.4.3.6   Placebo Testing

Another nice element of a DID design is that we can often further validate our results with a placebo test. We might still want to continue to test other hypotheses. In particular, we might want to run a placebo test. A placebo test is a way to validate a treatment effect by looking at another time or grouping and finding no effect when the treatment was not present. In this example, we could find DMAs over another period or similar DMAs over the same period that were not exposed to our commercial and see if they had similar effects.

Table 10.5 is an example of a placebo test where we look at two different DMAs that had no commercial, but are similar to our original DMAs. We can see that they do not have a significant difference in ATT, as expected. The results lend credence to the argument that the commercial had a significant effect.

Table 10.5   **Placebo Test Example**

Treatment	Before Commercial	After Commercial	Difference
DMA 1 (control)	2,250 downloads	3,535 downloads	1,285
DMA 2 (control)	2,300 downloads	3,548 downloads	1,248
	−50	−13	37 (ATT − DID)

From Table 10.6, the ATT of this placebo test is 37 downloads. The placebo test shows that in the two DMAs that did not air a commercial, the difference is small and that there is no significant causal effect during the treatment time period.

We could also look at the same treatment DMA and control DMA over a another non-treatment time period. If we see similar results, then we can assume that the commercial did indeed cause a huge spike in downloads.

Well-thought-out placebo tests in industry are extremely persuasive regarding the causal effect of your treatment and can lend credence to any DID design. You can find a placebo test for almost any DID design.

10.5   Actionable Insights

In this chapter, here are the actionable insights:

- Design is key for causal inference. Validation comes from design, not from results.

- Finding natural experiments can be an easy way to operationalize observational data.

- These potential experiments exist everywhere; sometimes they do not answer the exact question we are looking to answer, but rather a tangential question that changes the direction or understanding of a web product.

- Difference-in-difference is a powerful tool to remove post-treatment biases in natural experiments or when you have a persuasive counterfactual.

In this chapter, we learned the basics of causal inference from observational data. In the next chapter, we will cover another powerful design technique, known as regression discontinuity (RD), and one very important use-case of RD, interrupted time series.

The next chapter will also cover time-series modeling and seasonality decomposition. Although these are not causal inference methods, they can be very useful tools to model data within causal inference designs.

Finding natural experiments or DID designs is not always easy. Some problems really are not conducive to this framework. In this case, statistical matching is very helpful, as explained in Chapter 12.

In Pursuit of the
Experiment, Continued

In Chapter 10, we discussed the nuts and bolts of causal inference from observational data. We explored examples of natural experiments, where assignment into treatment and control groups occurs due to some natural process. We also went through an application of the difference-in-difference design. A difference-in-difference (DID) design can be used to model both natural experiments and quasi-experiments, which have a counterfactual, as in the designated market area (DMA) example.

Recall that a quasi-experimental design is used when the assignment process is not random. The reality is the vast majority of cases of causal inference from observational data are quasi-experiments, not natural experiments. To make these designs work, the researcher must control assignment into treatment and control groups. The idea of controlling assignment may seem abstract now, but you'll understand what that means after you see the examples in this chapter and Chapter 12.

In this section, we'll discuss a very popular quasi-experimental design technique, regression discontinuity (RD). This approach can be applied in a variety of cases, but adequate testing must be done to substantiate its validity. We will also cover time-series models and seasonality methods to improve estimation for the time-series case of RD, called interrupted time series (ITS).

Causal inference from observational data is difficult, as discussed in Chapter 10. Although causal inference generally takes more effort, it leads to the most prescriptive and *actionable* results. If we can utilize causal inference methods in addition to broader explanatory and predictive methods, we can understand our web product on a much deeper level.

With prediction, we can often throw everything but the kitchen sink at a problem. In contrast, with causal inference, our approach must be much more thoughtful. As described in earlier chapters, prediction can be validated and improved on a post hoc basis with external or test data; causal inference cannot. Causal inference relies on internal validity or the underlying logic of the design to drive the credibility in the results.

With causal inference, we must put on our detective hat, as we are always looking for ways to invalidate our designs. If a design has been invalidated, we can sometimes move to a smaller coverage area (or a smaller population for which there is support in the data, such as focusing on only male users for the dating website "liking" example), but often times we must start over or rethink our initial design. It's also a much more one-off endeavor, which means that as a data scientist, you must have an arsenal or large toolkit of methods that you shuffle through for each specific problem. In addition, you might have to be much more creative in your application or design than with predictive methodologies.

In this chapter, we will cover RD, a quasi-experimental method. In practice, RD is one of the hardest designs to implement correctly. Many situations may initially seem like good candidates for an RD design, but after further evaluation, it becomes obvious they are plagued by selection bias. It's not a one-size-fits-all approach, since we depend on the statistical estimation of the counterfactual, unlike natural experiments and DID methods. We'll discuss these issues throughout the next two sections on RD and ITS.

This chapter is one of the more technically rigorous chapters, as we will use advanced methods to model counterfactuals. If you don't understand the modeling methods, don't let that frighten you away. Unlike many other methods, many RD designs can be invalidated by graphing. In the best RD cases, the causal effect can be found visually. Also, applying high-level modeling methods is uncomplicated in R, and these modeling methods also can be visually invalidated. In the next section, we'll cover RD design and its applications.

11.1 Regression Discontinuity

In Chapter 10, we discussed DID modeling. When we use this approach, we've found a comparable counterfactual or control group to compare to our treated users. In contrast, regression discontinuity relies on a *break* or *level change* in our treatment variable or timing of our treatment variable to assign users to treatment and control.

11.1.1 Nuts and Bolts of RD

Suppose there is an arbitrary cut point or step change in a game or website feature. For instance, a user who gets 50 points within a specific time frame is awarded an enthusiast badge. This might be a good candidate for an RD design.

You will have users on both sides of this cut point—that is, a group of users at 49 points and a group of users at 51 points. Theoretically, these users on either side of the cut point are similar in terms of skill level, motivation, and time in product. The RD design assumes that users on both sides of the cut point are more similar to each other than to the other users in their own respective groups. For instance, a user who gets 75 points is substantially different from a user who gets 51 points, even though both received a badge. Similarly, a user with 20 points is a lot different from a user with 49 points, even though both do not progress to the next level.

The RD design finds the **local average treatment effects (LATE)**. We've already seen the ATE and the ATT. LATE is the average treatment effect defined in a local area of variation. Here the local area is defined around the cut point.

11.1.2 Potential RD Designs

Regression discontinuity exploits breaks in the treatment variable. Let's explore some potential examples to get a better understanding of where RD is best applied. Here are some non-web analytics examples of potential RD designs:

- The effect of a scholarship program on future earnings. Scholarships are given to participants who score an 80 or higher on a national standardized test. We assume getting a score of 79 or 80 is essentially random. Here the treatment is receiving the scholarship. The control group are students who score 79 and the treatment group are students who score 80. *The design can be invalidated if richer students with higher social status or with certain instructors are more likely to get an 80 than a 79, suggesting that there is selection at the cut point.*

- The effect of winning a U.S. House of Representatives election on personal wealth. The assumption here is that the winners of close elections are random. Thus, we can access the effect of winning a U.S. House seat by comparing personal wealth of near winners and losers. *This design would be invalidated if there was selection in terms of who won, based on other factors such as personal wealth, meaning that richer candidates were more likely to win in close elections than are poorer candidates.*

These examples are great candidates for RD, although they are not guaranteed to work. For instance, the elections example might ultimately fail because richer candidates and incumbents are able to squeeze out a win more often than not. Selection on wealth and incumbency means that the assumption of randomness at the cut point (i.e., who wins and loses election) is errone-ous, invalidating the design. This was found in practice by Caughey and Sekhon (2001).

Nevertheless, RD is better than many other modeling methods, because clustering or density at the cut point can be plotted and observed. We'll see examples of this in later sections. RD can also be invalidated quickly and easily, unlike pure modeling approaches.

11.1.3 The Enemy of the Good: Nonrandom Selection at the Cut Point

Now that we've seen some examples of successful and unsuccessful RD designs, let's consider the core assumption that is required for RD to work. The primary assumption is random selection at the cut point. In our game example, we assumed that users who progressed right at the cut point did so randomly. Those users who progressed could easily have not progressed; likewise, those users who did not progress could easily have progressed.

The users right at the cut point who did not progress become the control group for the users who did progress. We can then compare two groups to find the effect of progressing on product retention. The defined cut point, score, and treatment make this a *sharp* regression discontinuity design. There is also a *fuzzy* RD design that involves a gradual change; it is not discussed in this book, but can be explored in reference readings.

Similar to the other quasi-experimental designs, selection bias can invalidate this design. For instance, suppose that users who progressed were more likely to have been in the product for a few days, rather than it being their first day. They were also more likely to have friends in the product than the users who did not progress. If this is the case—that is, there is nonrandom selection at the cut point—then our estimated "causal" effect of gaining a badge is not valid. We cannot rule out that it is a spurious relationship, where, for instance, having more friends is driving gaining a badge and retention.

Our estimate could be measuring the slight advantages that helped certain users progress to higher levels, instead of our desired causal variable, "gaining a badge." Selection at the cut point breaks the randomness assumption. It means that the assumption that the users who progressed were similar to those who did not *fails*. We might be able to model the effects of confounders by adding them into our model estimator, but generally if there is one confounder, there's likely to be many confounders—and there might be no support for controlling for these confounders.

Let's explore this idea in a little more detail. To remove the effect of confounders, we theoretically need to find users in the treatment group who look like users in the control group. However, if there are one or more confounders, all users with a particular confounder may be found in the treatment group and not in the control group. For instance, suppose all users with friends in the product progress to 51 points, and there is no support for any users with friends in the 45–49 interval. We then cannot estimate the "causal" effect on the full population; that is, we might be able to estimate the effect only for users with no friends.

To model out confounders, we need to understand where the selection is occurring, have support in both the treatment and control groups, and properly model the selection. We might just need to drop observations where support in the treatment or control group is lacking.

Selection is a problem with all quasi-experimental designs and often drives "causal" effects, especially if they are particularly large. Selection at the cut point is actually very common in practice. Unfortunately, the more important (i.e., the larger) the causal effect, the more selection you'll likely see. The reason is that the more important this factor is for positive outcomes, the more users will try to "game the system," so to speak, making those who get a badge less and less random.

For instance, suppose we offered a $1,000 reward to everyone who progresses. You'd see some strong selection at the cut point. People would talk to one another in an effort to improve their game play, leading to selection. Generally, where regression discontinuity is most useful, it's also most likely to be wrong. The one exception is with time as the discontinuity variable. We'll discuss this special case when we consider interrupted time series. RD can require some advanced, or one-off, modeling techniques to estimate the LATE, but has some advantages over the DID design. In particular, it is easily observable, if data is plotted correctly, when RD's core assumptions fail.

11.1.4 RD Complexities

Three complexities arise with the RD design:

- Selection at the cut point

- RD is only defined in the limit

- "Clumpiness" in the data around the cut point

Generally, if you can handle these three issues, then the RD design is valid.

First, the difficulty with arbitrary human cut points is that there is often selection at the cut point. For instance, in two very popular examples of RD design, researchers have found rampant selection at the "random" cut points in both scholarships and elections. For instance, higher-income students and candidates with more campaign contributions are more likely to get scholarships and win elections, respectively. This is a *huge* problem. The benefit here is that it can be observable by plotting close to the cut point for all confounding variables.

The second complexity is that RD is only defined in the limit. If you remember back to your high school calculus class, the limit is the value that a function approaches as it gets closer and closer to some point, here the cut point. In our example, the arbitrary cut point is 50. It's only defined in extremely close increments from 50. However in practice, only 51 and 49 are defined, while 49.999999999 is undefined and no user can take this value. We then face the problem of how large the control group (left of the cut point) and the treatment group (right of the cut point) should be. How much data do we have close to the cut point? Is a player who scored 48 or 52 really still comparable? How about 45 and 55? We can do robustness checks and vary our sample sizes to see how much those changes affect the estimate. However, if the results strongly differ, which they theoretically should, we need to ask ourselves if there is enough coverage at the cut point.

The third problem is how to model "clumpiness" near the cut points. If different types of models get different estimates for the pre-treatment and post-treatment values, what model should we use? We'll see an example related to this issue in the next section, and suggest how to estimate the effect. Is there a true effect or is there rampant selection? Clumpiness at the cut point could also be a sign of selection. [You can test for clumpiness attributable to selection. While beyond the scope of this book, check out the McCrary density test described by McCrary (2008) and implemented in the R package 'rdd'. The idea here is that if there is no selection, there should be not be irregular clumpiness on either side of the cut point and both sides of the cut point should be proportionally similar.]

11.1.5   Graphing the Data

With RD, there's a simple rule: When in doubt, graph. How do we graph RD? The x-axis is the treatment variable, and we should focus on the area around the cut point. The y-axis is our outcome or confounder variables, which have occurred prior to treatment. Often with RD designs, the effect or selection in the data becomes visible by just graphing the data.

Graph the data closest to the cut point, because that is where RD is defined. Even if your assumptions may hold away from the cut point, that is largely irrelevant in an RD design. RD designs have been invalidated because of selection very close to the cut point. Even if a few, well-connected users are being selected for, that will invalidate your design.

When we have adequately accounted for these problems in the design, RD can be a useful tool. It is best applied when an arbitrary cut point is not well known by the players, so that no strategies or selection problems occur at the cut point. Now, we'll discuss a numeric regression discontinuity example.

11.2   Estimating the Causal Effect of Gaining a Badge

Let's say we create a badge for snowmobile enthusiasts who reach 50 points in the first day. Snowmobile enthusiasts can achieve a badge for doing a myriad of things like reviewing snowmobile products, completing their user profile, and signing up for our newsletter. There is no clear way of finding your points as a new user. You're given the badge if you reach 50 points on the first day. Otherwise, you do not receive the badge.

We want to find the effect on retention of gaining a snowmobile "enthusiast" badge. The "enthusiast" badge has a nice design and can be added to a user's profile page or flair when reviewing. It can affect how users feel about themselves and how other users view them. The hypothesis is that gaining this enthusiast badge leads to greater user retention in our product.

We decided to test this with an RD design. To ensure the validity of this design, we need to address the following issues:

1. Does this design meet the requirements of a RD design (i.e., cut point in treatment variable, hypothetical randomness)? **Check.**

2. Figure out how large a group we need or is sufficient for the treatment and control.

3. Create a model to estimate the y-value from either direction at the limit.

4. Check selection on other variables.

The data has five variables: user_retention (days), score at end of first day, profile_description_length (characters), user_friends (count), and viewed_pages. Note that all the variables, except user days, are all defined at the end of the first day.

In Figure 11.1, user score is plotted against user days in product, which is our core retention metric. The cut point is at 50, as discussed earlier. In this case, it's not particularly visually clear that there is an effect at the cut point. There does seem to be a difference in the estimates from the linear model as we get closer to the cut point. As we discussed, RD is only defined in the limit, so the closer we get to the cut point, the better the design. This graph is implemented in R in Listing 16.3.

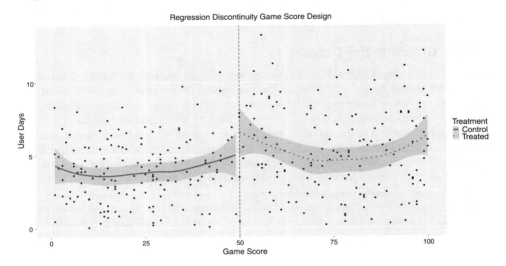

Figure 11.1 RD plot of the enthusiast badge example.

11.2.1 Comparing Models

In this section, we'll apply three models (really six models, since we need to apply the model from both sides) to the data to try to estimate the "causal" effect of gaining a badge on user days in product. The three models are plotted in Figure 11.2. We implement this in R in Listing 16.3 in Chapter 16.

First, we plot our data with user score on the x-axis and user days on the y-axis. Our outcome variable is user days. We need to estimate the user days, given a score of 50, using the data from both the right and the left.

The first model is an OLS model. We estimate the "causal" effect by estimating two regression models from the right and left sides at the cut point and subtracting the difference of the right model from the left model. The right model estimate at 50 minus the left model estimate at 50 is our LATE. Note that these models have only one x variable; that is, we're not including any confounders. (Listings 16.2 and 16.3 go through graphing and RD models in R.)

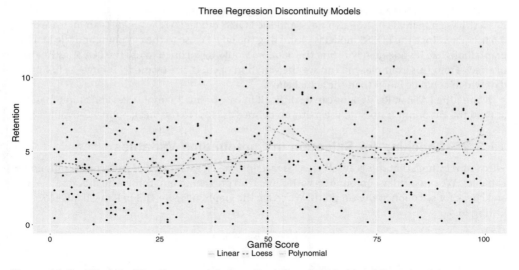

Figure 11.2 RD plot of the three models from the left and right side of the cut point.

The second modeling type is a quadratic model. We will fit a quadratic model to the right and left sides. For reference, the quadratic fit is based on the quadratic equation, $y = ax^2 + bx + c$.

Finally, we'll apply a localized regression model or a LOESS (locally estimated polynomial smoothing) model. LOESS is a localized estimator, meaning that we estimate using values within a small range (i.e., the bandwidth), rather than using the full data set as with the normal linear regression. We also weight the points closest more highly, compared to those located farther away. The modeler must set the bandwidth, which is the fraction of the data used to build the model. LOESS, then, fits a low-degree polynomial, generally either linear or quadratic, locally. If you're interested in a more technical explanation of these methods, check out Hastie et al.'s (2009) *The Elements of Statistical Learning*.

Generally, LOESS or some type of localized model will provide better estimates, since it's defined close to the cut point, compared to models over the full range for RD. Be wary of just modeling noise at the cut point as well. In cases of a low number of observations or very high outlier observations, this can radically drive up or down estimates at the cut point.

We find that the three models have different estimates of the LATE. We get the LATE by subtracting the left-hand model at $x = 50$ from the right-hand model estimate at $x = 500$ (Table 11.1). To see how this is estimated in R, see Listing 16.3.

Table 11.1 **RD-Estimated LATE for OLS, Quadratic, and LOESS Models**

	Left Estimate 50	Right Estimate 50	LATE Estimate
OLS model	4.46 user days	5.44 user days	0.98 user day
Quadratic model	5.07 user days	6.72 user days	1.65 user days
Loess model	5.17 user days	5.75 user days	0.58 user day

The OLS model has a LATE estimate of 1 user day increase in retention. The quadratic model LATE shows an increase of 1.65 user days, and the LOESS model LATE estimate is an increase of 0.6 user day. Since the LOESS model is estimating the effect close to the cut point and the LOESS graph looks like it's adequately fitting the data, we would be inclined to use the LOESS estimates of effect. From this example, you can see the variation of effect size by model is large—a full user day, which could be larger than the actual effect.

Estimating LATE in RD designs can be difficult in case of small sample sizes and clumpiness around the cut point. It's best to use methods defined as close to the break point as possible.

11.2.2 Checking for Selection in Confounding Variables

We cannot assume that this "causal" effect is real until we check for similar patterns in confounder variables. We can overlay confounders with those who progressed and those who did not, and check for selection at the cut point. We create the graph in Figure 11.3 in R in Chapter 16, Listing 16.4.

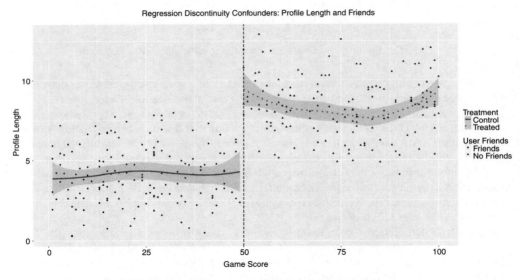

Figure 11.3   Confounder variables (user friends and length of profile).

In Figure 11.3, we can see that there is selection at the cut point in our confounder, length of profile, because there is a huge jump in our estimates at the cut point. Assuming we have completed our profile before we "gain" the badge, this means we are selecting users who have longer profiles and that "getting the badge" is, in fact, not random at the cut point. This would invalidate our design. Basically, users with longer profile descriptions also seem to have a discontinuity with game score. The discontinuity in this graph means that there is selection of users based on other variables into the enthusiasts' badge.

We can also overlay this plot and see selection with user friends: There is clumpiness of user friends on the left side compared to very few user friends on the right side. Thus, users with more friends are getting the badge, so once again there is nonrandom selection at the cut point.

An alternative hypothesis for the treatment effect could be that users with friends are more engaged in the product and likely to be retained longer, such that the enthusiast badge has no causal effect. At this point, we cannot differentiate between our original hypothesis and this alternative.

We might be able to drop all users with friends and see if this discontinuity at the cut point persists. If it does not, then we could try to estimate the effects on just that subpopulation. In this case, this approach is unlikely to work, as there seems to be a jump in the profile length variable as well.

Here are some tips when working through an RD design to improve "believability" of the results:

- *Compare a variety of models and sizes of treatment and control group.* What's the right model and the right sizes of groups? No one knows, and the best choices are data-specific. We can compare different types of models and group sizes and see how robust our results are. If we get the same effect sizes with different types of models and treatment and control group sizes, then the effect size is likely to be correct. In such a case, we need to check that it's not being driven by selection.

- *Check all potential confounder variables.* It is essential to check all confounding variables. If there is at least one confounding variable, the design becomes much harder to believe. We might be able to create a model with the confounder included (if it's relatively unimportant). In the regression example, for instance, we could add the confounder as the covariate. However, do not be lulled into a false sense of security. This could signal a much larger problem:

  - Selection at the cut point might actually signify core problems with the randomness assumption. Many RD designs do have confounding at the cut point on many variables because randomness does not exist. For instance, a popular RD design was to look at the effect of winning elections on policy outcomes. It was theorized that close elections were random. However, there was selection on key variables such as campaign donations and incumbency, meaning that candidates who had more money were more likely to get 50.0001% of the vote than 49.9999% of the vote. It could be impossible to control for campaign donations and incumbency advantage, and those two factors could be the driving force behind all policy outcomes you are looking at as an outcome variable. The close election example in majoritarian elections in the United States fails for this reason.

  - No coverage might signal a lack of support in the data, which means you'll have to look for a smaller subpopulation to consider. Lack of support means that selection is occurring at the cut point, leaving no users of a certain type in the control group and creating an unrepresentative or unbalanced treatment group. For instance, in our earlier example, perhaps users with friends are all progressing. A practitioner might even want to try statistical matching (described in Chapter 12) over RD. RD sometimes buries the selection issues because many practitioners do not adequately explore all the potential confounders and that step is not mandatory for carrying out the design. In many RD designs, there *are* confounding variables.

11.3   Interrupted Time Series

Interrupted time series (ITS) is a special case of RD design, where the break or level change is in the time variable. We can use time-series modeling techniques to model the data at the discontinuity. Time series discontinuities are some of the most believable RD designs in practice, so we'll cover this special case here. ITS relies on a break in time to operationalize the statistical estimate of the pre-treatment trend line. Let's unpack this a little more.

Suppose we have an intervention or some kind of treatment that varies by time. We can estimate the pre-intervention trend in the post-treatment period (control group) and compare that with the actual post-treatment data (treatment group). That's the core idea behind ITS.

Just as with DID estimation, we need clear pre- and post-treatment periods. That is, we need to know when treatment was implemented. In the example depicted in Figure 11.4, a promotional campaign offers a 20% discount on downloading a streaming game starting June 1, 2019. The pre-treatment period is the 50 days before May 31. We can use this pre-treatment period to estimate the trend in the post-treatment period of 50 days after June 1. Since this is a time-series example, we'll use the total profit in millions.

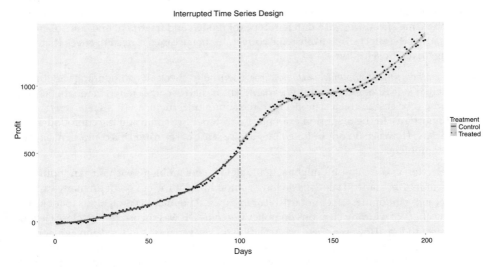

Figure 11.4   Interrupted time series design for downloads over time.

Since we're estimating the trend, rather than relying on the actual trend, we need to make some decisions about how to model it. First, we need to think about how the intervention will affect the outcome, or how a promotional campaign will affect profit. Is the effect gradual or an immediate step change? In this example, let's assume that we have both an immediate step change as the price immediately changes and a gradual change as the information about the promotion diffuses through the population.

In this section, we'll go over a number of different ways to model an ITS design. First, we'll examine a simple regression model; then, we'll apply time-series modeling methods to estimate

LATE. Before we apply time-series methods, we'll provide a brief introduction to major concepts and modeling techniques in time series.

11.3.1 Simple Regression Analysis

The easiest way to model the interrupted time series is with regression with dummy variables. Specifically, we can model ITS in the same way as we did with the DID design. The following is the regression equation that we will model:

$$y = \text{inter} + b1*\text{time} + b2*\text{treatment} + b3*(\text{time since treatment}) + \varepsilon$$

The outcome variable is profit, so we'll use an OLS regression. Note that we can fit this with other models. For instance, if the outcome was a count, such as number of downloads daily, we'd use a Poisson regression. If it's a binary outcome, we'd use a logistic regression.

The *time* variable is the time elapsed since the start of the study by unit of frequency—daily, in this case. The *treatment* is a dummy for the pre- or post-intervention period. The *time since treatment* is the days elapsed since treatment. The treatment effect (ATT) estimate is 269 downloads, which is a significant change (Table 11.2). We calculate this table in R Listing 16.5.

Table 11.2 **Summary of the ITS OLS Regression Results**

	Estimate	Std. error	z value	Pr(> |z|)
(Intercept)	–85.3292	10.4486	–8.167	3.82e-14 ***
treatment	270.1814	14.5952	18.512	< 2e-16 ***
time	4.7806	0.1814	26.35	< 2e-16 ***
timetx	1.2482	0.2528	4.937	1.69e-06 ***

Signif. codes: 0 '***' 0.001 '**' 0.01 '*' 0.05 '.' 0.1 ' ' 1

Residual standard error: 51.59 on 196 degrees of freedom

Multiple R-squared: 0.9864, Adjusted R-squared: 0.9862

F-statistic: 4737 on 3 and 196 DF, p-value: < 2.2e-16

In Figure 11.4, we can see nonlinearity and seasonality. Thus, in this case, a regression model would not lead to the best fit. When we plot the regression model overlaid with our data, we can see that it is a poor fit for the data. (Try this for yourself in the R section in Chapter 16 Listing 16.5.) We need to find a better model that will take into account some of the nonlinearity and seasonality, so that our model produces better elements.

A regression model is not well suited for ITS when the following conditions appear:

- Seasonality: Period variation that occurs in fixed intervals

- Time-varying confounders: Selection bias of other covariates

- Overdispersion: Greater variability in the data than is represented in the model

- Autocorrelation: Correlation between the process and itself in prior periods

In the next section, we'll explore time-series modeling techniques that statistically correct for some of these issues.

A Failed ITS Design: Look at Subpopulations

Sometimes it's very difficult to model the effect on the entire population. Theoretically, certain subpopulations might be affected much more by the treatment. This is generally true with almost all treatments. Just think about a policy change. For instance, raising the minimum wage initially will most strongly affect those workers who earn around the minimum wage or those areas with more workers at the minimum wage.

With ITS designs, we can look at subgroups that will likely have more clearly defined effects. If we find that they do have more clearly defined effects, that lends credence to an otherwise weak design. Be wary of randomly testing subgroups, however. This approach is most credible when the theory includes relevant mechanisms underlying why one group would be more affected by treatment than another group. In our example, we could focus on a subgroup that opened the promotional email.

11.3.2 Time-Series Modeling

Many types of user behavior (such as sales or downloads) occur over periods of time. As we saw in the DID design, we can operationalize time to understand causal effects.

In this section, we'll discuss the time-series modeling approaches for an ITS design. To get there, we'll discuss some basic principles of time series that will help improve our ITS model. Note that we'll discuss time-series concepts only in relation to quasi-experimental design techniques. If you are interested in using time-series modeling, it might be helpful to review the time-series concepts in Shumway and Stoffer's (2006) *Time Series Analysis and Its Applications: With R Examples*.

In the next section, we'll go over two core concepts in time-series analysis: autocorrelation and stationarity.

11.3.2.1 Autocorrelation and Stationarity

When the outcome variable is time, you'll deal with a few unique issues that might not be present in other types of independent variables. One of those issues is auto-correlation.

Autocorrelation

Autocorrelation is serial correlation between the values of the process at different times, as a function of the time lag. As discussed in Chapter 6, correlation is how two variables vary linearly with one another. In layman's terms, autocorrelation is how a set of time-series data varies linearly with itself at different points in time based on a lag of one or more periods. This basically means that prior periods are helping to explain the current data—which is a problem because it breaks common statistical assumptions. Statisticians love to assume that data is random, independent, and identically distributed (iid assumption). Independence refers to the fact that picking one observation does not mean you're more likely to get another, similar observation. Autocorrelation is pernicious because it breaks all these assumptions.

There are two ways to correct for autocorrelation in ITS design: (1) robust standard errors on the OLS estimates or (2) use of a time-series model. The OLS results from Table 11.2 remain approximately the same with robust standard errors. In this example, there are more problems than just autocorrelation, so we'll use a time-series model to fit the data.

Stationarity

The other core concept to understand when modeling time-series data is stationarity. **Stationarity** means that your mean and variance are constant over time. While a nonstationary process can vary greatly in the short run, a stationary process in the long run regresses back to its historical mean and variance. Stationarity is a nice property to see in time-series data, though it's not always present.

Stationarity is especially important for interrupted time series. The reason is rather obvious: It's much easier to identify a discontinuity in the data in a stationary process than in a nonstationary process. To identify a nonstationary process in the data, it generally takes a much longer pre-treatment period than post-treatment period, which may or may or may not be available. This approach may lead to errors as well, since theoretically the RD design is still only defined around the cut point.

Consider the DID modeling example from Chapter 10. In that case, the process was stationary and the effect size was large, so the effect was quite clear to the human eye. Conversely, in many other cases with the nonstationary processes, the effect is much more muffled by noise and an upward or downward trend that's larger than the small effect size. A nonstationary series takes a more experienced hand to correctly model the data, and even then the results may not be believable.

11.3.2.2   ARMA/ARIMA Model

A common approach to dealing with autocorrelation in an ITS design is to use a time-series model like an ARMA/ARIMA model. The ARMA/ARIMA model is a model with two core components: an autoregression (AR) model and a moving average (MA) model.

An autoregression model is a linear regression where we predict series values based on the lagged values of the series itself. In an AR(1) model, we model one period lag. In an AR(2) model, we model two period lags. In the moving average model, we model the future value of the series based on the average of prior values. Thus, an MA(1) model uses one past observation and an MA(2) model uses the average of two past observations. The difference between the ARMA and ARIMA is the "I"—that is, the integrated component indicates that data is replaced with the difference between itself and previous values.

Returning to our sales promotion, we'll apply an ARIMA model to our ITS example. Now, this may not solve all the underlying problems in our data set, but it may help us better fit our data and find the effects of the intervention.

Table 11.3 shows the result of the ARIMA fit with treatment modeled as both a step and a gradual change. In Chapter 16, Listing 16.6, we implement this ARIMA model.

Table 11.3   **Interrupted Time Series with ARIMA Model Fit**

Coefficients	Estimate	Std Error	Pr(> |t|)
ar1	−0.1018	0.3265	0.755
ma1	0.2905	0.3112	0.351
sar1	0.4878	0.0907	0.000***
sma1	0.2804	0.0997	0.000***
Treatment	2.0008	1.3723	0.145
Gradual treatment	−0.267	1.3841	0.847

From this model, we can see that there was not an effect of the treatment; neither the step change was significant, nor the gradual change was statistically significant. The model has a moving average (ma1), autoregression (ar1), and seasonal components (sar1, sma1). When we actually account for the autocorrelation and seasonality, there is not an effect of the intervention.

Modeling any counterfactual is extremely difficult. We'll return to this idea many times in upcoming chapters. Small modeling decisions can lead to large changes in effect sizes and other elements. Many of the models can be extremely sensitive to small changes because real data is highly complex, with annual, daily, and weekly seasonality, cyclic (like business cycle) and noncyclic trends (product growth/death), outliers, and more.

Similarly to the RD example, as data analysts we should try a variety of models and check all potential confounders as robustness checks. We presented an example of this work in the previous section, so we'll skip the confounder validation methods in this section. However, it's extremely important to not omit these steps in practice.

In the next section, we'll cover a very useful business tool—seasonality decomposition. When we want to extract the trendline from time-series data, we can use seasonality decomposition to help remove noise and cyclic patterns.

RD in Broader Context

In this chapter, we learned that the RD design can be a powerful tool for finding localized causal effects. RD is a useful tool for a few reasons. First, we are exploiting randomness in the forcing variable, which means that we do not have to implement an experiment ourselves. Second, RD lends itself to creative application, as there are many types of RD designs and the basic assumption is only a break or level change in the treatment variable. Unlike many other causal inference methods, RD is easily invalidated with a good graphing hand. Graphing RD can show us that selection is occurring at the cut point. It can even show us the confounding variables that are preventing causal inference.

One of the strongest use-cases for RD is the ITS design. ITS has the nice properties of an RD design and the nice aspects of using time as the force or treatment variable. ITS, DID, and other designs that have temporal variables can be improved with a better understanding of time-series modeling.

This chapter has offered another method to derive causal insights from observational data. As described in Chapter 3, causal insights are easily *actionable* and prescriptive, which make them more valuable than other types of insights for altering user behavior.

11.4 Seasonality Decomposition

Seasonality involves known patterns that are repeated over fixed time intervals. Cyclic patterns can occur on different time scales, such as daily, weekly, monthly, and yearly.

Seasonality can bias results in the ITS design in two ways. First, high variation or a period high during the treatment (such as the treatment period that covers Black Friday through Christmas for retailers) can bias results. Second, an autocorrelation effect can occur on top of seasonality, with mean or variance tethered to the prior periods.

In this section, we will not cover how to remove seasonality bias in its models, because of its statistical rigor and narrow applicability. Building a model that removes the effect of seasonality can be achieved with an ARIMA model or done with Fourier terms. Both of these methods are out of the scope of this text. Please refer to Bhaskaran et al. (2013) for more information on how to get seasonality-adjusted estimates.

Now we'll cover regular seasonality decomposition, which is useful in a variety of business contexts. In most cases, simple seasonality decomposition with understanding of the business cycle seasonality is sufficient to adequately assess the validity of these designs. We'll offer only a gentle introduction to seasonality decomposition; you can refer to reference texts for more technical rigor. In Chapter 16, Listing 16.7, we cover seasonality decomposition in R.

Seasonality decomposition is an extremely important technique in practice because almost all purchasing data (i.e., behavioral data) varies by hour, day, week, month, or some other time unit. To examine general time trends, it's often very useful to apply seasonality decomposition. For instance, with our snowmobile website, we may see more traffic and sales on weekends or before or during the Christmas season. We want to understand both how sales vary throughout the year and how the general trend looks over time.

Seasonality should not be confused with a general "cyclic" pattern, which we'll extract separately. Seasonality differs from a cyclic pattern in that it's fixed and occurs for a known period. For instance, the business cycle may lead to a secular trend in your data. There may also be nonrepeating cycles, irregular data, errors, and just general random noise. Seasonality decomposition is one way of trying to model and isolate individual components of data. These modeling techniques are generally relatively simple compared to the true complexity of the data. They provide one way to look at and think about the data. We will discuss their limitations at the end of this section.

In this section, we'll discuss how to extract the seasonal component from time-series data. If we're trying to understand causal relationships in time-series data, seasonality is always a potential confounder.

Seasonality decomposition has four components: (1) seasonal component, (2) cyclic component, (3) trend, and (4) error. Think back to sales of snowmobiles. The seasonal component would be the difference in monthly sales due to peaks in buying before Christmas. The cyclic component could be the business cycle. The trend component would be the actual movement of sales. The error component includes the irregular or outlier purchases made on certain days.

There are two main types of seasonality decomposition, the additive and multiplicative models. The multiplicative model assumes the height and width of fluctuations are proportional to the level or the average value in the series, while the additive model assumes the width and height of these changes are the same over time. Generally, the multiplicative model is more appropriate for user data.

Additive model:

$$Y = \text{Seasonal} + \text{Cyclic} + \text{Trend} + \text{Error}$$

Multiplicative model:

$$Y = \text{Seasonal} * \text{Cyclic} * \text{Trend} * \text{Error}$$

For our data, we'll use the multiplicative model.

Here we'll explain how the multiplicative seasonal decomposition is approximately calculated:

1. **Normalize by Mean**

   We divide all values in the series by the series mean. If the mean is zero, then we do not divide the values.

2. **Moving Averages**

   A core element of time-series models is calculating moving averages. A moving average is the sum of values from prior periods to predict future values. Suppose we had the following eight values: (2, 6, 5, 7, 1, 0, 8, 2). A three-component moving average would be: (NA, NA, NA, 4.34, 6, 4.34, 2.67, 3, 3.34). We're summing the value of the prior three values and dividing by 3 to calculate the moving average component in this example.

3. **Calculating the Trend**

   We calculate a trend based on the moving average. We use an OLS model to predict the outcomes (Y) from the moving average. The outcome is the moving averages and the predicted portion is the trend line.

4. **Calculating the Cycle**

   We calculate the cycle from the moving average divided by the trend.

5. **Calculating Seasonality**

   Then seasonality is the true outcomes (Y) divided by the moving averages. The outcome of this is seasonality plus error. To extract just seasonality, we then average all the same seasonal periods. For a yearly seasonal trend, we might sum up all historical December months to find the seasonal effect for December.

6. **Randomness or Error**

   The error is the residual of the true outcomes divided by the moving averages. We then divide seasonality by this outcome. The remaining value is the error.

Modern algorithms for seasonality decomposition are more complicated than this, but the presentation here gives you a general idea of how seasonality decomposition is calculated.

Let's take the sales data from the ITS in the sales example and break it into four quarters. Figure 11.5 shows the seasonality decomposition for our trend in the ITS example. There are many seasonal decomposition algorithms that are based on the concepts described here. The R function uses a LOESS method to do this seasonal decomposition, which we will discuss in a little more detail in Chapter 16 section 16.2.3.

This chapter introduced concepts in time series such as stationarity, autocorrelation, and seasonality decomposition. In business contexts, seasonality decomposition is extremely useful as there are often strong seasonal trends that make inference difficult.

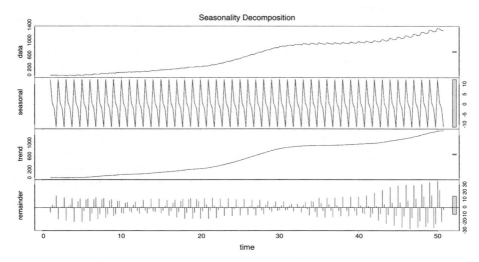

Figure 11.5   Seasonality decomposition.

> **Note**
>
> A final note on temporality and causality: A core aspect of "causality" is temporality. For a process to be causal, generally X must happen before Y. This means that causally related processes might be more likely to be correlated to a lagged version of the Y variable. Note that this could still be a spurious correlation.
>
> We can use the tools in this chapter to check the correlation between the X variables and lags in the Y variable. It adds credibility to a causality argument if a lagged Y by one or two periods is a lot more correlated to X than (1) X is correlated to Y and (2) X is correlated to a greater lagged Y. Chapter 12 describes how to contextualize these results and the other "causal" indicators to look for support for your hypothesis.

11.5   Actionable Insights

In this chapter, here are the actionable insights:

- Design is key for causal inference. Validation comes from design, not from results.

- Regression discontinuity is a design that can be used to operationalize many different types of randomness that occur naturally in web products; it's a creative design technique, rather just relying on a break or level change in the treatment variable.

- Understanding time-series data is key to modeling some of the best RD/natural experiments where treatment is a function of time.

- Seasonality decomposition is an extremely useful technique when working with time-series data.

Causal inference from observational data is vital to developing inference, since many difficult problems do not easily lend themselves to A/B testing. With a little thought, many designs in practice can be used to find causal factors.

Chapter 10 and 11 have demonstrated some of the most useful natural experimental and quasi-experimental designs for causal inference in observational data. The next chapter will cover statistical matching, another quasi-experimental design that's more applicable to all cases, and Hill's causality conditions, which we can use when all quasi-experimental designs fail.

Developing Heuristics in Practice

In the last two chapters, "In Pursuit of the Experiment" we went through natural experiments and quasi-experimental designs. In this chapter, we'll cover another quasi-experimental design technique, statistical matching. We'll also discuss logical tools that can be used to pare down factors to A/B test. Finally, we'll discuss Hill's causality conditions, which we can use when all else fails and we are not able to infer causation by any other means.

This chapter will cover the following topics:

- How to use statistical matching for causal inference

- Using matching as a heuristic

- Hill's causality conditions as a guide to identify causal relationships in practice

- Best practices when it comes to inferring causation in web/mobile products

In this chapter, we'll try to determine causal relationships from observational data, when there is not a clear experimental design. We'll use two techniques: statistical matching and Hill's causality conditions. Statistical matching is a method in which we search the control group for members that look like our treated group, and vice versa. Hill's causality conditions are a set of factors that, when present, make a correlative relationship more likely to be causal.

12.1   Determining Causation from Real-World Data

Suppose you were hired as a data scientist for a health company trying to determine the usefulness of a personal health coach in aiding people to quit smoking in an online support community. The company wants to see if its personalized messages to users are effective in keeping people from smoking. Personalized messages are not sent randomly, and there is no nice quasi-experimental design with personalized messages. If we just assumed that they are causally related to quitting smoking, we might waste a lot of resources finding out if this is indeed the case. We might ramp up the program and invest in lots of health coaches, but then see very little increase in the population that quits smoking and no change in growth or retention rates. Before we make a major investment, we might want to try to discern if the action of sending messages is causally related to helping members quit smoking or some other interesting variable.

What tools do we have in our statistical arsenal? One tool is matching, sometimes called propensity score matching. In **statistical matching**, we search for a control group that looks like our treated group. In the prior example, our treated group received personalized messages. Selection bias occurs when groups are not random—that is, when individuals or circumstances are forcing the creation of unrepresentative groups. These unrepresentative groups are driving differences between the treatment and control groups. Selection bias is the enemy of causal inference, so to estimate causal effects, we must do our best to eliminate this bias in the data.

Statistical matching allows us to correct for selection bias (at least the bias in the variables that we have collected). If we are able to correct for selection bias, we can use matching to make causal assessments such as "variable x is causing a 5% increase in variable y." For instance, suppose we find that messages sent out by health coaches increase quit rates by 5%. That's a huge increase, which can lead to a very prescriptive result: We should hire more health coaches. (Note this is very different from a high correlation. Correlation tells us nothing about whether one factor is driving the other and to what degree.) Causal inference is extremely powerful, as it can lead to clear actionable insights.

In many cases where we cannot correct for selection bias, statistical matching can be used as a heuristic to find causal confounders, or a few variables that could all be "causal" to A/B test. In most cases, we cannot determine which one variable or combination of variables is actually driving the effect from observational data. Usually, we can only A/B test a few factors, but statistical matching can pare down our variables to the most interesting ones to test.

In this chapter, we'll cover statistical matching and logical tools to help us access causal relationships in observational or real-world data. The first part of the chapter will cover statistical matching, and the second part will cover Hill's causality conditions and other heuristics to help with causal inference.

12.2 Statistical Matching

Matching is a process whereby we try to achieve similar distributions on observed variables for treatment and control. In essence, matching tries to correct for selection bias by creating roughly similar-looking populations, based on their attributes (including confounding variables) through selection. Confounding variables are variables that can drive both the variable of interest and the outcome.

12.2.1 Basics of Matching

Statistical matching is a technique to search for a control group in our population that looks like our treated group. What do we mean by "looks like"? Well, in this context, we mean that we are unable to statistically differentiate the two groups on *any* other variable except our treatment variable.

Matching tries to mimic an A/B test, as experimentation is the gold standard of statistical inference, but in a different way from our other quasi-experimental design techniques. Instead of trying to find randomness in the design (which is limited), we attempt to mimic the lack of selection in a real experiment, by selecting users in the control group who look most like our treated users.

The most important concept in statistical matching is balance.

> **Balance**
>
> In this context, balance means that a given variable, which is not the treatment, is statistically nondifferentiable between the treatment and control groups. For instance, we have equal or similar proportions of men and women in the treatment and control groups. Then, we can say we have achieved balance on this variable.

Matching works best when we have a small treated population and a large population of potential controls. We want to search through the control population for those who look most like our treated population. Historically, this was done using logistic regression to determine a propensity score. We'll go through this methodology as well as more modern approaches in the next few sections. Other methods are often computationally intensive, so for large data sets, propensity score matching is used.

12.2.2 What Features "Cause" a User to Buy?

A business owner might want to know what causes a user to make a purchase. The purchase could involve any product or service, such as a cup of coffee at Starbucks. There could be a large number of causal factors, which may include the user's desire for the product, being part of a routine, or an underlying shopping addiction. There could be any number of major and minor factors that cause a user to buy anything from a snowmobile to a cup of coffee on any given day at a particular time.

Since we don't know exactly what causes purchasing, we need to explore a whole host of variables that could be causal. One of the strongest reasons for matching is that we can find our core causal confounders from a large number of variables.

12.2.3 Matching Theory

In this section, we'll go over propensity score matching and will rely on the expertise built in Chapter 8 on logistic regression. Propensity score matching relies on a classification algorithm—in this case, the logistic regression—to assign a treatment score or a probability of being treated. As you may remember, logistic regression takes a binary label and outputs the probability of a class or event as the outcome.

But before we explore propensity score matching, let's clarify a few important concepts in matching. In matching, we are trying to find an optimal or "good" counterfactual group to our treatment group. Basically, we are looking through a control sample that resembles the treated group on features that are often confounders. First, we must determine the treatment and outcome we are interested in. Suppose we take the profile picture example. We want to find the causal effect of uploading a profile picture (or having the user pick an avatar) on retention. We are interested in the causal effect of having a profile picture, not the selection effect of those users who happen to upload or pick a profile picture on retention.

From there, we know our treatment is adding a profile picture and our outcome is retention or the number of days in product. Next, we need to think of confounder variables that might need to be included. Here are some of the potential features:

1. Other onboarding behavior (e.g., progression through the user funnel, completion in a user's first day, and more)

2. Social behavior in product

3. Demographics

4. Motivation

In our simple example, we'll have three variables: gender, completion of onboarding, and motivation level (surveyed). Table 12.1 shows the full data set. In our example, we have 10 users who are given an avatar for a profile picture (treatment group) and 20 who are not (control group). We'll keep the sample sizes in this example small so that we can demonstrate the process of matching.

Table 12.1 **Treated Group**

User	Treatment	Gender	Onboarding Completion	Motivation Level	Income (in thousands)	Retention (in days)
1	1	1	1	High	61	15
2	1	1	1	Medium	50	8
3	1	1	1	High	41	25
4	1	1	1	Low	85	3
5	1	1	0	Medium	120	2
6	1	1	1	Medium	90	45
7	1	0	1	High	50	79
8	1	0	1	High	42	4
9	1	0	0	low	10	8
10	1	0	1	High	180	30

Now let's look at a worksheet of our potential controls to pick from (Table 12.2).

Table 12.2 **Potential Controls**

User	Treatment	Gender	Onboarding Completion	Motivation	Income (in thousands)	Retention (in days)
11	0	1	0	Low	10	1
12	0	1	0	Medium	15	6
13	0	1	1	Low	35	18
14	0	1	1	High	46	45
15	0	1	0	Medium	98	6
16	0	1	1	Medium	60	20
17	0	1	0	High	65	15
18	0	1	1	Low	30	2
19	0	1	0	Medium	92	61

(Continues)

Table 12.2 **(Continued)**

User	Treatment	Gender	Onboarding Completion	Motivation	Income (in thousands)	Retention (in days)
20	0	1	0	Low	40	10
21	0	1	0	Medium	52	3
22	0	1	1	High	63	17
23	0	0	0	Low	15	0
24	0	0	0	Low	19	1
25	0	0	1	Low	81	14
26	0	0	1	Medium	76	57
27	0	0	0	Low	47	12
28	0	0	0	High	255	1
29	0	0	0	Low	12	0
30	0	0	1	Medium	48	10

Can you find specific treated users who look like specific controls in Table 12.3? How do they compare in the aggregate?

Table 12.3 **Summary of the Treated and Control Groups**

	Gender (Proportion)	Onboarding (Proportion)	Motivation (Proportions)	Income (Average)	Retention (Average) Outcome
Treated	Female (60%)	Completed (80%)	High: 50% Medium: 30% Low: 20%	$72,900	20.4 days
Control	Female (60%)	Completed (45%)	High: 20% Medium: 35% Low: 45%	$57,950	14.95 days

From Table 12.3, we can see that there is a balance on gender, meaning equal proportions of men and women in the treatment and control groups. However, for the other variables (i.e., onboarding completion, motivational level, and income), it's clear that there is no balance. We can also see from Figure 12.1 that not just the mean of income is very unbalanced—the full distribution is unbalanced. The controls have lower incomes than the treated users. We might not ever be able to understand how higher-income users are affected, even with matching, because there are no comparable control users.

This is *very* typical. Treatment groups *don't* look like control groups. The treatment group often looks substantially better on these core variables (when we are looking at positive behavior). The problem with treatment and control groups looking different is that we cannot tell if the profile picture or one of the other variables is causing the difference in retention between the two groups.

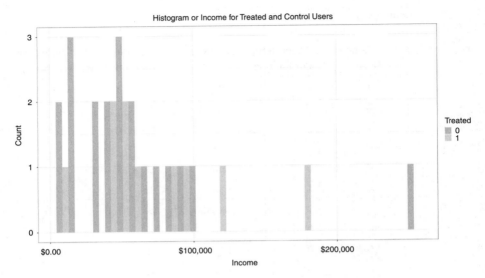

Figure 12.1   Distribution for income.

Now, we know this data is observational and unbalanced, so we can improve upon this with the matching framework. Can we find a control group that looks like our treated group? A number of methods that can find optimal control group are available. We'll investigate two of these methods here:

- Propensity score matching (with and without the caliper method)

- Genetic matching

We won't go too deeply into the mathematics of these methods. If you're interested in learning more about the derivations, see Rubin's (2006) *Matched Sampling for Causal Effects* and the article by Sekhon (2011).

To use propensity score matching, we need to calculate a propensity score. To do this, we need to run a logistic regression with our treatment variable as the outcome variable:

$$\text{treatment} \sim \text{constant} + b1*\text{gender} + b2*\text{onboarding} + b3*\text{motivation}$$

$$+$$

$$1b4*\text{motivation 2} + b5*\text{income\_normalized}$$

We use this regression to calculate the propensity score for individual users. We find control users who have similar propensity scores as our treated users. How do we determine what is similar? We use a **caliper**, the allowed difference in the propensity score between our treated user and our matched control. In this example, we will define the caliper to be less than a 0.25 difference in propensity score. This means that a treated user with a 0.70 propensity score can match with a control user with a propensity score between 0.95 and 0.45. Suppose our closest control user has a 0.44 or a 0.96 propensity score; then this user would have no comparable control and would drop out of our analyzed sample.

We'll come back to the caliper idea later in this section. Figure 12.2 shows the users in the treatment and control groups who perfectly overlap. This is an extreme example, but this often happens in real-world situations. A large number of users fall out because there is no perfectly adequate control or treatment counterpart. In this case, 18 observations fell out. They were basically treated users who looked nothing like the controls, so we cannot find an adequate match. Now that we have whittled down the possibilities, can you find treatment and control potential matches?

Propensity Matching Dataset

User	Treatment	Gender	On-boarding	Motivation	Income	Retention	Propensity Score
1	1	1	1	High	61	15	0.612
3	1	1	1	High	41	25	0.612
4	1	1	1	Low	85	3	0.184
5	1	1	0	Medium	120	2	0.5
7	1	0	1	High	50	79	0.851
8	1	0	1	High	42	4	0.851
10	1	0	1	High	180	30	0.851
12	0	1	0	Medium	15	6	0.5
13	0	1	1	Low	35	18	0.184
14	0	1	1	High	46	45	0.612
18	0	1	1	Low	30	2	0.184
22	0	1	1	High	63	17	0.612
25	0	0	1	Low	81	14	0.448

Figure 12.2   Control group chosen based on propensity score.

Because it radically lowers our sample size to find perfect matches, we must rely on a caliper. Let's find the closest matches for each treated user (with a caliper of 0.25), based on the propensity score model. How do you think they match up? Figure 12.3 shows the potential matches for the treated users.

In Figure 12.3, we can see that using a caliper whittles down the choices, but there is still sometimes more than one "good" match or two or more treated observations matched to only one control. The matching is far from perfect, but will generally do. However, it's good to check what's happening under the hood, because in an extreme case half the treated group could match with only one control. That would not be good, because you would not have coverage to move forward with statistical matching on that subset.

Now, let's check whether the groups are balanced. Just eyeballing it, they look somewhat balanced except for income. We can see that the treated group still has higher income.

Thus, the propensity method definitely helped make the comparison better, but there are still problems of lack of coverage (the treatment and control groups do not look sufficiently alike) and unbalanced variables.

Let's relax these concerns to explain how we would calculate the average treatment effect (ATE). The ATE is the causal effect of the program on retention. We'll even loosen our caliper assumption to pair users with their closest match, even if there is more than a 0.25 difference. Many of the dropped users will be matched to a single user; this is often a problem with non-caliper matching. But let's proceed.

Matching with Propensity Scores

User	Treatment	Gender	On-boarding	Motivation	Income	Retention	Propensity Score
4	1	1	1	Low	85	3	0.184
13	0	1	1	Low	35	18	0.184
18	0	1	1	Low	30	2	0.184
5	1	1	0	Medium	120	2	0.5
12	0	1	0	Medium	15	6	0.5
25	0	0	1	Low	81	14	0.448
1	1	1	1	High	61	15	0.612
3	1	1	1	High	41	25	0.612
14	0	1	1	High	46	45	0.612
22	0	1	1	High	63	17	0.612
7	1	0	1	High	50	79	0.851
8	1	0	1	High	42	4	0.851
10	1	0	1	High	180	30	0.851
22	0	1	1	High	63	17	0.612
14	0	1	1	High	46	45	0.612

Figure 12.3 Potential matches from the propensity score model with a caliper.

Now let's calculate the average treatment effect on the treated population (ATT), the average treatment effect on the control group (ATC), and ATE. We calculate ATT as the retention days of the treated user minus the retention days of the matched control.

Let's calculate ATC where every control user is matched with the closest treated user and we subtract the difference in retention. Then, we subtract the ATT from the ATC to get the ATE. Note that we must use a rule to determine ties so that every user has only one match, since many users might share the same propensity score in both the treatment and control groups. You can determine this based on what makes the most sense for your design.

The ATE for this example is –8.4 days without a caliper. This value is the predicted treatment effect of adding a profile picture or causal effect of adding a profile picture for the sample. The ATE is not statistically significant, meaning that we cannot be sure that this result is not due to random chance. In other words, the treatment could have had no effect in this example.

What about if we calculate ATE with a caliper? We know that the sample size is very small, so take this estimate with a grain of salt. We match with our caliper; unsurprisingly, it drops 20 observations, leaving 10 observations to match. We get an ATE of –8.5 days.

When we match users in this hypothetical example, we find that adding a profile picture actually leads to lower retention. We would not have noticed this effect in observational data because generally those users with a profile picture who are unmatched have higher retention. It is very common to find that (even imperfect) matching greatly lowers proportional differences, as discussed in Chapter 6. Proportional differences are simply the comparison of some effect on two or more groups. They are extremely misleading and should be used sparingly and along with other tools.

Here's an overview of the process of matching with a step-by-step approach for how to start the process.

1. Select the treatment and the outcome.

2. Select other variables that may also "cause" the outcome. (Always think about variables for which you might not have information.)

3. Use a matching method to find controls that look like the treated group.

4. Test whether the treatment and control groups' means or distributions are significantly different. See Chapter 16 section 16.3 for how this is implemented in R. Here are the steps to check whether the groups look similar across all the other variables except for treatment:

   i. Check graphs of distributions of variables.

   ii. Use statistical tests like the *t*-test, *k*-means, and others to show that they are the same. The function MatchBalance() from the 'Matching' R package will implement this for you.

5. Determine whether balance was achieved.

   i. If balance was achieved, proceed to calculate the ATT, ATC, and ATE.

   ii. If the balance is not achieved, use matching as a heuristic to find out where there is no balance.

In Chapter 16 section 16.3, we'll go through an example of statistical matching using the Lalonde data set to determine the effects of a jobs program on future earnings.

12.3 Problems with Propensity Score Matching

This section addresses possible problems with the propensity score matching approach, namely omitted variable bias and no coverage.

12.3.1 Omitted Variable Bias and Better Matching Methods

Almost all data in the world is observational, with the obvious exception of experimental data. The difficulty with observational data is the problem of selection, as we discussed in Chapter 6. Selection occurs when users are not randomly placed into the treatment and control groups, but rather are selected due to nonrandom conditions. It's a pernicious problem that staves off causal insight in most of the user data created.

Let's go back to the scenerio that we started this chapter with, you were asked to determine whether personal messages from a health coach will help our users quit smoking. Suppose we spent weeks building an adequate control data set and are finally able to achieve balance on about 50 core confounding variables. We are about to present results to the company's CTO when one of our coworkers asks us about a new variable used in a published paper on the topic—motivation. We realize that we missed this important confounding variable. Will our results still hold in this scenario?

Probably not. Even missing one variable will throw your conclusions into question. This problem is generally called **omitted variable bias**. For causality, omitted variable bias is a particularly pernicious problem because there is no easy way to verify causal claims without experimentation. We show causality in matching by removing alternative explanations—but if we cannot rule out all other explanations, we are unable to show causality. In practice, statistical matching for this reason is either for feature selection or of last resort when other methods will not work. Causal relationships are very difficult to verify when experimentation is not available.

In industry, incorrect causal inferences are not dire. A wrong result will likely not lead to untimely deaths, but results are still needed quickly. While not perfectly accurate, statistical matching in addition to logical causal tools can be used to identify likely causal relationships to A/B test or to ballpark causal effects.

Now back to the story: We might panic for a while in the face of the need to redo our analysis, but then we start problem solving. Suppose we collect data for user motivation regarding smoking cessation. Sadly for us, but true to form, adding motivation nullifies most of the causal effect of a personal quit coach on smoking cessation. Users who are more motivated are more likely to be online, and a quit coach is more likely to message them.

This is not unusual with causal inference: Effects can vary widely based on the observed variables that we included in our analysis. We might have missed key variables in our analysis that are actually driving the effect. In this case, motivation was likely driving the effect, while personalized messages were only spuriously related to smoking cessation.

As you can imagine, there are lots of variables for which we might not be able to get data and that are core to explaining an effect like motivation. We might also miss variables that are integral, but we fail to realize the core role they play.

This was a good lesson on the difficulty of causal inference in the absence of an A/B test. Finding the precise unbiased causal impact without an A/B test is difficult. However, the statistical methods laid out in this chapter, in addition to logic, are like a nightlight in a dark room. Use these methods as heuristics to help guide your understanding of users, but recognize that, unlike with A/B testing and predictive models for prediction, there is no easy validation so your results are always in doubt. The core problem with matching is the omitted variable bias problem. If we are missing core variables, then our estimates are *wrong*. The difficulty of matching is that our model will not tell us if we are missing core causal variables. This leaves us in a difficult position of deciding whether we want to believe our results.

We can use a number of strategies to find treated users who look like the controls. A popular way to achieve balance historically was to rely on propensity scores. We went through an example of this method in Section 12.4.2. A better way to do this is to rely on a genetic matching algorithm to iteratively build an aggregate control group. Because this is a much more complex method, we won't delve into it with much rigor. See the sidebar "Using GenMatch, a Genetic Matching Algorithm, to Find Control Groups" for an introduction to a genetic matching algorithm. Genetic matching generally finds us a control group that is more like our treated group than is possible with propensity score matching, allowing us to avoid the problem of no balance.

Using GenMatch, a Genetic Matching Algorithm, to Find Control Groups

In Chapter 15, we'll go through a GenMatch example in R. Basically, propensity score matching has been improved by newer algorithms that are better at achieving a balance between treatment and control groups.

GenMatch uses an evolutionary search algorithm to determine the weighting of each observation and create balance in the data set. It implements the same process as other matching algorithms do, including logistic regression. It just improves upon these user weights with each iteration. Instead of matching full users, it can weight users in different combinations to achieve better balance.

The current implementation is very slow because it grows exponentially by the size of the data set, so it can be used only on small data sets, limiting its applicability. Be wary if you are running it with a large data set, as it may crash your R program.

12.3.2   No Coverage

Another problem that is very common is a lack of coverage in the data; that is, the treated population may not look like the controls. The no-coverage problem can sometimes be solved by limiting the scope of your study or accepting multiple possible confounders in your conclusion. No coverage can come in two flavors.

First, there may be no controls who look like the treated users. For instance, there may be no women in the control group. Here's what you can do in that scenario:

- Drop users who have no coverage out of your analysis. You can't examine female users, so you must drop them from your analysis. However, you can potentially use this information to understand the selection effects that are occurring.

- Analyze other subgroups. If you have good coverage of male users, then you can estimate the effect for men.

Second, all selected variables may move in the same way, which prevents you from achieving balance. For instance, social class, education, and income may all move in the same direction and there is very little daylight between these factors. In such a case, you have narrowed down the pool of predictors to a few that you were unable to achieve balance on.

12.4   Matching as a Heuristic

Before we move on to other methods for causal inference, let's explore the use of matching as a heuristic. Suppose you were unable to find balance between your treatment and control groups: Can matching still be useful? This is actually not very uncommon. It tells you that basically your treatment users do *not* look like your control users. Strong selection effects are occurring in your social process.

Not all is lost. Matching can be a useful tool to whittle down the number of causal relationships that you need to test or examine. For instance, let's say we struggled to get balance on motivation and a socioeconomic variable. From this, we know that motivation and socioeconomic status are related to adding a profile picture and one of these variables (or some combination of them) is causing an increase in retention. We know that this change is not being caused by the other variables: gender, onboarding completion, or income.

From here, we can set up an experiment to separate these two variables' effects. Matching can show us where to focus our efforts. Recall from Chapter 6 that A/B testing will not search the space of treatments to test. Matching, however, can do just that. It can be a useful heuristic that saves time or money when A/B testing resources are in short supply.

Be aware that the actual variables themselves matter. As you'll remember from Chapter 3's discussion of human behavior change, some behaviors are much easier to change than others. If motivation is strongly related, motivation is a very difficult aspect of human behavior to influence. However, if onboarding completion is causing the effect, we can more easily nudge our users toward onboarding completion.

12.5   The Best Guess

Matching often fails when we are unable to achieve match balance because there are no controls that look sufficiently like the treated population. Other quasi-experiments also fail when the right situations don't occur, such as a discontinuity in our treatment variable. Difference-in-difference (DID) and regression discontinuity (RD) can be one-off endeavors whose results cannot be easily replicated in other contexts.

Essentially, quasi-experimental methods can fail when there is a poor or no counterfactual present. In those cases, we are essentially left without much in terms of inference. In fact, early causal inference work in smoking faced this exact problem. Researchers guessed that smoking "caused" cancer because it was unlikely that some other factor could produce such a large effect, but they had no way to prove that was the case.

In this section, we'll introduce some logical tools to help infer causal relationships. Suppose we have tried natural experiments and statistical matching to figure out if "friending" leads to greater retention in product. Can we use logic to make an educated guess to understand whether the two are causally related?

First, how large is the effect of friending on retention and how does it compare to other outgoing social behaviors? Table 12.4 shows an example of the odds ratio calculated for friending and other social behaviors. (Refer to Section 8.3.1.3, "Logistic Regression.")

Table 12.4   **Odds Ratio and Behavior**

	Friending	**Following**	**Liking**	**Commenting**	**Tagging**
Odds Ratio (Retention to Day 3)	50 times more likely to be retained	5 times more likely to be retained	8 times more likely to be retained	6 times more likely to be retained	4 times more likely to be retained
	As we can see, this odds ratio is substantially higher than for the other types of social behavior.				

Some simple metrics could help us make a causal argument for a variable when we have little else to go on. However, be aware that when the effects are not extremely clear, these simple heuristics *do not* work.

You might have a solid argument that friending could actually be causal, since there is a disproportionately large effect of friending on retention. Other confounders are not producing similar effects. If you are interested in any of the other variables, such as following, you don't have a strong argument that the relationship between those variables and retention is causal.

Another approach is calculate dosage effects. A **dosage effect** is how an outcome changes with unit increases in treatment. Let's calculate the dosage effect for the friending variable. This is just the proportional increase (Table 12.5).

Table 12.5 **Dosage Effects of Day in Product Based on an Additional Friend**

Treatment (Number of Friends)	Retention (Days)
1	20
2	26
3	32
4	45
5	56
6	64
. . .	

A dosage effect adds some legitimacy to the argument that our variable is causal. If a variable is causal (like a prescription), we would expect a higher amount to lead to a higher effect and each unit increase to result in a positive and potentially similar-sized increase. If we see this relationship pair out in the data, it suggests that this factor could be causal. However, remember that simply increasing is not enough (there has to be a similar-sized effect in the outcome variable with each unit increase in the treatment variable); the big confounder here is motivation. The number of friends could simply be an indicator of motivation. However, motivation may not be linearly distributed, so by looking at the dosage effect, we may be able to tease out the causal effect of "friends."

There are more sophisticated statistical methods to examine and calculate dosage effects. To explore them further, see *Nonlinear Regression Analysis and Its Applications* by Douglas Bates and Donald Watts (1988).

Finally, we can use placebo tests to guess at causal relationships. As you may remember, a placebo test is when we have a similar time or event without the treatment and we expect there to be no effect. It allows us to determine whether something else is causing the effect. To perform this kind of test, we use the same experimental design but vary one element related to treatment—that is, we specify when the treatment did not occur. We want to check whether there is still an effect. If an effect occurs, then it's likely that treatment did not cause that effect.

The example in Table 12.6 is a placebo test of our DID model from Chapter 11. Suppose we used the prior year around the same time as a placebo test. We use the same two designated market areas (DMAs), including one that received the treatment—a commercial on April 12, 2016. We'll look at the same period from the prior year with both DMAs. If we see no treatment effect on our outcome when relying on the same methods in the year prior, then it would lend credence to our belief that the promotion had a causal effect.

Table 12.6   **Placebo Test of a Promotion**

	Purchases (Before Promotion)	**Purchases (After Promotion)**	**Difference**
Promotion DMA April 12, 2015	576	725	149 (This might be a significant difference depending on the variation for the distribution of purchases)
No-Promotion DMA April 12, 2015	587	601	14 (This is probably just random noise, but we cannot be sure until we calculate the test statistic—see Chapter 6)

Calculating some of these comparison statistics and using dosage and placebo tests can help us guess at which factors are likely causal. But when all else fails, we can guess. Hill's 1965 guidelines for causality are a great place to go when we need to guess. Hill defined nine factors that may help establish support for causal relationships. As we have said throughout this chapter, there is no easy way to verify a relationship is indeed causal. However, many causal variables share some similarities that we can look for.

At the core of generating insight is causation, or "why something happens"—that is, causal inference. As we discussed in previous chapters, understanding *why* is difficult. Sometimes, it's even impossible. In product analytics, correlates are often used as a stand-in for causal relationships. When this occurs, it's often to the chagrin of those responsible, as the relationships are frequently found to be false and actions used to support those ends are in waste.

Hill's causality conditions are as follows:

1. *Strength of the effect:* Very large proportional effects are usually a sign of causality. For instance, if a smoker is 200 times more likely to get lung cancer, it's likely that smoking probably causes cancer. If one cannot easily think of another major candidate that could cause this large of an effect, it's likely to be causal.

2. *Consistency:* Has this factor been highly correlated in different places, among different groups, in different products, and at different times?

3. *Specificity of the association:* Is there a clear causal linkage with differing effects across groups and/or time? For example, strains of disease carried by rats caused the bubonic plague outbreaks in Europe. The linkage is clear and suggests that those persons living closer to places where rats might breed—that is, near sewage or densely populated areas—might be most affected by the plague. But the question of whether single parenthood causes lower earnings is murkier. In this case, there is no clear linkage and we cannot separate the effects on different groups. With the first example of the plague, there is a clear causal path or mechanism. With the second example, there could be many potential mechanisms— for example, single parenthood leads to lower parental attention, which leads to lower earnings. Single parenthood does not directly cause lower earnings. Instead, there are probably lots of intervening mechanisms between the two, making the causal linkage very hard to discern.

4. *Temporality:* Many interesting causal questions suffer from reverse causality. Did a recession cause the stock market crash, or did the stock market crash cause a recession? In some

cases, the temporality problem never arises because one event clearly precedes the other, as with disease and then death. [We can use more sophisticated statistical tools to look at temporality. We can lag the outcome and see if some variables become better predictors, using time series techniques; see Wooldridge's (2013) *Introductory Econometrics*. The topic of temporality was cursorily discussed in a concluding note in Chapter 11, after the overview of time-series methods. These tools are generally out of the scope of this book.]

5. *Dosage effects:* Does the strength of the effect increase with the more of the treatment that we get? For instance, does the proportion of smokers who get cancer increase with the number of cigarettes smoked each day? Finding a relationship between treatment increases and outcome increases lends credence to a causal relationship.

6. *Plausibility:* This consideration is also known as the smell test. Is it common sense? Although there is much about this world that we do not know, human beings do have extremely sophisticated ways of developing heuristics.

7. *Coherence:* Does the entire theory of user behavior mesh? Does it broadly fit other literature/ ideas on user behavior in a given circumstance?

8. *Experiment:* We discussed the use of experiments in the earlier sections.

9. *Analogy:* Is it analogous to some other phenomenon that you could easily test?

Hill's list is very useful for thinking through causal associations. These criteria force us to analyze the situation holistically and to calculate some extra pieces of information:

- Odds ratio. (Refer to Chapter 6 for explanation.)

- Dosage effect: The relationship between a unit increase in treatment and its effect on the outcome variable.

- Placebo tests: Find times or places that can be used to compare effects (as in the example presented earlier in the chapter).

- Temporality tests: Find how X correlates with lags in Y. This was briefly discussed in Chapter 11 and can be a useful technique to add credence to a causality argument if lagged Y by 1-3 periods is much more strongly correlated with X than a X is correlated with Y as-is or lagged Y greater than 5 periods.

In practice, these tools are very useful for identifying variables that could be causally related and warrant further exploration.

12.6   Final Thoughts

Statistical matching is a very powerful technique to better understand causal relationships in your data. Matching will estimate the size and direction of a causal effect without much design work, unlike the case with quasi-experimental designs. If you want to know the causal effect of profile pictures on retention, matching is where you should start.

If proper coverage and adequate confounding variables are added, you can generate insights such as "adding a profile picture causes a 5% increase in user retention." The ability to estimate a causal effect with observational data makes this approach very useful for industry settings.

A few problems do arise with statistical matching. Matching is not optimized for large data sets. This means that as a data scientist, you must find an adequate data sample for matching, which may at best get at the causal relationship between two factors. Matching also takes some analytical sophistication to get a good result. Propensity score matching will often not lead to balanced data sets, so you'll often have to rely on more sophisticated methods.

Matching can help you uncover the causal relationships and the approximate size of those relationships. However, in some situations where you lack coverage or are having a hard time trusting your statistical matching results, using Hill's causality conditions can lend credence to your findings. Hill's causality conditions are often a great way to start or approach a sticky causal web of factors. Generally, most variables are causally related but have a minor effect, and it's your job as a data scientist to find those few variables that have an outsized effect on the action or outcome in which you're interested. Statistical matching and Hill's causality conditions are very useful in practice for finding outsized causal factors.

12.7   Actionable Insights

In this chapter, here are the actionable insights:

- Matching can be used as a heuristic to find groups of variables that move in similar ways (your core confounders).

- Propensity score matching can be useful with large data sets, but GenMatch leads to better results for smaller groups.

- Logical tricks and simple techniques like large odds ratios, dosage effects, placebo tests, and temporality can lend credence to potential "causal" variables.

- Greater selection means there's less support in the data to make causal inferences. Some features with rampant selection can never be controlled for.

> **Note**
>
> This chapter did not explore this method in detail, but readings included in the Bibliography—particularly Bates and Watts's (1988) *Nonlinear Regression Analysis and Its Applications*—explore dose–response models that can help you infer causality in some scenarios.

Causal inference from observational data is vital to developing inference, as many difficult problems do not easily lend themselves to A/B testing or quasi-experimentation. Statistical matching is needed to understand intractable causal relationships. This chapter explored statistical matching, a tool that can determine causal effects in real-world data and help us piece together the relationships among variables and confounders in a causal framework.

Statistical matching helps us determine the group or aggregate causal effect. For instance, we found the treatment effect of adding a profile picture aggregated over all users. Theoretically, every user could have an individual "causal" or treatment effect of a profile picture.

Here's a more concrete example: Perhaps there is a very effective drug treatment, but it does not affect every person in the same way. Some participants, say men, react much better to the drug treatment and see a large treatment effect, while women experience a smaller treatment effect. With an A/B test, it's possible to explore the individual treatment or causal effect of a factor of interest. Chapter 13 explores uplift modeling, which is useful in estimating the individual treatment effects (or causal effects) for A/B test outcomes.

13

Uplift Modeling

In Chapter 12, we covered the topic of statistical matching in an effort to extrapolate causal relationships from observational data. In this chapter, we'll pivot to a whole different topic: We'll focus on situations in which we have A/B testing results and want to further understand the individual treatment effects. Individual treatment effects are the causal effect of a particular treatment on an individual, rather than an aggregate group.

Recall that in the introduction to causal inference in Chapter 10, we discussed a notable limitation of such inference: We are estimating the group-level treatment effect. However, in reality, treatment effects are individual. An individual will see some effect of the treatment, and it could be larger or smaller than the treatment effect on the group as a whole.

As we described in Chapter 6, an A/B test estimates the average treatment effect (ATE). This gives us the ATE over the full population. The ATE can be interpreted as the causal effect of the treatment variable on that outcome averaged over the full group, but the treatment or causal impact is not the same for every person or subgroup.

In reality, some users might see large treatment effects and other users small or negative treatment effects. In practice, we want to find those users who will benefit the most from treatment and expose them to treatment. This chapter will help us estimate individual treatment or causal effects from A/B test results and find users who are most affected by treatment. The statistical approach that we will use to estimate the individual treatment effect is called uplift modeling.

In this chapter, we'll go over examples, interpretations, and application of uplift models. Chapter 16 section 16.4 will apply these methods in R.

13.1 What Is Uplift?

Uplift modeling is a toolkit devoted to modeling the incremental impact of an action or "treatment" on a customer outcome. It is a useful behavioral targeting tool, created by combining the benefits of A/B tests (causal inference) with the validation properties of prediction. It's most effective when applied to acquisition of new users, conversion of nonpaying users to paying users, upselling, cross-selling, and modeling churn and retention. Note that uplift modeling can be useful in all four key areas of user development and behavior—acquisition, engagement, retention, and revenue.

Uplift modeling helps answer one key question, who to target—that is, who will react positively to some stimulus? We might be interested in staging a win-back campaign (to bring inactive users back into active status) or building a promotional marketing campaign to get users to buy a higher-valued product. One of the most effective methods to target and optimize your campaign is to build an uplift model.

As a toolkit, it's becoming widely popular, especially since its use in the 2012 election campaign of President Barack Obama. In that case, data scientists applied uplift models to determine which voters would react positively to Obama campaign mailers, ads, phone calls, and other outreach methods. Essentially, they were looking for voters whose behavior they could change—specifically, from abstaining from voting to getting them to the polls to vote for Obama. This targeting technique avoids people who could react negatively or would be unfazed by the outreach. Using uplift modeling can also test variants of positive and negative messaging strategies and personalize them for groups of voters most receptive to those types of messaging.

In this chapter, we explore the uses, methodology, and practical applications of uplift modeling with the Lalonde data set. The Lalonde data set comprises data obtained from an experimental jobs program. The goal of this study was to examine the effect of the jobs program on future earnings. We are using this data set because it's easily accessible (i.e., public data), commonly used to prove the efficacy of causal inference methods, and small. All of these techniques can be applied to your particular product A/B testing data.

13.2 Why Uplift?

Before uplift modeling became popular, many analysts used to rely on prediction to model retention and churn. Even today, uplift modeling is not as widely used as it could be. This is primarily because it requires two extensive processes: (1) a well-planned A/B test and (2) a subsequent sophisticated modeling effort.

Businesses often rely on predictive modeling because then they do not need to carry out an A/B test. Such modeling is better than nothing, but not very effective. To illustrate why, we'll explore a win-back campaign example. We're trying to prevent active users from becoming inactive. We build a predictive model to determine which users are likely to become inactive in the next month. We then send all of those users an email. Suppose a targeting marketing email costs $0.25 per user on average.

Some proportion of those users will not respond to our email, so we lose money on those users. But, more worrisome, we also might *lose* some users who respond negatively to our email. *We want to contact only those users who leave but will come back on receipt of an email.* That's a more nuanced proposition.

Predicting which users will return on receipt of the email is not solely predictive, but also causal in nature. As mentioned in Chapter 8, prediction modeling can be a poor targeting tool, especially in controversial campaigns, because it can be counterproductive. We may be sending out emails to people who would not otherwise leave, but may in fact choose to leave after receiving our email.

To avoid this problem, we combine the causal effect estimates via an A/B test with the elegance of predictive modeling to determine the individual treatment effect or causal effect of the treatment for an individual. At first, you might be wary of this approach because of the difficulty of its implementation for complex problems. Recall from Chapter 7 that variants of A/B tests grow factorially in the number of variations to the treatment. For very complex A/B tests and smaller sample sizes, this toolkit may not work well.

However, let's not throw the baby out with the bathwater. Uplift modeling should be in every analyst's toolkit because it can help you target treatments to the users who will benefit the most from those interventions.

Uplift modeling is different than statistical matching and other types of causal inference from observational data (discussed in Chapters 11 and 12) for two reasons: (1) It's based on an A/B test, or true randomization, and (2) it's focused on heterogeneous treatment effects, or the effect of treatment on the individual or small subgroups, rather than the average effect for the entire treatment group. When we focus on a heterogeneous treatment effect, we can determine who to target with treatment.

Now that we've explored uses of uplift modeling, we'll move on to a conceptual explanation of how uplift modeling works.

13.3 Understanding Uplift

Uplift modeling is based on the marketing concept of lift. **Lift** is the increase in sales attributable to a promotion or advertisement. Uplift modeling is a way to determine the lift attributable to a campaign or promotion. It uses predictive techniques on experimental data—that is, with treatment and control groups—to estimate lift.

Uplift modeling can predict the effect of a campaign on a subgroup of users by using control group users who look similar to treated individuals (as in matching). This allows us to model the subgroup counterfactuals (e.g., what if subgroup X did not receive treatment?).

The counterfactual is based on subgroups in the control group that look like the treated group *based on observed features*. You may notice that these are the same recurrent problems with modeling causation that we encountered in Chapter 11; they will affect our ability to understand heterogeneous causal effects as well. We'll discuss these issues throughout this chapter.

The goal of uplift modeling is to place users within these four groups:

- **Sure Things:** Users whom we will convert.

- **Persuadable:** Users who will convert given the marketing campaign (our target group).

- **Lost Causes:** Users who will never convert, and on whom the marketing campaign has no effect.

- **Do Not Disturbs:** Users will react negatively to the campaign.

With uplift modeling, we're trying to find the Persuadables—the users who would be persuaded to try out our product based on an ongoing promotion. We can find these users by building models based on our experimental data.

Next, we'll explore how uplift modeling differs from traditional predictive approaches (discussed in Chapter 8).

13.4 Prediction and Uplift

With predictive modeling, we cannot easily separate the four categories to find Persuadables, meaning we could be targeting the Do Not Disturbs.

With predictive models, we are also trying to predict an outcome such as voting or purchasing behavior. In contrast, with uplift modeling, we are more interested in who will modify their behavior based on the "actions" that we take. As you can see, this is a different framework from the conventional predictive framework. It also differs from the traditional causal inference problem, since we want to predict which treatment has the largest effect for a given individual (or, in actuality, one small subgroup), rather than estimate the treatment effect of one treatment for a group.

Traditional predictive modeling generally focuses on the treated users, without a comparative control group (in other words, it's often not randomized data). Since we do not have a control group in predictive modeling, we cannot model uplift. As discussed in Chapter 8, predictive modeling does not aid us in inferring causation.

A core difference between causal inference and prediction is the level of the approach, such as individual or group. In causal inference, we are (generally) able to estimate only ATE; in contrast, in prediction for user analytics, we (generally, though this does not have to be the case) estimate the fitted or predicted value for each individual or unit.

The ATE is the estimated treatment effect for the full population, both treatment and controls. To use predictive modeling of causal processes, we need to estimate the individual treatment effects. **Individual treatment effects** are the results of the treatment on a given individual.

[A side note: In this modeling framework, "predict" translates to "maximize the probability." We'll see how this is formalized in the uplift models in this chapter. To see a more formal mathematical explanation, refer to the readings in the bibliography.]

The individual treatment effects can vary greatly from the aggregate treatment effect. For instance, women might have a different cancer risk from smoking cigarettes than men do. It is possible that women might have a higher cancer risk, but the aggregate treatment effect might underestimate this risk for women. We'd want to know about these differences, so policy makers can target at-risk groups more successfully, thereby having an outsized effect on lowering the proportion of the population with cancer.

13.5   Difficulties with Uplift

A few major problems occur with uplift owing to the fact that we will never know the individual treatment effect. In most cases, the individual will not be in both the treatment group and the control group (the true comparative controls). Thus, we still need to find individuals who "look like" those treated in the control population and estimate the individual treatment effects for users. The best that we can do in reality is estimate the **subpopulation treatment effect (STE)** based on important observed features, such as gender.

The STE has two caveats that leave it short of true causal inference:

- Personal treatment effects: Subpopulation treatments could still be wrong for a given individual, just like ATE!

- Non-observed features: Unobserved features could be driving the magnitude of the causal effect, so that our models will fail to capture the true effect. This is a problem that constantly rears its ugly head in causal inference from observational data.

Unfortunately, at this time, discovering STE is the best that we can do. Even so, it's important to recognize how this modeling approach can go wrong.

Before we move on, let's define two concepts:

- **Main effect:** The primary causal effect of the treatment.

- **Heterogeneous treatment effect:** Effects of treatment in subpopulation groups.

While these effects vary depending on the actual example that we are looking at, oftentimes the main effect of treatment is *larger*, sometimes substantially, than the heterogeneous effects. For instance, there might be smaller differences in the effects of smoking on cancer risk between men and women, than between smoking and nonsmoking. With uplift modeling, we're trying to find these heterogeneous effects, but since they are smaller, erroneous models or the main effect of treatment can easily mask them.

Since there is no way for us to validate the causal effects (only predictive outcomes), it's difficult to determine the "best" models and validate variable selection methods. We'll discuss what seems to work in practice in later sections.

13.5.1 Lalonde Data Set

In this section, we will take a little time to explain the data set we will be working with in this chapter as well as in R listings in Chapter 16.

The Lalonde data set is a popular data set used in economics. It was obtained from a randomized experiment on the effects on a jobs program of future earnings. The treatment was the National Work Demonstration Jobs Program, a short-term program targeted at people who struggled to gain a foothold in the employment market. For instance, the main participant population consisted of individuals who were recently released from prison, released from rehabilitation facilities for drug or other maladies, and high school dropouts.

We can already see this is not a random sample of the general population, but rather a subset of individuals engaged with government and community institutions who lack steady employment. Note that the data from this experiment has internal validity, meaning that it holds for those involved (users who are similar to the participant population), but we cannot extrapolate the results to the general population (external validation).

The program offered minimum-wage, subsidized jobs to participants for a period of 12 months from 1975 to 1977. It also provided close supervision and supportive components to participants. It's a public data set, used by Lalonde (1986) and Dehejia and Wahba (1999), which contains 445 participants, of whom 185 received treatment. It has the following covariates: age, gender, education, Black ethnicity, Hispanic ethnicity, marriage status, degree (yes or no), earnings in 1974, and earnings in 1975. The treatment variable is whether someone participated in the program. The outcome variable is earnings in 1978.

Although this is not a product analytics data set, it's a very popular data set with which to examine these ideas because of the easy understanding of the variables and context. You can use a similar setup when working with product data sets.

13.5.2 Uplift Modeling

Now that we have introduced uplift modeling and the Lalonde data set, let's see an overview of the statistical techniques for uplift modeling. In this next section, we'll explore a variety of empirical approaches, starting with the earliest setups and working our way to more modern techniques. We'll go through three separate types of models: (1) the two-model approach, (2) the interaction model, and (3) tree-based models. Within tree-based models, we'll explore uplift forests and causal conditional inference forests. In this section, we'll also explore the basics of random forests as a predictive method.

In the two-model approach, we model the treatment and control groups in two separate models. In the interaction model, we model treatment as an interaction effect with our independent variables. In the tree-based models, we use the decision rule to split groups according to size of uplift.

As explained earlier, all the methods in this section rely on the results of an A/B test. Chapter 6 described the A/B test setup. The treatment *must* be randomized for uplift modeling to work. For all of these models, we have a few basic components.

- *Outcome*: What we are interested in predicting? (For the Lalonde data set, it's future employment.)

- *Treatment*: The action that we are taking that has been randomized. (In our example, this is a jobs program and participation in the program has been randomized to the best of our ability.)

- *Control group*: The group that receives no treatment. (In our example, these are the individuals who were not invited to participate in the jobs program.)

- *Treatment group*: The group that received the treatment. (In our example, this is the group that participated in the jobs program.)

13.5.3 Two-Model Approach

The most straightforward approach to uplift modeling (and the least accurate approach in practice) is the two-model approach. This approach works to model both the treatment and control groups separately and then subtract the predictions to calculate uplift.

Here are the steps:

1. Build a model to predict the outcome for the treatment group.

2. Build a model to predict the outcome for the control group.

3. Subtract the outcome predictions from the two models to calculate uplift.

We generally build the two models using the same type of model (in our example, a logistic regression) and the same predictors (the set described in Section 13.5.1). Listing 16.18 in Chapter 16 illustrates how to fit the two-model approach in R to the Lalonde data set.

While the two-model approach is a very straightforward strategy, it does not work well in practice. For the two-model approach to work properly, the prediction generated by each model *must* be correct for both the treatment and control groups for the subtracted difference to be uplift. As you can imagine, this is generally not true. Whereas prediction is focused on external validity, causation relies heavily on internal validity. We can end up with completely different, incorrect, or unreliable models for either or both treatment and control groups. We know that there is no way for us to easily validate this.

As mentioned earlier, the heterogeneous treatment effects are often small, so the effect might be lost when subtracting imperfect models. In addition, in building a predictive model we might remove variables that are impactful for uplift, but poor predictors. The underlying model might also be a poor fit for our treatment, control, or both data sets, resulting in poor predictive results.

Since we need perfect models for this method to hold, which rarely exist, the two-model approach is generally not useful. Note that a "good-enough" model will not suffice here. To overcome the drawbacks of the two-model approach, another uplift modeling technique known as the interaction model was developed. The next section discusses this approach in detail.

13.5.4   Interaction Model

It is apparent from the preceding section that the two-model approach does not generally produce good results in practice; thus a one-model approach was proposed using a logistic regression. Recall from Chapter 8 the modeling technique known as logistic regression. Lo (2002) describes the formal mathematical setup of interaction models.

The interaction model combines the two-model approach into one functional form using interaction terms to model the effect of treatment. Here are the steps to build such a model:

1. Build a logistic regression model with independent variables or features.

2. Add an interaction term (a binary variable indicating whether a user receives treatment) multiplied by your independent variables.

3. Subtract the model with interaction terms equal to 1 from the model with interaction terms equal to 0.

As explained Chapter 8, in the baseline logistic regression model, every term is 0 except the intercept. The baseline model in this context is the model for the controls. This is the model in which the interaction terms are equal to 0, but independent variables can be positive.

Let's explore a sample model setup using the Lalonde data set. Our outcome is predicting employment in the subsequent year. We'll retain three independent variables for simplicity (age, past earnings, and marital status). We'll use a treatment flag as our dummy variable for whether a user receives treatment (1 if they did, 0 if they did not). If we wanted to use the interaction model, we might set it up in the following way:

$$x = \text{intercept} + b1*\text{age} + b2*\text{past\_earnings} + b3*\text{marital\_status} +$$
$$c*\text{treatment\_flag} + d1*\text{treatment\_flag}*\text{age} + d2*\text{treatment\_flag}*$$
$$\text{past\_earnings} + d3*\text{treatment\_flag}*\text{marital\_status}$$

$$p = \frac{e^{(x)}}{1 + e^{(x)}}$$

Here for model setup, we used the logistic functional form; for a review of logistic regression setup, refer to Chapter 8 section 8.3.1.3. The outcome is the probability of finding employment. With this sample model, the b coefficients are the main effects of the independent variables (age, earnings, and marital status on employment), c is the main effect due to treatment (the effects of the jobs program), and the d coefficients are the effects of the independent variables due to treatment (age, past earnings, and marital status given they attended the jobs program). In Chapter 16, Listing 16.20, an interaction model is implemented on the Lalonde data set.

From Chapter 8, the coefficients of a logistic regression are interpreted as the log of the odds ratio, but can be converted into probabilities. Refer to Chapter 8 section 8.3.1.3 for a more formal introduction to log-odds and conversion to probabilities. We can interpret these coefficients in the context of our model to determine how each factor affects the probability of gaining employment.

We could calculate the "individual treatment effect" by considering a specific set of user characteristics such as age 18–25, female, no degree, and others. We could then plug this data into our model to obtain a probability of gaining employment. The reason that individual treatment effect is in quotes here is because it's actually a subpopulation treatment effect and may not include all the features that matter.

We could then calculate uplift for our full population by subtracting the treated model (treatment flag = 1) and the control model (treatment flag = 0).

Similarly to the two-model methodology, there are some problems with using interaction models.

- As we can tell from this example, a very real problem in practice is the large number of terms in this model. With so many similar variables, we can end up with a multicollinearity problem—that is, one variable may be predicted by one or more variables. Reduction is often needed, but it can be difficult to reduce the model effectively.

- Logistic regressions assume a very specific functional form. We might want to try some nonlinear methods that can break apart the subpopulations. In the next section, we'll investigate another type of modeling tool to help us model nonlinear subpopulation effects—tree-based models. Tree methods are naturally nonlinear and can accommodate subpopulation splits.

13.5.5   Tree-Based Methods

In Chapter 8, we explored decision trees for prediction. Decision tree models find the best partitions to classify a set of data into classes. When we introduced this concept, we compared decision trees to a game of "Twenty Questions" in which we are trying to guess which country a player is thinking about. A decision tree partitions the data into two groups at each node based on a decision rule. In that example, a potential rule could be "Is the country in Asia?" or "Does it start with the letter A?" We repeatedly ask questions until we get to the root node, where we classify our data.

How does a decision tree determine the optimal rule? A decision tree model runs through all potential variable splits and calculates a metric. In this section, we'll go over the most popular form of such trees—entropy—but there are lots of others. We will also cover only classification trees in this section.

Entropy can also be thought of as information gain. We gain information by creating groupings that are increasingly more similar (one class). Entropy in information theory is based on the following principle: The lower the probability of occurrence, the higher the information or entropy. We can consider measuring the entropy as 1/probability of occurrence. For example, the letters x and y have higher entropy compared to the letters a and e because they occur less frequently.

The mathematical definition of entropy associated with the proportion of data in each node of the decision tree is as follows:

$$= -\sum p(x) * log\big(p(x)\big)$$

where $p(x)$ is the proportion of observations in a class.

Now, let's explore this equation with two examples. We need the binary equation to calculate the values. Let's calculate the entropy value when the splits are 0.25 and 0.75.

$$= -\big(0.25 * log_2(0.25)\big) - \big((0.75) * log_2(0.75)\big) = 0.91$$

First, let's assume that we have the following splits:

p(x)	Entropy (approximate)
0.5, 0.5 (perfectly random)	1
0.334, 0.667	0.9
0.25, 0.75	0.8
0.2, 0.8	0.7
0, 1 (perfectly split)	0

We can see from this table when we have a perfect split because entropy is zero; that is, each node has objects of only one label. At this point, uncertainty is at its lowest point, and we have perfect information. When we gain no information from the split, then entropy is 1; this is when uncertainty is at its highest point. The random split occurs where uncertainty is the highest and entropy is 1. Other splits occur in between these two extreme points.

We will not go into the calculation of the information gain for a particular decision tree in detail. We can see from this discussion that we want splits that lower disorder by having more class homogeneity in each node.

Let's review the steps in a decision tree algorithm:

1. Search: At each node (starting with the root node), search for the optimal attribute to split the data into categories or classes. To do so, run a statistical test to determine the best attribute and split.

2. Apply the rule: Apply the rule and sort the training data into the appropriate split grouping.

3. Repeat steps 1 and 2 until the entire tree is constructed. This approach is called a "greedy algorithm" because it makes the best choice at each point with hopes of achieving a globally optimal solution.

Now that we have reviewed decision tree models, let's see how to use tree-based models to build uplift models and quantify the treatment effect on different subpopulations. We'll explore two different models: (1) a random forest uplift model and (2) a conditional inference forest model. First, however, we should examine random forests, as both of these models are variants of the random forest model.

13.5.6 Random Forests

Random forests are a collection of many decision tree models where the output for a case is either the mode (classification) or the average (regression) of the trees. Decision trees have a problem of overfitting, as we discussed in a sidebar in Chapter 8. Random forests correct for this problem, increase consistency of a given model, and are generally less likely to get stuck in poor local minima or local low points.

Trees solve the predictive problem by assuming the past nodes are optimal. Similar to forward induction in game theory, where we assume that past behavior was rational, forward induction can miss the global optima or best solution.

In computer science, we see this implementation often. Specifically, decision trees implement the greedy algorithm or top-down decision process, making optimal local decisions in hopes of finding the global optima. However, when we move forward in this way, it allows us to get stuck in a nonoptimal global solution.

In layman's terms, lots of trees are better than a single tree because, just as a single data point can vary a lot, the same is true with individual trees. For instance, we could have two very different trees with good predictive results. We want to use both trees because, by averaging them, we might get better predictive results than a single tree on its own.

In a traditional decision tree model, we seek to maximize information (i.e., entropy). Splitting criteria is the best approach when it increases the amount of information that we have, as it often leads to a relatively equal split at each node.

With tree-based methods for uplift, the models are somewhat different. We'll go over the splitting criteria for both the uplift and conditional inference models later in the section.

In traditional decision tree models, the leaves are the classes or predicted values for an object. In an uplift model, the leaves of the trees are the uplift or values. We'll see an example of a causal conditional forest at the end of the chapter. Before we jump into uplift tree–based models, we'll go over how to build a simple random forest. Both the uplift forest and causal conditional forest models will rely upon random forest models.

13.5.6.1 How Do Random Forests Work?

Now that we've discussed why a random forest is generally better than a decision tree model, we'll discuss the nuts and bolts of a random forest. The following steps are used to create a random forest model:

1. Randomly sample data. This simply means that we pick some observations at random to build our tree. For instance, we might pick 250 samples out of 1,000 to build a decision tree. Our sampling is without replacement. As mentioned in Chapter 3, *replacement* means that each pick does not change the composition of the distribution; that is, we return a picked choice back to the list we are picking from.

2. Randomly sample the variables or features of the data set. We pick a few to build each tree. For instance, let's say there are eight features, and we pick five to build our tree. We always keep some variables (at least one) separate and do not include them in our training data set. Different trees can be built with different sets of features.

3. Build the decision tree and calculate the associated metrics: out-of-bag error, proximities, and variable importance. These are described later in this section. We grow out the tree as big as we can, and do not prune it. Pruning, as described in Chapter 8, is when we reduce the size of our decision trees by getting rid of sections with little predictive power.

Now that we have built our decision tree model, what could go wrong? The quality of a random forest model depends on two factors:

- Low tree correlation—that is, how closely each tree is related. Tree correlation is lower when we include fewer features.

- The strength of prediction, which is higher when we include more features. We need to weigh these two goals to find the optimal number of features to include in building each model. We can do that by using both training and test data sets.

To assess the quality of the random forest model, we can utilize three matrices:

- **Out-of-bag (OOB) error:** This matrix accesses the internal model error. For every tree, one-third of cases are left out. We then use the model to predict the classification for each test case. Then, we take the majority class for all those test cases and compare it to the true result. The proportion of cases where the majority class was predicted incorrectly over all observations is the OOB error estimate.

- **Proximities:** This matrix determines relationships between cases or observations. It's an $N \times N$ matrix, where N is the length of the data set. If two cases are in the same terminal node, we increase the proximity by 1. We calculate this metric for all trees and normalize it by dividing by the number of trees. The output should be the proportion of times that these two cases are in the same terminal node.

- **Variable importance:** This matrix provides the relative importance of the individual features across many trees. The idea here is that if a variable is very important, it should greatly lower the predictive accuracy; it's not important, it shouldn't affect predictive accuracy. We calculate it in the following way:

  1. For a given test case, count the correctly classified instances of this case in the OOB estimates.

  2. Randomly change the value of a given variable and see how the OOB changes for this case. For instance, we can change married to not married and see how this affects the OOB estimate.

  3. Subtract the new correctly classified number from the old number without the permuted variable.

  4. Repeat steps 1 through 3 for all N cases in the data set. We normalize this by dividing by N; the result is the raw importance score for each variable.

Now that we've seen how random forest models work, we can apply these concepts to uplift forests and causal conditional inference trees in the next sections.

13.5.6.2 Uplift Forests

In the last section, we have explored the basics of random forests, we'll move on to uplift forests. We'll follow the same process we did with random forests by starting with a single tree model. In the next few paragraphs, we'll discuss an uplift tree. Recall that we defined uplift to be the incremental effect of treatment on the individual or case. To build an uplift tree, we need to have the following types of variables. These might differ from predictive random forest models.

- We need features like age or race that might lead to different effects of treatment. For instance, an 18-year-old might have a very different experience in a jobs program than a 25-year-old does. Age might be a good candidate to search for heterogeneous treatment effects of the jobs program on future earnings. A feature like an individual's height might be a poor candidate for heterogeneous treatment effects, even if it's a great predictor of earnings. Height likely does not affect the size of the treatment effect of the jobs program on earnings.

- We want to find controls with similar features to our treated group, so we can estimate the treatment effect for subgroups. Recall that we cannot determine the individual treatment effect when we don't have randomization, only the average treatment effect. Here, we're assuming that we have controls for people who look more like the treated group (because of randomization) to estimate the uplift for certain heterogeneous features of the population.

A key difference between a regular decision tree model and an uplift model is the splitting criteria. Splitting criteria, discussed in the prior section, are the rules used to divide cases into separate nodes. For an uplift model, we need splitting criteria that meet the following two goals:

- Find splitting criteria that are equivalent to zero if there is no effect of a variable on the difference between the treatment and control groups. Basically, there should be no split in the tree for height, but there should be one for age in our previous example.

- Find features that lead to the greatest gain or loss in the outcome based on the control group. One way to do this is to look for those features that maximize the difference between the treatment and control groups. We look at the feature distributions of the treatment and control groups at each split, and try to find the features that maximize the differences in the outcomes. Here the split is based on divergence between the probability distribution for treatment and control (KL metric). Refer to the bibliography for sources providing more technical details.

The model has added criteria to make it sensitive to the size of treatment and control groups in splits, and to prevent the data set from breaking into one branch being the control group and the rest of the tree being the treatment group.

This is just one tree. The algorithm then randomly samples a subsection of the training data and builds tree after tree, averaging the results just like in a random forest model.

13.5.6.3 Causal Conditional Inference Forest

Another algorithm to estimate uplift is the causal conditional forest developed by Leo Guelman, Montserret Guillen, and Ana Perez-Marin (2015). We'll be implementing this in R with their package (Uplift), as shown in Chapter 16, Listing 16.21.

This model tries to correct some of the problems of the uplift forest model. Here are two of the problems:

- *Overfitting:* We model patterns in the data that are not there.

- *Selection bias toward covariates with many splits:* We are more likely to pick covariates with more split options. For instance, age defined by year may have more splits than gender (male or female), but is equally useful for predicting uplift. Age is more likely to be selected.

With decision trees, overfitting is often corrected with pruning or removing portions of the tree that are not very predictive. In the case of uplift models, one suggestion is to remove variables with no interaction effect between the covariate and treatment variable. We then order the other covariates by the likelihood of an interaction between the covariate and the treatment. We determine whether there is an interaction effect with a statistical test. This will solve for both overfitting and selection bias to some degree. A detailed explanation of this methodology can be found in Guelman (2013).

13.5.6.4 Selection of Variables

In this book, we cursorily discussed feature selection in Chapter 7 with unsupervised methods like *k*-means and principal components analysis (PCA), and in Chapter 8 with supervised learning methods like lasso regression. There is a great deal of work on how to select features in machine learning and artificial intelligence (AI). Hastie et al. (2009) provide a more comprehensive overview of statistical feature selection.

It's important to select the right features for uplift modeling since we're looking for the subpopulation effects. We'll use the following criteria from Radcliffe and Surry (2011):

- *Fewer variables are better.* There is a high likelihood of overfitting with more variables. As mentioned in Chapter 6, overfitting occurs when the model fits noise rather than signal, resulting in worse prediction.

- *Remove highly correlated variables.* Highly correlated variables are a problem for causal inference. As mentioned in Chapter 4, spurious correlation is a nasty problem for causal inference. It makes determining what's causal, rather than spurious, difficult. For this reason, highly correlated variables lead to uninterpretable and unstable models.

- *Improve quality of the model and stability.* This criterion means that we need to test our models and find the best models, where the "best" means the most predictive and consistent model. Random forests, or multiple trees, are one way to remove models that are unstable since they aggregate many tree models.

- *Use primary factors rather than facilitating variables.* We can have a factor causing an outcome through a process or a facilitating variable. For instance, chimney sweeps used to have a very high rate of cancer. We could keep a primary variable such as the occupation of chimney sweep, or we could keep a facilitating variable such as the number of chimneys cleaned in a day. Instead of using chimneys swept in a day, we should use occupation. Don't worry—we can use number of chimneys swept in a day to determine dosage effects (as described in Chapter 12).

These criteria can be organized into three qualities to look for in feature selection for uplift models:

- Prediction

- Consistency of results

- Independence

In general, the first two are obtained by selecting variables for general predictive models. The third quality, independence, is useful for interpretation and implementation. If variables are too highly correlated, that condition leads to instability as well as failure to determine causal effects. This is especially problematic in user analytics, as so many variables are highly correlated.

13.5.6.5 Lalonde Outcomes

To make the concepts that we explored more concrete, we'll apply these concepts to the Lalonde data set. In Chapter 16, Listings 16.11–16.17, the previously described uplift models are applied in R. As discussed earlier in this chapter, the Lalonde data set is a randomized experiment, where treated individuals were enrolled in a jobs program. We can use uplift modeling to look at how the different subpopulations are affected by the jobs program. Uplift modeling will help us determine who we should target for future jobs programs.

For this example, our outcome variable is non-zero earnings (any employment in 1975). Our treatment variable is whether someone participated in the jobs program. We have a variety of variables to define subgroups, such as age, race, prior earnings, marital status, and more.

We will run the causal inference tree model using this data set to determine uplift. We will explore a measure of variables' importance for the causal inference tree model. We can look at which permuted features have the greatest impact on the treatment effect.

Recall that variable importance is a measure of how changes to features affect predictive accuracy. In other words, variables that are highly predictive will lead to a large increase in OOB error and have a high variable importance.

As shown in Figure 13.1, Hispanic ethnicity and education are the most important variables for increasing OOB error in the Lalonde data set, whereas marriage, prior income (1975), and age are of lesser importance. As you may have noticed, some of the variables of even lesser importance have been removed for simplicity's sake from Figure 13.1. We calculate net information in Listing 16.23.

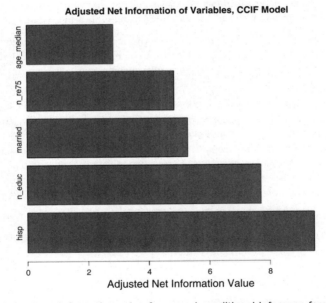

Figure 13.1   Adjusted net information value for causal conditional inference forest.

Figure 13.2 shows how these variables impact the treatment effect. First, the main effect was predicted to be about a 10% increase in having employment after the jobs program, while the true average treatment effect was 11%. Second, we can consider the heterogeneous treatment effects, or how certain attributes affect the size of the treatment effect on employment in 1978. We can see in Figure 13.2 that being Hispanic and participating in the jobs program had a negative effect on employment in 1978. In contrast, the other variables, particularly being married and having higher education, led to larger positive treatment effects.

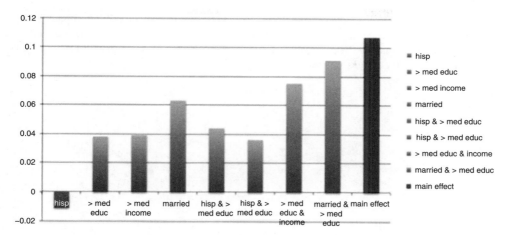

Figure 13.2   Difference in treatment effects for different population subgroups.

The first eight bars are not the absolute effects, but rather the difference related to a particular subgroup.

This section has shown us that many causal effects can, indeed, have heterogeneous effects on different groups. It's important to assess uplift by relevant subgroup. From there, we can find which groups are likely to see the greatest advantage from receiving the treatment or the largest causal effect. Note that these impacts are all estimated; they are not the "true" subgroup or individual treatment effects. In other words, these are our "best" guess at what smaller subgroup treatment effects are. We can see that some of the secondary effects are quite small and others are larger, but they are all smaller than the main effect. This is very typical for uplift modeling—the heterogeneous effects are generally smaller than the main effect.

13.5.6.6   Incremental Gains Curve Example

We can visualize the quality of our models with an incremental gains chart, which displays the gains against the percentile of users. Figure 13.3 shows the effect of targeting different quintiles of the population with an uplift random forest model and a causal conditional forest model. The user population is ranked in descending order in terms of effect. The incremental gains or the vertical axis can also be called "uplift." The baseline shows the uplift of random targeting. Note that with the last quintile, there is no difference between random targeting and either model.

For our example from the Lalonde data set, Figure 13.3 includes two models, the causal conditional inference tree model and the uplift random forest model, versus the random targeting model. We can see the causal conditional inference tree model is better.

13.5.6.7   Model Performance: Qini

Qini is a measure of the efficacy of the uplift. It is the area between the incremental gains curve (for each model) and the diagonal representing random targeting.

In Figure 13.3, for the causal conditional inference forest model, Qini is the area between the models—that is, the causal conditional forest model and the random targeting model. *Qini is 0.35 and 0.0045 for these two models, respectively, for the Lalonde data set.*

Qini—that is, the area under the curve—represents the improvement of uplift compared to random targeting. We calculate the incremental gains curve by applying our training model to our test data and calculating the gains of the model. Refer to Radcliffe and Surry (2011) for a more thorough examination of Qini and the effect of uplift on revenue.

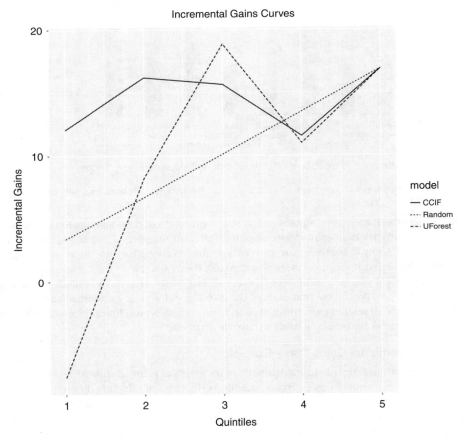

Figure 13.3   The incremental gains curve.

13.5.6.8 Causal Inference

How can we interpret our uplift results within the causal inference framework? In this chapter, we asked whether a jobs program causes an increase in employment in the next year. We asked what the magnitude of the causal effect is.

We first estimated that the jobs program caused about a 10% increase in the probability of having a job in the subsequent year. We could then access the cost of providing the program—for example, in terms of future taxes paid by recipients and the benefits to public budgets in terms of lower recidivism and less public program usage. Then, we could determine if we wanted to continue to run the jobs program.

Next, with uplift modeling, we were able to estimate the subgroup population effects or the causal effects of the jobs program on certain relevant subpopulations. From our uplift models, we estimated that being married increased the causal effect of the jobs program on employment about 6%, while higher education increased the causal effect of the jobs program on employment about 4%. Being Hispanic lowered the causal effect of the jobs program about 1%. We can see that the jobs program had different effects on different subpopulations.

If you were trying to target workers for a future jobs program, you might want to target those workers who would experience the largest positive effects. Alternatively, you might want to restructure your program to target those users who failed to gain much from the program. All of these potential plans of action are directly determined by causal insights derived from the data.

Keep in mind that since experimental results are defined by internal validity, these results might hold only for the population tested. In other words, since this program preselected individuals who were well connected with public institutions, the effect of the jobs program might be different for not-so-well-connected individuals. These individuals could have been preselected based on better social skills, thereby leading to a larger causal effect than other, less-connected populations might experience. You'll also see the problem of initial preselection in a web product, if your experiment or experimental design occurs later in the user funnel.

Overall, the key benefit of uplift modeling and the other causal methods described in this section is the clear prescriptive insights they provide. Causal inference gives us the information with which to make clear decisions that align with the goals of our organization. Our insights are defensible, clear, and prescriptive, and can lead to better outcomes in the future.

13.6 Actionable Insights

In this chapter, you learned about the following:

- For acquisition, engagement, retention, and revenue (all parts of the user development cycle), uplift modeling can deliver actionable information.

- For uplift modeling to work, you must have A/B testing data.

- Running an uplift model can be as simple as running a logistic regression with the correct setup.

- More complex models are available for nonlinear functional forms, as well as models that correct some of the traditional problems with uplift models.

- Uplift models offer the best of both worlds—predictive utility and causal inference.

Uplift modeling needs to be in every analyst's toolkit because of its powerful ability to estimate individual causal effects. It also provides a vital piece of information that you want to know—namely, how a particular treatment will affect different subpopulations.

You can also think of individual treatment effects as they apply to yourself. Should you take this drug regimen? Should you drink red wine? How should you change your behavior to live longer? This chapter has helped attack this problem in user analytics by explaining how uplift modeling works and how to implement it in practice.

The next section of this book will go over the R implementations for basic, predictive, and causal inference methods.

V

Basic, Predictive, and Causal Inference Methods in R

14

Metrics in R

The goal of the R portion of this book (Chapters 14–16) is not to teach R as a programming language, but through the command line for simple statistical analysis—how it's most commonly used in an analytics capacity. The R version used in Chapters 14–16 is R version 3.5.3 (2019-03-11), the Great Truth.

In this introductory R chapter, we'll do the following:

- Install R and RStudio.
- Learn the basics of R and RMarkdown.
- Create and analyze statistical distributions.
- Review metric creation.

In this chapter, we'll review the basics of R programming in combination with the concepts from Chapter 4 in R—that is, statistical distributions and metrics. Later chapters will go over implementation of A/B testing, prediction, causal inference from observational data, uplift modeling, and population projection in R.

14.1   Why R?

A point of view can be a dangerous luxury when substituted for insight and understanding.

—Marshall McLuhan

R, a statistical computing and visualization language, is one of the best software tools to help you turn your raw data into beautiful interactive insights. Why? Because R is an easy-to-use language that comes with features for complex statistical computing. R has some of the most comprehensive statistics libraries because of its use by academic statisticians. In addition, since R is open source under the GNU project, a large number of packages have been developed to support statistics and machine learning. R also has many programming functionalities (like being object-oriented) that make it a powerful way to analyze data. On top of that, it's free!

The data sets used in this book are small to help you learn about complex mathematical and statistical concepts. However, these techniques can be used with larger data sets. R has multi-threading capabilities, and R programs can interact with Hadoop and other Big Data applications.

The intended audience for the R portion of the book is readers with some familiarity with other programming languages. Nevertheless, you do not need proficiency in another language to use the book to learn R.

The beautiful thing about R is that it can be used through the command line as a simple statistical calculator or as a sophisticated programming language. So even if you are new to R and programming, you should be able to learn quite a lot and implement most of the applications discussed in this book on your own data sets.

The next section helps readers who are new to R to set up the R environment. If you already have R and RStudio installed and ready to go, feel free to skip the next section on R fundamentals.

14.2   R Fundamentals: A Very Basic Introduction to R and Its Setup

We start with a little history of the R language and then turn to installation and setup.

14.2.1   The R Language

Ross Ihaka and Robert Gentleman developed the R software environment at Bell Labs in the 1990s. R is easy to use, and a large number of statistical and domain-specific packages have been written for this language. It's based primarily on the C programming language. When working with large data stores in R, one important tip to help with your application development is that many R functions call C functions internally. It's better to rely on the iterating functions like `apply()`, than write for-loops. If written with a for-loop instead of a function, R will call C for each item in the loop versus once for the whole function.

To install R, go to this site: www.r-project.org/. You will have to choose the Windows, Mac, or Linux version as well as the CRAN mirror for your region. For Windows, the default installation location is "Program Files," which can cause problems because of the space in the name; thus, the program should be installed in Documents or some other directory instead. In addition to the R environment, it is advisable to get an integrated development environment (IDE) as well. For those new to programming, an IDE is simply an application that makes development easier by providing a nice design/format, code completion, and the ability to easily view output and run code. One of the best IDEs for R is RStudio.

Although other lightweight editors are available, this book will primarily use RStudio because of the great features that have been built in to make the R development environment easy to use. RStudio allows for subdivision of project space, easy version control (which is very important because the R environment cannot easily deal with multiple versions of packages), built-in RMarkdown (to create beautiful, professional documents), the ability to connect to a database and run database queries, and four tabs for ease of viewing code, output, graphics and the R environment. RStudio is also free (the personal development version) and can be downloaded here: www.rstudio.com/.

What Is an R Package?

A package is a set of functionalities that are available to users when the package is installed. For instance, we could have a {numbers} package, which allows us to use the "+" operator to add two numbers together. Another package that we might install is {dyplr}, which uses simple, intuitive functions to clean and manipulate data in R.

If you're working with a Mac, R should have been installed properly.

If you are working with Windows, you might encounter a problem loading R packages between R and RStudio. During the installation process, make sure they are installed at the same top-level directory. This will ensure both the R environment and RStudio are accessing the libraries from the same location. To find out where the libraries are installed, enter .libPaths() at the > prompt in R as well as in RStudio, and make sure both show the same location. Here is an example of the output from running this command and getting the default install location:

```
> libpaths() # in R
[1] "C:/PROGRAM/R/R-212~1.2/library"
```

14.2.2   RStudio

As mentioned earlier, RStudio is an IDE for developing R programs. It comes with a great editor to create and modify R programs and tools to visualize data and create reports.

As shown in Figure 14.1, RStudio has four panels. The panel on the top left-hand side is where you type your code; it is the input area for any code that you want to run. You can run this code by clicking the green arrow (or, alternatively, pressing Ctrl+Enter on the keyboard) at the top of the prompt. You can save your code by clicking the blue disk.

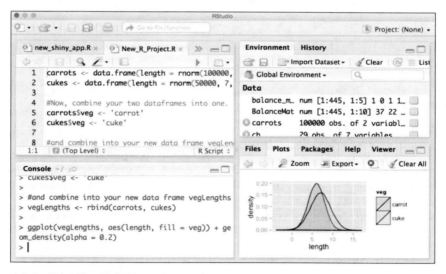

Figure 14.1   The RStudio window's four panels.

The bottom left-hand screen is the console where your code runs and you see the output as it executes. As shown in Figure 10.1, each ">" shows the executed line of code in blue. The output in black. The console also shows the trace of how the program was executed when an error occurs, and it is a great help in debugging your program. A trace will show you how your function reached its current point, by listing the functions backward from the current to the first function run.

The top right-hand panel provides a summary of your R environment. It shows the objects that you have created and the functions that you have defined. The top left-panel can hold your R script, RMarkdown, and more.

The panel on the bottom right also provides multiple functionalities. The Files tab acts like the File Explorer. It shows the local directory structure in your computer. You can navigate to any folder by clicking the appropriate folder icons and can launch the file by clicking the file name.

The Plot tab displays the plots you created. The Packages tab lists the packages installed in your R environment. The Help tab allows you to see the R documentation for functions.

RStudio is a great development environment that will allow you to run statistical analyses, display outputs, and plot data in the same window.

14.2.3   Installing Packages

To begin, open RStudio and go to "New Project" under the File menu located on the menu bar of RStudio. From there, create a new R project in a subdirectory of your choice.

The reason that we use RStudio projects is to subdivide the work. Each project has its own workspace, history, working directory, and supporting documents. This will make it easy for you to work with other developers and upload your code to repositories like GitHub.

To install a package, follow these steps:

1. Install: Run the command `install.packages("packageName")` to install an R package. It may pull up a question about the CRAN mirror. Pick the mirror closest to your geographic location. Mine is in Berkeley, California.

2. Load: Run the command `library("packageName")` to load the package for your current session.

Here is an example:

```
>install.packages("packrat")
>library(packrat)
```

Notice the name "packrat" appears in quotes because it's a string.

The reason that we installed the package packrat is so that we can use version control. Version control means that in a later session, you upload a later version of a package. This later version may have changed function names or a myriad of other changes, leaving your code unexecutable. This is where packrat comes in: It's a snapshot of your current packages at the version you need for a given project.

Once packrat is installed, you can run `packrat::init()` and the project becomes a packrat project, which means it has its own project package library. Now, when you run your program, package version changes will not affect it.

At this point, you've created a new packrat project and you're ready to get started with its development. The first project that we'll create is a simple RMarkdown document.

If you want to use packrat in the future, you don't need to install it again. Instead, just load it using the `library()` function.

14.2.4   RMarkdown

RMarkdown is an authoring framework that helps you create HTML, PDF, and MS Word documents and PowerPoint or HTML presentations, with R code and output. If you have worked with HTML, XML, or LaTeX, you are aware of what a markup language is. These languages use tags to define elements in a document. RMarkdown uses Markdown, which is also a markup language, to create beautiful writing, code, and output without having to use tags as in other markup languages. RMarkdown allows you to save your analysis or calculations if you use R as a statistical calculator, as you sometimes might.

RMarkdown comes pre-installed in later versions of RStudio. In case your version does not have it, run the following command in your project environment to install RMarkdown:

```
# install.packages("rmarkdown")
```

RMarkdown is quite easy to use. It includes three important aspects:

- Formatting text
- Chunking
- Compilation

14.2.4.1   Formatting Text

Users cannot control spacing in general. However, there are some exceptions to this rule. Pressing the Enter key will create a new paragraph, for example. There are also more complex exceptions that we will not discuss here.

While this is useful, if you desire other types of spacing, it is more difficult to implement in the way that you want. You'll have to play around with spacing, moving back and forth between output and the Markdown document.

Let's start by writing a simple document in RMarkdown. Table 14.1 summarizes the simple writing tools available in the Markdown language. It shows the syntax for creating headers, lists, and tables. Study the list for a few minutes to understand how to start writing. In RMarkdown, emphasized and strong statements get rendered as italic and bold, respectively, by default.

Table 14.1   **Markdown Writing Syntax**

Writing Tool	Markdown Syntax
Header	`# Header`
List	
■ Item 1	`*Item 1`
■ Item 2	`*Item 2`
■ Item 3	`*Item 3`
Italics (emphasized)	`_italics_`
Bold (strong)	`**bold**`

RMarkdown can contain chunks of R code. To add a chunk of R code, you simply click on the Chunks button at the top of the working frame or add ```{r} at the start of a chunk and ``` at the end of a chunk. Alternatively, you could use the keyboard shortcut Ctrl+Alt+I. Within that code chunk, you can put executable code that creates an output. To show the code, we use `echo = TRUE`. To not evaluate a code chunk, we can use `eval = FALSE`. You can also suppress warning and error messages with `warning = FALSE` and `errors = FALSE`, respectively. Also, smaller code chucks are better because when you compile the program, RMarkdown will not show you where the error is located within a given code chunk.

There are other arguments about whether to cache the output and how figures and text are printed. You find more information about these details at yihui.name/knitr/. Don't forget to install all of the packages and functions that are needed.

To reference variables in the text, outside of a code chunk, you just refer to them as `'''r mean(1:10)'''`.

You can write a few sentences using some of this syntax from Table 14.1. Here is a sample that you can try to modify:

```
# First RMarkdown
This is my first RMarkdown. It is exciting and cool.
This is the string that I printed: Hello World
```

Once the document has been written, the last step is to compile the document into the format that you want. To compile, click the Knit button or, alternatively, press Ctrl+Shift+K. RStudio compiles your document and sends the output to the RMarkdown tab on the lower-left panel. Once the compilation is complete, the document is generated in a new window.

You can also render your document directly by running `rmarkdown::render("")`. If your Markdown object compiled, then a new document in your given format will be created in the project directory.

14.2.5 Reading Data into R

We can read most data formats into R with one function. To read a comma-separated file (CSV), all you need to do is run `read.csv("file_path")`. We can use the argument `stringsAsFactors=FALSE` in `read.csv()` if we want the strings to be read in as strings rather than as factors. Recall that a string is a sequence of characters, whereas factors in R are a set of strings that map to numeric values. For instance, suppose we had a dummy variable for "male" and "female." We might then create the following factor: "male" maps to 1 and "female" maps to 2.

If you have a tab-delimited file (TAB), run `read.table(file_name, sep="\t")`. The function `read.table()` is quite versatile; it is capable of reading different data formats and should generally be used when data is not in a CSV format.

```
# Reading in a CSV file
dataset <- read.csv("~/Projects/practice_csv.csv")
# Reading in a TAB file
dataset <- read.table("~/Projects/practice_tab.tab", sep="\t")
```

If you build a data set in R and need to save it or some other object, you can save it as an R data object with `saveRDS()`. You can read in an R data object very easily with `readRDS()`. The R data object has the extension `.rdata`. Note that for most of these input types, the first row is taken as the header row, unless otherwise specified.

Finally, to read web formats such as JSON or XML, use the appropriate packages ("jsonlite," "xml2") to read data into R.

The next section addresses blank and missing values in data sets.

14.2.6 NAs in R

Many data sets will have blank values. This is a problem when working with data in R. R takes any blanks that you have in a data set and turns them into NAs—that is, placeholders. However if you don't deal with your NAs, you'll get error messages or your function will return NA.

You can change an NA by simply overwriting it with a numeric or other value. If this makes sense in your context, you should write in the correct values. The other way to deal with NAs is to simply remove them from a data set. R will remove all the rows with NA values.

```
# Removing rows where any column has an NA value
dataset_na_removed <- na.omit(dataset)
```

Many functions have an argument for how to handle NAs. For instance, with the mean function, mean(), we have to set na.rm = TRUE. This means that we will remove NAs from the calculation of the mean. Check the documentation for the exact syntax for a given function.

```
# Removing NA values from the mean function
mean_your_data <- mean(data[,1], na.rm = TRUE)
```

NaN and Inf should not be confused with NAs. NaN and Inf indicate that the number is infinite, indeterminate, or complex.

In the next section, we will use R to visualize and demonstrate the topics in Chapter 4 on distributions and Chapter 5 on metrics development. We will primarily focus on the normal and exponential distributions in this discussion.

14.3 Sampling from Distributions in R

In Chapter 4 section 4.1, we spent some time discussing normal distributions and discovering their usefulness. We can use the rnorm() function to generate random numbers from a normal distribution with our chosen mean and standard deviation. We can imagine these randomly generated numbers as "potential" user data. Of course, real user data will never be this nice, but our random numbers data set is easy to work and learn with.

Let's see how these normal distributions vary given different base criteria. Sampling means that we draw examples from a distribution to estimate the characteristics of the distribution. In Listing 14.1, we sample from three normal distributions with the same means, but different standard deviations. The standard deviations are 1, 3, and 3, respectively. We also vary the number of observations and see how that changes the shape of the distribution. The third normal distribution has 10 times the number of observations as the first two distributions. Can you guess what will happen to the third normal distribution?

Listing 14.1 **Sampling from the Normal Distribution**

```
# Library ggplot2
library(ggplot2)
# Setting Random Seed
set.seed(100)

# Sampling from some normal distributions and putting them into a data frame
normal_data = data.frame(
  normal1 = rnorm(100, 1, 1),
  normal2 = rnorm(100, 1, 3),
  normal3 = rnorm(1000, 1, 3)
)
```

```
# Density plots of these distributions
a <- ggplot(normal_data, aes(x = normal1)) +
      # Density Plot
      a + geom_density() +
      # Title
      ggtitle("Normal Distribution: Standard Deviation = 1, Observations = 100") +
      # X and Y Axes Titling
      ylab("Density") + xlab("Normal 1") +
      # Title Formatting
      theme(plot.title = element_text(hjust = 0.5))

b <- ggplot(normal_data, aes(x= normal2))
      b + geom_density() + ggtitle("Normal Distribution: Standard Deviation = 3,
        Observations = 100") +
      xlab("Normal 2") + ylab("Density") + theme(plot.title =
        element_text(hjust = 0.5))

c <- ggplot(normal_data, aes(x= normal3))
      c + geom_density() + ggtitle("Normal Distribution: Standard Deviation = 3,
        Observations = 1,000") +
      xlab("Normal 3") + ylab("Density") + theme(plot.title =
        element_text(hjust = 0.5))
```

Before we sample from a normal distribution, we need to set a random seed, so that we can replicate the results for future reference. We plot the first normal distribution in Figure 14.2, the second in Figure 14.3, and the third in Figure 14.4. We use a density plot, which can be thought of as a smooth histogram. The higher the density, the more points match that value.

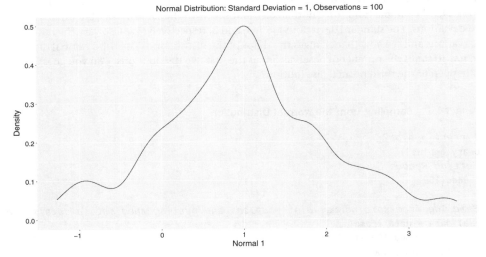

Figure 14.2   Density plot of a normal distribution, SD = 1, observations = 100.

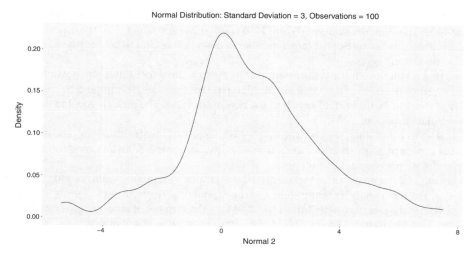

Figure 14.3   Density plot of the second normal distribution, SD = 3, observations = 100.

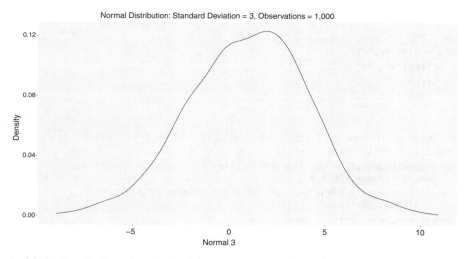

Figure 14.4   Density plot of the third normal distribution, SD = 5, observations = 1,000.

In this section, we'll use a data frame, which is an R object often used to hold data sets. We can create one with `data.frame()`. Then, we'll use both base plotting in R and the package {ggplot2} to create graphics in the next few chapters.

The sets of plots in this section are created using ggplot2. This package works in the following way. First, we load our data with the `ggplot()` function. We then add specifics for our plot with other functions, such as a title with `ggtitle()`, and the plot type. In Figures 14.2–14.4, the density plot is specified with the `geom_density()`.

The first normal distribution (Figure 14.2) is narrower than the second normal distribution (Figure 14.3). The third distribution (Figure 14.4) is smoother and wider than the other distributions. It's smoother because of the larger number of observations and wider because of the larger standard deviation.

Note that for all three normal distributions, the mean is the same: 1. It is also possible to vary the mean. Since the form of a normal distribution remains the same, this implies that the highest density of the distribution would switch to the new mean value. The mean is equal to the mode in a normal distribution.

To make this interesting, suppose we sample from some exponential distributions. We discussed exponential distributions in section 4.1.8. In R, to sample from an exponential distribution, we use the `rexp()` function.

In Listing 14.2, we create three exponential distributions by sampling while varying the rate parameter. The rate parameter tells us how fast the exponential distribution will grow. In this case, we'll vary the rate parameter from 1 to 3 and vary the number of observations from 100 to 1,000, respectively. Figures 14.5–14.7 plot these three exponential distributions.

Listing 14.2 Sampling from an Exponential Distribution

```r
# Setting Random Seed
set.seed(100)

# Sampling from random exponential distributions
exp_data = data.frame(
  exp1 = rexp(100, 1),
  exp2 = rexp(100, 3),
  exp3 = rexp(1000, 3)
)

# Density plot for each of the distributions
a <- ggplot(exp_data, aes(x = exp1))
    a + geom_density() + ggtitle("Exponential Distribution: Rate = 1,
        Observations = 100") +
    ylab("Density") + xlab("Exponential 1") + theme(plot.title =
        element_text(hjust = 0.5))
b <- ggplot(exp_data, aes(x = exp2))
    b + geom_density() + ggtitle("Exponential Distribution: Rate = 3,
        Observations = 100") +
    ylab("Density") + xlab("Exponential 2") + theme(plot.title =
        element_text(hjust = 0.5))
c <- ggplot(exp_data, aes(x = exp3))
    c + geom_density() + ggtitle("Exponential Distribution: Rate = 3,
        Observations = 1,000") +
    ylab("Density") + xlab("Exponential 3") + theme(plot.title =
        element_text(hjust = 0.5))
```

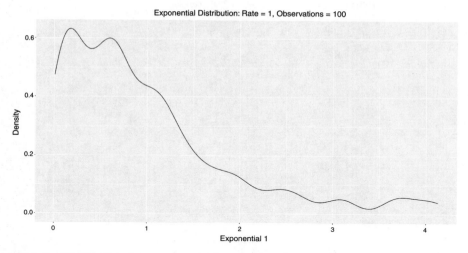

Figure 14.5   Density plot of an exponential distribution, rate = 1, observations = 100.

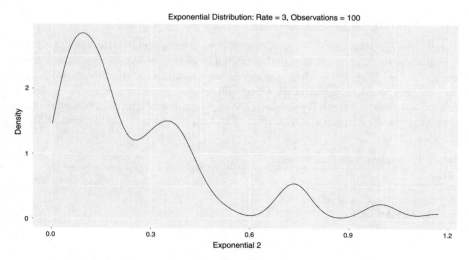

Figure 14.6   Density plot of an exponential distribution, rate = 3, observations = 100.

We can see that the higher the rate parameter, the faster the distribution tends toward zero. Again, the larger the number of observations, the smoother the distribution will be.

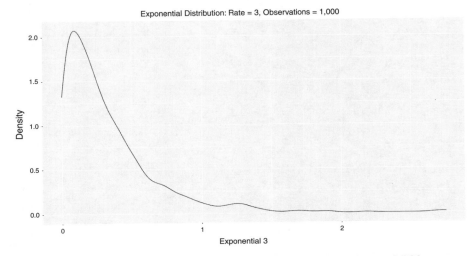

Figure 14.7   Density plot of exponential distribution, rate = 3, observations = 1,000.

14.4   Summary Statistics

Now that we've sampled from some normal and exponential distributions in R, let's find the mean, median and standard deviation of these samples. We discussed mean, median and standard deviation in sections 4.1.4-6. To do so, we can use R built-ins like the `mean()` function. This is pretty straightforward, unless there are NAs or NaNs, in which case we just have to declare what we want the function to do with these values. Listing 14.3 produces the basic summary statistics for the first normal distribution and the exponential distribution created in Section 14.3.

Listing 14.3   **Summary of Functionality**

```
# Creating data easy for use
normal1 <- normal_data$normal1
exp1 <- exp_data$exp1

# Finding the mean of a distribution
mean(normal1)
## [1] 1.002913

mean(exp1)
## [1] 0.9874761

# Finding the median of the distribution
median(normal1)
## [1] 0.9405801

median(exp1)
## [1] 0.6955635
```

```
# Finding the standard deviation of the distribution
sd(normal1)
## [1] 1.016102

sd(exp1)
## [1] 0.9242444

summary(normal1)

summary(exp1)
```

We can also call the `summary()` function in R, which has different meanings depending on the object. For a distribution, it will give you the mean, median, minimum, maximum, and quartile values.

```
# Summary Statistics in R
summary(normal1)
##    Min.  1st Qu. Median  Mean   3rd Qu. Max.
## -1.2720  0.3912  0.9406  1.0030  1.6560  3.5820

summary(exp1)
##    Min.    1st Qu.   Median    Mean    3rd Qu.    Max.
## 0.008003 0.325817 0.695564 0.987476 1.295371 4.129465
```

We can observe that the median and the mean are roughly the same for the normal distribution, but not for the exponential distribution.

We know that a normal distribution has some nice properties. How do we know if our user data is, indeed, a normal distribution? We can use a Q-Q plot to determine whether our data is approximately normal.

14.5   Q-Q Plot

A Q-Q plot is a modeling technique that can help us decide if the data that we have likely came from the same distribution that we want to compare it to. The idea of a Q-Q plot is that the percentiles of data should be similar if the data comes from the same distribution. For instance, if 90% of the data is less than 5 in a given distribution, then the percentage should be the same for the other distribution. If the two distributions' percentiles match, the Q-Q plot should match the 45-degree line (i.e., the red line in Figure 14.8).

Let's see how the normal Q-Q plot works for our two distributions. The plot for the normal distribution we randomly created should match the Q-Q plot for the normal distribution. Does it match in this example?

Listing 14.4 plots the Q-Q plots to determine normality for our first sample from the normal distribution (Figure 14.8) and our first sample from the exponential distribution (Figure 14.9). We will also apply the Shapiro-Wilk normality test to verify our results. The Shapiro-Wilks test of normality assumes that the distribution is normal; if it's likely not normal, then it returns a significant result.

Listing 14.4   **Q-Q plots**

```
# Q-Q plot of the distributions to determine normality
# Normal
qqnorm(normal1, main=c("Normal Q-Q Plot"), xlab="Normal Theoretical Quantiles",
  ylab="Normal Data Quantiles")
qqline(normal1, col = 2)

# Exponential
qqnorm(exp1, main=c("Exponential Q-Q Plot"), xlab="Normal Theoretical Quantiles",
  ylab="Exponential Data Quantiles")
qqline(exp1, col = 2)

# We can also use a normality test - in this case, the Shapiro-Wilks
# normality test
shapiro.test(normal1)

##
## Shapiro-Wilks normality test
##
## data:  normal1
## W = 0.98699, p-value = 9.355e-08

shapiro.test(exp1)
##
## Shapiro-Wilks normality test
##
## data:  exp1
## W = 0.8457, p-value < 2.2e-16
```

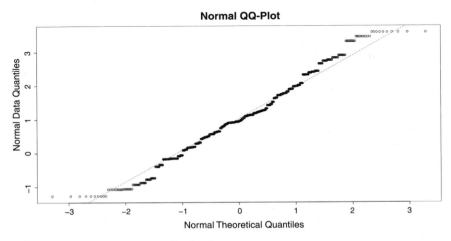

Figure 14.8   Q-Q plot of the normal distribution.

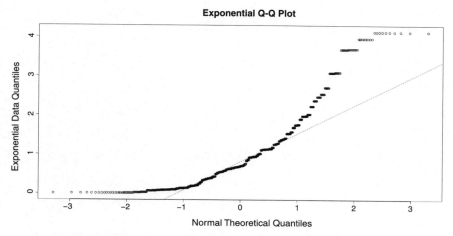

Figure 14.9   Q-Q plot of the exponential distribution.

From plotting the Q-Q plot, we can tell that the exponential data is not normal because the points in Figure 14.9 do not form a 45-degree line as in Figure 14.8. That, of course, is correct!

14.6   Calculating Variance and Higher Moments

We need to sometimes look at more complex metrics from distributions. We explored these more complex metrics in section 4.1.7. In this section, we'll calculate in R some other metrics from distributions. As we know from Chapter 4, variance is the square of the standard deviation.

Skew and kurtosis are some of the higher moments. In layperson's terms, skew is how much the distribution is pushed to one side or the other, and kurtosis is the thickness of the tails. Practically, this means how many observations lie at the extremes.

For simple calculation of these higher-order moments, load the {e1071} library. In this section, we show the R code to calculate variance, skew, and kurtosis for the first normal and exponential distribution examples.

You can also use the `library()` function or the `require()` function. These functions are analogous, except that if the library does not load, the `require()` function will return FALSE and a warning rather than an error. Listing 14.5 calculates the higher moments in R.

Listing 14.5   **Calculating Variance and Higher Moments**

```
# Installing the e1071 library
#install.packages('e1071')
library(e1071)

# Calculating the variance
var(normal1)
## [1] 1.032464
```

```
var(exp1)
## [1] 0.8542278

# Calculating skew
skewness(normal1)
## [1] 0.1661437

skewness(exp1)
## [1] 1.499829

# Calculating kurtosis
kurtosis(normal1)
## [1] -0.03226981

kurtosis(exp1)
## [1] 2.039756
```

14.7   Histograms and Binning

Creating histograms in R is very simple and a nice visualization tool. Let's create some histograms of the distributions that we have created. Histograms and binning was discussed in section 4.1.3 in Chapter 4.

In Listing 14.6, we'll build a histogram from our first normal distribution sample and our exponential distribution sample. Figure 14.10 is the histogram of our first normal sample and Figure 14.11 is the histogram of our first exponential distribution sample. In Section 14.3, we plotted the density plots of these distributions. Density plots are similar to histograms in that they provide a visualization of where the majority of the points lie. However, histograms have an extra component of binning.

Listing 14.6   **Plotting Histograms**

```
ggplot(normal_data, aes(x=normal1)) +
  # Histogram Plot
  geom_histogram() +
  # Titling and Title Formatting
  ggtitle("Histogram of a Normal Distribution") +
  ylab("Count") +
  xlab("Normal 1") +
  theme(plot.title = element_text(hjust = 0.5))

ggplot(exp_data, aes(x=exp1)) +
  geom_histogram() +
  ggtitle("Histogram of an Exponential Distribution") +
  xlab("Exponential 1") +
  ylab("Count") +
  theme(plot.title = element_text(hjust = 0.5))
```

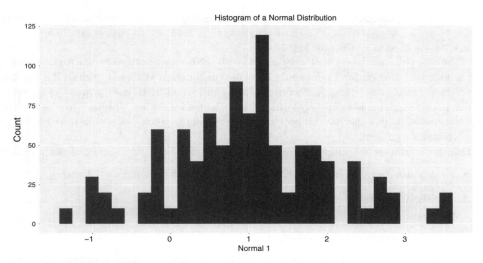

Figure 14.10 Histogram of the normal distribution.

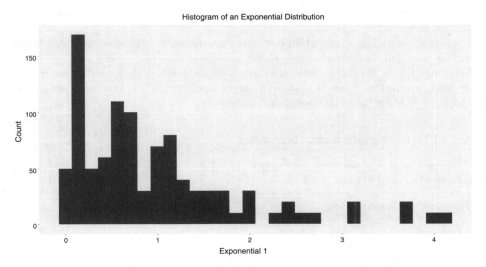

Figure 14.11 Histogram of the exponential distribution.

With histograms, we bin the data. How should we decide how many bins to use? It's often an art as much as a science. We can play with the number of bins and see how our distribution changes.

Notice that ggplot complains if we run the code in Listing 14.6. We get the following warning: `'stat_bin()' using 'bins = 30'. Pick better value with 'binwidth'`. This simply means that we need to set the number of bins.

In the next few paragraphs, we'll play around with the binning options for the first normal and exponential distribution examples. In R, we use the function `stat_bin()` to set the number of bins in our histogram in ggplot. We can also plot a histogram from base R with a `hist()` plot (which is a very quick way to initially visualize data), where we control binning with the `breaks` argument. `stat_bin()` also has this option, and its `breaks` argument works like the base R histogram's `breaks` argument.

There are a number of options that we have at our disposal when we use the `breaks` argument:

- We can give it a number that will define the number of bars (what we'll do here).

- We can give it a vector of breakpoints.

- We can provide a function to compute breakpoints.

- We can provide a function to compute the number of bars.

- We can give it the string name of the function to compute the number of bars.

In this introductory example, we'll just vary the number of cells. If we choose the number of cells, R then computes the breakpoints. It does this by taking the range of your variables' values and dividing that range by your number of cells plus 1. It will find the best equally spaced, round values that represent the full space.

The default for the binning function is the Sturges formula: ceiling(log2(length(x)) + 1). It's essentially the log of the length of your variable.

In Listing 14.7, we will vary the cell value by three designations—25, 50, and 100—for both the normal distribution. Figure 14.12 shows a histogram with the `hist()` function and 25 breaks. Figures 14.13–14.15 are the other histograms, respectively.

Listing 14.7 **Binning for a Normal Distribution**

```
# Different binning options (normal)
# Base histogram, breaks = 25
hist(normal1, main = "Histogram of a Normal Distribution", xlab="Normal 1",
  ylab="Count", breaks = 25)

# ggplot histogram, breaks = 25
ggplot(normal_data, aes(x = normal1)) +
  # Histogram binnings
  stat_bin(bins = 25) +
  # Titling
  ggtitle("Normal Distribution, Breaks = 25") +
  xlab("Normal 1") + ylab("Count") +
  # Title formatting
  theme(plot.title = element_text(hjust = 0.5))
```

```
ggplot(normal_data, aes(x = normal1)) + stat_bin(bins = 50) +
  ggtitle("Normal Distribution, Breaks = 50") +
  xlab("Normal 1") + ylab("Count") + theme(plot.title = element_text(hjust = 0.5))

ggplot(normal_data, aes(x = normal1)) + stat_bin(bins = 100) +
  ggtitle("Normal Distribution, Breaks = 100") +
  xlab("Normal 1") + ylab("Count") + theme(plot.title = element_text(hjust = 0.5))
```

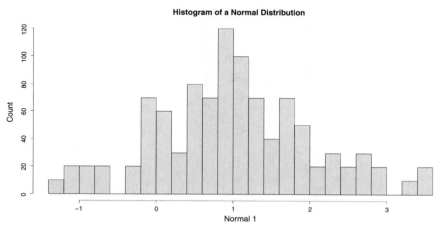

Figure 14.12   Histogram of a normal distribution, breaks = 25.

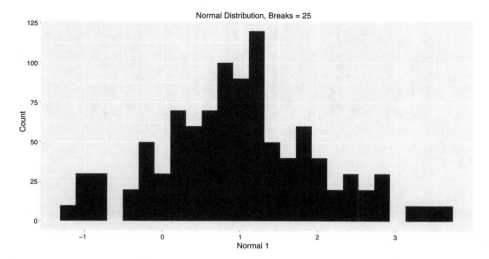

Figure 14.13   Histogram of a normal distribution, breaks = 25.

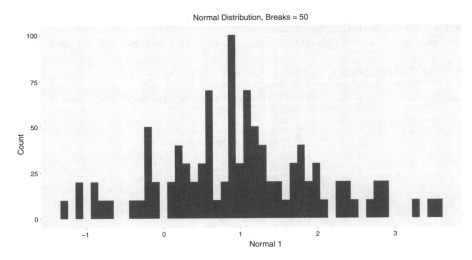

Figure 14.14   Histogram of a normal distribution, breaks = 50.

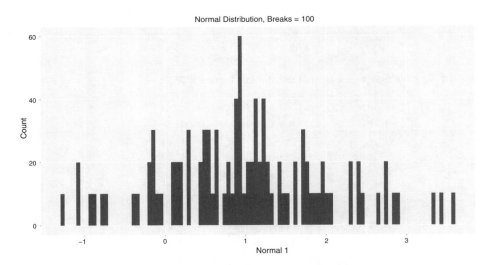

Figure 14.15   Histogram of a normal distribution, breaks = 100.

We can see in these three normal histograms that the number of bars greatly changes the looks of these distributions. The data is less smooth with more bars, but arguably is more true to its original form. We are also more likely to get lost in the noise. It's like a good story: A good story needs to leave out some details, so the reader does not get overwhelmed, but must still stay true to its form and have all the core components—the setting, characters, plot, and more.

Next, we'll visualize binning of the first exponential distribution while varying the sizes of the breaks again. In Listing 14.8, we will vary the cell value by three designations—25, 50, and

100—for both the exponential distribution. Figures 14.16–14.18 are the exponential histograms varying the bin sizes by the same amount, respectively.

Listing 14.8 **Binning for an Exponential Distribution**

```
# Different binning options (exponential)
ggplot(exp_data, aes(x = exp1)) +
  # Histogram Binning
  stat_bin(bins = 25) +
  # Titling
  ggtitle("Exponential Distribution, Breaks = 25") + xlab("Exponential 1") +
  ylab("Count") +
  # Title Formatting
  theme(plot.title = element_text(hjust = 0.5))

  ggplot(exp_data, aes(x = exp1)) + stat_bin(bins = 50) + ggtitle("Exponential
  Distribution, Breaks = 50") +
  ylab("Count") + xlab("Exponential 1") + theme(plot.title = element_text
  (hjust = 0.5))

  ggplot(exp_data, aes(x = exp1)) + stat_bin(bins = 100) + ggtitle("Exponential
  Distribution, Breaks = 100") +
  ylab("Count") + xlab("Exponential 1") + theme(plot.title = element_text
  (hjust = 0.5))
```

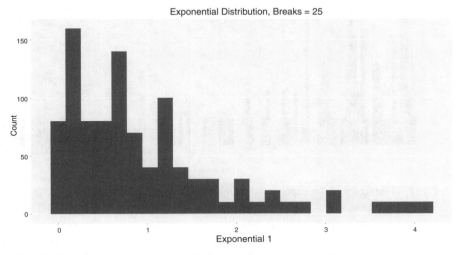

Figure 14.16   Histogram of the exponential distribution, breaks = 25.

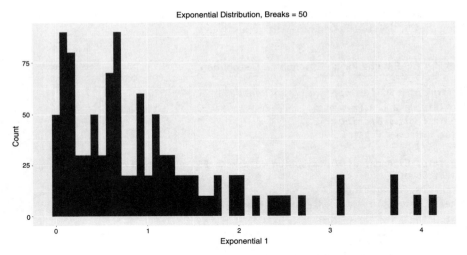

Figure 14.17   Histogram of the exponential distribution, breaks = 50.

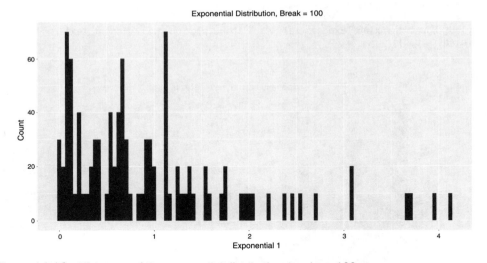

Figure 14.18   Histogram of the exponential distribution, breaks = 100.

With histograms, it's important to understand that how we bin data can lead to different—and sometimes misleading—interpretations. We should always explore more than just our first binning attempt. More sophisticated methods for determining the optimal binning exist, but are beyond the scope of this book. In this section, since histograms are very prevalent in user analytics, we just wanted to show how important selection of bins is for a histogram.

14.8 Bivariate Distribution and Correlation

In this section, we look at the relationship between two distributions. We discussed this topic in section 4.1.9 in Chapter 4. Suppose we assume that the first normal distribution is days in product and the exponential distribution is profile picture Likes. We're interested in seeing how these two distributions are related.

In Listing 14.9, we plot the two distributions together. Then, we'll calculate the linear correlation between the two variables. Finally, we'll calculate the regression line.

Listing 14.9 **Plotting the Bivariate Distribution**

```
# Plotting the relationship between our normal and exponential
# distributions, i.e. days in product
# Add Hmisc package
library(Hmisc)

# and likes
likes <- data.frame(cbind(normal1, exp1))
colnames(likes)<- c("Days", "Likes")

ggplot(likes,aes(Days, Likes))+
  stat_summary(fun.data=mean_cl_normal) +
  geom_smooth(method='lm',formula=y~x) +
  ggtitle("Relationship Between Days and Likes") +
  theme(plot.title = element_text(hjust = 0.5))

# With histograms, we bin the data. # Finding the correlation
cor(normal1, exp1)
## [1] 0.01346588
```

In Listing 14.9, we first build the data set by using cbind(), a simple function to bind vectors of columns together. The data consists of our normal and exponential samples that we are combining into a data frame with two columns. We can also use rbind(), which will bind vectors as rows. We then name our columns, so they will be readable when we plot them in our graph.

Next, we create a graph with the ggplot function. We add a regression line and the confidence interval for our regression line. We do this with the following functions. First, geom_smooth (method = 'lm', formula = y~x) builds our regression line. Note that we are defining the formula in the arguments, so we could define other formulas as well. Next, we add confidence intervals with stat_summary() function. Figure 14.19 shows these results for the example of the first normal and exponential distributions, assumed to be days and Likes. Finally, we can calculate correlation, using the cor() function.

We can see that the correlation between the two distributions is low—exactly what we would expect, since both distributions are independent of each other. The regression line is also basically flat, suggesting that there is no linear relationship, positive or negative, between days and Likes.

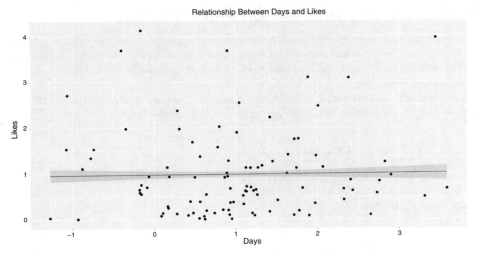

Figure 14.19   Bivariate plot of Days and Likes (includes linear regression line).

14.8.1 Calculating Metrics

In this next section, we'll go through some of the metric creation techniques discussed in Chapter 5 sections 5.1.5-5.1.7. We start by calculating period and cohort metrics.

We'll sample from an exponential distribution to create user data from a hypothetical web product over three months. Each month has a group of new users, and we want to determine how long they remained in the product. Listing 14.10 calculates period and cohort retention for this example. Figure 14.20 shows the distribution of all three cohorts together.

Listing 14.10   **Calculating Period and Cohort Metrics**

```
# Setting the seed
set.seed(100)

# Data frame with the different cohorts that we have created
cohort_model <- data.frame(
  cohort_number = factor(c(rep(1, each = 1000), rep(2, each = 2000),
    rep(3, each = 4000))),
  cohort_data = c(cohort1 <- rexp(1000, 1),
                  cohort2 <- rexp(2000, 1.5),
                  cohort3 <- rexp(4000, 3))
                  )

# Density plot by cohort
ggplot(cohort_model, aes(x=cohort_data, color=cohort_number)) +
  # Density Plot
  geom_density() +
```

```r
# Grayscale
scale_color_grey() +
theme_classic() +
# Titling
labs(title = "Cohort Days in Product", x = "Product in Days", y = "Density",
  color = "Cohort", linetype = "Cohort") +
# Title Formatting
theme(plot.title = element_text(hjust = 0.5))

# Average and median months in product over the full population
mean(cohort_model$cohort_data)
## [1] 0.5220862
median(cohort_model$cohort_data)
## [1] 0.3204659


# Average months in product by cohort
means_cohort <- tapply(cohort_model$cohort_data, cohort_model$cohort_number, mean)
medians_cohort <- tapply(cohort_model$cohort_data, cohort_model$cohort_number, median)

# Average months in product by cohort
mat_cohort <- matrix(c(means_cohort, medians_cohort), 3, 2)
rownames(mat_cohort)<-c("cohort1", "cohort2", "cohort3")
colnames(mat_cohort)<- c("mean", "median")
mat_cohort
## mean      median
## cohort1 0.9714811 0.6734068
## cohort2 0.6660809 0.4735058
## cohort3 0.3377401 0.2317998


# Adjusting for the users in each cohort
total_length <- length(cohort_model$cohort_data)
size_cohort <- c(table(cohort_model$cohort_number))

# Multiplying the cohort numbers by the number of users
colSums(mat_cohort*(size_cohort/total_length))
## mean      median
## 0.5220862 0.3639454
# Note: This is the same result as above

# We could equally weight each cohort
colSums(mat_cohort*(1/3))
   mean      median
## 0.6584341 0.4595708
```

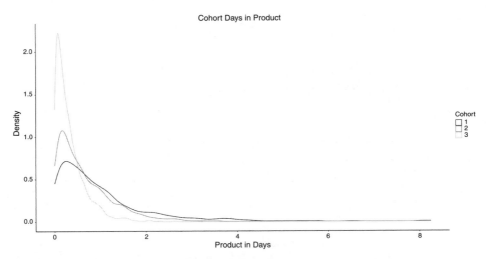

Figure 14.20   Three cohorts' user days plotted together.

Next, we calculate the simplest version—that is, retention over the full period. We do this by taking the mean of all the cohorts together.

```
# Average and median months in product over the full population
mean(cohort_model$cohort_data)
## [1] 0.5220862
median(cohort_model$cohort_data)
## [1] 0.3204659
```

Let's calculate the average and median number of user days by cohort. We can get aggregate metrics by relying on `tapply()`, which is in the family of `apply()` functions. These functions are replacements for for-loops and often faster to use than writing for-loops by hand in R. A for-loop is a function that will iterate over a set of data, usually performing a task. In our example, we will iterate over cohorts, calculating their mean and median.

We'll then put our data into a matrix, which is another R data structure. A matrix is very useful for carrying out linear algebraic operations like matrix multiplication and calculating eigenvectors (we'll see this in code listings in Chapter 16). We create a matrix object with the `matrix()` function. The first argument is the data, the second argument is the number of rows, and the third argument is the number of columns.

```
# Average months in product by cohort
means_cohort <- tapply(cohort_model$cohort_data, cohort_model$cohort_number, mean)
medians_cohort <- tapply(cohort_model$cohort_data, cohort_model$cohort_number, median)

# Average months in product by cohort
mat_cohort <- matrix(c(means_cohort, medians_cohort), 3, 2)
rownames(mat_cohort)<-c("cohort1", "cohort2", "cohort3")
colnames(mat_cohort)<- c("mean", "median")
mat_cohort
```

```
           mean      median
## cohort1 0.9714811 0.6734068
## cohort2 0.6660809 0.4735058
## cohort3 0.3377401 0.2317998
```

Here we calculated the simple period and cohort number for average months in product.

Let's say that we want to standardize our data by cohort size. We can also standardize by assuming equal weights for the different cohorts (as we did in Chapter 5 section 5.1.8) and see how this changes the outcome. We'll use some new functions in the next code block. Specifically, `table()` allows us to sum the length of each cohort by the number of elements in each cohort. `colSums()` is a great function because it allows us to sum up the columns of a matrix in one line.

```
# Adjusting for the users in each cohort
total_length <- length(cohort_model$cohort_data)
size_cohort <- c(table(cohort_model$cohort_number))

# Multiplying the cohort numbers by the number of users
colSums(mat_cohort*(size_cohort/total_length))
     mean      median
## 0.5220862 0.3639454
 # Note: This is the same result as above

 # We could equally weight each cohort
 colSums(mat_cohort*(1/3))
     mean      median
## 0.6584341 0.4595708
```

Suppose we want to standardize our data by cohort size. In this example, equal-sized cohorts increased our mean and median.

14.9 Parity Progression Ratios

The last topic that we will cover in this section is parity progression ratios (PPRs). We'll calculate these ratios and plot them to see where the breakpoints appear.

In this discussion, we're returning to the example from Section 5.2.6, "Revenue." We create a function to calculate the ratio by dividing the number of users who reached x purchases at their maximum from the number who reached $x - 1$ at their maximum. We then plot these ratios in a graph.

First, we create a vector of our original data. A vector is an R data type in which all the values are of the same type. Here, the vector comprises the progression or proportion of our user base that makes it to each subsequent purchase. Then we create an R function to calculate the ratio. To do so, we take the vector of numbers from two to the end and divide by the list shifted back by one. This process will calculate our full vector of ratios.

Next, we use the `function()` command to create a new function with arguments inside the parentheses. Here the only argument is a vector of the users at each step. A function generally takes arguments, performs some operation on the inputs, and then outputs something. In this case, this function will calculate the progression ratios and output that result. We'll use this example to demonstrate a function.

In this example, `calculate_ratio` is the name of the function. We use the `return()` function to return the vector. This function returns only one object. If you want to return more than one vector or matrix in R, you need to save it as a list, which is another R data type.

The ratio can be calculated by dividing the number of users who progress to the next step by those who progressed only to the prior step as of time *t*. We can then plot this result and look at how the ratio changes as we move toward higher and higher purchasing.

Listing 14.11 illustrates how to calculate the PPR. Figure 14.21 is the plotted progression ratios from our function.

Listing 14.11 **Parity Progression Ratio**

```
# Original vector of progression by users. It consists of the same numbers as
# in Chapter 3.
user_progression <- c(10000, 7800, 3560, 2875, 2000, 1876,1450, 1000, 543, 500, 450,
  425, 410)

# Function to calculate the progression ratios
calculate_ratio <- function(list_progress){
                  # Create a matrix
                  len_list <- length(list_progress)
                  ratios <- matrix(c(NA), len_list-1, 1)
                  # Calculate ratios
                  ratios <- list_progress[2:len_list]/
                  list_progress[1:len_list -1]
                  # Return list
                  return(ratios)
                  }


# Or we can skip the function altogether and just use two commands
progression_length <- length(user_progression)
progression_ratios <- user_progression[-1] / user_progression[-progression_length]


# Here we call the function and return the list that we calculated
progression_ratios <- calculate_ratio(user_progression)

# Plot the outcome
prog_ratios <- data.frame(cbind(c(1:length(progression_ratios)), progression_ratios))
colnames(prog_ratios)<-c("purchases", "ratios")

ggplot(data=prog_ratios, aes(x = purchases, y = ratios)) +
    # Line
    geom_line() +
    # Points
    geom_point() +
    # Titling
```

```
ggtitle("Purchasing Parity Progression Ratios") +
xlab("Purchases") +
ylab("Ratios") +
# Title Formatting
theme(plot.title = element_text(hjust = 0.5))
```

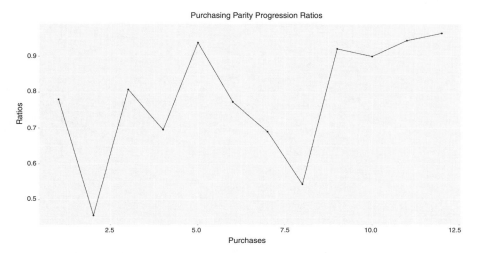

Figure 14.21   Parity progression purchasing example.

A very sticky product will approach a ratio of 1 very quickly. This is true for this purchasing example: By the ninth purchase, users progress to 1.

14.10   Summary

In this chapter, you were successfully able to:

- Run R in RStudio.

- Build a new R project and render RMarkdown documents.

- Plot distributions and calculate statistical moments.

- Create functions and metrics.

In the next chapter, we will work through A/B testing examples and predictive modeling in R.

A/B Testing, Predictive Modeling, and Population Projection in R

In the last chapter, we learned how to set up our R environment and R data objects, and how to sample from distributions. This chapter covers R implementation of A/B testing, predictive modeling, and population projection, as described in Chapters 6–9. By the end of this chapter, you should be able to:

- Run an A/B test in R.
- Analyze the results of an A/B test in R.
- Build simple clustering and predictive models in R.
- Cross-validate those models in R.
- Project populations from your web product.
- Understand and plot the long run dynamics of populations.

In this section, we'll go through the technical aspects of defining, building, and analyzing an A/B test. First, we'll build an experimental data set to implement and test out these ideas. Then, we'll implement the predictive models from Chapters 7–9.

15.1 A/B Testing in R

In the first part of this chapter, we'll build a data set by sampling from the distributions that we saw in Chapter 4. Once we have created some contrived data, we can test whether there is a statistical difference between treatment and control groups in our promotion example. The benefit of contrived data is that we know what the results of our statistical test should be. A copy of this data set is available on the book's website. The book's website also includes a real, labels-changed product analytics data set for readers to try out these techniques on real data.

When working with real data, you have to consider the data-generating process: What activities are your users engaging in to create this data? You also have to think about what metric you are interested in—for instance, the mean or the median. Another aspect you'll have to consider is whether the distribution follows a common statistical distribution, such as a normal or exponential distribution, to determine the right statistical test. Chapter 6 provides some examples of types of data/questions and the right statistical tests for them. This chapter will walk you through a few examples of A/B testing in R, where we know the "true" underlying distribution. Although this will never occur in real life, it will help us understand the concepts better.

As discussed in Chapter 6, an A/B test has treatment and control groups. The goal of each statistical test is to decide whether the desired metric is similar for both groups. If the metric is different, we'd like to know the size and the direction of the difference.

15.1.1   Statistical Testing

In this section, we'll demonstrate an example of running a number of A/B tests in R based on the content from Chapter 6 Section 6.5. Imagine that we run an A/B test on a new promotional banner on our website. We want to test its efficacy before we deploy it for all users. The treatment group will see the banner, and the control group will see the placebo or another similar banner without the promotion. To validate the banner's usefulness, we can calculate the effect of this promotion with a few key metrics.

In Listing 15.1, we build the data for the A/B testing section. Here, as we did in Chapter 14, we first set a random seed, so that the data is replicable. Then, we run our statistical tests on our metrics. Finally, we validate if our statistical test worked. In real life, the testing process will not be this cut and dry, but it's nice to work with clear-cut distributions when you start. Since we are sampling from known distributions, we'll know if the statistical test is correct.

Listing 15.1   **Creation of A/B testing data**

```
# Creation of A/B testing data
set.seed(101)

# Creating the A/B testing outcomes
# Exponential distribution, time on webpage
treated_timeonpage <- rexp(2000, 1.5)
control_timeonpage <- rexp(2000, .5)

# Normal distribution, average revenue
treated_averev <- rnorm(2000, 10, 5)
control_averev <- rnorm(2000, 15, 5)

# Poisson distribution, number of purchases
treated_purchases <- rpois(2000, 2)
control_purchases <- rpois(2000, 2)

# Binomial distribution, CTR
treated_CTR <- rbinom(2000, 0:1, .5)
control_CTR <- rbinom(2000, 0:1, .57)
```

```
# Putting all the variables together
# Treatment data set
user_treated <- data.frame(user_id = 1:2000, treated = as.factor(1), time_in_product =
    treated_timeonpage, purchases = treated_purchases, rev_user = treated_averev,
    CTR = treated_CTR, region = sample(LETTERS[1:4], 2000, replace = T), gender =
    rep(c("F", "M"), 1000))

# Control data set
user_control <- data.frame(user_id = 1:2000, treated = as.factor(0), time_in_product =
    control_timeonpage, purchases = control_purchases, rev_user = control_averev,
    CTR = control_CTR, region = sample(LETTERS[1:4], 2000, replace = T), gender =
    rep(c("F", "M"), 1000))

# Let's look at some of the data
full_data <- rbind(user_treated, user_control)
```

In this first section, we'll create the treatment and control groups' user distributions for each metric. The metrics are time on website, average revenue, number of purchases, and click-through rate (CTR). Before we start, see if you can determine which statistical test we will use for each metric.

As shown in Listing 15.1, we've put all the contrived data into two data frames: a treatment data frame and a control data frame. Next, we'll look at the first five values to verify that our data is combined correctly. As shown in Listing 15.2, running the head() function for user_treated displays the treated data set.

Listing 15.2 **View of Treated Data Set**

```
#15.2 View of data set
head(full_data)

##   user_id treated time_in_product purchases  rev_user CTR region gender
## 1       1       1       0.7879605         0  3.738263   0      D      F
## 2       2       1       2.1166552         2 18.977046   1      D      M
## 3       3       1       0.2795787         4 23.063693   0      A      F
## 4       4       1       0.2102539         0  7.167367   1      C      M
## 5       5       1       1.0628510         1  6.828969   0      B      F
## 6       6       1       0.3266455         1  9.516845   1      C      M
```

The next step is to run some statistical tests. The first metric that we will consider is average revenue. First, we plot the two distributions of average revenue per user (ARPU) in Figure 15.1. For all graphs in this section, we'll follow the following convention where treatment is the full line and the control is the dotted line.

Then, we run Welch's *t*-test (which is different from the Student's *t*-test we used in Chapter 6 section 6.5.4.2). The Student's *t*-test is easier to calculate and will give us the general idea, but in practice it is not the best choice. Welch's *t*-test is preferred in an empirical setting because it is likely that samples have different variances and/or sample sizes. The null hypothesis for Welch's *t*-test is that ARPU is the same for both the treatment and control groups. We run Welch's *t*-test in R with the t.test() function.

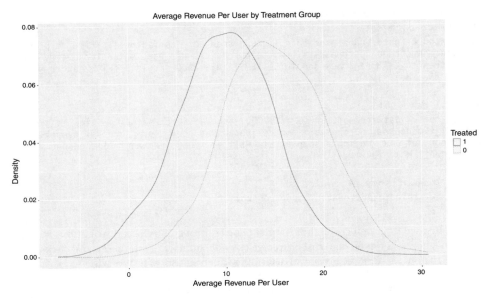

Figure 15.1   Treatment and control ARPU distributions.

Listing 15.3 gives the R output of Welch's *t*-test. The estimated difference between the two distributions is –$5. The *p* value is almost zero, meaning it's highly likely that the treatment and control distributions are different. The result can be interpreted in the following way: The promotion made users spend $5 less on average.

Listing 15.3   **Running an Analysis of A/B Outcomes**

```
# Run some analysis of the A/B testing outcomes
# t-Test
# In this example, we want to see if there is a difference between average
# revenue from the users who saw the promo and those who did not.

# Load ggplot package
library(ggplot2)

# Density plot of ARPU By treatment and control
ggplot(full_data, aes(x = rev_user, color = treated)) +
  geom_density(aes(linetype = treated)) +
  labs(title = "Average Revenue Per User by Treatment Group",
       x = "Average Revenue Per User", y = "Density",
       color = "Treated", linetype = "Treated") +
  theme(plot.title = element_text(hjust = 0.5))

# Running a t-test
t.test(user_treated$rev_user, user_control$rev_user)
```

```
##  Welch two-sample t-test
##
## data:  user_treated$rev_user and user_control$rev_user
## t = -31.741, df = 3997.3, p value < 2.2e-16
## alternative hypothesis: true difference in means is not equal to 0
## 95 percent confidence interval:
##   -5.333737 -4.713168
## sample estimates:
## mean of x mean of y
##   9.896065 14.919518
```

If the p value is higher, you have to make a determination of when to reject the null hypothesis. A good way of looking at it is as the likelihood of a false positive (or Type I error). If you use a p value of 0.05, you'll have a 1 in 20 chance of a false-positive result. Suppose you have 20 metrics for an A/B test; this confidence level means that one will have a significant difference in means that is not actually significant. A p value of 0.01 can be thought of as a 1 in 100 chance of a false-positive result. Thus, if you have 100 metrics, one will have a false positive result.

Okay, great—well, not so great for this product, but good for us that we found out this information! As described in Chapter 6, it's easy to be content with one or two metrics. That's generally a bad idea: You need to test out many metrics, over both the short and long runs, to determine the efficacy of a feature change.

Now, let's see how the banner promotion affected users' CTR to purchasing. Our null hypothesis is that the CTRs are the same for the treatment and control users. First, we'll plot the two distributions, as shown in Figure 15.2. Then, we'll use a chi-squared test to assess whether there is a difference in CTR, as we saw in Chapter 6 section 6.5.4.1. To run the chi-squared test in R, we use the `chisq.test()` function as shown in Listing 15.4.

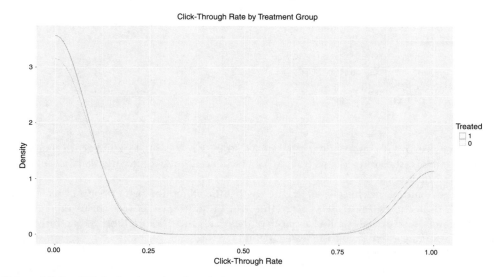

Figure 15.2   CTR for treatment and control groups.

Listing 15.4 **Running a Chi-Squared Test**

```r
# Chi-squared test
# In this example, we want to see if there is a difference in click-through
# rate (CTR) to purchase between those users who saw the promo and those
# who did not

# Density plot of CTR by treatment
ggplot(full_data, aes(x = CTR, color = treated)) +
  geom_density(aes(linetype = treated)) +
  labs(title = "Click-Through Rate by Treatment Group",  x = "Click-Through Rate",
       y = 'Density', color = "Treated", linetype = "Treated") +
  theme(plot.title = element_text(hjust = 0.5))

# Run the chi-squared test
ct <- chisq.test(user_treated$CTR, user_control$CTR)
ct

##   Pearson's chi-squared test with Yates's continuity correction
##
## data:  user_treated$CTR and user_control$CTR
## X-squared = 229.52, df = 1, p value < 2.2e-16

ct$expected

##                 user_control$CTR
## user_treated$CTR        0        1
##               0 1069.0325 441.9675
##               1  345.9675 143.0325

ct$observed

##                 user_control$CTR
## user_treated$CTR    0    1
##               0 1202  309
##               1  213  276
```

For reference, this is a sample from a binomial distribution. We won't go into depth about what a binomial distribution is here. Refer to Ashenfelter et al.'s (2006) *Statistics and Econometrics* for more information.

From the results of the chi-squared test, we see that the promotion had a negative effect on the CTR of the treated users. Fewer users clicked through. The difference between the treatment and control groups is statistically significant. Both of these early metrics are telling us that the promotion is not working as expected to increase CTR and revenue.

This is interesting. Let's look at a few more metrics and see if we can understand better what is actually happening. Next, we'll consider how long users spend on the page with the promotion. We can use survival analysis to visualize and understand this difference. Note that this is a popular way to look at how a feature affects user retention (length of time in product).

In Listing 15.5, we carry out survival analysis which was discussed in Chapter 6 section 6.5.4.3. The `surv_curv()` function defined in Listing 15.5 takes our data and builds a survival curve. The function works in the following way: (1) We need to discretize the steps to carry it out, so we round our data to the first decimal place; and (2) we need to calculate the proportion surviving at each step, so we sum the number of users where the time surviving is greater than the step number.

Listing 15.5 Survival Curve Analysis

```
# Library survival
library(survival)

# Function to calculate survival curves
sur_curve <- function(treated_rd, steps){
  # Create output object
    survival_mat <- matrix(c(NA), length(steps), 1)
    for(i in 1:length(steps)){
      # Calculate proportion surviving
      survival_mat[i] <-
      sum(ifelse(treated_rd >= steps[i], 1, 0))/length(treated_rd)
    }
    # Return matrix
    return(survival_mat)
}

# Round data and calculate steps for survival curve
treated_rd <- round(user_treated$time_in_product, 1)
steps <- seq(from = 0, to = max(treated_rd), by = .1)
control_rd <- round(user_control$time_in_product, 1)

# Call survival function to plot data
survival_treated <- sur_curve(treated_rd, steps)
survival_control <- sur_curve(control_rd, steps)

# Plot survival curves for treatment and control groups
full_survival <- as.data.frame(cbind(survival_treated, survival_control))
colnames(full_survival) <- c("treated", "control")
full_survival$seconds <- c(1:48)

ggplot(full_survival) +
  geom_line(aes(seconds, treated, linetype = "1")) +
  geom_line(aes(seconds, control, linetype = "0")) +
  labs(title = "Probability of Survival by Treatment Group",x= "Seconds",
       y = "Proportion", linetype='Treated') +
  theme(plot.title = element_text(hjust = 0.5))
```

Although `survival` does come with prebuilt function, `survfit()`, which can be plotted as a curve with `plot()`, in Listing 15.5 we include our own function to build a survival curve. Writing your own functions allows for greater flexibility in parameters, visualizations, and more.

As we saw with binning, how you chose to discretize the data (or the steps you create) can have a huge effect on what the curve looks like. Similar to binning, it can be useful to try different product-specific values. Here a step value of 0.1 second is used. Figure 15.3 shows the survival curve created by plotting the proportion surviving over time.

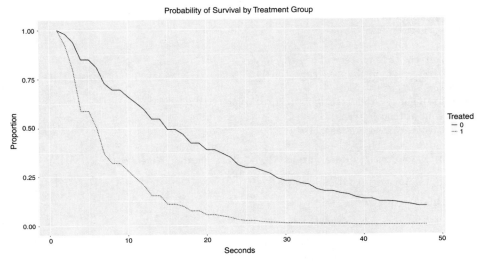

Figure 15.3   Survival curve for treatment and control on banner page.

Now, we'd like to know if our survival curves are different. To determine this, we calculate the log-rank test described in the sidebar in section 6.5.4.3, which is the statistical test for whether two survival curves are indeed the same. Our null hypothesis is that the survival curves are the same for the treatment and control groups. We need the package "survival" for easy calculation. We use the function `survdiff()` to calculate the log-rank test. Refer to Listing 15.6 to see how the log rank test is run.

Listing 15.6   **Running the log-rank test**

```
# Let's calculate the log-rank test between the treatment and control
# groups' time from click-to-purchase

# Survival analysis, log-rank test
fit <- survdiff(Surv(as.numeric(as.character(full_data$time_in_product)))
  ~ full_data$treated)
fit

## Call:
## survdiff(formula =
          Surv(as.numeric(as.character(full_data$time_in_product))) ~
##     full_data$treated)
```

```
##
##                          N Observed Expected (O-E)^2/E (O-E)^2/V
## full_data$treated=1 2000     2000     1121       688       1089
## full_data$treated=0 2000     2000     2879       268       1089
##
##  Chisq= 1089  on 1 degrees of freedom, p= <2e-16
```

From the plotted survival curves in Figure 15.3, we can see that the length of time on the web page is significantly longer for the control group than for the treatment group. The two survival curves are significantly different based on the low *p* value of the log-rank test. From all of the different metrics, we're beginning to see that the effect of the promotional banner on time on page, revenue, and CTR is negative.

Let's check one more important metric, purchasing: How has the promotion affected purchasing? We'll use a Poisson test, which is a statistical test to compare two Poisson distributions. A Poisson distribution models the probability of a given number of events occurring in a fixed interval—here, the number of purchases. Our null hypothesis is that the average number of purchases by users is the same for the treatment and control groups. Listing 15.7 shows how to run a Poisson test.

Listing 15.7 **Running a Poisson Test**

```
# Load MASS package
library(MASS)

# Poisson process model, number of purchases

# Density plot of CTR by treatment
ggplot(full_data, aes(x = purchases, color = treated)) +
  geom_density(aes(linetype=treated)) +
  labs(title = "Purchases by Treatment Group", x = "Purchases", y = 'Density',
       color = "Treatment",linetype = "Treatment") +
  theme(plot.title = element_text(hjust = 0.5))

# Poisson test: Are they different?
parms_t <- fitdistr(user_treated$purchases, "poisson")
parms_c <- fitdistr(user_control$purchases, "poisson")
n <- nrow(user_treated)

poisson.test(c(n, n), c(as.numeric(parms_t$estimate), as.numeric(parms_c$estimate)))

##  Comparison of Poisson rates
##
## data:  c(n, n) time base: c(as.numeric(parms_t$estimate),
## as.numeric(parms_c$estimate))
## count1 = 2000,  expected count1 = 2014, p value = 0.658
## alternative hypothesis: true rate ratio is not equal to 1
## 95 percent confidence interval:
```

```
## 0.9263576 1.0496602
## sample estimates:
## rate ratio
## 0.9860835
```

Note that the outcome here is a count variable—in other words, a positive integer. First, as with the other statistical tests, we plot the two distributions together in Figure 15.4. Then, we calculate the Poisson test using the "MASS" package, a popular R statistical computing package.

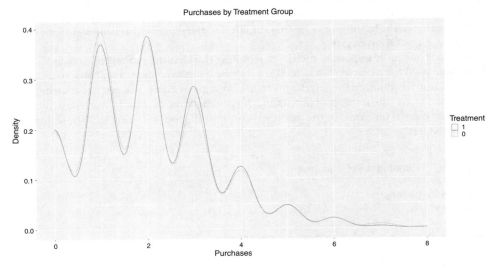

Figure 15.4 Distribution of purchases for treatment and control groups.

We can see that the *p* value is equal to 0.658. Hence, these distributions are actually the same in terms of purchasing—there is no difference in the number of purchases per user in the treatment and control groups.

The treatment had a negative effect on revenue, CTR, and length of time on the web page, but the user purchasing behavior remained the same. Users bought the same number of goods, but they were cheaper after the promotion. We can deduce from this final metric that the promotion might have had the intended effect by making purchases cheaper, but it did not cause users to buy more. Overall, we might not try this promotion again, since it negatively affected revenue and CTR and did not increase purchasing behavior.

In the next section, we'll carry out power analysis to determine the sample size needed for our example in Chapter 6.

15.1.2 Power Analysis

Power analysis is used to determine the sample size needed for an A/B test, when we want to meet certain criteria. A larger sample size is better, but sometimes there is a cost to adding users. How do we find the floor—that is, the minimum number of users that we need? We can use power analysis. We explored an example of power analysis in Chapter 6 section 6.5.5.

Here are our basic criteria from that example:

- We have 1 million users. Suppose one of their outcomes is normally distributed.
- Their mean spending is currently $5.25.
- The standard deviation is equal to $1.
- We want a high level of statistical significance, let's say 0.01 or below.
- The power is 0.90.
- We'd like to see a $0.50 change at a minimum.

This is how we can calculate the sample size needed. First, we need to get the corresponding Z values for the test significance and power that are desired. Then we multiply those added Z values by the standard deviation. Finally, we divide that number by the desired difference in the distributions squared. Listing 15.8 presents this in code.

Listing 15.8 **Power Analysis**

```
# Power analysis
# Let's work through the example in Chapter 7

# Equation: N = sigma^2 (Z1 +Z2) / (mean_difference)^2
z1 <- qnorm(.99) # Statistical significance of the t-test
z2 <- qnorm(.90) # Power of the statistical test
sigma <- 1 # Standard deviation
change <- 5.75 - 5.25 # Estimate of the effect

# Calculating the numerator
num <- sigma^2*(z1+z2)^2
num
## [1] 13.01694

# Calculating the denominator
denom <- change^2

# Sample size for treatment (and control)
(2*num)/denom
## [1] 104.1355
```

From this analysis, we can surmise that at a minimum we need 106 participants, or 53 participants in the treatment group and 53 participants in the control group. We must round up to the next even number as there are two groups that we must create. There are other ways to calculate the statistical power for different quantities or distributions, but this gives you a quick overview of how it works for a common example.

In this section, we implemented an A/B test and power analysis in R. In the next section, we'll go over the predictive modeling examples from Chapters 7–9.

15.2   Clustering

This section will implement supervised and unsupervised learning methods in R. First, we'll apply unsupervised learning techniques of *k*-means and principal components analysis (PCA) on our small sample data set from Chapter 7.

15.2.1   *k*-Means

As described in Chapter 7 section 7.2.1.2, *k*-means is a clustering algorithm that segments a population into a user-specified number of groups. In this case, we wanted to divide the population into two groups, whales and wallflowers.

In the implementation shown in Listing 15.9, we first load the data into R. Then we apply *k*-means to the data to find two clusters. We use the R function kmeans() to calculate the *k*-means object, and we get the centers by using the command kmeans()$centers. The argument for *k*-means algorithm is the whales data frame. The data set called book_whales_k_means_chapter_11.csv for this example and is available on the book's website.

Listing 15.9   ***k*-Means Implementation for the Whales and Wallflowers Example**

```
# Example of k-means for whales and wallflowers

# Load the data from your directory
whales <- read.csv("whales_k_means.csv")

# Get first 6 rows of the data set
head(whales)

##   usernum socialbeh profiledesc level2day1 userfriends
## 1       1         1         121          1           2
## 2       2         1          54          0           4
## 3       3         1          16          1           3
## 4       4         1          87          1          12
## 5       5         1         291          1           5
## 6       6         1         111          0          12

# Calculate centers
whales_kmeans <- kmeans(whales[, 2:5], centers = 2)
round(whales_kmeans$centers, 2)
##   socialbeh profiledesc level2day1 userfriends
## 1      0.25       21.33       0.42        2.67
## 2      0.50      163.25       0.62        6.62

# add clustering to our dataset
whales$kmeans <- whales_kmeans$cluster
```

The *k*-means algorithm found two clusters. Group 1 could be wallflowers and group 2 could be whales. Whales are different from the wallflowers because, on average, they have more friends (7 versus 3), have longer profiles (163 characters versus 21), and are more likely to engage in social behavior and reach level 2 on the first day.

We can get other information from the *k*-means object, such as which group each user is in, by calling kmeans()$clusters. We can get goodness-of-fit metrics, such as within-cluster sum of squares, from this object by running whales_means$withinss. Run ?kmeans() for more information.

15.2.2   Principal Components Analysis

Next, let's apply PCA to better understand our variables. Just as in Chapter 7, we're going to add a retention variable to make the data set more interesting. This data is added in this section.

We will explore the variation in our numeric variables. PCA is used to understand variation in our confounder variables as well as preforms dimension reduction. Dimension reduction in the context of PCA means taking a high-dimensional (i.e., large) variable set, linearly transforming it, and selecting a smaller set that explains most of the variation. The PCA biplot shows the compression of information to 2-dimensions. Refer to Chapter 7 section 7.2.1.3 for an intuitive explanation of PCA and an introductory technical explanation.

PCA works best with numeric variables, so we drop all the other types of variables from our analysis to keep it simple. We'll look at profile length, number of friends, and retention. Listing 15.10 shows how to run PCA using the prcomp() function. We'll take the log of the profile description, user friends, and days in product to lower the right skewness of the data. We want to scale and center the data so the results are not affected by the magnitude differences between variables. A general rule of thumb with transformation of input data is that we want numeric variables to be as close to normal as possible and categorical data to be binary. This usually will give us the best results, though your mileage will vary depending on the algorithm.

Listing 15.10   **Running PCA for Whales and Wallflowers Data**

```
# PCA for whales and wallflowers data

# First, add a new retention variable to the data set
whales$daysproduct <- c(12, 2, 5, 0, 1, 5, 5, 0, 1, 1, 3, 15, 6, 0, 5, 10, 1, 3, 2, 4)

# Let's create a PCA data.frame with just numeric variables
pca_data <- data.frame(profile_len = log(whales$profiledesc + 1),
  friends = log(whales$userfriends + 1), retention = log(whales$daysproduct + 1))

# Let's run PCA on the scaled and centered data
pca <- prcomp(pca_data, scale = TRUE, center = TRUE)

# Rotation by component
pca

## Standard deviations:
## [1] 1.3572668 0.9133865 0.5688162
```

```
##
## Rotation:
##                       PC1          PC2          PC3
## profile_len -0.6659015  0.07732564  0.7420215
## friends     -0.5780273  0.57533240 -0.5786856
## retention   -0.4716563 -0.81425634 -0.3384184

# Let's calculate how much variance is explained by each factor
cumulative_prop <- data.frame("components" = c("first", "second", "third"),
                              "prop"= (pca$sdev)^2/sum(pca$sdev^2))

# Plot the variation explained by each factor (bar graph)
ggplot(data = cumlative_prop, aes(x = components, y = prop)) +
  geom_bar(stat = "identity") +
  labs(title = "Variation Explained by Component", x='Components', y = "Proportion") +
  theme(plot.title = element_text(hjust = 0.5))
```

Now that we have run the PCA, we create a PCA object. From that object, we can calculate the proportion of each component by squaring the standard deviation to get the variance and dividing each component by the total variance.

The size of each component is plotted in Figure 15.5. We want to calculate the rotation of each component, which we can find the rotation by calling our PCA object; see Listing 15.10.

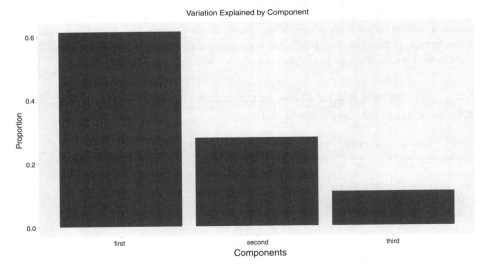

Figure 15.5   PCA components proportions.

Now that we know the size of our components and the rotation, we want to look at the biplot of the data. We'll use another PCA algorithm, `princomp()`, available in R, to calculate the same (or similar—sometimes the results are slightly different) object and plot it using a biplot, a two-dimensional view with both points and lines. See Listing 15.11.

Listing 15.11   **Plotting Biplot**

```
# Plot biplot
pca2 <- princomp(scale(pca_data, center = TRUE, scale=TRUE))
biplot(pca2, expand = .85, col = c("black", "blue"), cex = 1, pc.biplot = 2,
  main = "Whales and Wallflowers Biplot")
```

In Figure 15.5, the bar graph is a plot of the relative size of each component. These proportions add up to 1; we can see that more than 60% of the variation is explained by the first component. From the rotation, we know that the first component is primarily profile length and number of friends. The second component explains almost 30% and is primarily retention and number of friends. The rotation helps us understand where most of our variation is coming from.

In Figure 15.6, we can see the position on the biplot of each of our points plotted based on their values for the first and second components. We can also see the vectors for each of our three numeric factors and how they relate to each user.

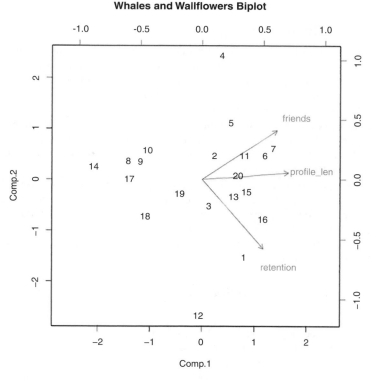

Figure 15.6   Biplot of the whales and wallflowers example.

The biplot in Figure 15.6 helps us visualize the PCA results in two dimensions. A biplot is a mix of points and vectors. The points are the individual observations plotted in a two-dimensional space in the direction of the first and second components, on the *x*- and *y*-axes, respectively. The vectors represent the individual features of retention, profile length, and number of friends. We can see that our whales are almost entirely on the right-hand side (points 6, 7, 11, 13, 15, 16, and 20) and our wallflowers on the left. The wallflowers are more varied than the whales in terms of the first two components.

Both *k*-means and PCA are unsupervised learning techniques, in that there is no outcome variable or classifier. For example, there are no labels for type (whales and wallflowers) in our data set that we are trying to classify. We are just exploring the variables that we might use to classify the data.

In the next section, we'll examine predictive techniques in which all our models will have an outcome variable.

15.3 Predictive Modeling

Next, we'll cover linear regression, logistic regression, decision trees, and support vector machines. We'll move through the topics in the exact same order as we did in Chapter 8 starting with linear regression.

15.3.1 Linear Regression

The most widely taught predictive model is linear regression. We went through a descriptive, graphical, and numerical explanation of this model in Chapter 8 section 8.3.1.2. In this section, we'll use regression to try to predict the number of days a user stays in product, based on our other variables. Note that we take the logs of the exponentially distributed variables to ensure a better model fit, similar to what we did for PCA.

This regression, like the rest of the examples, is intended purely to show the methods. A data set of 20 observations is much too small to trust the effects of the model. Generally, you need at least 10–20 observations per covariate. Thus, we'd like to have at least 40–80 observations if we wanted to trust the effects of this model.

Listing 15.12 shows an implementation of linear regression in R. Here, we use the `lm()` function (its name stands for "linear model") with our model formula and `data = our_dataset`. When we call the `summary()` function on our regression object, we get the coefficients, their levels of significance, and the *R*-squared or goodness-of-fit measure. In R, typing the object name and running it, using the `summary()` or `print()` function, will often print useful information about most R objects' features.

Listing 15.12 **Implementing Linear Regression**

```
# Linear regression
lm_retention <- lm(log(daysproduct + 1) ~ socialbeh +
            log(profiledesc + 1) + level2day1 +
            log(userfriends + 1), data = whales)

# Summary table
summary(lm_retention)

## Call:
## lm(formula = log(daysproduct + 1) ~ socialbeh + log(profiledesc +
##     1) + level2day1 + log(userfriends + 1), data = whales)
##
```

```
## Residuals:
##      Min      1Q   Median      3Q      Max
## -1.42820 -0.30614 -0.01349  0.55797  1.20845
##
## Coefficients:
##                       Estimate Std. Error t value Pr(>|t|)
## (Intercept)            0.80194    0.39157   2.048   0.0585 .
## socialbeh             -0.22654    0.47011  -0.482   0.6368
## log(profiledesc + 1)   0.23126    0.11789   1.962   0.0686 .
## level2day1            -0.11218    0.41212  -0.272   0.7892
## log(userfriends + 1)  -0.07531    0.31632  -0.238   0.8150
## ---
## Signif. codes:  0 '***' 0.001 '**' 0.01 '*' 0.05 '.' 0.1 ' ' 1
##
## Residual standard error: 0.8202 on 15 degrees of freedom
## Multiple R-squared:  0.2292, Adjusted R-squared:  0.02361
## F statistic: 1.115 on 4 and 15 DF, p value: 0.386
```

When we run the model in R, it produces the summary table in Listing 15.12. Note that the first piece of the output is the model. We're trying to predict the log of days in product based on social behavior, log of profile description, reaching level 2 in the first day, and log of user's friends. In the summary table for this model, we can see the coefficients, standard errors, *p* values, and *R*-squared. We talked about how to interpret these results in Chapter 8 section 8.3.1.2.

If we could believe this model (if it had more data and met the assumptions of ordinary least squares [OLS] analysis), we might note that the only coefficient that is significant under the 10% level is the length of the profile description. The adjusted *R*-squared value is low for this model, meaning that we are not explaining much variation. The adjusted *R*-squared is like a metric for error on the training set. We also want to understand how it looks on our test set.

We can forecast the outcome for each user based on our linear model by using predict(), as shown in Listing 15.13, to access the quality of our models. To get our prediction in days, we need to take the exponential value of the estimate to get the user days in product.

Listing 15.13   **Implementing Predictions**

```
# Predictions
table_pred <- data.frame(cbind(exp(predict(lm_retention, whales) + 1),
  whales$daysproduct))
colnames(table_pred) <- c("Predictions", "Actual")
table_pred

##     Predictions Actual
## 1     12.078797     12
## 2     10.814897      2
## 3      7.493380      5
## 4     10.028931      0
## 5     14.028321      1
## 6     11.863053      5
## 7     11.309127      5
## 8     11.338501      0
```

```
## 9      5.580107      1
## 10     4.881043      1
## 11    15.388456      3
## 12    12.989416     15
## 13    10.772847      6
## 14     6.061418      0
## 15    16.324663      5
## 16    17.176782     10
## 17     5.753125      1
## 18     5.753125      3
## 19    10.924661      2
## 20    15.363480      4
```

We can see that the actual days and the predicted days in product are close for some individuals, such as user 1. They are extremely far apart for other individuals, such as user 2. The error is high in this model.

15.3.2 Logistic Regression

In Chapter 8 section 8.3.1.3, we wanted to use a logistic regression to find the probability that a user sends a message. A logistic regression outputs a probability of a given outcome.

In the whales and wallflowers example, let's assume the social behavior variable denotes whether the user sent a direct message. Again, let's fit a simple model. We have not done any feature selection or model validation.

As shown in Listing 15.14, to run a logistic regression, we use the `glm()` function (its name stands for "generalized linear model") with the model formula as the first argument, `family = binomial` as the second argument, and our data as the third argument. The `summary()` for the `glm` object will print the model first, then the regression results. The main elements of interest that it will print are the coefficients (here the log odds), *p* values, and, at the end, the AIC (or a logistic goodness-of-fit measure). We will change the log odds into probabilities to interpret this model.

Listing 15.14 **Building the Logistic Regression**

```
# Building the logistic regression
glm_social <- glm(socialbeh ~ level2day1 + log(daysproduct + 1) + log(profiledesc + 1)
    + log(userfriends + 1), family = binomial, data = whales)

# Summary table
summary(glm_social)

## Call:
## glm(formula = socialbeh ~ level2day1 + log(daysproduct + 1) +
##     log(profiledesc + 1) + log(userfriends + 1), family = binomial,
##        data = whales)
##
## Deviance Residuals:
```

```
##     Min       1Q   Median       3Q      Max
## -1.5198  -0.6933  -0.2430   0.6180   1.6072
##
## Coefficients:
##                         Estimate Std. Error z value Pr(>|z|)
## (Intercept)              -4.3374     2.5070  -1.730   0.0836 .
## level2day1                0.6835     1.2259   0.558   0.5771
## log(daysproduct + 1)     -0.2366     0.9624  -0.246   0.8058
## log(profiledesc + 1)      0.3386     0.4840   0.700   0.4842
## log(userfriends + 1)      1.5497     1.2408   1.249   0.2117
## ---
## Signif. codes:  0 '***' 0.001 '**' 0.01 '*' 0.05 '.' 0.1 ' ' 1
##
## (Dispersion parameter for binomial family taken to be 1)
##
##     Null deviance: 25.898  on 19  degrees of freedom
## Residual deviance: 17.674  on 15  degrees of freedom
## AIC: 27.674
##
## Number of Fisher Scoring iterations: 5
```

If we are to believe this model, suppose we have a higher sample size, days in product has a negative effect on social behavior, and every other variable is positively related. There are no significant variables. We'll calculate the probability of our base model and then generalize the function. To calculate the probabilities from the coefficients, we need to use the find_prob() function:

```
# Probabilities
p = exp(glm_social$coef[1])/(1 + exp(glm_social$coef[1]))
p
## (Intercept)
##   0.0129019
```

```
# Finding probability function, useful for finding specific probabilities
find_prob <- function(coef){
  p = exp(coef)/(1 + exp(coef))
  return(p)
}
```

The base model means that every dummy and numeric variable is equal to zero, meaning the user has no friends, no messages, and the like. In this model, there is 1.3% chance of sending a message. The number of friends has a dramatic effect on the odds of sending a message, with the other variables being much smaller factors in this model.

15.3.3 Decision Trees

In this section, we'll apply a classification tree algorithm to predict whether a user will exhibit some form of social behavior. We'll also calculate the precision, recall, and $F1$ score—all metrics used to assess the quality of a binary predictor. The precision metric tells us how good we are at correctly classifying selected observations, and the recall metric tells us how good we are at identifying which observations to classify positively. $F1$ score is a combination of these two metrics.

A decision tree is a method by which one finds the "best" binary splits based on some decision rule to classify data (see Chapter 8 section 8.3.1.4 and Chapter 13 section 13.5.5). R has many packages that can apply these models with different specifications to run a decision tree. We use the function rpart() in the "rpart" package to build a decision tree with our data.

When we run the decision tree model on this data set, we get the results shown in Listing 15.15. We can see that when we use summary() on the rpart() object, R prints a few important pieces of information, OOB error estimates, variable importance, the decision tree splits (which we will plot; see Figure 15.7), and a goodness-of-fit measure, mean squared error. See Chapter 8 section 8.3.1.4 and Chapter 13 section 13.5.5 for an in-depth explanation of these variables and results.

Listing 15.15 **Building a Decision Tree**

```
# Decision tree
library(rpart) # Decision tree package
library(rattle) # Nice plotting of trees

## Loading required package: rpart
# Building a decision tree
tree_social <- rpart(socialbeh ~ level2day1 + log(daysproduct + 1) +
  log(profiledesc + 1) + log(userfriends + 1), data = whales)

# Summary of the tree model
summary(tree_social)

## Call:
## rpart(formula = socialbeh ~ level2day1 + log(daysproduct + 1) +
##     log(profiledesc + 1) + log(userfriends + 1), data = whales)
##   n= 20
##
##           CP nsplit rel error    xerror      xstd
## 1 0.2747253      0 1.0000000 1.105684 0.1571116
## 2 0.0100000      1 0.7252747 1.105684 0.1571116
##
## Variable importance
## log(profiledesc + 1) log(userfriends + 1) log(daysproduct + 1)
##                   43                   35                   13
##           level2day1
##                    9
##
## Node number 1: 20 observations,     complexity param=0.2747253
##     mean=0.35, MSE=0.2275
##     left son=2 (10 obs) right son=3 (10 obs)
##     Primary splits:
##         log(profiledesc + 1) < 3.781341  to the left,  improve=0.27472530,
##             (0 missing)
##         log(userfriends + 1) < 1.242453  to the left,  improve=0.14835160,
##             (0 missing)
##         level2day1           < 0.5       to the left,  improve=0.09890110,
##             (0 missing)
```

```
##          log(daysproduct + 1) < 1.700599  to the left,  improve=0.06593407,
##              (0 missing)
##    Surrogate splits:
##          log(userfriends + 1) < 1.497866  to the left,  agree=0.90, adj=0.8, (0 split)
##          log(daysproduct + 1) < 0.8958797 to the left,  agree=0.65, adj=0.3, (0 split)
##          level2day1           < 0.5       to the left,  agree=0.60, adj=0.2, (0 split)
##
## Node number 2: 10 observations
##    mean=0.1, MSE=0.09
##
## Node number 3: 10 observations
##    mean=0.6, MSE=0.24
```

```
# Plotting the tree
fancyRpartPlot(tree_social, main = "Decision Tree To \n Predict Whales and
  WallFlowers")
```

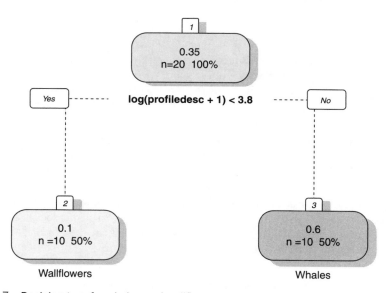

Figure 15.7   Decision tree for whales and wallflowers.

We can see that there is only one split on profile description length. If the length is greater than 43 characters, we classify it as a 1; otherwise, we classify it as a 0. The output includes surrogate splits that we could use if our primary split did not work—for example, in the case of missing data. Decision trees are a great choice when you have missing data, which happens often in practice.

Next, we'll calculate the error of this decision tree model. We calculate precision, recall, and the *F*1 score in Listing 15.16 discussed in sidebar in Chapter 8 section 8.4.2.

Listing 15.16   **Calculating Precision and Recall Metrics**

```
# Calculating precision and recall from tree split
whales$pred_social <- predict(tree_social, type = 'vector')
tabs <- table(whales$pred_social, whales$socialbeh)

precision <- tabs[1,1]/(tabs[1,1] + tabs[1,2])
precision
## [1] 0.9

recall <- tabs[1,1]/(tabs[1,1] + tabs[2,1])
recall
## [1] 0.6923077
# Precision is high, recall is low

# Calculating the F1_score
f1_score <- 2/((1/recall) + (1/precision))
f1_score
## [1] 0.7826087
```

We can infer from the error rate that precision is relatively high or we are classifying most observations correctly. The rate of recall is not so good: We're struggling to identify the observations that we should classify as true. Since the *F*1 score is a combination of the two, it's pretty mediocre. If we want to improve this model, we should focus on improving our rate of recall.

15.3.4 Support Vector Machines

The last classification algorithm we will explore in this subsection on predictive modeling is a support vector machine (SVM) explored in Chapter 8 section 8.3.1.5. Again, we'll apply SVMs to the whales and wallflowers data set to predict the social behavior outcome, or whether the user is a whale or a wallflower. In R, two packages implement SVMs: the "e1071" package and the "ksvm" package.

In Listing 15.17, we apply SVM model using the e1017 package to predict social behavior. We can try different kernels and use the predict() function to calculate the *F*1 score, just as we did in the prior section. Try calculating the *F*1 score here on your own.

Listing 15.17   **Fitting our SVM model**

```
# Loading the library and setting the seed
library(e1071)
set.seed(101)

# Fitting a simple SVM with radial basis kernel
svm_fit <- svm(socialbeh ~ profiledesc + level2day1 + userfriends, data = whales)
summary(svm_fit)
```

```
## Call:
## svm(formula = socialbeh ~ profiledesc + level2day1 + userfriends, data = whales)
##
## Parameters:
##    SVM-Type:  eps-regression
## SVM-Kernel:  radial
##        cost:  1
##       gamma:  0.3333333
##     epsilon:  0.1
##
##
## Number of Support Vectors:   16

# Tuning the SVM by searching for the best parameters with 10-fold CV
obj = tune.svm(socialbeh ~., data=whales,cost=seq(1:10),gamma=2^(-2:2))
obj

## Parameter tuning of 'svm':
##
## - sampling method: 10-fold cross-validation
##
## - best parameters:
##  gamma cost
##   0.25    3
##
## - best performance: 0.1430022
```

We also search for optimal cost and gamma parameters. We can use the tune.svm() function to specify the values for cost and gamma that we want to test. Since this data set is small, it's nice to illustrate these ideas, but it's not large enough to effectively predict the outcome.

In Listing 15.17, we fit our model with the radial basis kernel. We then search a set of cost parameters, from 1 to 10, and gamma parameters, from 0.25 to 4, for the optimal parameters to tune our model. In this example, we use 10-fold cross-validation and find the best parameters are a gamma parameter of 0.25 and a cost parameter of 3.

You can do a lot more with SVMs in R, including plotting the decision boundary, writing your own kernels, and better model tuning. However, as this is an introduction, we will not go into greater depth here. There are a number of great books on SVMs, including that by Hastie et al. (2009).

15.3.5 Cross-Validation

In this section, we'll demonstrate one cross-validation method discussed in Chapter 8 section 8.4.2. We will validate our linear regression results with leave-one-out cross-validation. There are a number of different ways to cross-validate data. In leave-one-out cross-validation, we leave out one observation and run the model on the rest of the data set; we repeat this for every observation in the data set.

In this example, we will build 20 models, leaving one observation out each time. We will then assess our regression error rate from the test observation across the 20 models.

Recall that the linear regression had a real outcome, number of days in product. Let's implement a for-loop to run that model 20 times and predict each left-out observation. A number of packages will do this for you, but it's nice to at least write out the process a few times to understand what's going on (see Listing 15.18). The actual outcome versus the predicted outcome is plotted in Figure 15.8. How good is this model at predicting user days in product?

Listing 15.18   Leave-One-Out Cross-Validation

```
# Leave-one-out cross-validation
# Set seed
set.seed(101)

# Create data.frame to save data
CV_outcome <- data.frame("predicted" = as.factor(rep(0:1, 20)), "test" = rep(1:20,
  each = 2), "retention" = NA)

# Run this model 20 times and save the test data
for(i in 1:20){
  # Create 19 obs training set
  training <- whales[-i,]

  # Build linear regression model
  lm_ret <- lm(log(daysproduct + 1) ~ socialbeh +
                  log(profiledesc + 1) + level2day1 +
                  log(userfriends + 1), data = training)

  # Predict test data outcome
  pred <- predict(lm_ret, whales[i,])

  # Save actual outcome to compare
  test <- log(whales$daysproduct[i] + 1)

  # Save in data.frame
  CV_outcome$retention[((2*i)-1)] <- test
  CV_outcome$retention[2*i] <- pred
}

# Plot the result (difference)
ggplot(data = CV_outcome, aes(x = test, y = retention,
        group = predicted)) +
  geom_line(aes(linetype = predicted)) + geom_point() +
  labs(title = "Leave-one-out Cross Validation Results", x='Test', y = "Retention",
      linetype='Predicted') +
  theme(plot.title = element_text(hjust = 0.5))
```

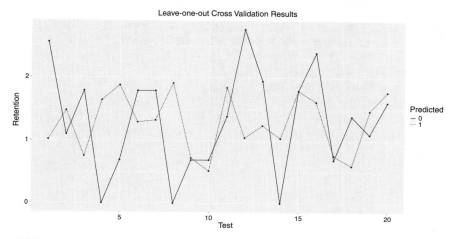

Figure 15.8   Prediction for leave-one-out cross-validation.

From the leave-one-out cross-validation, we can see that there is more variation in the data set than in the model. This is to be expected. We struggle to predict certain observations, such as points 4, 5, 8 and 12.

In this section, we examined the predictive modeling techniques from Chapter 8. In the next section, we'll move to a completely new topic, population projection discussed in Chapter 9. There is a natural break here, as this material does not build on the material covered thus far in this chapter.

15.4   Population Projection

In this section, we'll go through the projection models from Chapter 9. Please take some time to understand the methods covered in Chapter 9. Doing so will help you get the most out of the R methods described in this section, as we will provide the R code to explore all the examples discussed in Chapter 9. We will go over the general transition matrix example, user death by a thousand cuts, and the exemplary example.

In the first part of Chapter 9 section 9.3.2 on the 'Snowmobile Transition Example', we discussed the transition matrix and simple population projection. We'll project the population from the transition matrix later in this section.

We can project population a period forward by multiplying the transition matrix by the population from the last period to get the new population. In Listing 15.19, we project the population of this web product forward by 20 periods to look at the distributions of the different groups over time. Figure 15.9 shows the total population projected over 20 periods, and Figure 15.10 shows the subgroup population projected over 20 periods.

Listing 15.19   **Population Projection**

```
### Building the transition matrix
row1 <- c(1.25, 0, 0, 0, 0)
row2 <- c(.5, .5, .4, .05, 0)
row3 <- c(0, .2, .1, .05, 0)
row4 <- c(.5, .25, .5, .8, 0)
```

```
row5 <- c(0, .05, 0, .1, 1)
trans_mat <- matrix(rbind(row1, row2, row3, row4, row5), nrow = 5, ncol = 5)
initial_pop <- matrix(c(1000, 1000, 1000, 1000, 1000), nrow = 5, ncol = 1)

# Population projection, 1 period
new_pop <- trans_mat %*% initial_pop
new_pop
##         [,1]
## [1,] 1250
## [2,] 1450
## [3,]   350
## [4,] 2050
## [5,] 1150

# Population projection, 20 periods
mat_new <- matrix(NA, nrow = 5, ncol = 20)

library(expm)

mat_new <- matrix(NA, 5, 20)
for(i in 1:20){
            mat_new[, i] <- trans_mat %^% i %*% initial_pop
            }

# Plotting the population projection
# Total population
pop_frame <- data.frame(population = colSums(mat_new), period = 1:20)

ggplot(pop_frame, aes(x = period, y = population)) +
  geom_line() + geom_point() + labs(title = "Population over 20 Periods", x ='Period',
    y = "Population") +
  theme(plot.title = element_text(hjust = 0.5))

# Subgroup population
# Building a data frame
subpop_frame <- data.frame(c(mat_new), rep(1:5, 20), rep(1:20, each = 5))
names(subpop_frame) <- c("population", "subgroups", "period")

# Plotting subgroup population growth over 20 periods
subpop_frame$subgroups <- as.factor(subpop_frame$subgroups)
ggplot(subpop_frame, aes(x = period, y = population, group = subgroups)) +
  geom_line(aes(linetype = subgroups)) +
  labs(title = "Subgroup Population over 20 Periods", x = 'Period', y = "Population",
    linetype = 'Subgroups') +
  theme(plot.title = element_text(hjust = 0.5))
```

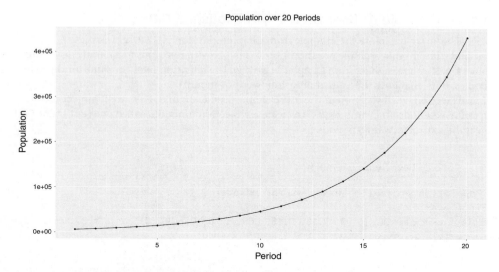

Figure 15.9   Projection of population over 20 periods.

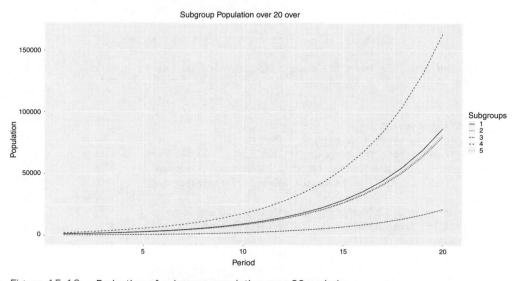

Figure 15.10   Projection of subgroup population over 20 periods.

Population projection is a useful tool to predict how subpopulations in our product will change over time. As we can see in Figure 15.10, although each group is growing, a group's proportion can decline over time, changing the social dynamics of our web product.

In the next section, we'll move on to the two projection examples from Section 9.4. In these models, we add diffusion (i.e., word-of-mouth growth) to our model.

15.4.1   Example 1: User Death by a Thousand Cuts

In this section, we'll explore the example from Chapter 9 section 9.4.2 'User Death By A Thousand Cuts.' In this example, we show how a small growth rate leads to a rapidly declining population. If you remember from Chapter 9, we keep the retention rates the same for the two examples, only changing the rates of diffusion (word-of-mouth).

In this section, we'll go through the first example user death in R. First, we'll project population out five periods. In Listing 15.20, we create a projection function, called `project_func()`, to project the matrix forward 5 periods.

Listing 15.20   **User Death Example**

```
## Population projection examples for Chapter 9
# First example
example_1 <- t(matrix(c(0.09, 0.13, 0.13, .65, 0, 0, 0, .36, 0), nrow = 3, ncol = 3))
pop <- matrix(c(100000, 50000, 25000), nrow = 3, ncol = 1)

# Projection function
project_func <- function(trans_mat, initial_pop, periods){
  # Defining the output object
  mat_new <- matrix(NA, nrow = dim(trans_mat)[1], ncol = periods)
  # Projecting the population out n periods
  for(i in 1:periods){
                mat_new[, i] <- trans_mat %^% i %*% initial_pop
}
# Returning a matrix with the population in each period by subgroup
return(mat_new)
}

# Projecting population out 5 periods
example1_mat <- project_func(example_1, pop, 5)
example1_frame <- data.frame(c(example1_mat), rep(1:3, 5), rep(1:5, each = 3))
names(example1_frame) <- c("population", "subgroups", "period")
example1_frame$subgroups <- as.factor(example1_frame$subgroups)

# Plotting subgroup population growth over 20 periods
ggplot(example1_frame, aes(x = period, y = population,
      group = subgroups)) +
  geom_line(aes(linetype = subgroups)) +
  labs(title = "Subgroup Growth over 5 Periods", x = 'Period', y = "Population",
      linetype = 'Subgroups') +
  theme(plot.title = element_text(hjust = 0.5))
```

In Figure 15.11, we can see that the population of all subgroups declines over time. However, the size of cohort 3 actually increases before it declines. Cohort 2 sees the most radical population decline.

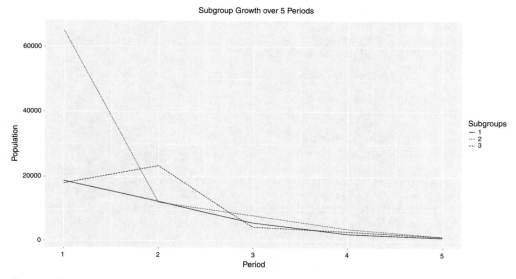

Figure 15.11   Population projected over 5 periods for example 1.

Next, we'll calculate eigenvectors and population oscillations which we discussed in section 9.4.2.5 and the sidebar in section 9.4.3.3. First, to calculate eigenvectors in R, we can use the base function `eigen()`. We then get an object with `object$value` equal to the eigenvectors for our matrix.

To view how the population will oscillate over time, we have to first convert the imaginary eigenvalues into polar coordinates, and then convert that information back to a readable format so that we cam view the oscillations by period. Listing 15.21 calculates the eigenvectors and oscillations for the user death example.

Listing 15.21   **Calculating Eigenvectors**

```
# We calculate the eigenvectors so that we can understand how our population
# will change over time.
# Calculating the eigenvalues
e <- eigen(example_1)

## Plotting population oscillations
e$values
## [1]  0.439616+0.0000000i -0.174808+0.19656791 -0.174808-0.19656791

## Function for creating the eigen plot
eigen_plot <- function(e_value){
  # Calculating the polar coordinates to model oscillations
  a <- Re(e_value)
  b <- Im(e_value)
  magnitude <- sqrt(a^2 + b^2)
  theta <- atan(b/a)
```

```
# Calculating the oscillations
x = c(1:20)
y = (magnitude^x)*2*cos(theta*x)
list_eigen <- list("x_values" = x, "y_values" = y)
return(list_eigen)
}

# Plotting
# Creating the data.frame
plot_object <- eigen_plot(e$values[2])
eigen_frame <- data.frame(plot_object)

# Plotting population oscillations over the first few periods
ggplot(eigen_frame[1:6, ], aes(x = x_values, y = y_values)) +
  geom_line() + labs(title = "Population Oscillations over Periods 1-6", x = "Period",
    y = "Eigen + Conj") +
  theme(plot.title = element_text(hjust = 0.5))
```

In Figure 15.12, we can see the oscillations of the user death example. We already know that our population will decline, but we can tell that there is one major population oscillation (in period 2) and after that, a few much smaller oscillations as the population trends to zero.

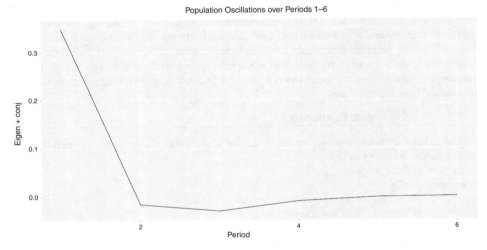

Figure 15.12   Oscillations from example 1 over six periods.

Next, we'll look for the long-term growth rate that would keep the population proportions unchanging. We can plot Lokta's equation and find where it equals 1. (See the sidebar in Chapter 9 section 9.4.3.2 for the calculation of this equation.) Listing 15.22 calculates Lokta's R.

Listing 15.22 **Calculating Lokta's R**

```
# Finding the stationary population
y = function(x){
                .099*exp(-1*x) + .135*exp(-2*x) + .07*exp(-3*x)
                }
ggplot(data.frame(x = c(-1, 0)), aes(x)) +
  stat_function(fun = y) + geom_hline(yintercept = 1, linetype = "dashed") +
  labs(title = "Stationary Population - Lokta's R", x = 'X', y = 'Y') +
  theme(plot.title = element_text(hjust = 0.5))
```

In Figure 15.13, we can see that this equation crosses the line 1 at –0.58. The long-term growth rate solutions to Lokta's equation is –0.58.

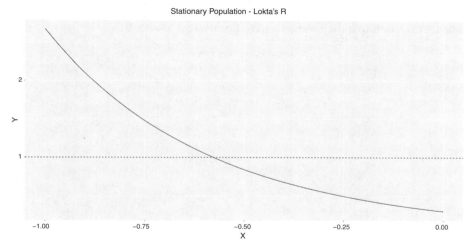

Figure 15.13   Calculation of Lokta's R.

15.4.2 Example 2: The Exponential Growth Example

Next, let's explore the exemplary example discussed in Chapter 9 section 9.4.3. Similar to what we did with the user death example, we'll project population out over five periods. Figure 15.14 shows the population for the exemplary example projected out over five periods. We calculate and plot the complex eigenvalues and find the stationary population growth rate as we did in the last example. Thus, Listing 15.23 carries out the same process for the exponential growth example as for the user death example.

Listing 15.23 **Implementing the Exemplary Example**

```
# Example 2
example2 <- matrix(c(1.66, .65, 0,1.89, 0, .36, 1.7, 0, 0), 3, 3)
pop2 <- matrix(c(100000, 50000, 25000), nrow = 3, ncol = 1)
```

```
# Plotting the population
example2_mat <- project_func(example2, pop2, 5)
example2_frame <- data.frame(c(example2_mat), rep(1:3, 5), rep(1:5, each = 3))
names(example2_frame) <- c("population", "subgroups", "period")
example2_frame$subgroups <- as.factor(example2_frame$subgroups)

# Plotting subgroup population growth over 5 periods
ggplot(example2_frame, aes(x = period, y = population, group = subgroups)) +
  geom_line(aes(linetype = subgroups)) +
  labs(title = "Subgroup Growth over 5 Periods", x = 'Period', y = "Population",
  linetype = 'Subgroups') +
  theme(plot.title = element_text(hjust = 0.5))
```

In Figure 15.14, we can see that the population is rapidly growing for all cohorts, but growth is strongest for cohort 1. Remember that the retention rates are the same in this example as in example 1. This means that the effect is entirely driven by the growth rates.

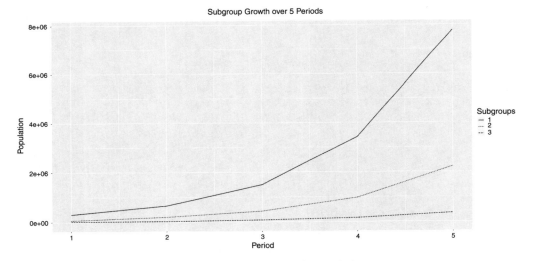

Figure 15.14   Population projection of example 2 over five periods.

Again, as we did for the user death example, we plot the population oscillations over six periods for the exemplary example in Figure 15.15. In Listing 15.24, we calculate the eigenvectors for example 2. We can tell from this example that there is a bigger oscillation in the population initially, and then smaller or dampened oscillations at later periods.

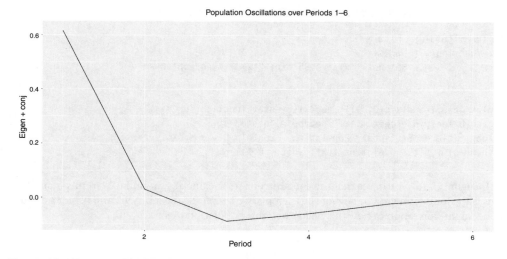

Figure 15.15 Population oscillation for example 2 over six periods.

Listing 15.24 **Calculating Eigenvectors Exemplary Example**

```
# Calculating the eigenvalues for example 2
e2 <- eigen(example2)

> e2$values
## [1] 2.2764258+0.0000000i -0.3082129+0.2824047i -0.3082129-0.2824047i

# Plotting the population oscillations for example 2
plot_object2 <- eigen_plot(e2$values[2])

# Creating the data.frame
plot_object2 <- eigen_plot(e2$values[2])
eigen2_frame <- data.frame(plot_object2)

# Plotting population oscillations over the first few periods
ggplot(eigen2_frame[1:6,], aes(x = x_values, y = y_values)) +
      geom_line() +
  labs(title = "Population Oscillations over Periods 1-6", x = "Period",
      y = "Eigen + Conj") +
  theme(plot.title = element_text(hjust = 0.5))
```

For more information on population oscillations and the long-run dynamics of populations, refer to Keyfitz and Caswell's (2005) *Applied Mathematical Demography*.

Next, in Listing 15.25, we calculate long-run growth rates for a stable population, or Lokta's *R*.

Listing 15.25   **Calculating Lokta's R for Exemplary Example**

```
## Calculating Lokta's R
y = function(x){
                .85*exp(-1*x) + 1.95*exp(-2*x) + 1.44*exp(-3*x)
                }

ggplot(data.frame(x=c(0, 1)), aes(x)) + stat_function(fun = y) +
  geom_hline(yintercept = 1, linetype = "dashed") +
  labs(title = "Stationary Population - Lokta's R", x = 'X', y = 'Y') +
  theme(plot.title = element_text(hjust = 0.5))
```

In Figure 15.16, we can see that the equation crosses the line at 1 around 0.75 in this example. This is the long-term growth rate for the exemplary example. See Sections 9.3 and 9.4 for a discussion and interpretation of how this relates to stable population theory.

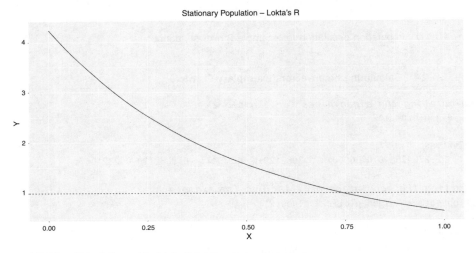

Figure 15.16   Calculation of Lokta's *R* for the second example.

15.5 Actionable Insights

In this chapter, we covered a variety of very useful techniques for A/B testing, supervised and unsupervised learning, and population projection in R. These techniques are the core of any analyst's toolkit and, as you've seen, can be implemented in R. R can be used like STATA and SAS as a statistical programming language in which it's key to know the theory and the functions that will carry out the statistical operations.

For a more in-depth exploration of these topics, see the advanced readings suggested in the Bibliography. R has much greater functionality for predictive modeling and validation, which you can start to see by exploring the "caret" package. Chapter 16 covers the causal inference methods in R discussed in Chapters 10–13.

Regression Discontinuity, Matching, and Uplift in R

Chapter 15 covered A/B testing and predictive modeling. This chapter covers R implementation for the last subsection of the book on causal inference methods—that is, the implementation in R of difference-in-difference (DID) modeling, regression discontinuity (RD), statistical matching, and uplift modeling, discussed in Chapters 10–13. We'll work with the Lalonde data set, which contains data from an experimental jobs program described in Chapter 13, for statistical matching and uplift modeling.

By the end of the chapter, you will be able to:

- Estimate a difference-in-difference model.

- Remove the effects of seasonality.

- Calculate the effect size in a regression discontinuity or interrupted time series (ITS) model.

- Implement statistical matching, including assessing model balance and matching quality.

- Estimate uplift from four different types of models.

- Calculate the Qini and the most important heterogeneous subgroups effects.

This chapter is meant to be read in conjunction with the chapters on theory. Please refer back to the theory chapters to help clarify graphs and interpretation of results.

16.1 Difference-in-Difference Modeling

In this section, we will go over DID modeling for the TV promotion example in Chapter 10 section 10.4.3. We'll create the data set with normal distributions. Then, we'll calculate the average treatment effect on the treated group (ATT) and run a regression to estimate the standard errors and p values.

This example involves a TV commercial run in the first direct marketing area (DMA) but not in the second DMA. The two periods are before and after treatment, which for the treated group is having the commercial run in their media market. We are trying to estimate the effect of the television commercial on the number of downloads; see Listing 16.1.

Listing 16.1   **Difference-in-Difference Estimation**

```
# Setting the seed
set.seed(101)

# Let's build an example of the DID example from Chapter 7
# We're running a TV experiment in DMA 1 and we're using
# DMA 2 # # as a "control"
# Pre and post are before and after the commercial ran
DMA_1_pre <- rnorm(100, 2100, 25)
DMA_2_pre <- rnorm(100, 2300, 25)
DMA_1_post <- rnorm(100, 4230, 25)
DMA_2_post <- rnorm(100, 3548, 25)

# Build treatment effect table
table_com <- matrix(c(mean(DMA_1_pre), mean(DMA_2_pre), mean(DMA_1_post),
  mean(DMA_2_post)), 2, 2)
table_com



##          [,1]      [,2]
## [1,] 2099.07 4230.052
## [2,] 2298.95 3547.363

# Calculating the ATT
ATT <- (table_com[1, 2]-table_com[2,2]) - (table_com[1,1]-table_com[2,1])
ATT
## [1] 882.5681
```

We can see that there is a large effect of the promotion. It increased the number of downloads by 882 per day in a given DMA.

Next, let's run a regression discussed in Chapter 10 section 10.4.3.4 to see if these effects are significant (Listing 16.2). First, we need to create dummy variables for treatment (whether it is the control or treated DMA) and time (whether pre or post commercial). Finally, an interaction between treatment and time is the ATT, or the average "causal effect" of the treatment on the treated group. (See Listing 15.19.)

Listing 16.2   **Difference-in-Difference Regression**

```
# DID regression

# First, build the data set as described above, two dummy variables for
# time and treatment
diff_data <- data.frame(rbind(cbind(DMA_1_pre, 1, 0),
                              cbind(DMA_1_post, 1, 1),
                              cbind(DMA_2_pre, 0, 0),
                              cbind(DMA_2_post, 0, 1)))
names(diff_data) <- c("downloads", "treated", "time")
```

```
# DID regression model
diff_model <- lm(downloads ~ treated + time + treated*time, data = diff_data)


summary(diff_model)

##
## Call:
## lm(formula = downloads ~ treated + time + treated * time, data = diff_data)
##
## Residuals:
##     Min      1Q  Median      3Q     Max
## -78.794 -16.219  -0.429  15.197  65.305
##
## Coefficients:
##               Estimate Std. Error t value Pr(>|t|)
## (Intercept)   2298.950      2.420   949.9   <2e-16 ***
## treated       -199.880      3.423   -58.4   <2e-16 ***
## time          1248.413      3.423   364.7   <2e-16 ***
## treated:time   882.568      4.841   182.3   <2e-16 ***
## ---
## Signif. codes:  0 '***' 0.001 '**' 0.01 '*' 0.05 '.' 0.1 ' ' 1
##
## Residual standard error: 24.2 on 396 degrees of freedom
## Multiple R-squared:  0.9993, Adjusted R-squared:  0.9992
## F-statistic: 1.769e+05 on 3 and 396 DF, p-value: < 2.2e-16


# Plot the experiment
diff_data$days <- c(rep(1:200, 2))
diff_data$treated <- factor(diff_data$treated, levels = c(1, 0),
  labels = c("DMA1", "DMA2"))

ggplot(diff_data, aes(days, downloads, color = treated)) +
  geom_line(aes(linetype = treated)) +
  scale_linetype_manual(values = c("solid", "dashed")) +
  scale_color_manual(values = c("black", "blue")) +
  labs(title = "Before/After Commercial, DMA 1 & DMA 2",
    x = "Days", y = "Downloads", color = NULL,
      linetype = NULL)   +
  theme(plot.title = element_text(hjust = 0.5))
```

We plot both periods and the treatment and control groups in Figure 16.1. We can see that downloads for both the treatment and control groups increased during that period, but downloads for the treatment group increased more.

In difference-in-difference modeling, we run a regression with three variables. The first is the treatment, a dummy variable indicating whether an observation was in treatment or control; the second is time, a dummy variable indicating whether the observation is either pre or post treatment; and the third is an interaction effect between treatment and time. An interaction effect is the simultaneous effect of two variables on the dependent variable, here downloads.

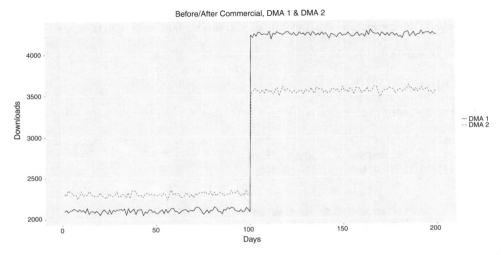

Figure 16.1   Difference-in-difference example.

We can see that the ATT is statistically significant. In this case, the time and treatment variables are also statistically significant. This is not a great example, because all the variables are highly significant. In practice, we're only looking for the interaction effect between treatment and time to be significant and have a large magnitude.

Recall that the estimate is the same as what we estimated in the simple table by subtracting the effect in both groups. We run the regression to find out if the effect is statistically significant after calculation of the standard errors. If it's significant, then we could have support for a causal effect, given that our design makes sense.

Also, note that we can often graph effects in a difference-in-difference design. From the graph, this process is stationary as discussed in Chapter 12 section, such that the mean and variance remain consistent over time. It's much easier to tell if we have a good design in a stationary process, but many real-world examples are not stationary. This means that we need more data defining the pre-treatment period and might need to remove seasonality. We'll demonstrate how to remove seasonality in Listing 16.7.

Difference-in-difference modeling can be a powerful technique to find causal effects in observational data. It's also a technique where graphing can give us a lot of information. In the next section, we'll go over another useful technique to extract insight from observational data or regression discontinuity.

16.2   Regression Discontinuity and Time-Series Modeling

In the last section, we discussed the implementation of difference-in-difference modeling in R. In this section, we'll go through another useful quasi-experimental design in R, regression discontinuity. We covered the theory behind regression discontinuity in Chapter 11. In this section, we'll show you how to implement regression discontinuity in R.

16.2.1   Regression Discontinuity

The first example that we discussed in the regression discontinuity section 11.1 of Chapter 11 was a sharp RD design related to a user's score. Users with a score above 50 automatically gain an enthusiast badge, while users who do not get 50 points fail to earn the badge. The outcome in which we are most interested is whether this enthusiast badge leads to greater retention. Recall that we can explore this by modeling the data around the cut point.

In Listing 16.3, we'll fit three models as discussed in Chapter 11 section 11.2.1 (regression, quadratic, and LOESS) to estimate the "causal" effect of gaining the enthusiast badge on retention or days in product. To fit the RD model, we need to estimate the models from both the left and right sides at the cut point, which is 50 in this example.

Listing 16.3   **RD Game Score Cut Point Example**

```
# First, let's load the data
 rd_data <- read.csv('rd_data.csv')
# Here is a summary of the data in the file
 summary(rd_data[,(3:4)])

##    game_score      retention
##    Min.   :  1.0   Min.   : 0.02959
##    1st Qu.: 22.0   1st Qu.: 2.67194
##    Median : 49.5   Median : 4.29894
##    Mean   : 49.4   Mean   : 4.59727
##    3rd Qu.: 77.0   3rd Qu.: 6.21584
##    Max.   :100.0   Max.   :13.20937

# ggplot for initial cut point data
treat.ind <- ifelse(rd_data$game_score > 49, 1, 0)
ggplot(rd_data, aes(game_score, retention, linetype = as.factor(treat.ind))) +
  # Points
  geom_point() +
  # Loess model
  stat_smooth(size=1.5, method = 'loess') +
  # Cut-point line
  geom_vline(xintercept=50, linetype="longdash") +
  # Titling
  ggtitle("Regression Discontinuity Game Score Design") + xlab("Game Score") +
  ylab("User Days") +
  # Legend
  scale_linetype_manual(values = c(1,3), labels = c("Control", "Treated"),
  name='Treatment') +
  # Title Formatting
  theme(plot.title = element_text(hjust = 0.5))

# Regression
## Regression fit from the left side
fun_left <- lm(retention ~ game_score, data=rd_data, subset=game_score <= 50)
```

```r
## Regression fit from the right side
fun_right <- lm(retention ~ game_score, data = rd_data, subset=game_score >= 50)

## Predict data from left and plot
new_left <- data.frame(game_score = rd_data$game_score[rd_data$game_score <= 50])
pred_left <- predict(fun_left,new_left)

## Predict data from right and plot
new_right <- data.frame(game_score = rd_data$game_score[rd_data$game_score >= 50])
pred_right <- predict(fun_right,new_right)

# Quadratic fit
## Quadratic model from the left side
fit1 <- lm(retention ~ poly(game_score,2, raw=TRUE), data=rd_data,
  subset=game_score <= 50)

## Predict
left <- sort(rd_data$game_score[rd_data$game_score <= 50])
quadratic1 <- fit1$coefficients[3]*left^2 + fit1$coefficients[2]*left +
  fit1$coefficients[1]

## Quadratic model from the right side
fit2 <- lm(retention ~ poly(game_score,2, raw=TRUE), data=rd_data,
  subset=game_score >= 50)

## Predict
right <- sort(rd_data$game_score[rd_data$game_score >= 50])
quadratic <- fit2$coefficients[3]*right^2 + fit2$coefficients[2]*right +
  fit2$coefficients[1]


## LOESS fit
## LOESS fit from the left side
lo_left <- loess.smooth(
  rd_data$game_score[rd_data$game_score <= 50],
  rd_data$retention[rd_data$game_score <= 50],
  data = rd_data, family=c("gaussian"), span=.25)

## LOESS fit from the right side
lo_right <- loess.smooth(rd_data$game_score[rd_data$game_score >= 50],
  rd_data$retention[rd_data$game_score >= 50],
  data = rd_data, family=c("gaussian"), span=.25)


# Estimates for the three models
## Regression estimate
est <- data.frame("game_score" = c(50))
predict(fun_right, est) - predict(fun_left, est)
## 0.9756212
```

```
## Quadratic estimate
(fit2$coefficient[3]*(50)^2 + fit2$coefficient[2]*50 + fit2$coefficient[1]) -
  (fit1$coefficient[3]*(50)^2 + fit1$coefficient[2]*(50) + fit1$coefficient[1])
## 1.653323

# LOESS estimate
lo_right$y[1]-lo_left$y[50]
## 0.582847

## Plot the three model estimates
rd_data$Side <- ifelse(rd_data$game_score > 49, 'Right', 'Left')
ggplot(rd_data, aes(x=game_score, y=retention, group=Side)) +
  # Points
  geom_point() +
  # Vertical line
  geom_vline(xintercept=50, color='black', linetype=4) +
  # Linear models
  geom_smooth(method='lm', se=FALSE, data=rd_data,
              aes(linetype='Linear', color='Linear')) +
  # Polynomial curve
  geom_smooth(method='lm', se=FALSE,
              formula=y ~ poly(x, 2, raw=TRUE), data=rd_data,
              aes(linetype='Polynomial', color='Polynomial')) +
  # LOESS curve
  geom_smooth(method='loess', se=FALSE, span=0.25, data=rd_data,
              aes(linetype='Loess', color='Loess')) +
  # Legend
  scale_color_brewer(NULL, palette='Paired', guide='legend') + scale_linetype_
    discrete(NULL) +
  # Titling
  labs(title="Three Regression Discontinuity Models", x = 'Game Score',
    y = 'Retention') +
  # Formatting
  theme(legend.position='bottom', plot.title=element_text(hjust=0.5))
```

We use the lm() function to plot both the linear and quadratic equations. To plot the quadratic equation, we'll use the poly() function, with the argument 2 to specify squaring the *x* variable within our regression function. Then, we use the estimated regression coefficients on the quadratic form to estimate the *y* value at the cut point. Finally, we use the loess.smooth() function to estimate the LOESS model from both the right and left sides. We use the bandwidth argument of 0.25 in this case. Try to play with the bandwidths in this example to see how much they change the LOESS results.

Regression discontinuity designs do not have a standard functional form, so we need to find the model that is most defensible. The more robust the model is, the more data that is close to the cut point; and the less selection bias that we see, the more defensible the model is.

In Figure 16.2 and Figure 16.3, we plot these three models from both the right and left sides of the cut point to see how well each of these models fits the data. It's very useful to plot your RD data and models.

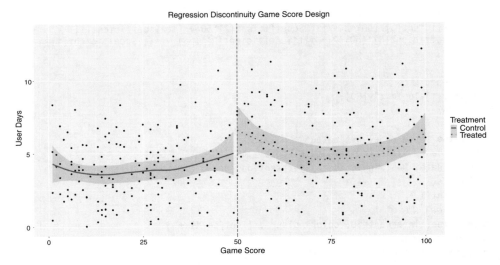

Figure 16.2   Regression discontinuity plot.

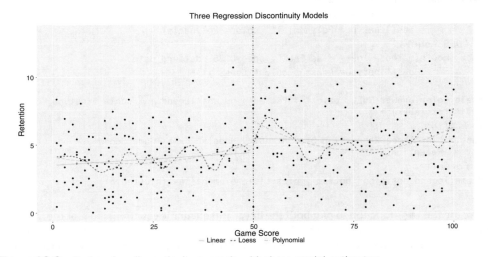

Figure 16.3   Regression discontinuity example with three model estimates.

We can see from this example that the estimates for local average treatment effects (LATE) vary greatly, with a range of [0.6, 1.6], based on the model that we are using and how we specify that model. The only way to access models is by looking at how well they fit the data close to the cut point. In this case, the LOESS and quadratic models seem to be best at modeling the true difference. Why?

The best model is one that fits the data closest to the cut point, rather than data farther away. We can get rid of regression immediately in this case because it is best at modeling data in the middle, about scores of 25 and 75 (which makes sense given how a regression line is calculated, but does not work well in this example). The quadratic fit seems to be a little high and the LOESS fit seems a little low. We can pick the LOESS estimation as it seems to fit the data best closest to the cut point which is around 1 day increased retention due to getting an enthusiast badge. The estimation of the LATE is not an exact science, but you can use graphing to guide your choice of the model that fits the data best.

Next, we want to look at how other confounding variables vary at the same cut point as discussed in Chapter 11 section 11.2.2. In Listing 16.4 and Figure 16.4, we plot the user profile length and number of friends by game score.

Listing 16.4   **RD Confounder Plot**

```
# Plotting the confounders
ggplot(rd_data, aes(game_score, profile_len, linetype=as.factor(treat.ind))) +
  # Points
  geom_point(aes(shape=as.factor(user_friends))) +
  # LOESS model
  stat_smooth(size=1.5, method = 'loess') +
  # Cutpoint line
  geom_vline(xintercept=50, linetype="longdash") +
  # shape for user friends
  scale_shape(name="User Friends",breaks=c("0","1"), labels=c("Friends", "No
  Friends")) +
  # Legend
  scale_linetype_manual(values = c(1,3), labels = c("Control", "Treated"),
  name='Treatment')
  # Titling and title formatting
  ggtitle("Regression Discontinuity Confounders: Profile Length and Friends") +
    xlab("Game Score") +
    ylab("Profile Length") +
    theme(plot.title = element_text(hjust = 0.5))
```

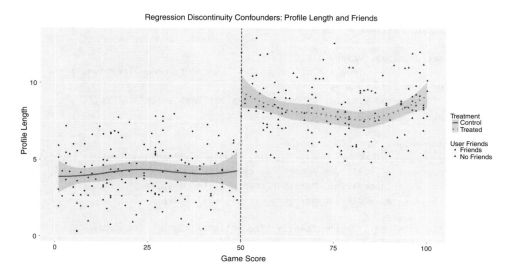

Figure 16.4   RD confounders in game score example.

We can see that both confounding variables, the profile length and user friends, break at the cut point. For this reason, this RD design is not valid. Since both user friends and profile length were established before a user gains a badge, either of these variables, or a combination of them, could be causing the LATE that we are seeing. We cannot determine the causal effect of gaining an "enthusiast" badge on the cut point.

16.2.2 Interrupted Time Series

A special case of regression discontinuity is interrupted time series which was explored in section 11.3 in Chapter 11. In an ITS design, the treatment variable with a break or discontinuity is time. For this example of the ITS design, we will model the effects of a 20% promotional discount on the annual revenue of a video game company. We'll assume that there was a change in the commercials mid-period on the 50th day, where there is a line in Figure 16.5. Figure 16.5 is a plot of the average revenue per user over 100 days.

Listing 16.5   **Interrupted Time Series Plotting and OLS Model**

```
# Install packages
library(forecast)
# First, let's load the data
its_data <- read.csv("its_data.csv")

# Plot the data
treat.its <- ifelse(its_data$days > 99, 1, 0)
ggplot(its_data, aes(x = time, y = profit, linetype=as.factor(treat.its))) +
  # Points
  geom_point() +
  # Cutpoint Line
  geom_vline(xintercept=100, linetype="longdash") +
  # Loess Model
  stat_smooth(size=1.5, method = 'loess') +
  # geom_smooth(method = 'lm') +
  # Legend
  scale_linetype_manual(values = c(1,3),
                        labels = c("Control", "Treated"), name='Treatment') +
  # Titling and Title Formatting
  ggtitle("Interrupted Time Series Design") + xlab("Days") + ylab("Profit") +
  theme(plot.title=element_text(hjust=0.5))

# Regression model for ITS example
## Creating the variables for the regression; they are already included in the data set
its_data$treatment <- ifelse(as.numeric(as.character(rownames(its_data))) < 100, 0, 1)
its_data$time <- as.numeric(as.character(rownames(its_data)))
its_data$timetx <- as.vector(rbind(c(rep(0, 100), c(1:100))))

reg <- lm(its_data$profit ~ treatment + time + timetx, data = its_data)
summary(reg, robust=T)
```

```
##Call:
##lm(formula = its_data$profit ~ treatment + time + timetx, data = its_data)

##Residuals:
     Min       1Q    Median       3Q       Max
-130.574  -36.186   -8.402   37.089   148.324

##Coefficients:
               Estimate Std. Error t value Pr(>|t|)
##(Intercept) -85.3292   10.4486   -8.167 3.82e-14 ***
##treatment   270.1814   14.5952   18.512  < 2e-16 ***
##time          4.7806    0.1814   26.350  < 2e-16 ***
##timetx        1.2482    0.2528    4.937 1.69e-06 ***
---
##Signif. codes:  0 '***' 0.001 '**' 0.01 '*' 0.05 '.' 0.1 ' ' 1

##Residual standard error: 51.59 on 196 degrees of freedom
##Multiple R-squared:  0.9864,   Adjusted R-squared:  0.9862
##F-statistic:  4737 on 3 and 196 DF,  p-value: < 2.2e-16
```

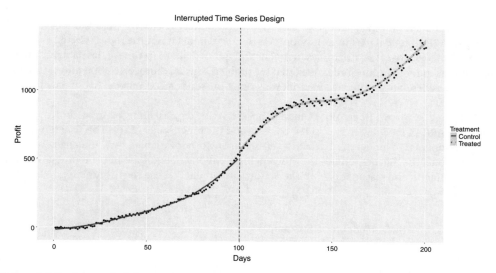

Figure 16.5   Interrupted time series example.

This regression model is not a good fit for the data. Try and plot it yourself. To do so, add geom_smooth(method = "lm") + and remove stat_smooth(size=1.5, method = 'loess') + to the ggplot code in Listing 16.5. The resulting plot is shown in Figure 16.6.

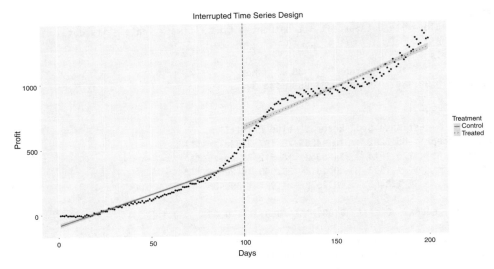

Figure 16.6   Interrupted time series linear fit.

Now that you have plotted it, it does not seem as if the linear model is a good fit near the cut point. The data is nonlinear close to the cut point. (Note that the data for this example is created using an ARIMA model plus some randomness. A linear model is not the right fit here.)

We'll need to try some other ways to model time-series data. With time-series data, we have data points indexed in time order. We often see problems such as autocorrelation and seasonality with time-series data. In the next section, we'll fit a time series ARIMA model to our data to estimate LATE.

In Listing 16.6, we'll fit an ARIMA model to the revenue data as discussed in section 11.3.2.2. We fit an ARIMA model with the "stats" package and the function `arima()`. This function takes a few arguments. To model the interaction effects or any other variables, we'll use `xreg`. Then, we can model the AR component, the differencing component, and the MA component with the order argument, and seasonality with the seasonal argument. We use the ts() function to build a time series data vector.

Listing 16.6   ARIMA Model for ITS Example

```
# Interaction effects
IntReg <- cbind(It=(1:200)>100, It.w=((1:200)>100)*(1:100))
basic_interaction <- Arima(ts(its_data$profit, frequency=4), xreg=IntReg,
  order=c(1,1,1), seasonal=c(1,1,1))
summary(basic_interaction)
```

```
## Coefficients:
## ar1 ma1 sar1 sma1 It It.w
## -0.1018 0.2905 0.4878 0.2804 2.0008 -0.2670
## s.e. 0.3265 0.3112 0.0907 0.0997 1.3723 1.3841
##
## sigma^2 estimated as 7.698: log likelihood=-473.88
## AIC=961.76 AICc=962.36 BIC=984.67
##
## Training set error measures:
## ME RMSE MAE MPE MAPE MASE ACF1
## Training set 0.0604637 2.697216 2.135684 3.25818 5.831864 0.07681414
## -0.0004501119

# Calculating the p values for this model
(1-pnorm(abs(basic_interaction$coef)/sqrt(diag(basic_interaction$var.coef))))*2
## ar1 ma1 sar1 sma1 It It.w
## 1.842833e-01 1.909077e-10 7.495600e-08 4.936081e-03 9.318723e-02 8.742326e-08
```

Lagged Effect Model:

```
gradual_effect <- Arima(ts(its_data$profit, frequency=4), order = c(1,1,1),
    seasonal=c(1,1,1), xreg=IntReg)

gradual_effect
## Coefficients:
## ar1 ma1 sar1 sma1 It It.w It.lh
## 0.0099 0.0505 0.4970 0.0737 -264.0825 -7.5659 0.4921
## s.e. 0.6493 0.6466 0.1031 0.1150 39.9907 1.6988 0.0736
##
## sigma^2 estimated as 6.148: log likelihood=-450.93
## AIC=917.85 AICc=918.63 BIC=944.04
## Training set error measures:
## ME RMSE MAE MPE MAPE MASE ACF1
## Training set 0.1096493 2.403986 1.801487 2.890285 5.65562 0.06479407 -0.001792034

#Calculating the p values for this model
(1-pnorm(abs(gradual_effect$coef)/sqrt(diag(gradual_effect$var.coef))))*2
## ar1 ma1 sar1 sma1 It It.w It.lh
## 0.0000000 0.0000000 1.417557e-06 5.212685e-01 0.0000000 0.9378504 0.0000000
```

The first model that we fit has two added terms—it and it.w. One denoting the period and one for the gradual effect of period. In the second model, we add an additional another term, a lagged *x* variable during treatment.

In the first model, the main effect of treatment is not significant under the 1% level, but the gradual effect of treatment is significant under the 1% level.

The second model is not relevant to this example, but just here to show you how to model lagged effects in ARIMA models. It has shows a significant effect. We should not use a lagged x variable in this example, because there is no good reasoning why this model would have lagged effects of the treatment, as the treatment shows up immediately (, i.e., a 20% discount).

16.2.3   Seasonality Decomposition

A very useful technique is seasonality decomposition, especially for user data, as we discussed in Chapter 11 section 11.4. Most user data has daily, weekly and yearly periodicity. It's helpful to separate the seasonality from the trend line.

Seasonality decomposition in R can be done with the `stl()` function. Generally, `stl()` does not use the technique discussed in Chapter 11 section 11.4. Instead, it uses LOESS smoothing to the periodic subseries (e.g., all December months). However, when we use the argument `s.window = 'periodic'` smoothing is replaced by the mean.

In Listing 16.7, we apply `stl()` to the time-series data from the ITS example. This data set actually has four intervals, even though we used only the first one in the prior example. Figure 16.7 plots this seasonality decomposition.

Listing 16.7   **Seasonality Decomposition**

```
# Library
library(forecast)

# Seasonality decomposition
arima.stl = stl(ts(its_data$profit, frequency=4), s.window="periodic")

plot(arima.stl,  main = "Seasonality Decomposition")
```

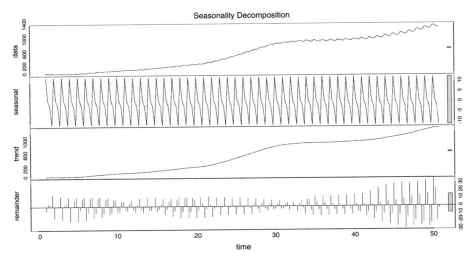

Figure 16.7   Plot of seasonality decomposition with `stl()`.

The stl() function creates three separate components from the data we feed it: the seasonal piece, the trend, and the remainder. Sometimes we want to remove seasonality and can use the trend line to estimate our pre- and post-treatment effects. Seasonality decomposition might not remove annual seasonality (if not enough data is provided) or other types of seasonality unique to your data. You might have to use the theory developed in Chapter 11 section 11.4 to try to remove some of those effects yourself.

16.3   Statistical Matching

In the next two sections, we'll go over the implementation of statistical matching and uplift modeling described in Chapters 12 and 13 with the Lalonde data set.

To carry out this analysis, we will work with a few popular R packages: "Matching," "genmoud," "uplift," "caret," and "stats." All of these packages can be loaded with the library() function after installation of R. The primary package we'll be using for statistical matching is "Matching," which was created by Jasdeep Sekhon. To implement uplift modeling, we'll use the package "uplift" developed by Leo Guelman. This package will help us implement both uplift forest models and causal inference uplift models. Listing 16.8 shows the commands to install and load packages.

Listing 16.8   **Loading the Required Packages**

```
# Load the packages needed for this chapter
install.packages(c("Matching", "rgenoud", "uplift", "caret", "skimr"),
  repos='http://cran.us.r-project.org')

## There are binary versions available (and will be installed) but
## the source versions are later:
## binary  source
## Matching 4.8-3.4  4.9-3
## rgenoud   5.7-12 5.8-2.0
## caret     6.0-47 6.0-80
library("Matching")
library("rgenoud")
library("uplift")
library("caret")
library("skimr")
```

First, let's look at the Lalonde data set, which is included in the "Matching" package. Listing 16.9 shows the first six rows with the head() function of the Lalonde data set. Next, we'll look at the summary of each of the variables with the summary() function.

Listing 16.9   **Lalonde Data Set**

```
# Data set
data(lalonde, package = 'Matching')

# The first few rows
head(lalonde)
```

```
##    age educ black hisp married nodegr re74 re75      re78 u74 u75 treat
## 1   37   11     1    0       1      1    0    0   9930.05   1   1     1
## 2   22    9     0    1       0      1    0    0   3595.89   1   1     1
## 3   30   12     1    0       0      0    0    0  24909.50   1   1     1
## 4   27   11     1    0       0      1    0    0   7506.15   1   1     1
## 5   33    8     1    0       0      1    0    0    289.79   1   1     1
## 6   22    9     1    0       0      1    0    0   4056.49   1   1     1
```

```
# Summary of the data
skimr::skim(lalonde)
```

```
## Skim summary statistics
## n obs: 445
## n variables: 12
##
## __ Variable type:integer _____
## variable missing complete   n   mean    sd  p0 p25 p50 p75 p100   hist
##      age       0      445  445 25.37   7.1  17  20  24  28   55  ▆▇▁▁▁
##    black       0      445  445  0.83  0.37   0   1   1   1    1  ▁▁▁▁▇
##     educ       0      445  445 10.2   1.79   3   9  10  11   16  ▁▁▁▆▂
##     hisp       0      445  445  0.088 0.28   0   0   0   0    1  ▇▁▁▁▁
##  married       0      445  445  0.17  0.37   0   0   0   0    1  ▇▁▁▁▂
##   nodegr       0      445  445  0.78  0.41   0   1   1   1    1  ▁▁▁▁▇
##    treat       0      445  445  0.42  0.49   0   0   0   1    1  ▇▁▁▁▆
##      u74       0      445  445  0.73  0.44   0   0   1   1    1  ▃▁▁▁▇
##      u75       0      445  445  0.65  0.48   0   0   1   1    1  ▅▁▁▁▇
##
## __ Variable type:numeric_____
## variable missing complete   n   mean       sd p0 p25    p50     p75    p100
    hist
##     re74       0      445  445 2102.27 5363.58  0   0      0  824.39 39570.7
 ▇▁▁▁▁
##     re75       0      445  445 1377.14 3150.96  0   0      0 1220.84 25142.2
 ▇▁▁▁▁
##     re78       0      445  445 5300.77 6631.49  0   0 3701.81 8124.72 60307.9
 ▇▁▁▁▁
```

We discussed the LaLonde data set in Chapter 13 section 13.5.1. The Lalonde data set is a randomized experiment, not observational data. Although we will apply matching algorithms to it, it's not generally the type of data set to which we want to apply matching, since it's **not** observational. However, for the sake of having consistency for both the matching and uplift examples, we'll be using the Lalonde data set to find treated and control users to compare. Unlike in A/B testing, it's harder to achieve randomization in the general population. Hence matching on the Lalonde data set does make sense in that context.

Since this is an experimental data set, we can calculate the ATE right away. In Listing 16.10, we calculate the ATE for the jobs program.

Listing 16.10 **Computing ATE**

```
# ATE
mean(lalonde$re78[lalonde$treat == 1]) -
    mean(lalonde$re78[lalonde$treat == 0])

## [1] 1794.343

median(lalonde$re78[lalonde$treat == 1]) -
    median(lalonde$re78[lalonde$treat == 0])

## [1] 1093.515
```

Before we move into modeling, we need to clean up the Lalonde data set. Listing 16.11 creates the data set that we will use for our models. The outcome will be binary (whether participants had any income in 1978). The treatment is whether they participated in the jobs program. More details of the jobs program are discussed in Chapter 13 section 13.5.1.

Then, we select the features to use in our model and modify them for our models. The features in this sample data set include the following: (1) age (a dummy variable for age divided by median age, or 25), (2) education (years completed of schooling), (3) no degree (a dummy variable for whether participants completed high school), (4) race (Hispanic or Black), (5) married (a dummy variable for whether participants are married), and (6) income in 1974 and 1975.

We also add a dummy variable for no earnings in either 1974 or 1975, and take the log of earnings in both 1974 and 1975. We'll normalize earnings and education before we put it into our model. Normalizing is taking numeric variables measured on different scales and putting them in a comparable scale. In Listing 16.11, w build the variables to model the data.

Listing 16.11 **Building Variables**

```
# Fit model with binary outcome (whether participants had income in 1978)
lalonde$outcome_binary <- as.numeric(lalonde$re78 > 0)

# Building the features
lalonde$age_median <- lalonde$age > median(lalonde$age)
lalonde$no_earnings <- lalonde$re75 == 0 | lalonde$re74 == 0
lalonde$log_re74 <- log(lalonde$re74 + 1)
lalonde$log_re75 <- log(lalonde$re75 + 1)

## or with dplyr
library(dplyr)
lalonde <-
    lalonde %>%
    mutate(outcome_binary = as.numeric(lalonde$re78 > 0),
           age_median = age > median(age),
           no_earnings = re75 == 0 | re74 == 0,
           log_re74 = log(re74 + 1),
           log_re75 = log(re75 + 1))
```

```
# Z Normalizing function
zVar <- function(var){
  normal <- (var - mean(var)) / sd(var)
  return(normal)
}

lalonde$n_re74 <- zVar(lalonde$log_re74)
lalonde$n_re75 <- zVar(lalonde$log_re75)
lalonde$n_educ <- zVar(lalonde$educ)

## or using built in functions
lalonde$n_re74 <- as.numeric(scale(lalonde$log_re74))
lalonde$n_re75 <- as.numeric(scale(lalonde$log_re75))
lalonde$n_educ <- as.numeric(scale(lalonde$educ))

#ATE for employed
mean(lalonde$outcome_binary[lalonde$treat == 1]) -
    mean(lalonde$outcome_binary[lalonde$treat == 0])
## [1] 0.1106029
```

In Listing 16.12, we set up the basic functional forms (or formulas) for the matching models that will come later in this section. Note that the features chosen for this section rely on common techniques for fitting models, such as creating dummy variables when possible, normalizing numeric variables, and taking the log for log-normal variables that were created in Listing 16.11. When building predictive or other types of models, it's often useful to rely on these techniques.

Listing 16.12 **Model**

```
### Full model
form <- outcome_binary ~ trt(treat) + age_median + n_educ + hisp + black + married +
  nodegr + no_earnings + n_re74 + n_re75

### Smaller model
form2 <- outcome_binary ~ trt(treat) + age_median + n_educ + hisp + married + n_re75
```

We'll show two different methods for statistical matching in this chapter—namely, propensity score matching and GenMatch, an evolutionary search algorithm for matching. The first model that we will run is the propensity score model, which matches users based on their propensity score. We explored propensity score matching in Chapter 12 section 12.2. A propensity score model will fit a logistic regression predicting treatment. We will then use the fitted values of the model to find people in the control group who look like the treatment group members, by matching people based on their scores. For instance, say a person in the treatment group had a propensity score of 0.79 of receiving treatment and we found the closest control user with a score of 0.80 of receiving treatment. We could match those users and find the difference in outcome. If we were to do this over the full data set, we would find the ATE.

We use the `Match()` function in R to calculate the ATE, ATT, or ATC. We also get the statistical significance of that estimate. Listing 16.13 implements the propensity score model and calculates the ATE for earnings in 1978.

Listing 16.13 **Propensity Score Model**

```
# Estimate the propensity model

# First, let's define the functional form
form_prop <- as.formula("treat ~ age_median + n_educ + hisp + black + married +
  nodegr + no_earnings + n_re74 + n_re75")

# Fitting a logistic regression model predicting treatment
prop_model <- glm(form_prop, family = binomial, data = lalonde)

# Let's use the Match function to calculate the average treatment effect
# Note that the "M=1" option means one-to-one matching, but
# multiple #users can be matched to the same control.

# Calculate the average treatment effect
match_relationship <- Match(Y = lalonde$outcome_binary, Tr = lalonde$treat,
  X = prop_model$fitted, estimand = "ATE", M = 1)

summary(match_relationship)

##
## Estimate... 0.11535
## AI SE...... 0.049992
## T-stat..... 2.3073
## p.val...... 0.021039
##
## Original number of observations.............. 445
## Original number of treated obs.............. 185
## Matched number of observations.............. 445
## Matched number of observations  (unweighted). 2035
```

From Listing 16.13, we can see that our ATE estimate is 11.5% and it's significant. It increased with matching of the participants.

We need to visualize how the covariate balance has changed after fitting the propensity score model to decide whether this model was indeed good. As you will remember from Chapter 12 section 12.2.1, balance means that the treatment and control groups are indistinguishable from each other. In particular, we look at their means and distributions to tell if the treatment and control groups are similar for each feature. We can use the function `MatchBalance()` to determine this information. The `match.out()` argument is the `Match()` object. The `MatchBalance` object prints the results for each variable of a number of statistical tests for balance. The "Before Matching" column shows how the treatment and control groups compare prior to our matching of the treated and control groups. The "After Matching" column shows how the treatment and control groups compare once we have matched them.

The printout shown in Listing 16.14 includes a comparison of means, eQQ (based on the Q-Q plot in Chapter 10), and the cumulative density function (another distributional comparison) of the treatment and control groups before and after matching for each variable. It also includes the results of the *t*-test and the distributional *KS*-test for numeric variables, which can be reviewed to determine whether the two means or distributions are the same. A low *p* value in the "Before Matching" or "After Matching" category denotes that the mean and the distribution are the same according to the *t*-test and *KS*-test, respectively. In Listing 16.14, notice the features plotted in Figure 16.8. Can you find where we failed to achieve balance?

Listing 16.14 **Match Balance Output**

```
# We want to check how the covariate balance has changed and plot it.
match_balance <- MatchBalance(form_prop, data=lalonde, match.out = match_
  relationship, nboots = 100)


##
## ***** (V1) age_medianTRUE *****
##                           Before Matching         After Matching
## mean treatment........      0.52432                0.50225
## mean control..........      0.46538                0.50773
## std mean diff.........        11.77                 -1.0956
##
## mean raw eQQ diff.....     0.059459                0.007371
## med   raw eQQ diff.....            0                      0
## max   raw eQQ diff.....            1                      1
##
## mean eCDF diff........      0.02947               0.0036855
## med  eCDF diff........      0.02947               0.0036855
## max  eCDF diff........      0.05894                0.007371
##
## var ratio (Tr/Co).....        1.004                 1.0002
## T-test p-value........      0.22142                0.81504
##
##
## ***** (V2) n_educ *****
##                           Before Matching         After Matching
## mean treatment........     0.083945                0.061652
## mean control..........     -0.05973                0.067569
## std mean diff.........       12.806                -0.58331
##
## mean raw eQQ diff.....      0.22622                0.044421
## med   raw eQQ diff.....            0                      0
## max   raw eQQ diff.....        1.116                  1.116
##
## mean eCDF diff........     0.028698               0.0056862
## med  eCDF diff........     0.012682               0.0034398
## max  eCDF diff........      0.12651                0.022113
##
```

```
## var ratio (Tr/Co).....      1.5513             1.2525
## T-test p-value........      0.15017            0.89538
## KS Bootstrap p-value..      0.01               0.23
## KS Naive p-value......      0.062873           0.70228
## KS Statistic.........       0.12651            0.022113
##
##
## ***** (V3) hisp *****
##                         Before Matching    After Matching
## mean treatment........     0.059459           0.075281
## mean control.........      0.10769            0.089888
## std mean diff........      -20.341            -5.5299
##
## mean raw eQQ diff.....     0.048649           0.007371
## med  raw eQQ diff.....     0                  0
## max  raw eQQ diff.....     1                  1
##
## mean eCDF diff........     0.024116           0.0036855
## med  eCDF diff........     0.024116           0.0036855
## max  eCDF diff........     0.048233           0.007371
##
## var ratio (Tr/Co).....     0.58288            0.85094
## T-test p-value........     0.064043           0.11994
##
##
## ***** (V4) black *****
##                         Before Matching    After Matching
## mean treatment........     0.84324            0.83933
## mean control.........      0.82692            0.83933
## std mean diff........      4.4767             0
##
## mean raw eQQ diff.....     0.016216           0.0039312
## med  raw eQQ diff.....     0                  0
## max  raw eQQ diff.....     1                  1
##
## mean eCDF diff........     0.0081601          0.0019656
## med  eCDF diff........     0.0081601          0.0019656
## max  eCDF diff........     0.01632            0.0039312
##
## var ratio (Tr/Co).....     0.92503            1
## T-test p-value........     0.64736            1
##
##
## ***** (V5) married *****
##                         Before Matching    After Matching
## mean treatment........     0.18919            0.17303
## mean control.........      0.15385            0.16303
## std mean diff........      8.9995             2.642
##
```

```
## mean raw eQQ diff.....    0.037838          0.002457
## med   raw eQQ diff.....           0                 0
## max   raw eQQ diff.....           1                 1
##
## mean eCDF diff........    0.017672         0.0012285
## med   eCDF diff........    0.017672         0.0012285
## max   eCDF diff........    0.035343          0.002457
##
## var ratio (Tr/Co).....      1.1802            1.0487
## T-test p-value........     0.33425           0.63625
##
##
## ***** (V6) nodegr *****
##                     Before Matching     After Matching
## mean treatment........     0.70811           0.75843
## mean control.........      0.83462           0.76742
## std mean diff........      -27.751           -2.0976
##
## mean raw eQQ diff.....     0.12432         0.0044226
## med   raw eQQ diff.....           0                 0
## max   raw eQQ diff.....           1                 1
##
## mean eCDF diff........     0.063254         0.0022113
## med   eCDF diff........     0.063254         0.0022113
## max   eCDF diff........     0.12651         0.0044226
##
## var ratio (Tr/Co).....      1.4998            1.0265
## T-test p-value........   0.0020368           0.49285
##
##
## ***** (V7) no_earningsTRUE *****
##                     Before Matching     After Matching
## mean treatment........     0.71892           0.75955
## mean control.........      0.77692           0.76778
## std mean diff........      -12.868           -1.9246
##
## mean raw eQQ diff.....    0.054054          0.002457
## med   raw eQQ diff.....           0                 0
## max   raw eQQ diff.....           1                 1
##
## mean eCDF diff........    0.029002         0.0012285
## med   eCDF diff........    0.029002         0.0012285
## max   eCDF diff........    0.058004          0.002457
##
## var ratio (Tr/Co).....      1.1678            1.0244
## T-test p-value........     0.16849           0.72005
##
##
```

```
## ***** (V8) n_re74 *****
##                        Before Matching      After Matching
## mean treatment........   0.050829             0.02376
## mean control..........  -0.036167            -0.036084
## std mean diff........     8.5079               5.8291
##
## mean raw eQQ diff.....    0.096692             0.017754
## med  raw eQQ diff.....    0                    0
## max  raw eQQ diff.....    1.887                1.887
##
## mean eCDF diff........    0.019223             0.006249
## med  eCDF diff........    0.0158               0.0058968
## max  eCDF diff........    0.047089             0.014742
##
## var ratio (Tr/Co).....    1.0798               1.0944
## T-test p-value........    0.36951              0.27748
## KS Bootstrap p-value..    0.61                 0.14
## KS Naive p-value......    0.97023              0.97987
## KS Statistic..........    0.047089             0.014742
##
##
## ***** (V9) n_re75 *****
##                        Before Matching      After Matching
## mean treatment........   0.10609             -0.024267
## mean control..........  -0.075484            -0.015784
## std mean diff........    17.578               -0.84561
##
## mean raw eQQ diff.....    0.1893               0.012719
## med  raw eQQ diff.....    0                    0
## max  raw eQQ diff.....    1.8277               1.3657
##
## mean eCDF diff........    0.050834             0.0066403
## med  eCDF diff........    0.061954             0.007371
## max  eCDF diff........    0.10748              0.015233
##
## var ratio (Tr/Co).....    1.132                1.0407
## T-test p-value........    0.061767             0.84965
## KS Bootstrap p-value..    0.03                 0.13
## KS Naive p-value......    0.16449              0.97224
## KS Statistic..........    0.10748              0.015233
##
##
## Before Matching Minimum p.value: 0.0020368
## Variable Name(s): nodegr  Number(s): 6
##
## After Matching Minimum p.value: 0.11994
## Variable Name(s): hisp  Number(s): 3
```

16.3.1   Plotting Balance

We will use a function created by Mark Huberty, shown in the appendix of this chapter, to plot the results from the `MatchBalance()` function. It takes the results from a `MatchBalance` object and puts it into a graph, where the *p* values for the *t*-test and *KS*-test are plotted. The *t*-test before matching is represented by the darker shaded dot and the *t*-test after matching is represented by the triangle. The *KS*-test before matching is a lighter shaded dot and the *KS*-test after matching is the diamond. We want to see that the triangle and diamond are not less than the 10% level for any variable. In Figure 16.8, the match balance for the propensity score model is plotted.

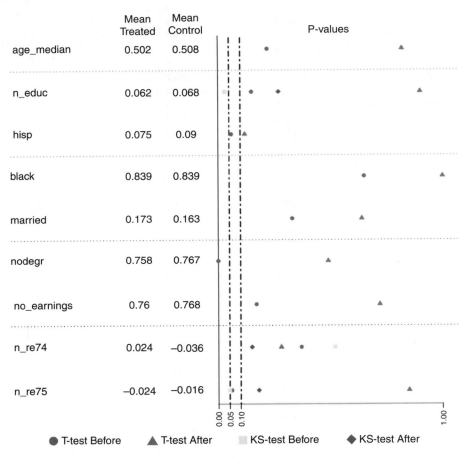

Figure 16.8   Match balance for Lalonde example.

We can tell from the `MatchBalance()` function whether we are able to achieve balance with the propensity score model. Prior to matching, we were not able to achieve balance on a few variables: education, Hispanic ethnicity, no degree (nodegr), and earnings in 1974. After we matched on the propensity score, we were able to achieve balance on all features. Often, we are not able to achieve balance even with the propensity score model, so another potential strategy is to try matching with a caliper.

16.3.2 Caliper Matching

As you will remember from Chapter 12 section 12.2.3, a caliper restricts the amount of difference in the propensity score between treatment and control participants. For instance, suppose we have a treated user with a propensity score of 0.1, but the closest control user has a propensity score of 0.50. We can't truly match these users because they are too different. However, in our current model, we are matching these disparate users. A caliper will restrict the distance between two users' propensity scores. It will drop users for whom there is no close match.

Here, we'll set the caliper to 0.05 of a standard deviation (propensity score). We'll limit matches to similar users based on the underlying distribution. To run this in R, we add a `caliper` argument to our `Match()` function. Listing 16.15 shows the ATE based on our caliper.

Listing 16.15 **Caliper Matching**

```
# Rematch the model with a caliper so that scores equal to or less than
# 0.05 standard deviation of each covariate are dropped
match_caliper <- Match(Y = lalonde$outcome_binary, estimand = "ATE",
  Tr = lalonde$treat, X = prop_model$fitted, M = 1, caliper = .05)


summary(match_caliper)

##
## Estimate...  0.11575
## AI SE......  0.048587
## T-stat.....  2.3824
## p.val......  0.017202
##
## Original number of observations..............  445
## Original number of treated obs..............  185
## Matched number of observations..............  424
## Matched number of observations  (unweighted).  2005
##
## Caliper (SDs).......................................  0.05
## Number of obs dropped by 'exact' or 'caliper'  21

# Calculating match balance
caliper_bal <- MatchBalance(form_prop, data = lalonde, match.out = match_caliper,
  nboots = 100, print.level = 0)

# We need to define the covariates to include when we plot
covariates <- cbind(lalonde$age_median, lalonde$n_educ, lalonde$hisp, lalonde$black,
  lalonde$married, lalonde$nodegr, lalonde$no_earnings, lalonde$n_re74, lalonde$n_
  re75)
colnames(covariates) <- c("age_median", "n_educ", "hisp", "black", "married",
  "nodegr", "no_earnings", "n_re74", "n_re75")

# Plotting result; plot.pval is in the appendix
plot.pval(colnames(covariates), caliper_bal, legend = TRUE)
```

Using a caliper in this example forced us to drop 21 observations where there wasn't a comparable treated or control user. From Figure 16.9, a plot of the new balance with the caliper method, we can see that we have again achieved balance.

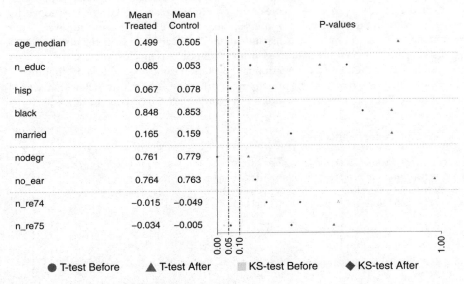

Figure 16.9   Match balance for the caliper model.

Another potential option is `GenMatch()`, an evolutionary search algorithm. We'll show an example of `GenMatch()` in the next section.

16.3.3 GenMatch()

In this section, we'll try to use the GenMatch function to create a balanced data set. GenMatch was covered in the sidebar in Chapter 12 section 12.3.1 as a why to deal with poor balance in the propensity score model. `GenMatch()` searches for the optimal weighting to achieve balance between the treatment and control groups on each variable. We need to create a BalanceMat— that is, a matrix of covariates that we'd like to achieve balance on. The result is a long printout, which provides the output for each generation while searching for an optimal weighting.

As mentioned earlier, this is an extremely computationally intensive algorithm, so you should be wary about data set size. It's best used for data sets with fewer than 1,000 users. Listing 16.16 runs the GenMatch algorithm on our data set.

Listing 16.16   **Running** GenMatch()

```
# Setting the seed
set.seed(101)
```

```
# Balance Matrix
balance_mat <- cbind(lalonde$age_median, lalonde$n_educ, lalonde$hisp,
  lalonde$married, lalonde$n_re75, lalonde$nodegr)

## or with dplyr
balance_mat <-
  lalonde %>%
  dyplr::select(age_median, n_educ, hisp, married, n_re75, nodegr) %>%
  as.matrix()


# Call genmatch
genout <- GenMatch(Tr = lalonde$treat, X = covariates, BalanceMatrix = balance_mat,
  estimand = "ATE", M = 1, pop.size = 16, max.generations = 10, wait.generations = 1)
```

The GenMatch() function completed and found the optimal weights. Now we can look at how it affected the ATE (Figure 16.10). Listing 16.17 shows the ATE after we matched the Lalonde data set using the GenMatch algorithm.

Listing 16.17 **GenMatch ATE**

```
# Now that GenMatch() has found the optimal weights, let's estimate
# our causal effect of interest using those weights
#
Genmatch_out <- Match(Y = lalonde$outcome_binary, Tr = lalonde$treat, X = covariates,
  estimand = "ATE", Weight.matrix = genout)
summary(Genmatch_out)

##
## Estimate...  0.10164
## AI SE......  0.049571
## T-stat.....  2.0504
## p.val......  0.040323
##
## Original number of observations..............  445
## Original number of treated obs...............  185
## Matched number of observations...............  445
## Matched number of observations  (unweighted).  1996


# Let's determine if balance has actually been obtained on the variables of
  interest
#
match_gen <- MatchBalance(form_prop, data = lalonde,
                          match.out = Genmatch_out, nboots = 500,
                          print.level = 0)

# Plot the match balance outcome
plot.pval(colnames(covariates), match_gen, legend=TRUE)
```

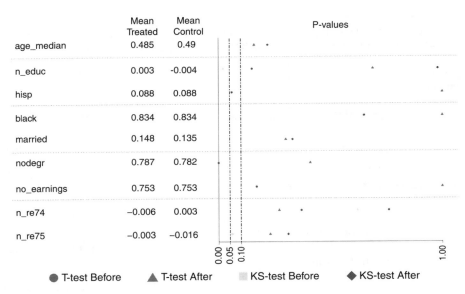

Figure 16.10   Match balance for GenMatch.

Listing 16.17 shows that the ATE decreased from 11.5% to 10%, which is a slight decline compared with the matched data set. We are able to achieve balance between the treatment and control groups. The GenMatch model worked better than the propensity score model under the *KS*-test. In the propensity score model, for the variable earnings in 1974, the *p* value was 0.13 after matching, while in this model it's closer to 0.25. Great—we've achieved balance again.

If we could not achieve balance, then perhaps the effect of treatment is not causal or was not estimated correctly. GenMatch often works substantially better than the propensity score model, but cannot always be used because of the data set's size. Regardless of the quality of the matching algorithm used, if there are core deficiencies in the data set, then matching will not work. If there is no coverage, matching of the full population will not work, but smaller subgrouping may have coverage and can be matched. Coverage means that strong selection effects are present and there are no control users who look like a portion of the treated users.

However, in that situation, at least we can determine the primary confounding variables. For instance, if we found that education was a confounder, then we could try to correct for it in the next experiment by stratifying our samples based on education (or limiting the variance in education of participants by cohort) or making sure that the sample is truly randomized on education of the participants.

In the next section, we'll go through techniques for uplift modeling based on the material from Chapter 13.

16.4   Uplift Modeling

In this section, we'll go over the techniques to determine the effects of treatment on subgroups of the population. We'll use the Lalonde data set again to show how to calculate uplift and subgroup heterogeneous treatment effects. Keep in mind that we should probably not apply both statistical matching and uplift modeling to the same data set in real life. The reason for this is that generally they are applied to different types of data—uplift modeling is appropriate for experimental data, and statistical matching is best used for observational data.

16.4.1   Two-Model Solution

In this section, we'll follow the organization of Chapter 13. We'll implement four types of uplift models in R: (1) the two-model approach, (2) the interaction model, (3) causal conditional inference forests, and (4) uplift forests.

In Listing 16.18, we'll estimate uplift using the two-model approach. As we discussed in Chapter 13 section 13.5.3, this is often not the best approach to estimate uplift, but it's useful to understand how it's implemented and how it compares to other approaches. We'll assume that both the treatment and control groups can be modeled by a logistic regression with the same functional form. In the two-model approach, we use the following process:

1. Use the treated data to build a treatment model and the control data to build a control model.

2. Get predictions for the full data set from both the treatment and control models.

3. Subtract the treatment predictions from the control predictions to estimate uplift.

We implement these steps in Listing 16.18. With the two-model approach, the general estimate of uplift is often good, but subgroup effects might not be very accurate.

Listing 16.18   **Implementation of Two-Model Uplift Solution**

```
# Two-model solution (simple)
# Treated model
treatment <- glm(form, family = binomial, data = lalonde, subset = treat == 1)

# Control model
control <- glm(form, family=binomial, data=lalonde, subset = lalonde$treat == 0)

# Calculating uplift
uplift_glm <- cbind(
  predict(treatment, newdata=lalonde, type="response"),
  predict(control, newdata=lalonde, type="response"))
  colnames(uplift_glm) <- c("treat_model", "control_model")
  model1 <- cbind(lalonde, uplift_glm)

# Predicted average treatment effect
model1$uplift <- model1$treat_model - model1$control_model
mean(model1$uplift)
## [1] 0.1045998

median(model1$uplift)
## [1] 0.06561073
```

Average predicted uplift is 10.5% and median uplift is 6.6%.

Next, we look at how this model predicted uplift on a random sample of users (in Listing 16.19). A great way to understand how your model is working by looking at individual cases.

Listing 16.19 **Individual Users' Uplift**

```
# Sample users
set.seed(101)
sample_uplift <- sample(nrow(model1), 5)
model1[sample_uplift,]
```

##		age	educ	black	hisp	married	nodegr	re74	re75	re78	u74	u75
##	166	19	10	0	0	0	1	0.00	5324.11	13829.60	1	0
##	20	26	12	1	0	0	0	0.00	0.00	10747.40	1	1
##	315	25	10	1	0	1	1	0.00	0.00	0.00	1	1
##	291	33	11	1	0	0	1	0.00	0.00	0.00	1	1
##	111	20	9	1	0	0	1	6083.99	0.00	8881.67	0	1

##		treat	outcome	outcome_binary	age_median	no_earnings	log_re74
##	166	1	[74.3,25142.2]	1	0	1	0.00000
##	20	1	0.0	1	1	1	0.00000
##	315	0	0.0	0	1	1	0.00000
##	291	0	0.0	0	1	1	0.00000
##	111	1	0.0	1	0	1	8.71358

##		log_re75	n_re74	n_re75	n_educ	treat_model	control_model
##	166	8.580189	-0.5971577	1.5708308	-0.1090919	0.9877164	0.6741084
##	20	0.000000	-0.5971577	-0.7209076	1.0069053	0.7310072	0.6107346
##	315	0.000000	-0.5971577	-0.7209076	-0.1090919	0.7720531	0.5517217
##	291	0.000000	-0.5971577	-0.7209076	0.4489067	0.5876612	0.5618551
##	111	0.000000	1.6979470	-0.7209076	-0.6670904	0.4679087	0.6853267

##		uplift
##	166	0.31360800
##	20	0.12027256
##	315	0.22033143
##	291	0.02580618
##	111	-0.21741795

```
## or the dplyr way
## sample_n(model1, size=5)
```

We can see the predicted individual treatment effects differ dramatically, ranging from –31% to 22%. That's a huge difference.

16.4.2 Interaction Model

As described in Chapter 13 section 13.5.3, the interaction model is another way to model uplift. The interaction model is applied with a logistic regression. The steps to carry out this process are the following:

1. Build a model in which the predictor variables interact with the treatment variables.

2. Fit a model for the treated group and fit a model for the control group.

3. Subtract the estimates for the treated group from the estimates for the control group to find uplift.

We calculate the effect by assuming treatment is 1 and control is 0. The interaction effects are how the treatment affects the predictor variables. We can estimate uplift for this data set by subtracting the treated predictions from the control predictions. Listing 16.20 implements the interaction model.

Listing 16.20 **Implementing Interaction Model**

```
# Interaction model, logistic regression
set.seed(101)

form_int <- outcome_binary ~ age_median + n_educ + hisp + black +
  married + nodegr + n_re74 + n_re75 + treat*age_median + treat*n_educ + treat*hisp +
  treat*black + treat*married + treat*nodegr + treat*n_re74 + treat*n_re75

interaction_md <- glm(form_int, family=binomial, data=lalonde)

summary(interaction_md)

##
## Call:
## glm(formula = form_int, family = binomial, data = lalonde)
##
## Deviance Residuals:
##     Min       1Q   Median       3Q      Max
## -2.2518  -1.3004   0.6614   0.9454   1.7129
##
## Coefficients:
##                   Estimate Std. Error z value Pr(>|z|)
## (Intercept)        1.81258    0.72408   2.503  0.01230 *
## treat              0.65674    1.13926   0.576  0.56430
## age_median        -0.16917    0.28783  -0.588  0.55670
## n_educ            -0.07650    0.19246  -0.397  0.69101
## hisp              -0.07571    0.82443  -0.092  0.92683
## black             -1.05700    0.66533  -1.589  0.11213
## married           -0.11194    0.39019  -0.287  0.77419
## nodegr            -0.23625    0.45349  -0.521  0.60240
## n_re74             0.43241    0.21843   1.980  0.04774 *
## n_re75            -0.25560    0.21636  -1.181  0.23747
## treat:age_median  -0.17018    0.47914  -0.355  0.72246
## treat:n_educ       0.01032    0.28235   0.037  0.97085
## treat:hisp        14.63231  686.74896   0.021  0.98300
## treat:black        0.12404    1.03436   0.120  0.90454
## treat:married      1.02582    0.69198   1.482  0.13823
## treat:nodegr      -0.41435    0.71095  -0.583  0.56002
## treat:n_re74      -1.30460    0.43954  -2.968  0.00300 **
## treat:n_re75       1.16248    0.44977   2.585  0.00975 **
## ---
## Signif. codes:  0 '***' 0.001 '**' 0.01 '*' 0.05 '.' 0.1 ' ' 1
##
```

```
## (Dispersion parameter for binomial family taken to be 1)
##
##      Null deviance: 549.47  on 444  degrees of freedom
## Residual deviance: 509.37  on 427  degrees of freedom
## AIC: 545.37
##
## Number of Fisher scoring iterations: 15
# Build a treat model
lalonde_treat <- lalonde
lalonde_treat$treat <- 1
treat_prediction <- predict(interaction_md, lalonde_treat, type = "response")

# Build a control model
lalonde_control <- lalonde
lalonde_control$treat <- 0
control_prediction <- predict(interaction_md, lalonde_control, type = "response")

# Predicted uplift
mean(treat_prediction - control_prediction)
## [1] 0.1035318

## or with dplyr
lalonde %>%
  mutate(treat_old = treat) %>%
  mutate(treat = 1) %>%
  mutate(pred_treat = predict(interaction_md, ., type = "response")) %>%
  mutate(treat = 0) %>%
  mutate(pred_control = predict(interaction_md, ., type = "response")) %>%
  mutate(difference = pred_treat - pred_control) %>%
  dplyr::summarize(mean(difference))
```

Note that you'll get a warning when you run the interaction model—"prediction from a rank-deficient fit may be misleading"—because the interaction has a large number of terms, such that we don't have the necessary observations to properly fit the model. This is a problem when trying to fit an interaction model with a large number of terms: you'll need more data to make it work. This approach is probably not the right approach to fitting this data, but may work well in other situations with more data.

The following are a few useful features of this model:

- We can just build one model.

- We can understand how our variables affect our uplift predictions (although not that easily when there are many interaction effects).

- Logistic regression is relatively easy to understand.

We can interpret these coefficients similarly to the logistic regression in Chapter 8 section 8.3.1.3. From the model, earnings in 1974 is significant and the interaction with the treatment is also significant at the 5% level (this is the accepted standard for academic publishing in many disciplines, but there has been a growing movement toward adopting a lower standard). We can see that the average predicted uplift of this model is about 10.3%.

In the next section, we'll fit a causal conditional inference forest and an uplift forest model. Both of these methods are described in detail in Chapter 13.

16.4.3 Causal Conditional Inference Forest and Uplift Forest Models

In this section, we'll go over the uplift tree models, causal conditional inference forests (CCIF), and uplift forests that we discussed in detail in Chapter 13 section 13.5.6.2. Both of these methods will be implemented in R with the "uplift" package. We'll also compare these models with the Qini coefficient, also discussed in Chapter 13 section 13.5.6.7.

In this section, we'll add a model validation component. Instead of more complex methods, we will simply divide our data into a training set and a test set. Various aspects of cross-validation are covered in Chapter 8 section 8.4. Here, we'll just assess model quality in a simple way by dividing the data into 80% for training and 20% for testing. We'll compare the CCIF model and the uplift forest model.

As you'll remember from Chapter 8, the CCIF trees model has additional criteria to correct for overfitting and selection bias toward covariates with many splits. The uplift forest model is a random forest model with special splitting criteria for modeling uplift.

In Listing 16.21, we fit the model and then predict the treated and control probability for having a job in 1978 for each participant. We can use the "caret" package and the `createData-Partition()` function to create our training and test data sets. We then use the `ccif()` function from the "uplift" package to run the CCIF model. We can alter parameters in the CCIF function like split, p value, and others. We will demonstrate that here, but you can use cross-validation to find the optimal hyperparameters for your model.

Listing 16.21 **Implementation of Causal Inference Forest**

```
# Set random seed
set.seed(78)

#Load libraries
library('rsample')

# Create a training set and a test set
a <- createDataPartition(lalonde$outcome_binary, p = 0.8, list = FALSE)
training <- lalonde[a, ]
test <- lalonde[-a, ]

library(rsample)
data_split <- initial_split(data = lalonde, prop = 0.8)
training <- analysis(data_split)
test <- assessment(data_split)
```

```
### Fit causal conditional inference tree model
ccif_training <- ccif(formula = form,
                      data = training,
                      ntree = 100,
                      split_method = "KL",
                      distribution = approximate (nresample = 999),
                      pvalue = 0.1,
                      verbose = TRUE)


pred <- predict(ccif_training, test)
```

Once we have run our model, we can evaluate the model performance on our test data set. In Listing 16.22, we first plot uplift by quintile and then use an incremental gains curve to compare uplift forests to CCIF. We also calculate the Qini coefficient, or the improvement over the random targeting model.

Listing 16.22 **Evaluating Model Performance**

```
### Evaluate model performance
perf <- performance(pred[, 1], pred[, 2], test$outcome_binary, test$treat,
  direction = 1, groups = 5)

## ggplot of quintiles
ggplot(data.frame(perf[, c("group", "uplift")]), aes(x = group, y = uplift)) +
  geom_line() +
  labs(title = 'Uplift Quintile Results, Causal Conditional Inference Forest Model',
  x= "Quintiles", y='Uplift') +
  theme(plot.title=element_text(hjust=0.5))

Q <- qini(perf, plotit=TRUE, main="Causal Conditional Inference Forest Model versus
  Random Targeting")

Q #Qini Object Output


## $Qini
## [1] 0.03466893
##
## $inc.gains
## [1] 0.1205433 0.1618563 0.1561969 0.1154499 0.1686474
##
## $random.inc.gains
## [1] 0.03372949 0.06745897 0.10118846 0.13491794 0.16864743
```

The quintile plot assumes that there are five separate subgroups (built by ranking the subgroups from those with the greatest estimated uplift to those with the least). The value that you see for each group is the actual difference between the treatment and control subgroups for each grouping. The uplift for these quintiles is plotted in Figure 16.11. Figure 16.12 plots the incremental gains curve for the CCIF model. From this, we'll calculate the Qini, which is discussed in Chapter 13 section 13.5.6.7.

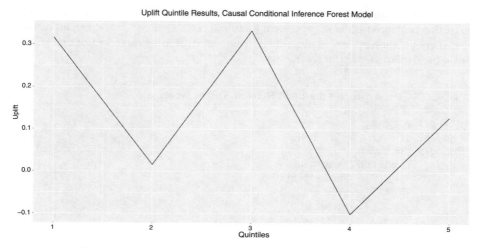

Figure 16.11   CCIF model uplift by subpopulation group.

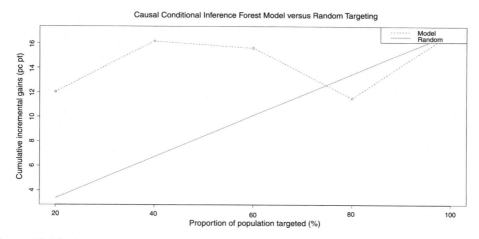

Figure 16.12   Improvement of the CCIF model over random targeting.

> **Note**
>
> The results in this section vary by random seed and could vary by R version. The best approach would be to take a bootstrap sample, but that was not used in this section for simplicity reasons. The R version used to generate these results is version 3.5.3, "The Great Truth."

The Qini coefficient for the CCIF model is 0.035. We'll compare this to the Qini coefficient for the uplift forest model in the next section. (Note this is the result for our random seed. To replicate the results presented here, use the same random seed.)

In Listing 16.23, we compare the CCIF model to the plain random forest uplift model to see if the CCIF model is indeed an improvement for this data set. Figure 16.13 is the uplift based on our five subpopulation groups. Figure 16.14 is the incremental gains curve for this model. We also calculate the Qini coefficient for this model.

Listing 16.23   Implementing the Uplift Random Forest Model

```
# Setting the seed
set.seed(78)
### Fit upliftRF model
RF_training <- upliftRF(form,
                        data = training,
                        mtry = 3,
                        ntree = 100,
                        split_method = "KL",
                        minsplit = 3,
                        verbose = TRUE)


pred_RF <- predict(RF_training, test)

### Evaluate model performance
perf_RF <- performance(pred_RF[, 1], pred_RF[, 2], test$outcome_binary, test$treat,
  direction = 1, groups = 5)

## ggplot of quintiles
ggplot(data.frame(perf_RF[, c("group", "uplift")]), aes(x=group, y=uplift))
  + geom_line() +
  labs(title = 'Uplift Quintile Results, Random Forest Model', x= "Quintiles",
  y='Uplift') +
  theme(plot.title=element_text(hjust=0.5))

Q_RF <- qini(perf_RF, plotit = TRUE, main="Random Forest Model versus Random
  Targeting")

# Qini object output
Q_RF


## $Qini
## [1] 0.00450481
##
## $inc.gains
## [1] -0.07583475  0.08262592  0.18845501  0.10979061  0.16864743
##
## $random.inc.gains
## [1] 0.03372949 0.06745897 0.10118846 0.13491794 0.16864743
```

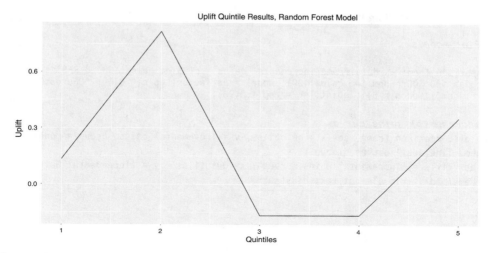

Figure 16.13   Random forest uplift model on the five subgroups.

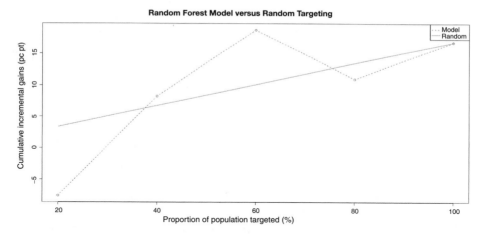

Figure 16.14   Incremental gains curve for the random forest uplift model.

The Qini coefficient for this model is 0.0045. That's much lower than the Qini coefficient for the CCIF tree model. For this reason, we prefer the CCIF model to this random forest uplift model.

In Listing 16.24, we plot both models in one graph so we can compare the two together. Figure 16.15 is the incremental gains curves for both models over the five quintiles.

Listing 16.24   **Plotting the Models**

```
# Plot models

comparison_frame <- data.frame(incremental_gains = c(Q$inc.gains*100, Q_RF$inc.
   gains*100, Q$random.inc.gains*100), model = as.factor(rep(c("CCIF", "UForest",
   "Random"), each = 5)), quintiles = rep(1:5, 3))

# Incremental gains curves
ggplot(comparison_frame, aes(x = quintiles, y = incremental_gains, group = model)) +
   geom_line(aes(linetype = model)) +
   labs(title = "Incremental Gains Curves", x='Quintiles', y = 'Incremental Gains')+
   theme(plot.title=element_text(hjust=0.5))
```

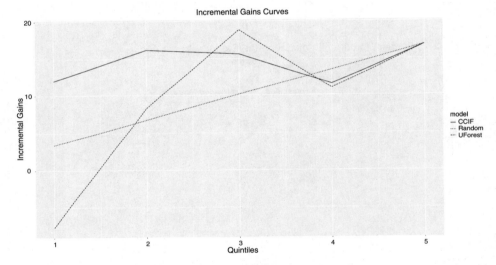

Figure 16.15   CCIF and random forest model incremental gains curves.

Let's try to better understand the features within the model. We'll look at the primary subgroups (married, Hispanic, and others) from this model. In Chapter 13, we did some more analysis and calculated the heterogeneous treatment effects by group; we plotted them in Figure 13.3.

We know that the CCIF model is better than the uplift forest model from our results in the last section with the test set. We can now run the better model (CCIF) model on the full data set, so that we can determine variable importance.

By plotting the variable importance, we can tell which features help us predict uplift. In Listing 16.25, we calculate variable importance for our better model, the CCIF model. We plot the variable importance in Figure 16.16.

Listing 16.25   **Finding Variable Importance for the CCIF Model**

```
# Set the seed
set.seed(78)

#Causal conditional inference model on the full data set
ccif1 <- ccif(formula = form2,
              data = lalonde,
              ntree = 100,
              split_method = "KL",
              distribution = approximate(nresample = 999),
              pvalue = 0.1,
              verbose = TRUE)


summary(ccif1)

## $importance
##          var   rel.imp
## 1     n_educ 54.305408
## 2      n_re75 26.064842
## 3    married 12.864070
## 4 age_median  4.575095
## 5       hisp  2.190585
## $ntree
## [1] 100
##
## $mtry
## [1] 2
##
## $split_method
## [1] "KL"

# Variable importance
varImportance(ccif1, plotit = TRUE, normalize = TRUE, main="Relative Importance of
  Variables, CCIF Model")

# Adjusted net information value
niv_out <- niv(form2, data = lalonde, main="Adjusted Net Information of Variables,
  CCIF Model")
niv_out

## $niv_val
##               niv penalty adj_niv
## age_median  1.799  0.8711  0.9279
## n_educ     15.287  4.5315 10.7555
## hisp       10.734  2.0018  8.7322
## married     5.140  1.4209  3.7191
## n_re75     16.727  6.8211  9.9059
```

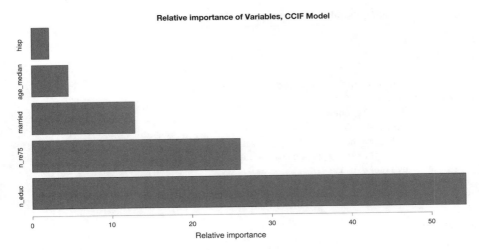

Figure 16.16   Variable importance for CCIF model.

Figure 16.17 is the adjusted net information value of each of the variables for the CCIF model. The net information value determines the predictive power of each variable for uplift. We can see that Hispanic ethnicity, education, marital status, and prior earnings in 1975, respectively, are the most important features that we can use for targeting. We illustrated their effects in Figure 13.1 in Chapter 13.

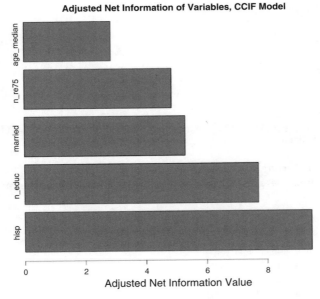

Figure 16.17   Adjusted net information value for CCIF model.

The "uplift" package also has a ModelProfile() function that can break up our user base into groups for targeting. We will not discuss it further here.

16.5   Actionable Insights

In this chapter, we worked through the R implementation of statistical matching, uplift modeling, and population projection described in Chapters 10–12. We used the Lalonde data set to implement statistical matching. We learned how to check and plot match balance, how to create a matched control, and how to calculate the ATE after matching.

We also implemented uplift modeling, including all the methods described in Chapter 13: the two-model approach, an interaction model, uplift forests, and causal conditional inference trees.

While we have gone over the core elements, there is much more to R than has been covered in this chapter. A good place to start would be to look at the "uplift," "caret," and "MASS" packages, as well as the R packages used in Chapters 14 and 15. You can also peruse the advanced readings for more in-depth treatment of these ideas.

Appendix

Listing 16.26 provides the `plot.pval()` function, which plots match balance across variables.

Listing 16.26   **Match Balance**

```
# Match balance
# This function was created by Mark Huberty at UC Berkeley

plot.pval <- function(covariates, bal.out, title=NULL, legend,legendx=0.15,lege
  ndy=2.2, textsize=0.9, parcex=0.8, at1=-0.35, at2=-0.15, at3=-0.9,xlim1=-0.85) {

  balanceMat <- function(cov, mbresults){

    # Calculate the number of covariates
    n <- ifelse(class(covariates)=="matrix", dim(covariates)[2], length(covariates))

    # Determine how the covariate names are provided, and then grab them
    if(class(covariates)=="matrix") rnames <- dimnames(covariates)[[2]]
    if(class(covariates)=="character") rnames <- covariates

    # Construct the matrix of statistics from the MatchBalance data and
    attach it to the covariate names
    z <- t(sapply(1:n, function(x){
      c(rnames[x],
        round(bal.out$AfterMatching[[x]]$mean.Tr,3),
        round(bal.out$AfterMatching[[x]]$mean.Co,3),
        round(bal.out$BeforeMatching[[x]]$tt$p.value,2),
        round(bal.out$AfterMatching[[x]]$tt$p.value,2),
        round(bal.out$BeforeMatching[[x]]$tt$statistic,2),
        round(bal.out$AfterMatching[[x]]$tt$statistic,2),
        ifelse(is.null(bal.out$BeforeMatching[[x]]$ks$ks.boot.pvalue) ==
                 0,round(bal.out$BeforeMatching[[x]]$ks$ks.boot.pvalue,2),
                 NA),
```

```
            ifelse(is.null(bal.out$AfterMatching[[x]]$ks$ks.boot.pvalue) ==
                0, round(bal.out$AfterMatching[[x]]$ks$ks.boot.pvalue,2),
                NA))
})))
z <- as.data.frame(z)
# return(z)

z[,2:9] <- apply(z[,2:9], 2, function(x){as.numeric(x)})
mat <- z[,2:9]

# Apply the correct column names
names(mat)<- c("Mean Tr.",
                "Mean Con.",
                "BM t p-value",
                "AM t p-value",
                "BM t stat",
                "AM t stat",
                "BM KS p-value",
                "AM KS p-value")
# Apply the correct row names
dimnames(mat)[[1]] <- z[,1]
mat
}

# Take the function above and apply it to the data supplied in the command
results <- balanceMat(covariates, bal.out)

# Set values of different parameters
xlim = c(xlim1,1); pchset = c(21,24,22,23); pchcolset = c("blue","red", "yellow",
  "darkgreen")

# Set margins and letter size
par(cex=parcex, mai = c(0.5, 0.35, 1.1, 0.35))

# Set number of rows
ny = nrow(results)

# Create the empty figure
if(!is.null(title))  plot(x=NULL,axes=F, xlim=xlim, ylim=c(1,ny),xlab="",ylab="",
  main=title)
if(is.null(title))   plot(x=NULL,axes=F, xlim=xlim, ylim=c(1,ny),xlab="",ylab="")

# Add the 0, 0.05, and 0.1 vertical lines
abline(v=c(0,0.05,0.1),lty=c(1,4,4), lwd=c(1,2,2))
axis(side=1,at=c(0,0.05,0.1,1),tick=TRUE, las=2, cex.axis=0.7)
```

```r
# Add labels on top of the three areas of the graph
axis(side=3,at=at1,labels="Mean\nTreated",tick=FALSE, padj=0.5,cex.axis=textsize)
axis(side=3,at=at2,labels="Mean\nControl",tick=FALSE, padj=0.5,cex.axis=textsize)
axis(side=3,at=0.5,labels="P-values",tick=FALSE, padj=0.5,cex.axis=textsize)

# Fill the figure with the information which is inside the 'results' matrix
## Add the p values of the t statistics as points
for(i in 3:4) points(results[,i],ny:1, pch = pchset[i-3+1], col = pchcolset[i-3+1],
    bg = pchcolset[i-3+1])

## Add the p values of the KS statistics as points
for(i in 7:8) points(results[,i],ny:1, pch = pchset[i-5+1], col = pchcolset[i-5+1],
    bg = pchcolset[i-5+1])

# Second, add each variable name and the means for treated and control
for(i in 1:ny) {
   text(at3,ny-i+1,dimnames(results)[[1]][i],adj = 0,cex=textsize)
                                                  # variable name
   text(at1,ny-i+1,results[i,1], cex=textsize)    # treatment mean
   text(at2,ny-i+1,results[i,2], cex=textsize)    # control mean
}

# Add dotted horizontal lines every two variables to make it prettier
for(i in seq(2,by=2,length.out=floor((ny-1)/2))) abline(h = i+0.5, lty = 3)

# Add legend
if(legend) legend(x=-1,y=-1, c(colnames(results)[3:4], colnames(results)[7:8]),
    pch=pchset, pt.bg = pchcolset, cex=0.8, ncol=2, xpd=NA)
}
```

Conclusion

In Academia, I always felt the "truth" rested between the highly siloed disciplines. That's why I wanted to write a multidisciplinary book blending qualitative and quantitative tools. I also felt that there was little movement forward in understanding human behavior because of the focus on singular connections, rather than on holistic theories of human behavior.

In academic social science settings, papers would often try to show that X causes Y. I always felt this was too simplistic and that social processes don't follow this linear equation-like formats, but rather demonstrate a more complex, multidimensional, circular relationship. Y may also cause X through Z and T, but X may be related to Z, but not through Y, and so on. This is where my desire to write a book based on the scientific method started. I yearned for a "theory of the social universe," so to speak, where we employ a variety of tools to validate it. Natural scientists should not be the only scientists with complex, holistic theories of the world.

As you may have noticed, this book also relies on tools from a variety of domains. I was tired of seeing books repeat the same few tools again and again because of their origin in the same discipline. A lot of methodological development to me in certain disciplines felt very path dependent, rather than being based on practical benefits. In this book, nothing is siloed. You've see tools from computer science, sociology, psychology, statistics, and economics. It doesn't matter where the tool comes from; you should select the best tool for the job. It's really just the beginning, once you get out there and explore. There are applicable tools in a whole host of other disciplines.

Don't limit yourself to the current "data science" box. It is and will be insufficient. Understanding user behavior is often so difficult that we need a broadened toolkit from multiple disciplines to begin to understand and model this complex behavior.

The goal of this book is to provide an overview of the latest tools for understanding behavior in a web setting. There are two core takeaways of this book:

- *The importance of the integration of qualitative and quantitative tools when trying to understand user behavior.* The development of theories, baselines, and metrics relies on qualitative ideas about conceptualization. Many supposedly quantitative metrics are really qualitative, because they are based on arbitrary inclusion rules and definitions. Not all qualitative metrics are equal. Effort needs to be spent on the development of qualitative techniques. Without intuitive qualitative baselines, the quantitative metrics can be meaningless and even deceptive.

- *The importance of causal inference when modeling human behavior.* Prediction sheds light on only a small subset of potential "actionable insights." Most insight relies upon causal inference, which is not supported by most of the 2.5 quintillion bytes of data created daily. What does this mean for us going forward? We must work to improve causal inference tools for behavior change, while understanding the limitations and correct uses of prediction.

While this book covers a variety of tools, ranging from sociological conceptual development techniques to statistical matching, it's far from sufficient to let us answer some of the most difficult causal questions regarding customer behavior. Some of these questions may be answerable given the right design, but we still lack the tools/designs necessary to answer *all* questions.

Human beings don't randomize their behavior, so most social data is and always has been observational. While the Internet age has opened up some great opportunities for easy A/B testing and collecting massive amounts of observational data, it has not made it much easier to draw complex causal linkages.

People have been theorizing about relationships in social behavior for thousands of years—but the validation is still difficult. Causal inference from observational data is both a science and an art in practice. Validating an effect without an innovative design or A/B test is nearly impossible. The world is better this way. If it were easy to show causal relationships, human beings would be predictable, simple, and boring. This book provides a framework to explore the easiest questions, facilitates the integration of distinct toolkits, and sheds light on major analytics mistakes.

In these concluding remarks, I wanted to explore some of the open questions in this space. The current data-rich world has created more questions than it has answered. Now that we have gone through some of the basics, here are some questions still left to consider:

- What are the limits of prediction in a world with infinite (or close to infinite) relevant user data? Can human behavior ever be perfectly (or close to perfectly) predicted? This is a deeply intriguing question that gets to the heart of the growth in machine learning (ML)/artificial intelligence (AI) in recent years. AI is moving to a variety of domains, from prescribing treatments for disease to predicting crime. If there are serious limits to prediction, these need to be understood and documented to prevent false attribution. How wrong are we? Are certain people just aberrant from the predicted norms? How biased is our data? Even with good data, are there things that we will never be able to predict?

- What are the limits to human behavior change? Is causal inference really useful in changing behavior? Just because we can understand why something occurs, that doesn't always mean we can easily change it or anticipate the consequences when we change it. We really understand very little about behavior change over the course of a person's life. When does it happen, how often? Is behavior change more difficult for some people than for others?

- Are we using data to stifle creativity? The focus of many companies is on short-term assessment of behavior change. For instance, we assess our recommendation system based on whether a user watched a recommended movie. However, every movie recommended was a horror movie and after watching a few of these films, the user gets bored and leaves. Prediction can force users into stable and consistent behavior that does not reflect their true desires or natural creativity. How big of a problem is this in creating products? Creativity is good for humanity. Being able to predict the future and thinking you're good at it, when you're really not, is a dangerous thing.

- How addictive can we make web products, and who is getting addicted? By increasing the stickiness of products, we are addicting some users to certain behaviors. Who are these users? What are the long-run effects on people's lives?

- Finally, how do online behaviors and interactions affect a person's real life and psychological state? The Internet allows us to interact with a much larger world. Users often choose an echo chamber of similar people or might engage with people whom they are unlikely to meet in real life (in a foreign country, of different ages). How does this affect self-perception, motivation, and real-life behavior? We know very little about how social interaction on the Internet differs from interaction in real life.

These questions may never be completely answered, but can guide us as we work to better understand users and even people more generally.

The social sciences have never settled on one predominant toolkit because there is no easy validation of social behavior, especially complex behavior that cannot be randomized. We have seen this throughout the book. Social processes are multidimensional, open, fuzzy outcomes, characterized by incomplete information and millions of potential causal linkages. They are incredibly hard to quantify and model. But the current world allows us to randomize, track small behavioral movements, and change environments (both social and systemic). For this reason, the answers to some of these questions are almost within our grasp. We can make headway into understanding human behavior and its causal linkages.

Bibliography

Aberson, Christopher. *Applied Power Analysis for Behavioral Science*. New York: Routledge, 2010.

Andersen, Hanne, and Hepburn, Brian. "The Scientific Method." In *The Stanford Encyclopedia of Philosophy*, edited by Edward Zalta. 2015. https://plato.stanford.edu/cite.html.

Angrist, Joshua, and Evans, William. "Children and Their Parent's Labor Supply: Evidence from Exogenous Variation in Family Size." *American Economic Review,* 88 (1988), 450–477.

Angrist, Joshua, and Krueger, Alan. "Empirical Strategies in Labor Economics." *Handbook of Labor Economics,* Vol. 3A, edited by Orley Ashenfelter and David Card. North Holland: Elsevier, 1999.

Angrist, Joshua, and Pischke, Jörn-Steffen. *Mostly Harmless Econometrics: An Empiricist's Companion*. Princeton, NJ: Princeton University Press, 2008.

Applegate, David, Bixby, Robert, Chvátal, Vasek, and Cook, William. *The Traveling Salesman Problem*. Princeton, NJ: Princeton University Press, 2006.

Ashcraft, Adam, Fernández-Val, Ivan, and Lang, Kevin. "The Consequences of Teenage Childbearing: Consistent Estimates When Abortion Makes Miscarriage Nonrandom." *Economic Journal, 123*, no. 571 (2013): 875–905.

Ashenfelter, Orley, Levine, Phillip, and Zimmerman, David. *Statistics and Econometrics: Methods and Applications*. Danvers, MA: Wiley, 2006.

Bates, Douglas, and Watts, Donald G. *Nonlinear Regression Analysis and Its Applications*. New York: Wiley, 1988.

Bhaskaran, Krishnan, et al. "Time Series Regression Studies in Environmental Epidemiology." *International Journal of Epidemiology* 42, no. 4 (2013): 1187–1195. https://doi.org/10.1093/ije/dyt092.

Breiman, Leo. "Bagging Predictors." *Machine Learning* 24 (1996): 123–140.

Breiman, Leo. "Random Forests." *Machine Learning* 45, no. 1 (2001): 5–32.

Breiman, Leo, Friedman, Jerome, Olshen, Richard, and Stone, Charles. *Classification and Regression Trees*. Boca Raton, FL: Chapman and Hall, 1984.

Caraballo, Ralph, Shafer, Paul, Patel, Deesha, Davis, Kevin, and McAfee, Timothy. "Quit Methods Used by US Adult Cigarette Smokers, 2014–2016." *Preventing Chronic Disease* 14 (2017): E32.

Card, David, and Krueger, Alan. "Minimum Wages and Employment: A Case Study of the Fast-Food Industry in New Jersey and Pennsylvania." *American Economic Review* 84, no. 4 (1994): 772–793.

Casella, George, and Berger, Roger. *Statistical Inference*. Belmont: Duxbury, 2002.

Centers for Disease Control. *How Tobacco Smoke Causes Disease: The Biology and Behavioral Basis for Smoking-Attributable Disease: A Report of the Surgeon General.* Atlanta, GA: U.S. Department of Health and Human Services, 2010.

Chaiton, Michael, Diemert, Lori, Cohen, Joanna, et al. "Estimating the Number of Quit Attempts It Takes to Quit Smoking Successfully in a Longitudinal Cohort of Smokers." *BMJ Open,* 6, no. 6 (2016).

Chambliss, Daniel. *Making Sense of the Social World: Methods of Investigation.* Los Angeles: Sage, 2016.

Copeland, Jack. "The Turing Test." *Minds and Machines* 10, no. 4 (2000): 519–539.

Crevier, Daniel. *AI: The Tumultuous Search for Artificial Intelligence.* New York: BasicBooks, 1993.

Dehejia, Rajeev, and Wahba, Sadek. "Causal Effects in Non-experimental Studies: Reevaluating the Evaluation of Training Programs." *Journal of the American Statistical Association* 94, no. 448 (December 1999): 1053–1062.

Dehejia, Rajeev, and Wahba, Sadek. "Propensity Score Matching Methods for Non-experimental Causal Studies." *Review of Economics and Statistics* 84 (February 2002): 151–161.

Fearon, James, and Laitin, David. "Ethnicity, Insurgency, and Civil War." *American Political Science Review* 97, no. 1 (2003): 75–90.

Ferster, Charles, and Skinner, B. F. *Schedules of Reinforcement.* New York: Appleton-Century-Crofts, 1957.

Fiore, M. C., Bailey, W. C., and Cohen, S. J. *Treating Tobacco Use and Dependence (Clinical Practice Guideline).* Rockville, MD: U.S. Department of Health Human Services, Public Health Service, 2000.

Fisher, Ronald. *The Design of Experiments.* Edinburgh: Oliver & Boyd, 1935.

Fogg, B. J. "A Behavior Model for Persuasive Design." In *Proceedings of the 4th international Conference on Persuasive Technology,* ACM, 2009, p. 40.

Fogg, B. J. *Persuasive Technology: Using Computers to Change What We Think and Do (Interactive Technology).* San Francisco: Morgan Kaufmann Publishers, 2003.

Geisser, Seymour. *Predictive Inference.* New York: Chapman and Hall, 1993.

Giddens, Anthony, Duneier, Mitchel, Appelbaum, Richard, and Carr, Deborah. *Introduction to Sociology.* New York: W. W. Norton, 2009.

Guelman, Leo, Guillen, Montserret, and Perez-Marin, Ana. "Optimal Personalized Treatment Rules for Marketing Interventions: A Review of Methods, a New Proposal, and an Insurance Case Study." *UB Risk Center Working Papers Series,* 2014.

Guelman, Leo, Guillen, Montserret, and Perez-Marin, Ana. "Uplift Random Forests." *Cybernetics & Systems* 46, no. 3 (2015): 230–248.

Hastie, Trevor, Tibshirani, Robert, and Friedman, Jerome. *The Elements of Statistical Learning.* New York: Springer, 2009.

Henke, Nicolaus, Bughin, Jacques, Chui, Michael, Manyika, James, Saleh, Tamin, Wiseman, Bill, and Sethupathy, Guru. *The Age of Analytics: Competing in a Data-Driven World.* McKinsey Global Institute, 2003. https://www.mckinsey.com/business-functions/mckinsey-analytics/our-insights/the-age-of-analytics-competing-in-a-data-driven-world. Accessed June 6, 2018.

Hill, Austin Bradford. "The Environment and Disease: Association or Causation?" *Proceedings of the Royal Society of Medicine* 58, no. 5 (1965): 295–300.

Höfler, Michael. "The Bradford Hill Considerations on Causality: A Counterfactual Perspective?" *Emerging Themes in Epidemiology* 2, no. 1 (2005): 2–11.

Holton, Gerald. *Thematic Origins of Scientific Thought, Kepler to Einstein.* Cambridge. MA: Harvard University Press, 1988.

Hosmer, David, Lemeshow, Stanley, and May, Susanne. *Applied Survival Analysis.* Hoboken, NJ: Wiley & Sons, 2008.

Johnston, James, and Pennypacker, Henry. *Readings for Strategies and Tactics of Behavioral Research* (2nd ed.). Hillsdale, NJ: Erlbaum, 1993.

Kahneman, Daniel, Knetsch, Jack, and Thaler, Richard. "Experimental Tests of the Endowment Effect and the Coase Theorem." *Journal of Political Economy* 98 (1990): 1325–1348.

Kahneman, Daniel, Knetsch, Jack, and Thaler, Richard. "Fairness and the Assumptions of Economics." *Journal of Business* 59 (1986): S285–S300.

Kahneman, Daniel, Knetsch, Jack, and Thaler, Richard. "The Endowment Effect, Loss Aversion, and Status Quo Bias." *Journal of Economic Perspectives* 5 (1991): 193–206.

Keyfitz, Nathan, and Caswell, Hal. *Applied Mathematical Demography.* New York: Springer, 2005.

LaLonde, Robert. "Evaluating the Econometric Evaluations of Training Programs." *American Economic Review* 76 (1986): 604–620.

Lange, Paul, Kruglanski, Arie, and Higgins, Tory. *Handbook of Theories of Social Psychology: Collection: Volumes 1 & 2.* London: Sage, 2011.

Leatherdale, Scott. "Natural Experiment Methodology for Research: A Review of How Different Methods Can Support Real-World Research." *International Journal of Social Research Methodology* 22, no. 1 (2019): 19–35.

Lehmann, Erich, and Romano, Joseph. *Testing Statistical Hypotheses* (3rd ed.). New York: Springer, 2005.

Lemmens, Valery, Oenema, Anke, Knut, Knut-Inge, and Brug, Johannes. "Effectiveness of Smoking Cessation Interventions Among Adults: A Systematic Review of Reviews." *European Journal of Cancer Prevention* 17, no. 6 (2008): 535–44.

Lo, Victor. "The True Lift Model: A Novel Data Mining Approach to Response Modeling in Database Marketing." *SIGKDD Explorations* 4, no. 2 (2002): 78–86.

Maji, Subhransu, and Malik, Jitendra. *Fast and Accurate Digit Classification.* Technical Report UCB/EECS-2009-159. Berkeley, CA: EECS Department, University of California, Berkeley, November 2009.

Manyika, James, Chui, Michael, Brown, Brad, Bughin, Jacques, Dobbs, Richard, Roxburg, Charles, and Byers, Angela. *Big Data: The Next Frontier for Innovation, Competition, and Productivity.* McKinsey Global Institute, 2011. https://www.mckinsey.com/business-functions/digital-mckinsey/our-insights/big-data-the-next-frontier-for-innovation. Accessed June 6, 2018.

Matloff, Norman. *The Art of R Programming: A Tour of Statistical Software Design*. San Francisco: No Starch Press, 2011.

McCrary, Justin. "Manipulation of the Running Variable in the Regression Discontinuity Design: A Density Test," *Journal of Econometrics* 142, no. 2 (2008): 698–714.

Miller, Rupert. *Survival Analysis*. New York: John Wiley & Sons, 1997.

Norcross, John, Mrykalo, Matthew, and Blagys, Marci. "Auld Lang Syne: Success Predictors, Change Processes, and Self-Reported Outcomes of New Year's Resolvers and Non-resolvers." *Journal of Clinical Psychology* 58, no. 4 (2002): 397–405.

Oakes, Michael. *Statistical Inference: A Commentary for the Social and Behavioural Sciences*. New York: Wiley, 1986.

O'Neil, Cathy. *Weapons of Math Destruction: How Big Data Increases Inequality and Threatens Democracy*. New York: Crown Publishers, 2016.

Phillips, Carl, and Goodman, Karen. "Causal Criteria and Counterfactuals: Nothing More (or Less) Than Scientific Common Sense?" *Emerging Themes in Epidemiology* 3, no. 1 (2006): 3–5.

Popper, Karl. "Conjectures and Refutations." In *Readings in the Philosophy of Science*, edited by Theodore Schick. Mountain View, CA: Mayfield, 1963.

Powers, Daniel, and Xie, Yu. *Statistical Methods for Categorical Analysis*. San Diego: Academic Press, 2000.

Prochaska, James, and Velicer, Wayne. "The Transtheoretical Model of Health Behavior Change." *American Journal of Health Promotion* 12, no. 1 (1997): 38–48.

Radcliffe, Nicholas. "Hillstrom's Mine That Data Email Analytics Challenge: An Approach Using Uplift Modelling." *Stochastic Solutions Limited* 1 (2008): 1–19.

Radcliffe, Nicholas. "Using Control Groups to Target on Predicted Lift: Building and Assessing Uplift Models." *Direct Marketing Journal* 1 (2007): 14–21.

Radcliffe, Nicholas, and Surry, Patrick. "Real-World Uplift Modelling with Significance Based Uplift Trees." White Paper TR-2011-1. *Stochastic Solutions*, 2011.

Reinhart, Alex. *Statistics Done Wrong: The Woefully Incomplete Guide*. San Francisco: No Starch Press, 2015.

Rogers, Everett. *Diffusion of Innovation* (5th ed.). New York: Simon and Schuster, 2003.

Rosen, Laura, Galili, Tal, Kott, Jeffrey, Goodman, Mark, and Freedman, Laurence. "Diminishing Benefit of Smoking Cessation Medications During the First Year: A Meta-Analysis of Randomized Controlled Trials." *Addiction* 113, no. 5 (2018): 805–816.

Rosenbaum, Paul. "The Case-Only Odds Ratio as a Causal Parameter." *Biometrics* 60 (2004): 233–240.

Rosenbaum, Paul, and Rubin, Donald. "Assessing Sensitivity to an Unobserved Binary Covariate in an Observational Study with Binary Outcome." *Journal of the Royal Statistical Society* B45 (1983): 212–218.

Rosenbaum, Paul, and Rubin, Donald. "Reducing Bias in Observational Studies Using Subclassification on the Propensity Score." *Journal of the American Statistical Association* 79 (1984): 516–524.

Rosenbaum, Paul, and Rubin, Donald. "The Central Role of the Propensity Score in Observational Studies for Causal Effects." *Biometrika* 70 (1983): 41–55.

Rubin, Donald. "Estimating Causal Effects of Treatments in Randomized and Nonrandomized Studies." *Journal of Educational Psychology*, 66, no. 5 (1974): 688–701.

Rubin, Donald. *Matched Sampling for Causal Effects*. Cambridge, UK: Cambridge University Press, 2006.

Rzepakowski, Piotr, and Jaroszewicz, Szymon. "Decision Trees for Uplift Modeling with Single and Multiple Treatments." *Knowledge and Information Systems* 32, no. 2 (2012): 303–327.

Sekhon, Jasdeep. "Multivariate and Propensity Score Matching Software with Automated Balance Optimization: The Matching Package for R." *Journal of Statistical Software* 42, no. 7 (2011): 1–52.

Shumway, Robert H., and Stoffer, David S. *Time Series Analysis and Its Applications: With R Examples*. New York: Springer, 2006.

Soltys, Michal, Jaroszewicz, Szymon, and Rzepakowski, Piotr. "Ensemble Methods for Uplift Modeling." *Data Mining and Knowledge Discovery* 29, no. 6 (2015): 1531–1559.

Su, Xiaogang, Kang, Joseph, Fan, Juanjuan, Levine, Richard, and Yan, Xin. "Facilitating Score and Causal Inference Trees for Large Observational Studies." *Journal of Machine Learning Research* 13 (2012): 2955–2994.

Su, Xiaogang, Tsai, Chih-Ling, Wang, Hansheng, Nickerson, David, and Li, Bogong. "Subgroup Analysis via Recursive Partitioning." *Journal of Machine Learning Research* 10 (2009): 141–158.

Thaler, Richard, and Sunstein, Cass. *Nudge: Improving Decisions About Health, Wealth, and Happiness*. New Haven, CT: Yale University Press, 2008.

Valente, Thomas, and Rogers, Everett. "The Origins and Development of the Diffusion of Innovations Paradigm as an Example of Scientific Growth." *Science Communication* 16, no. 3 (1995): 242–273.

Vigen, Tyler. "Spurious Correlations." http://tylervigen.com/spurious-correlations. Accessed June 21, 2018.

Wachter, Kenneth. *Essential Demographic Methods*. Cambridge, MA: Harvard University Press, 2004.

Wheelan, Charles J. *Naked Statistics: Stripping the Dread from the Data*. New York: W. W. Norton, 2013.

Wickham, Hadley. *Advanced R*. Boca Raton, FL: CRC Press, 2015.

Wooldridge, Jeffrey. *Introductory Econometrics: A Modern Approach* (5th international ed.). Mason, OH: South-Western, 2013.

Yeung, See. "Hypernudge: Big Data as a Mode of Regulation by Design." *Information Communication & Society* 20, no. 1 (May 2016): 118–136.

Ziman, John. *Real Science: What It Is, and What It Means*. Cambridge, UK: Cambridge University Press, 2000.

Index

E

N

O

Q

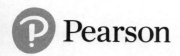

Photo by izusek/gettyimages

Register Your Product at informit.com/register

Access additional benefits and **save 35%** on your next purchase

- Automatically receive a coupon for 35% off your next purchase, valid for 30 days. Look for your code in your InformIT cart or the Manage Codes section of your account page.

- Download available product updates.

- Access bonus material if available.*

- Check the box to hear from us and receive exclusive offers on new editions and related products.

Registration benefits vary by product. Benefits will be listed on your account page under Registered Products.

InformIT.com—The Trusted Technology Learning Source

InformIT is the online home of information technology brands at Pearson, the world's foremost education company. At InformIT.com, you can:
- Shop our books, eBooks, software, and video training
- Take advantage of our special offers and promotions (informit.com/promotions)
- Sign up for special offers and content newsletter (informit.com/newsletters)
- Access thousands of free chapters and video lessons

Connect with InformIT—Visit informit.com/community

the trusted technology learning source

Addison-Wesley • Adobe Press • Cisco Press • Microsoft Press • Pearson IT Certification • Que • Sams • Peachpit Press

 Pearson